WEST GROUP
HIGH COURT
CASE SUMMARIES ™

Editor in Chief	**Dana L. Blatt, J.D., Esq.**
Managing Editor	**Marie H. Stedman**
Written By	**Phillip J. Valdivia, J.D., Esq.**
	Annette L. Anderson, J.D., Esq.
	Jennifer A. Weinzierl, J.D., Esq.
	Jason L. Baumetz, J.D., Esq.
	Susannah J. May, J.D., Esq.
	Daniel R. Dinger, J.D., Esq.
Memory Graphics	**Norman Vance**
Page Design	**Terri Asher**
Chief Administrator	**Richard A. Strober**

**Adaptable to
Courses Utilizing
Yeazell's Casebook
on Civil Procedure,
5th Edition**

Published by **WEST GROUP**
610 Opperman Drive
Eagan, MN
55123

Copyright © 2002 West Group
    610 Opperman Drive
    P.O. Box 64526
    St. Paul, MN 55164-0526

ISBN 0-314-25817-5

Printed in the United States of America

3rd reprint 2003

A Message from Dana L. Blatt, J.D., Editor In Chief
West Group High Court Case Summaries

As Editor in Chief of West Group's High Court Case Summaries, I am pleased to be associated with West Group and its tradition of providing the highest quality law student study aids such as Nutshells, Hornbooks, the Black Letter Series, and Sum and Substance products. I am also pleased that West Group, as the new publisher of High Court Case Summaries, will continue its tradition of providing students with the best quality student briefs available today. When you use these High Court Case Summaries, you will know that you have the advantage of using the best-written and most comprehensive student briefs available, with the most thorough analyses. Law students cannot afford to waste a minute of their time. That's why you need High Court Case Summaries. You'll find that with High Court you not only save time, but also have the competitive edge with our exclusive features such as memory graphics, "party lines," overview outlines, and case vocabulary. The following two pages will introduce you to the format of a High Court Brief.

Dana L. Blatt, J.D., Editor In Chief

FORMAT FOR A HIGH COURT BRIEF

THE HEADNOTE

Like a headline in a newspaper, the headnote provides you with a brief statement highlighting the importance of the case to the course.

"PARTY" LINE

A quick memory aid. For instantaneous recollection of the names of the parties and their relationship to each other.

MEMORY GRAPHIC

"A picture is worth a thousand words." Our professional cartoonists have created an entertaining "picture of the facts." To assist you in remembering what a particular case is about, simply glance at the picture.

INSTANT FACTS

Another great memory aid. A quick scan of a single sentence will instantly remind you of all of the facts of the case.

BLACK LETTER RULE

This section contains the single most important rule of the case (determined by reference to the chapter of the casebook where the case can be found). Read together with instant facts, you have a perfect mini brief.

CASE VOCABULARY

Every new or unusual legal, Latin or English word found in the original case is briefly defined in this section. This timesaver eliminates constant references to separate dictionaries.

PROCEDURAL BASIS

In a single sentence we summarize what happened, procedurally, to cause the case to be on appeal.

FACTS

"Just the facts ma'am..." Our facts are clearer and easier to understand than the original case. In fact, you can have a complete understanding of the original case without ever having to read it. Just read our brief.

ISSUE

Utilizing our I.R.A.C. format (Issue, Rule, Application, Conclusion), we put it all in focus by simply stating the single most important question of every case.

DECISION AND RATIONALE

We know you need to understand the rationale of every case to learn the law. In a clear, concise, and meticulous fashion we lay it all out for you. We do the work of separating what is important from what is not. Yet, we provide you with a thorough summary of every essential element of every case. Every concurrence and dissent is summarized as well.

ANALYSIS

We provide you with an extensive analysis of every single case. Here you will learn what you want to know about every case. What is the history or background of the litigation? What do authorities say about the opinion? How does it fit in with the course? How does each case compare with others in the casebook? Is it a majority or minority opinion? What is the importance of the case and why did the casebook author choose to include it as a major opinion in the casebook? What types of things will the professor be asking about the case? What will be said about the opinion in class? Will people criticize or applaud it? What would you want to say about the case if called upon in class to brief it? In other words, what are the "secret" essential things that one must know and understand about each case in order to do well in the course? We answer these and many other questions for you. Nobody else comes close to giving you the in-depth analysis that we give!

A Great All-Around Study Aid!

Henningsen v. Bloomfield Motors, Inc.

(Auto Purchaser) v. (Auto Dealer)

32 N.J. 358, 161 A.2d 69 (N.J. 1960)

M E M O R Y   G R A P H I C

Instant Facts

An automobile purchaser sued the dealer and manufacturer for breach of an implied warranty of merchantability, although the express contractual terms of the sale disclaimed all implied warranties.

Black Letter Rule

A contract of adhesion does not trump statutory implied warranties of merchantability.

Case Vocabulary

CAVEAT EMPTOR: Let the buyer beware.

CONTRACT OF ADHESION: A contract between parties of unequal bargaining position, where the buyer must "take it or leave it."

IMPLIED WARRANTY OF MERCHANTABILITY: A warranty that means that the thing sold must be reasonably fit for the general purpose for which it is manufactured and sold.

Procedural Basis: Certification to New Jersey Supreme Court of appeal of judgment awarding damages for breach of implied warranty.

Facts: Mr. Henningsen purchased a car from Bloomfield Motors Inc. (D), a retail dealer. The car had been manufactured by Chrysler Corporation (D). Mr. Henningsen gave the car to his wife for Christmas. Mrs. Henningsen (P) was badly injured a few days later when the steering gear failed and the car turned right into a wall. When he purchased the car, Mr. Henningsen signed a contract without reading the fine print. The fine print contained a "warranty" clause which disclaimed all implied warranties and which granted an express warranty for all defects within 90 days or 4000 miles, whichever came first. Mrs. Henningsen (P) sued Bloomfield (D) and Chrysler (D). The trial court dismissed her negligence counts but ruled for Mrs. Henningsen (P) based on the implied warranty of merchantability. Bloomfield (D) and Chrysler (D) appealed.

Issue: Does a contract of adhesion trump statutory implied warranties of merchantability?

Decision and Rationale: (Francis, J.) No. A contract of adhesion does not trump statutory implied warranties of merchantability. In order to ameliorate the harsh effects of the doctrine of caveat emptor, most states have imposed an implied warranty of merchantability on all sales transactions. This warranty simply means that the thing sold must be reasonably fit for the general purpose for which it is manufactured and sold. The warranty extends to all foreseeable users of the product, not merely those in privity of contract with the seller. In order to avoid the implied warranty obligations, many manufacturers, including Chrysler (D) and all other automobile manufacturers, include an express warranty provision which disclaims all statutory implied warranties. We must determine what effect to give this express warranty. Under traditional principles of freedom of contract, the law allows parties to contract away obligations. However, in the auto sales context, the fine-print disclaimer of implied warranties is a contract of adhesion. It is a standardized form contract, and the purchaser has no opportunity to bargain for different terms. He must "take it or leave it," and he cannot shop around to different dealers because all of them use the same standard contract. Because the purchaser and seller occupy grossly inequal bargaining positions, we feel that justice must trump the principle of freedom of contract. Chrysler's (D) attempted disclaimer of an implied warranty of merchantability is so inimical to the public good as to compel an adjudication of its invalidity. Affirmed.

Analysis:

This well-written opinion presents an excellent exegesis of several areas of law, ranging from products liability to various contract principles. The opinion notes several conflicting interests and principles which the court must weigh. First, the traditional principle of caveat emptor faces the modern doctrine of implied warranties of merchantability. The court has little difficulty in holding that modern commercial transactions require protection for purchasers. An implied warranty of merchantability is imposed in all auto sales transactions in order to protect the buyer. Second, the requirement of privity of contract is weighed against an implied warranty. The court notes that, in modern sales transactions, a warranty safeguards all consumers of a product, not merely those in direct contractual privity with the seller. Third, the principle of freedom of contract is weighed against this implied warranty. Freedom of contract is one of the fundamental tenets of the law. Parties should be free to contract for any provisions, and generally parties are bound by the terms of their contract. However, an important exception exists when a contract is one of adhesion. Contracts of adhesion typically involve terms in fine print, written by a powerful seller to limit liabilities or impose responsibilities upon an unsuspecting buyer. No bargaining occurs for these terms, and indeed the buyer is in no position to bargain. If the buyer attempts to change the terms of the contract, the seller simply will not complete the transaction. In order for a contract to be considered "adhesive" or "unconscionable," the buyer usually has nowhere else to go. As in the case at bar, all sellers of a particular type of goods may include similar terms in their adhesive contracts. Weighing all of these factors, a court may rule that the express contractual terms are invalid, notwithstanding the principle of freedom of contract. The arguments for and against this approach are easy to see. On one hand, a buyer should not be allowed to benefit from his failure to read the terms of a contract or to attempt to change some unwanted terms. On the other hand, social justice requires that the buyer be protected from an all-powerful seller, especially where the buyer has no other option but to accept the contract as written. All in all, public policy, and not traditional law, shapes this court's opinion.

Table of Contents

Alphabetical Table of Cases

Chapter 1

Civil procedure is a system. It tells lawyers what court to file suit in, when to file a complaint and how to answer a complaint, who can be parties to a suit, and how the suit can be brought to an end before, during, and after trial. Civil procedure is about the strategies that lawyers employ to win cases, and it is about the strategy that legislators and the courts employ to make sure that the outcome of each case is just. Procedure tries to balance society's competing goals in resolving disputes: Society wants to find truth and at the same time it wants to minimize conflict. Civil procedure creates a framework that lawyers can use to search for the truth, but it also places a limit on how much time a lawyer can spend in his search.

Most disputes are resolved outside of the legal system because the stakes are too small to provide an incentive to sue, or because an adequate settlement is offered before the formal complaint is filed, or because the prospective plaintiff cannot find a lawyer who is willing to represent him.

How does a dispute enter the legal system? The first step is for the plaintiff to find a lawyer. The lawyer's job is to use his specialized knowledge to navigate his client through the legal system and to design a winning strategy.

The second step is for the lawyer to decide which court to file suit in. Can the action be brought in state court? Can it be brought in federal court? Which court system would be the most convenient for the client? The best tactical choice? In deciding which court to bring the action in, the lawyer will find out which courts have subject matter jurisdiction over the dispute. Some courts are courts of general jurisdiction and can hear a wide variety of cases, but other courts can only hear a narrow range of cases, for example: family courts can usually only hear cases involving juveniles and family disputes. The lawyer will then determine which courts have personal jurisdiction over the defendant. Personal jurisdiction is the power a court has to enforce a judgment against a particular defendant, and usually only state and federal courts within the state where the defendant lives or does business will have personal jurisdiction over him. Finally, the lawyer will find out in which court venue is proper. Venue rules allocate cases between courts in cases where more than one court has jurisdiction over the dispute.

The third step is for the lawyer to draft a complaint, file the complaint with the court, and notify the defendant that the suit has begun. State courts generally require that complaints be specific and lay out clearly the nature of the action and the basic facts that support the plaintiff's allegations. The rule that governs complaints in federal courts is less strict. A plaintiff can file a complaint in federal court even if he has only accumulated a small amount of evidence to support his position.

The fourth step is for the defendant's lawyer to draft a response to the complaint. The defendant's lawyer can try to persuade the court to dismiss the complaint by using one of several forms of preanswer motion or he can answer the complaint with defenses and maybe some complaints of his own. Preanswer motions can be made because there is some reason why the court should dismiss the complaint that has nothing to do with the substance of the complaint. The complaint may have been filed in a court that did not have jurisdiction over the complaint or the defendant, for example. Preanswer motions can also be made when the plaintiff has stated a claim that the relevant law of the jurisdiction does not recognize, or when the plaintiff's complaint is vague and difficult for the defendant to understand. Unlike preanswer motions, answers express the defendant's position on the truth of the plaintiff's allegations. The defendant can answer a complaint by simply denying its truth or by asserting claims that would serve to defeat the plaintiff's claim. For example, the defendant might claim that the statute of limitations on the plaintiff's claim has run.

Not all cases are between a single plaintiff and a single defendant. Rules of civil procedure govern who is allowed to be joined to a lawsuit as a plaintiff or a defendant, who must be joined, and who can choose to be joined. The federal rules allow a plaintiff to choose who may be joined as a co-plaintiff or a co-defendant. This is called permissive joinder. Compulsory joinder is when a party is joined to the lawsuit by a court order because the court has determined that the party would be affected by the outcome of the case. A third party can seek to enter the lawsuit through a process called intervention when he believes that the lawsuit would inflict some hardship on him if it were conducted without him. Class actions involve cases where the number of potential plaintiffs is so great that joinder would be impractical. In a class action suit, a few plaintiffs represent the cases of the entire group of similarly situated parties.

The fifth stage in the lawsuit is discovery. During discovery, the parties to the suit use various techniques provided in the procedural rules to gather factual information from each other and from outsiders to the lawsuit, such as expert witnesses. There are five main methods of discovery: initial disclosures, document production, oral depositions, written interrogatories, and physical and mental examinations. The initial disclosures are the basic information, such as the names of witnesses, that all parties are required to reveal to each other. Procedural rules allow the parties to request documents from each other and from nonparties and provide for a means of enforcing these requests. Parties are also allowed to question witnesses under oath, but outside the presence of a judge, through the deposition process. Parties can also request other parties to answer a series of written questions, called interrogatories. Finally, parties can make a motion to obtain a physical or mental examination of another party.

There are various means of ending a lawsuit before it gets to trial. The methods of pretrial disposition include settlement, dismissal during the pleadings stage, and summary judgment. Motions for summary judgment are not usually granted until after the discovery phase. In a motion for summary judgment, a party is saying: "There is no dispute about the facts. But, given the facts, the moving party must win under the law."

If the methods of pretrial disposition fail, the lawsuit will proceed to trial. Procedural rules govern the various stages in the trial. First, the court notifies the parties of the trial date. Second, a jury is selected through an elaborate process involving the questioning of each potential juror by all parties and the judge, and the eventual elimination of unsuitable jurors. After jury selection, the trial begins. Each party makes an opening statement. Then the plaintiff presents his case, and the defendant can respond by moving for a judgment as a matter of law, which is similar to a summary judgment. If the motion fails, the defendant presents his case, and either party will move for a judgment as a matter of law. If these motions fail, the parties make their arguments to the jury, the judge gives the jury instructions on how to apply the law to the facts of the case, and the jury retires to deliberate. When the jury has reached a verdict, the trial usually ends. However, the losing party can make a final motion for a judgment as a matter of law, or a judgment notwithstanding the verdict. If that fails, the losing party can appeal to a higher court. However, after trial the parties are prohibited by procedural rules from bringing the same case, or a case that is based on the same legal issue against each other a second time.

Chapter 1

NOTE: THE PURPOSE OF THIS OUTLINE IS TO ORGANIZE THE CASES SO THAT ONE CAN QUICKLY UNDERSTAND THE RELEVANCE OF EACH CASE TO THE COURSE. NO ATTEMPT IS MADE IN THIS OVERVIEW TO ADDRESS EVERY CONCEPT THAT MUST BE STUDIED. BE SURE TO READ THE ENTIRE CASEBOOK AND/OR OTHER MATERIALS TO GAIN A FULL UNDERSTANDING OF ALL CONCEPTS.

I. Civil Procedure: Theory and Practice
   A. Civil Procedure in the Scheme of Things
      1. Civil procedure is about lawyers' relationships with courts, their clients, and with the legal profession.
      2. Civil procedure defines the various steps in and sets the rules of the litigation process. It tells a party where and how he can bring a lawsuit, how he can obtain necessary information from the opposing party, and what kind of remedy he can obtain. It also tells a party how he can avoid litigation.
      3. Civil procedure tries to enable society to define and seek truth and justice. Society has an interest in deciding disputes by analyzing the merits of the opposing cases. Civil procedure is used to facilitate this analysis. A rule of civil procedure can be understood by asking how that rule can lead to a just decision based on the merits of each case.
      4. An important theme in civil procedure is the attempt to balance the interest society has in pursuing truth and justice with its interest in the efficient disposition of lawsuits. Although litigation can be seen as a force for social justice and reform, there is a movement afoot to reduce expensive and time-consuming trials with quicker and cheaper alternative forms of dispute resolution.
   B. Civil Procedure and the Lawyer-Client Relationship
      1. Disputes are resolved without a trial either because a prospective plaintiff has no grounds for a lawsuit or cannot find a lawyer who will represent him, or because he is offered a settlement by the prospective defendant. It is only the rare case that enters the litigation process.
      2. The first step for any plaintiff is to find a lawyer. An individual hires a lawyer to guide him through the litigation process in pursuit of a legal remedy for his injury.
      3. The legal system treats the lawyer's choices as if they are the client's choices. The problem with this is that sometimes lawyer's make mistakes. When

a mistake is made, the procedural system has to resolve the conflict between what is fair to the individual whose lawyer has made the mistake and what is fair to the opposing party, who may have acted in reliance on the lawyer's mistaken decision. The system resolves this conflict by allowing a certain amount of procedural flexibility, and also by allowing a legal malpractice cause of action.

II. Which Court Can Hear the Case?
   A. Why Should a Party Care Where Suit Is Brought?
      1. Convenience: It may be more convenient and cost-effective to bring a lawsuit in a nearby court, where the judges are familiar. A court that is convenient for one party usually has the additional benefit of being inconvenient for the opposing party.
      2. Tactics: A jury in one location might be more sympathetic than a jury in another location. A court in one location might have a backlog of cases that would have the effect of lengthening the amount of time it would take to resolve the dispute.
      3. Issues of convenience and tactics also affect the decision to bring a case in federal as opposed to state court. For example:
         a. Federal judges are appointed for life, and are therefore immune from the political pressures faced by state-court judges, who are often elected.
         b. Some federal district courts have lighter caseloads than their state counterparts, which allows cases to be resolved more quickly.
         c. The opposing party may not be familiar with the federal court system's fast pace and more formal procedural rules.
   B. Subject Matter Jurisdiction: 28 U.S.C. §§1331 and 1332
      1. Subject matter jurisdiction refers to the ability of a court to hear a particular type of dispute. For example: a family court will only hear cases involving family matters such as child custody.
      2. Some courts are courts of general jurisdiction, and can hear any case, unless a statute requires that a certain type of case be heard in a special court. A court of limited jurisdiction is one that was set up by statute to hear only a particular type of dispute.
      3. All federal courts are courts of limited jurisdiction.

The limits of federal jurisdiction are defined in Article III, Section 2 of the Constitution. 28 U.S.C. §§1331 and 1332 are the most important of the statutes that Congress has passed to authorize federal subject matter jurisdiction.

4. §1331 grants federal courts federal question jurisdiction, or subject matter jurisdiction over any claim that arises under federal law.

5. §1332 grants federal courts diversity jurisdiction, which is jurisdiction over any case where the amount in controversy is over $75,000 and where the case is between citizens of different states; or between citizens of a state and citizens of a foreign country.

    a. For diversity jurisdiction purposes, an individual is a citizen of a state if he resides there with the intention of remaining there indefinitely. *Gordon v. Steele*

C. Personal Jurisdiction

1. In addition to subject matter jurisdiction, a court has to have personal jurisdiction over the defendant. Personal jurisdiction determines which state a case can be brought in. Personal jurisdiction is the same for both federal and state courts within the same state.

2. Courts can assert personal jurisdiction over defendants even when process has not been served on the defendant within the state. Citizens of a state and individuals and corporations that engage in certain types of activity within a state are always subject to personal jurisdiction within that state, even when not personally served there.

D. Venue: 28 U.S.C. §1391

1. After determining whether a court has subject matter and personal jurisdiction, the next determination is whether venue is appropriate. Venue involves the question of the proper locality of the court that is to hear the matter. In cases where more than one court has both subject matter and personal jurisdiction, venue rules determine which court the case can be brought in.

2. In the federal court system, cases are first brought and tried in district courts. There may be more than one district court in a given state. In a case where all the federal district courts in a state have subject matter and personal jurisdiction, 28 U.S.C. §1391 is applied to determine where venue lies.

3. Each state court system has its own venue rules. Most state judicial districts are set up along county lines. Under most state venue statutes, a case may be brought in the district where one party or the other resides or does business or in the district where the claim arose.

E. Service of Process: Rule 4

1. After determining in which court to bring suit, the plaintiff will draft a complaint and file it with the court. Then the plaintiff must notify the defendant of the lawsuit.

2. Rule 4 sets out two basic methods of notice:

    a. Waiver of service is the less formal and less expensive method. The plaintiff mails the defendant a copy of the complaint and copies of Form 1A and Form 1B. The suit can proceed if the defendant mails back a signed copy of Form 1B.

    b. If the defendant does not mail a signed waiver form to the plaintiff, the plaintiff must move on to the second, more formal method of service. The plaintiff drafts a summons, which is then signed and sealed by the clerk of the court. The summons and complaint are then delivered to the defendant by a process server.

III. Stating the Case

A. The Lawyer's Responsibility for Drafting a Proper Complaint: Rule 11

1. A complaint is an application to the judicial system to use its power to grant relief. A complaint cannot be made for improper or frivolous purposes.

2. Rule 11 sets out the lawyer's responsibility to determine, after a reasonable inquiry, that the complaint is not being made for any improper purpose and that the claim is well-grounded in fact and existing law.

3. Rule 11 empowers courts to impose sanctions, including the payment of the opposing party's legal expenses, on party's that violate the rule. Courts can impose sanctions on their own initiative, or in response to a party's motion for sanctions.

    a. Rule 11 sanctions are designed to deter improper conduct and will only be applied in exceptional circumstances where the claim is patently frivolous. *Bridges v. Diesel Services*

B. The Complaint

1. After determining that the complaint is not being made for improper purposes and that it is well-grounded in fact and law the plaintiff has to determine how to draft the complaint. What information must be included in a well-pleaded complaint?

2. State court systems frequently have different requirements for what should be included in a

complaint than the federal court system. However:

   a. A federal court is not required to apply a state well-pleaded complaint rule even when the case originated in state court under state substantive law. *Bell v. Novick Transfer Co.*

C. The Response—Motions and Answers

   1. After the plaintiff notifies the defendant of his claim, the defendant is required by federal and state civil procedure rules to respond. There are two basic types of responses:

   a. Motions ask the court to take some action in the defendant's favor: either to dismiss the plaintiff's complaint, or to change the nature of the suit. There are several types of motions:

     (1) The defendant may have found a reason why the action cannot proceed in the particular court in which the plaintiff filed it. The court may not have subject matter jurisdiction or personal jurisdiction, or the venue may not be proper. The summons may have been defective or served improperly. These motions are covered by Rule 12(b)(1)-(5).

     (2) The defendant may believe that the plaintiff has no right to relief under the substantive law of the jurisdiction in which the complaint was filed. This motion is covered by Rule 12(b)(6).

     (3) The defendant may not understand the complaint because the complaint is too vague. The defendant will move for a "more definite statement" under Rule 12(c).

   b. Answers respond to the specific allegations contained in the complaint. There are two types of answer:

     (1) If the defendant believes that an allegation is untrue, or does not know whether the allegation is true, he can deny the allegation under Rule 8(b).

     (2) The defendant can make affirmative defenses under Rule 8(c), for example that the plaintiff has waived his right to make a claim or that the statute of limitations has expired, that would effectively defeat the plaintiff's complaint.

   2. The motions outlined above are pre-answer motions, and must be made before an answer is filed. This is because the motions are preliminary by nature—they do not address the substance of the plaintiff's complaint and so do not require any factual development.

   a. Usually, a defendant will use more than one of the options listed above to fight the plaintiff's complaint. If his motions are denied, he then must file an answer.

   3. The defendant can also use counterclaims, cross claims, and third-party claims to assert claims against the plaintiff or against another defendant.

   a. Counterclaims: Under Rule 13, a defendant may file a counterclaim against the plaintiff if he decides that he has a complaint against the plaintiff. There are two types of counterclaim:

     (1) A compulsory counterclaim arises out of the same transaction that gave rise to the plaintiff's complaint.

     (2) A permissive counterclaim does not arise out of the same transaction as the plaintiff's complaint.

   b. Cross claims: If the plaintiff sues more than one defendant, the defendants can file cross claims against each other under Rule 13(g) as long as the cross claims arise out of the same transaction that gave rise to the plaintiff's claim.

   c. Third-party claims: A defendant can file a third-party claim under Rule 14 if he believes that there is a party liable to him for any damages claimed by the plaintiff.

D. Amendment of Pleadings

   1. The federal rules allow parties to amend their pleadings as the case proceeds through the discovery phase and new facts come to light that might alter the nature of the action.

   2. Rule 15 deals with the amendment of pleadings. Rule 15(a) sets out the general rules. Rule 15(b) deals with amendments made during the trial as new evidence is introduced.

IV. Parties to the Lawsuit

A. Permissive Joinder

   1. Rule 20 deals with permissive joinder, or the parties who may be joined to a lawsuit, as co-plaintiffs or codefendants, by the original plaintiff.

B. Compulsory Joinder

   1. Under Rule 13 a court can order, on a motion by the defendant, that a third party be brought into the suit as a coplaintiff or codefendant because the outcome of the lawsuit might affect the third party's interests.

   2. Courts order joinder when the substantive law applied in the suit will involve the rights or liabilities of a third party, or when more than one party is claiming the same property, or when the relief granted to one party will affect the interests of a third party. However:

   a. It is not always necessary to make all joint tortfeasors parties to the same lawsuit. *Temple v. Synthes Corp.*

3. Compulsory joinder creates a tension between the right of parties to a lawsuit to control their own claims and strategy and the principle that the courts should decide on the claims of all parties who will be affected by the outcome of the lawsuit.

C. Intervention

1. Under Rule 24, a party can petition the court to allow him to intervene as a codefendant or co-plaintiff if he can show that the suit would inflict hardship on him if conducted without him.

D. Class Actions

1. The class action is a controversial alternative to the joinder of multiple plaintiffs. It is used when the number of potential plaintiffs is so great that it makes more sense to allow a few parties to represent the entire class in the lawsuit.

2. Rule 23 governs class actions.

V. Factual Development—Discovery

A. The discovery rules allow parties to obtain information from each other and from individuals and entities that are not parties to the suit. There are five principal means of discovery:

B. Required Disclosures. Under Rule 26(a)(1) the parties to the lawsuit are required to provide each other with certain basic information.

C. Inspection of Documents

1. Under Rule 34 a party can request that the opposing party provide him with documents.

2. Under Rule 45 a party can obtain documents from other witnesses by subpoena.

3. "Documents" include printed and written papers and records as well as sound recordings, videotapes, photographs, and email.

D. Oral Depositions. Under Rules 30 and 45 a party can question any witness with information about the suit under oath in the absence of a judge.

E. Written Interrogatories. Under Rule 33 a party can send another party written questions to be answered in writing. Written interrogatories cannot be used to gain information from nonparties.

F. Physical and Mental Examinations. Under Rule 35, a party may move for a court order allowing him to obtain a physical or mental examination of another party. A party can obtain a court order if he shows that the condition to be examined is a matter in dispute.

G. A legal privilege can be used to protect information from discovery under Rule 26. *Butler v. Rigby*

VI. Pretrial Disposition—Summary Judgment

A. Policy concerns addressed by pretrial disposition.

1. The federal rules provide relaxed pleading requirements and allow for broad discovery in order to serve a policy interest in allowing both parties to develop as much factual information as possible before their suit can be dismissed.

2. There is a competing policy interest in disposing of cases before trial as often as possible in order to reduce the administrative costs of unnecessary trials.

3. Summary judgment allows a court to dispose of cases where trial is not necessary and would serve no purpose.

B. Rule 56 governs summary judgment. Motions for summary judgment can be made at any time, but are not usually granted until after discovery.

1. Rule 56(c) allows courts to grant a motion for summary judgment when the case presents "no genuine issue as to any material fact." But it is not always easy to tell when there is a factual issue that justifies a trial. For example:

2. In *Houchens v. American Home Assurance Co.*, the court granted summary judgment under Rule 56(c) because although the plaintiff could show that her husband had disappeared and had been declared legally dead by a state court, she could not show that he had in fact died or that he had died by accident. Therefore there was no issue of material fact in her case against the carrier of her husband's accidental-death insurance policy.

C. Other methods of pretrial disposition include:

1. Default judgment. Under Rule 55, if a defendant fails to answer the complaint or fails to defend his case, the court will enter a judgment for the plaintiff.

2. Dismissal. Under Rule 41(b), if a plaintiff does not obey a court order during the pretrial proceedings, the court can dismiss the case. Under Rule 41(a), the plaintiff can apply for a voluntary dismissal.

D. Methods for streamlining the trial include:

1. Request for admission. Under Rule 36, a party can seek admission of the truth of certain facts or the acknowledgment of the genuineness of specific documents.

2. Pretrial conference. Under Rule 16, a court can order a conference between the parties. Parties can use this conference to discuss settlement terms.

VII. Trial

A. Fewer than 5% of federal cases go to trial. However,

the trial process exerts an influence over the pretrial process in that the parties' estimations of the likely outcome at trial affect their approaches to trial preparation and settlement.

B. There are a number of steps in the trial process:

1. The court notifies the parties of the trial date.

2. The jury is selected.

   a. Prospective jurors are seated in the jury box and are told briefly about the nature of the case.

   b. The judge and attorneys for both parties question the prospective jurors both individually and as a group.

   c. Both parties may challenge jurors for cause, or may make peremptory challenges, challenges for which no cause is stated.

3. The attorneys for each side make their opening statements.

4. The plaintiff makes his case-in-chief.

   a. The plaintiff introduces evidence and calls his witnesses and each witness is examined and cross-examined.

   b. After cross-examination, the plaintiff can redirect testimony, and the defendant is given the opportunity to recross.

5. After the plaintiff has presented his case, the defendant has the opportunity to move for judgment as a matter of law (also known as directed verdict) under Rule 50(a).

   a. A motion for judgment as a matter of law is the defendant's way of saying that even if everything the plaintiff has said is true, under the substantive law applied in the case the plaintiff has no right to relief.

6. The defendant presents his case.

   a. After the defendant has presented his case, the plaintiff can move for judgment as a matter of law.

7. The plaintiff rebuts the defendant's case. And the defendant is given the opportunity to rebut the plaintiff's rebuttal.

   a. The general rule is that a party can only rebut new issues that were raised in the previous stage of the trial.

8. After both sides have rested, either party can move for judgment as a matter of law under Rule 50(a). The judge does not usually grant the motion. Most courts prefer to reserve judgment at this stage until after the jury has delivered a verdict.

9. Both parties make their closing arguments to the jury and the judge then gives the jury his charge, or instructions.

   a. The charge explains to the jury what law applies to the evidence in the case. Under Rule 51, the parties can object to any portion of the charge that they think is erroneous.

10. The jury deliberates, and then returns a verdict. The jurors are usually polled to find out if they all agree with the verdict.

11. Under Rules 50(b) and 59, the losing party can move for a new trial or for a judgment as a matter of law, also known as a judgment notwithstanding the verdict, up to 10 days after the jury has returned its verdict.

12. If the losing party raised a point during the trial that he believes was disposed of erroneously, he can appeal the court's final judgment.

13. Under very limited circumstances, such as evidence of criminal conduct by the judge, a party can move to set aside the judgment under Rule 60(b).

C. Despite the strong public policy interest in jury trials, evidenced in the Seventh Amendment, there are occasions where a jury is not permitted to hear a case.

1. The court can dispose of a case on a motion for judgment as a matter of law when the party that carries the burden of proof cannot produce enough evidence to meet that burden. Courts will grant a motion for judgment as a matter of law when they believe that a reasonable jury could arrive at only one verdict.

2. It is the jury's job to weigh material issues of fact and to decide the credibility of witnesses. In deciding whether to grant a motion for judgment notwithstanding the verdict, a court will not take the witnesses' credibility into account.

   a. In *Norton v. Snapper Power Equipment*, an appellate court decided that the trial court had erred in granting the defendant's motion for judgment notwithstanding the verdict because a reasonable jury could have found for the plaintiff based on the facts presented and because a reasonable jury could have found the plaintiff's expert witnesses to be more credible than the defendant's.

VIII. Former Adjudication

A. The former adjudication principle in civil procedure is similar to the double jeopardy rule in criminal procedure. If a party to a case is not happy with the case's outcome, he should not be allowed to bring the same case again.

B. The difficult issue that former adjudication raises is: How should a court decide which issues can be litigated in a second action? This issue is addressed in two ways:

1. Claim preclusion (also known as res judicata). If a plaintiff loses a case, he cannot bring another action based on the same claim. If a defendant loses, he cannot bring a second action in order to set aside the first judgment.
   a. It is not always easy to determine whether the second claim is the same as the first one.
2. Issue preclusion (also known as collateral estoppel). Under the doctrine of issue preclusion, if the party to a case raises an argument based on the set of facts in that case and is unsuccessful, he cannot use that same argument based on those same facts in a second action with the same opposing party. Conversely, if a party prevails on an issue, he may assert that issue as binding in a subsequent matter.
   a. For example, if A sues B on a promissory note and B alleges fraud as a defense, if B loses he will not be able to assert fraud based on the same events in any subsequent promissory-note suit that A brings.
C. The court in *Rush v. City of Maple Heights* deals with issues of both claim preclusion and issue preclusion.
   1. Under *Rush*, whether or not injuries to both person and property resulting from the same wrongful act are to be treated as injuries to separate rights or as separate items of damage, a plaintiff may maintain only one action to enforce his rights existing at the time such action is commenced.

IX. Appeals
A. The right of appeal does not guarantee that any error by the trial court will be corrected. This is because under the procedural rules a party can only appeal an adverse ruling at certain times during the trial process. Procedural rules also determine how strictly an appellate court can scrutinize a trial court's decision.
   1. Under the final judgment rule, 28 U.S.C. §1291, appellate courts can only review trial court decisions that have the effect of disposing of the case finally.
   2. Non-final court decisions, also known as interlocutory orders, may not be appealed. For example, an order to produce information under Rule 34 is an interlocutory order and cannot be appealed. *Apex Hosiery Co. v. Leader.*
B. Appellate Structure and Jurisdiction
   1. At the federal level, parties can appeal from the district court to the circuit court of appeals. If a party loses in the court of appeals, he can petition the Supreme Court to grant a writ of certiorari.
   2. At the state level, judgments can be appealed from a trial court of general jurisdiction to an appellate court. And like the United States Supreme Court, the highest court in the state has the discretion to choose which cases it will hear. Decisions of the highest state court can be reviewed by the United States Supreme Court if they raise questions of federal law.
   3. The Supreme Court's power to review cases is governed by 28 U.S.C. §§1253-1258.
C. Civil Procedure in Your Substantive Courses
   1. Procedural issues are often discussed in substantive courses such as contracts and torts. This is because procedural issues are often interrelated with the substantive issues discussed within a court's opinion.
   2. Focusing on the procedural issues raised by a case will enable you to understand how and why a case arrived in a particular court. It will also enable you to determine how much of the opinion relies on an assessment of the substantive law applied in the case and how much depends on an assessment of the facts.
      a. For example, on a motion for summary judgment the court must analyze both the legal issues and the factual issues the case presents whereas on a Rule 12(b)(6) motion the court only examines the legal issue of whether the plaintiff can be granted relief for his claim rather than the factual issue of whether the plaintiff can meet his burden.

Gordon v. Steele

(College Student) v. (Doctors and Hospital)
376 F. Supp. 575 (W.D. Pa. 1974)

M E M O R Y   G R A P H I C

 ## Instant Facts

A college student injured in Pennsylvania was able bring a state-law malpractice suit in federal court against two Pennsylvania doctors and a hospital because her moving to Idaho to attend college made her a citizen of Idaho for diversity jurisdiction purposes.

Black Letter Rule

An individual is a citizen of a state if he resides there with the intention to remain indefinitely.

Case Vocabulary

ANIMO MANENDI: Intent to remain
DOMICILE: Place where, for legal purposes, a party is said to reside.
EMANCIPATION: The release of a minor child from the control of and dependence on his parents.

Procedural Basis: Motion to dismiss for lack of diversity jurisdiction in a malpractice action for damages.

Facts: Susan Gordon (P) suffered a wrist injury in February, 1972, when she was 18. Two physicians (D) and an osteopathic hospital (D) in Erie County, Pennsylvania, failed to diagnose fractures in her wrist, and as a result, Gordon (P) endured pain and hospitalization. Her wrist and hand continued to be partially disabled. In August of 1972, Gordon (P) enrolled in Ricks College in Rexburg, Idaho. Gordon (P) filed suit in federal court against the doctors (D) and hospital (D) in April of 1973. The doctors (D) and hospital (D) moved to dismiss for lack of diversity of citizenship. Under 28 U.S.C. §1332(a)(1), a federal court can hear a civil action arising out of state law if the damages total more than $75,000 and the parties on both sides of the suit are citizens of different states. The doctors (D) and hospital (D) argued that Gordon (P) is a citizen of Pennsylvania because: 1) when she was admitted to Ricks College she gave her address as Erie, Pennsylvania; 2) the college records for the 1972-1973 school year show her address as Erie, Pennsylvania; 3) she worked in Erie during her summer vacations; 4) she has a Pennsylvania driver's license and holds a bank account in Erie; 5) she goes to Erie for Christmas vacations, and 6) although Ricks College is a Mormon institution, Gordon (P), as a woman, will not be required to perform the extended missionary work abroad that male students are expected to perform. Gordon (P) argues that she is a citizen of Idaho, not Pennsylvania, because: 1) she has expressed her intention to not return to Pennsylvania; 2) she regards her apartment in Rexburg as her residence; 3) she returned to Erie in the summer of 1973 only to receive treatment for eye problems; 4) she visited Erie during Christmas in 1973 only to be deposed and to keep medical appointments, and has not returned to Erie for any other school vacations; 5) her goal is to marry someone of her faith, and she has a greater opportunity to achieve this in Idaho than in Pennsylvania; 6) she has been a member of Blue Cross in Idaho since 1972; and 7) after graduation, she may relocate anywhere in the United States or abroad.

Issue: Can an 18-year-old college student be considered, for diversity purposes, a citizen of the state where she attends college rather than the state where her parents reside?

Decision and Rationale: (Knox, J.) Yes. An 18-year-old college student can be considered a citizen of the state where she attends college for diversity purposes if the court finds that she resides in that state and intends to remain there indefinitely. The legal status of college students has raised problems in the area of diversity jurisdiction. This is because while the age of majority in almost all states is 18, the traditional procedural rule is that a college student is financially dependent on his parents and therefore will remain a citizen of the state in which his parents live rather than the state in which he attends college. The most recent treatments of the law in the Third Circuit applied the rule that an individual is a citizen of a state when he resides there with the intent to remain indefinitely—he does not have to intend to remain permanently. It is the state of citizenship at the time of filing suit that matters for diversity purposes, not the individual's state of citizenship at the time of the injury. In order to determine intent, the court will look at a number of factors including the individual's expressed intent, where he votes and pays his taxes, and the locations of his home and place of business. The court will look only to the intent of the individual at the time he moved to the state. In light of the rules set out by the Third Circuit and taking into account the facts that the age of majority in Pennsylvania is 18, that Gordon (P) rented an apartment in Rexburg, Idaho, and had expressed the intention to not return to Pennsylvania, it is clear that Gordon (P) is a citizen of Idaho for diversity purposes. Motion to dismiss denied.

Analysis:

In this case the court articulates the rule for determining an individual's citizenship for diversity jurisdiction purposes and applies it in a difficult case involving an 18-year-old who goes to college in Idaho, but whose parents live in Pennsylvania. 28 U.S.C. §1332(a)(1) allows federal courts to hear cases that involve state law causes of action where the damages total $75,000 and the parties on both sides of the dispute are citizens of different states. Presumably, Gordon's (P) damages total $75,000. Her status as a citizen of a different state than the doctors (D) and hospital (D) is less clear. At the time of her wrist injury and the doctors' (D) diagnosis, she was a citizen of Pennsylvania. By the time she brought suit, however, she had moved to Idaho to attend college. The court reached its conclusion that Gordon (P) was an Idaho citizen by taking into account her renting an apartment in Idaho and by examining her subjective intention to remain in Idaho indefinitely. Because she was a college student, the argument could be made that she had no intention to remain in Idaho indefinitely, but was planning to leave the state when she graduated. This argument is supported by the facts that Gordon (P) had spent school vacations in Erie and had not given up her Pennsylvania driver's license or Erie bank account. The court was not persuaded by this argument because Gordon (P) expressed an intention to remain in Idaho indefinitely as she would have a better opportunity to marry within her faith if she remained in Idaho. The court is also persuaded by the fact that Gordon (P) has leased an apartment in Rexburg. This represents an exercise of her right, as a legal or "emancipated" adult, to enter contracts. Gordon (P) is taking advantage of her legal status as an adult and her independence from her parents. Had she moved into a dormitory, the court might not have reached the same determination because she would not have signed a long-term lease signifying a commitment to Idaho and she would not have demonstrated that she had established a residence independent from her parents.

Bridges v. Diesel Service, Inc.

(Disabled Man) v. (Former Employer)
1994 U.S. Dist. LEXIS 9429 (E.D. Pa. 1994).

M E M O R Y   G R A P H I C

Instant Facts

An attorney representing a plaintiff in an employment discrimination case violates Rule 11(b) because she does not perform a competent level of legal research in preparing the complaint, but the court determines that Rule 11 sanctions are not appropriate under the circumstances.

Black Letter Rule

Rule 11 sanctions are designed to deter improper conduct and will only be applied in exceptional circumstances where the claim is patently frivolous. Procedural errors likely will not result in sanctions.

Case Vocabulary

CONDITION PRECEDENT: The condition that must be performed or event that must occur before a party can perform an obligation.

Procedural Basis: Defendant's motion for sanctions for plaintiff's violation of Rule 11(b)

Facts: James Bridges (P) sued Diesel Services, Inc. ("Diesel") (D), his former employer on the grounds that Diesel had terminated his employment because of his disability in violation of the Americans with Disabilities Act ("ADA"). The ADA requires that all administrative action be exhausted before a discrimination suit can be brought. Bridges' (P) attorney did not exhaust all administrative remedies before filing the complaint. She failed to file a charge with the Equal Employment Opportunity Commission ("EEOC") as required by the ADA. The court dismissed Bridges complaint for failure to exhaust administrative remedies. Diesel (D) moved for sanctions under Rule 11(c) of the Federal Rules of Civil Procedure, claiming that Bridges had violated Rule 11(b)(2)'s provision that by presenting a complaint to the court, an attorney is certifying that to the best of his knowledge, information, and belief, formed after a reasonable inquiry, that the claims in the complaint are warranted by existing law. Rule 11(c) allows the court to award sanctions for violations of Rule 11. The court can order the violator to pay the moving party's legal expenses.

Issue: Is the court obligated to impose sanctions under Rule 11(c) for any violation of Rule 11(b)?

Decision and Rationale: (Huyett, J.) No. The court is not obligated to impose sanctions for every violation of Rule 11(b). Rule 11(b) requires counsel to "'Stop, Think, Investigate and Research'" before filing a complaint. An attorney violates Rule 11(b) if signing the complaint is objectively unreasonable under the circumstances. An attorney's signature is a certification that the pleading is supported by a reasonable amount of factual investigation and a competent level of legal research. In this case, Bridges' (P) attorney did not demonstrate a competent level of research because she would have discovered the EEOC filing requirement after even a cursory examination of the ADA case law. However, although there is precedent for awarding Rule 11 sanctions for failure to exhaust administrative remedies, sanctions are not appropriate in this case. Rule 11 is designed to deter improper conduct and in this case there is no evidence that sanctions are necessary to deter future improper conduct by Bridges' (P) attorney. Bridges' (P) attorney acknowledges her error and filed the charge with the EEOC. Bridges' (P) complaint was dismissed and can be re-filed once the administrative remedies are finally exhausted. Rule 11(c) sanctions are only appropriate in exceptional circumstances, where the claim is patently frivolous. In this case, the attorney's mistake was not substantive, but procedural and possibly caused by a mistaken interpretation of a Supreme Court ruling on a matter involving an EEOC filing requirement. There is also a policy rationale for denying sanctions in cases such as this one: the possibility that plaintiffs would have to pay defendant's legal fees if the plaintiff's attorneys make procedural mistakes in filing pleadings would have a chilling effect on discrimination litigation. Motion for sanctions denied.

Analysis:

Rule 11(c) states that the court may impose sanctions for violations of Rule 11(b). Courts have discretion in deciding under what circumstances they will impose sanctions. In this case, the court decided that it would not impose sanctions where the defect in the complaint is minor and merely procedural rather than substantive. The defect in this case was easy to cure and Bridges' (P) attorney did so promptly. The court advances an important policy reason for not imposing sanctions for minor violations in discrimination cases. The court does not want to discourage litigation under Title VII by making such litigation prohibitively risky or costly. Responding to Diesel's (D) motion for sanctions cost Bridges (P) money, and had Diesel (D) prevailed, Bridges (P) would have had to pay the company's legal expenses. The court balances the need to avoid chilling Title VII litigation with the need to deter future violations of Rule 11 by naming Bridges' (P) attorney in the opinion and questioning her professional competence. [The fear of seeing his name linked with professional incompetence in law school civil procedure textbooks may effectively motivate an attorney to scrupulously adhere to the provisions of Rule 11(b).]

Bell v. Novick Transfer Co.

(Injured Automobile Passenger) v. (Owner of Tractor-Trailer Truck)
17 F.R.D. 279 (D. Md. 1955)

M E M O R Y   G R A P H I C

 ## Instant Facts

A minor child injured when a tractor-trailer truck crashed into the car in which he was a passenger sues the truck driver and his employer in federal court; and although the court applies state substantive law, it decides to apply federal procedural rules.

Black Letter Rule

A federal court is not required to apply a state "well-pleaded complaint" rule even when the case originated in state court under state substantive law.

Case Vocabulary

DECLARATION: Usually a statement under penalty of perjury; document which sets forth the plaintiff's cause of action and facts which sustain the cause of action, which advise defendant of the grounds upon which he is being sued.
DISCOVERY: The process through which both parties obtain the information that they intend to use as evidence at trial or to use in preparing their cases.
INTERROGATORY: Questions submitted by one party to the other party; interrogatories can be written, or they can be oral, in which case they take place during depositions.

Procedural Basis: Motion to dismiss for failure to state a compensable claim in a negligence action for damages.

Facts: Ronald Bell (P), a minor, was injured after the car he was riding in was hit from the side by a tractor-trailer truck [ouch!]. The truck was owned by Novick Transfer Company ("Novick") (D) and Katie Marie Parsons (D) and was operated by Morris Jarrett Coburn, III (D). Bell (P) filed a negligence claim in Maryland state court. The case was removed to federal court on Novick's (D) motion under 28 U.S.C. §§1441 and 1446. Novick (D) then moved to dismiss the case because Bell's (P) complaint failed to state a claim under which relief could be granted. Novick (P) argued that the complaint failed to state a compensable claim under Maryland rules of civil procedure because it did not allege any specific act of negligence that resulted in an injury to Bell (P). The complaint alleged that on August 14, 1954, Bell (P) was riding in a car on Race Road in Baltimore County, Maryland when, at the intersection of Race Road and Pulaski Highway, the car was struck on the passenger side by a tractor-trailer truck owned by Novick (D) and Parsons (D) and operated by Coburn (D). Coburn had been driving the truck in a reckless and negligent manner. The complaint listed Bell's (P) injuries and damages and asserted that they were caused by Novick's (D) negligence.

Issue: Is a federal court required to apply a state" well-pleaded complaint" rule when the case originated in state court under state substantive law?

Decision and Rationale: (Thompsen, J.) No. A federal court is not required to apply a state "well-pleaded complaint" rule, even thought the case originated in state court under state substantive law. Rule 8 of the Federal Rules of Civil Procedure requires only that a complaint be "a short and plain statement of the claim showing that the pleader is entitled to relief." Bell's (P) complaint satisfies this requirement by alleging negligence on Novick's (D) part and asserting that this negligence caused Bell's (P) injuries. Novick (D) also is not entitled to a "more definite statement" under Rule 12(e), because the information that Bell (P) would have to provide can be obtained during the discovery phase of the litigation. In this case, a more definite statement is not necessary to enable Novick (D) to form an adequate response to the complaint. Motion to dismiss denied.

Analysis:

This case highlights a difficult problem in civil procedure: how specific should a plaintiff's complaint be in order to survive a motion to dismiss for failure to state a compensable claim? How many facts does the plaintiff have to include in his complaint? The injured party is not always in a position to know all the facts relating to his cause of action. The factual development of a case happens during discovery. The discovery phase of litigation is where the parties spend most of their time and money. At the complaint stage, the plaintiff will have very little evidence—he may only have suspicions and theories. But it may not be fair to slap the defendant with a lawsuit, forcing him to hire a lawyer and incur fees and expenses, on the basis of suspicions and theories with little factual support. This case shows how different the federal approach to pleading can be from the state approach. Maryland rules of procedure require plaintiffs to do at least some factual development before filing a complaint. Maryland rules would have required Bell (P) to assert all four elements of the negligence claim: to describe what Novick's (D) duty was, how Novick (D) breached that duty, and how the breach caused Bell's (P) injury. Bell's (P) complaint only asserted injury and alleged that Coburn (D) was driving in a negligent manner. Rule 8 requires only a short and simple statement of the claim under which the plaintiff is entitled to relief. Bell's complaint satisfies this requirement. More detailed factual development will happen during discovery. As a result, Maryland's rule is more defendant-friendly than the federal rule. Maryland protects potential defendants from being forced into expensive frivolous lawsuits by requiring plaintiffs to back their complaints with some factual support. Rule 8 allows plaintiffs who may not be in a position to know all the facts to at least clear the first hurdle in litigation and get as far as the discovery phase. Getting as far as the discovery process allows the plaintiff to obtain information that the defendant might be trying to hide.

Temple v. Synthes Corp.

(Patient) v. (Implant Manufacturer)
498 U.S. 5 (1990)

M E M O R Y   G R A P H I C

Instant Facts

Temple (P) sued his doctor, the hospital, and a medical manufacturer in separate proceedings, for injuries sustained when a metal plate and screw device malfunctioned.

Black Letter Rule

It is not always necessary to make all joint tortfeasors parties to the same lawsuit.

Case Vocabulary

ADMINISTRATIVE PROCEEDING: A form of litigation before administrative agencies, rather than before a court.

DIVERSITY JURISDICTION: A means of federal subject-matter jurisdiction based on parties residing in different states.

JOINDER: The addition of persons or entities as parties to a lawsuit.

PER CURIAM: A phrase meaning "by the court," used to distinguish opinions written by the entire panel of judges rather than by a single judge.

WITH PREJUDICE: The dismissal of a claim which results in precluding the claim from being brought at a later time.

Facts: Temple (P) underwent a surgery in which a plate and screw device, manufactured by Synthes, Ltd. (D), was inserted in Temple's (P) spine. Following the surgery, the device's screws broke off inside Temple's (P) back. Temple (P) sued Synthes (D) in a Louisiana federal district court based on diversity jurisdiction, alleging that the design and manufacture of the device were defective. In addition, Temple (P) initiated a state administrative proceeding against the surgeon and the hospital in which the surgery was performed. [Why didn't Temple bring only one action? Did he have a screw loose?] At the conclusion of the administrative proceeding, Temple (P) sued the doctor and hospital in a state court in Louisiana. Synthes (D) filed a motion to dismiss the original claim for failure to join the doctor and hospital in the suit. The District Court ordered Temple (P) to join those parties. However, Temple (P) refused, and the District Court dismissed the action with prejudice. The Fifth Circuit Court of Appeals affirmed the dismissal, on the grounds that Synthes (D) was prejudiced by not having the doctor and the hospital present in the original litigation, since one of Synthes' (D) defenses might be that the doctor and hospital were negligent. The Supreme Court granted certiorari.

Issue: Must all interested entities always be made parties to a lawsuit?

Decision and Rationale: (Per Curiam) No. All interested entities do not necessarily have to be made parties to a lawsuit. Rule 19 of the Federal Rules of Civil Procedure governs the joinder of parties. Rule 19(a) dictates when parties must be joined, and Rule 19(b) allows a court to dismiss a suit if such joinder is not feasible. In the case at hand, the Court of Appeals held that the doctor and hospital should have been joined pursuant to Rule 19(a). However, we agree with Temple (P) that it was error to label the joint tortfeasors as indispensable parties and dismiss the lawsuit under Rule 19(b). As stated in the Advisory Committee Notes to Rule 19(a), it is not necessary that all joint tortfeasors be named as defendants to a lawsuit. Rather, the doctor and the hospital were merely permissive parties, whose joinder is not required. We reverse the judgment of the Court of Appeals and remand for further proceedings consistent with this opinion. Reversed and remanded.

Analysis:

This case provides an early glimpse into the complex rules of joinder in federal courts. Basically, the Federal Rules of Civil Procedure detail the circumstances under which a party must be joined to a pending lawsuit. For example, if complete relief cannot be afforded without the presence of a certain party, he must be made a party to the lawsuit. This rule accomplishes the overriding goal of judicial efficiency, as it is in the public interest to have all related claims tried in the same lawsuit. While it is not yet necessary to understand all of the workings of joinder at this point in the course, close attention should be paid to the recurring theme of judicial efficiency. Often judicial efficiency, in itself, mandates certain steps in a civil trial. However, these policy considerations are balanced by the rights of the parties. In the case at hand, Temple (P) was not required to bring suit against all of the defendants in the same action, although this certainly would have been more efficient. Notice that Temple (P) benefits from not having to sue the manufacturer, doctor and hospital in the same proceeding, since the parties cannot argue that the other's negligence actually caused the injury. It can also be inferred that certain jurisdictional benefits attach to the lack of joinder in this case. Perhaps the state laws of Louisiana were more favorable to Temple's (P) case. However, if he was required to sue all of the defendants in one forum, then they could have removed the case to the presumably less-favorable setting of a federal district court. All of these choice-of-law and jurisdictional issues will be considered in depth throughout this course. For now, just realize that there are numerous factors which come into play in deciding whom to sue and in which forum to bring suit.

Butler v. Rigby

(Automobile Accident Victims) v. (Negligent Party)
1998 U.S. Dist. LEXIS 4618 (E.D.La. 1998)

M E M O R Y   G R A P H I C

Instant Facts

The defendant in a lawsuit arising from a car accident requested information from the plaintiffs' health care providers and the providers objected on the grounds that the information was confidential.

Black Letter Rule

A legal privilege can be used to protect information from discovery under Rule 26.

Case Vocabulary

AFFIDAVIT: a written statement that has been signed and notarized.

Procedural Basis: Appeal of Magistrate Judge's denial of expert witnesses' motion for a protective order under Rule 26(c).

Facts: The lawsuit arose from an automobile accident. Butler and the other plaintiffs in the case (P) received medical treatment from the American Medical Group ("AMG") and from Midtown Health Center ("MHC"). Rigby (D) served AMG and MHC with notices of depositions requesting documents and other information. Rigby (D) asked AMG and MHC to provide any documents and other evidence that reflect: a listing of the total number of patients treated by AMG and MHC since 1992 that are now involved in the lawsuit and a list of patients referred to AMG and MHC by specific personal-injury lawyers. Rule 26(c) allows individuals from whom discovery is sought to move for a protective order even if they are not parties to the suit. Rule 26(b)(1) allows parties to obtain discovery "regarding any matter, not privileged, which is relevant to the subject matter involved in the pending action." Rule 26(b)(2) allows courts to restrict discovery if "the burden or expense of the proposed discovery outweighs its likely benefit." AMG and MHC moved for a protective order prohibiting Rigby's (D) discovery on the grounds that the list of patients referred by certain personal-injury lawyers was not relevant to the lawsuit under Rule 26(b)(1), that the listing of the number of current AMG and MHC patients was protected by the doctor-patient privilege, and that the request for information was unduly burdensome under Rule 26(b)(2) and (c). Rigby (D) argued that the listing of patients referred to AMG and MHC by specific personal-injury lawyers was relevant because it would show that AMG and MHC receive income from the lawyers who had originally represented Butler (P). The magistrate judge denied AMG's and MHC's motion.

Issue: Can a privilege, such as the doctor-patient privilege, protect certain information from discovery even when that information is relevant to the case under Rule 26(b)(1) and the request is not unduly burdensome under Rule 26(b)(2)?

Decision and Rationale: (Sarah Vance, J.) Yes. A privilege, such as the doctor-patient privilege, can protect certain information from discovery, even when the information is relevant to the subject of the lawsuit under Rule 26(b)(1) and the request was not unduly burdensome under Rule 26(b)(2). Rule 26 authorizes a broad definition of relevance. However, discovery can be limited when the request for information is unreasonably cumulative or duplicative or where the burden imposed outweighs the likely benefit of obtaining the information. AMG and MHC argued that the listing of all patients referred by certain personal-injury lawyers was both irrelevant and burdensome. Rigby (D) argued that the information was necessary to establish that AMG and MHC had received substantial income from attorneys who had represented Butler, et al. (P) and that AMG and MHC were biased as a result. Evidence of a "special relationship" between an attorney and his expert witness is relevant to establishing bias. Discovery that is designed to produce such evidence is allowed when the request for information is not too burdensome. In this case, the burden imposed on AMG and MHC does not outweigh the likely benefit to Rigby (D). However, because AMG and MHC will be put to considerable expense to provide lists of patients, and research the source of their referrals, Rigby (D) will have to pay half of AMG and MHC's costs. The listing of patients treated by AMG and MHC since 1992 would include a list of both current and past patients. The identities of a health care provider's past and current patients are protected under Louisiana case law by the doctor-patient privilege and are therefore not discoverable under Rule 26(b)(1). As an additional matter, it is unclear whether a list of past and current patients would be relevant to the subject matter of the lawsuit. Affirmed in part and reversed in part.

Analysis:

This case demonstrates how interested Congress and the courts are in protecting certain privileged communications. Courts generally prefer not to intervene during the discovery process, and to that end they tend to interpret relevance under Rule 26 very broadly. Under Rule 26(b)(1), information can be relevant for purposes of discovery even when it would be considered inadmissible at trial. This means that parties are allowed to obtain information from other parties and from witnesses that they have no realistic intention of using in the actual trial. Why has Congress given protection from discovery to certain legally-recognized types of privileged communications when other types of inadmissible evidence are not protected from discovery? Congress and the courts may want to encourage individuals to make these kinds of communications. Society has an interest in encouraging individuals to disclose their identities and the nature of their injuries to doctors. Patients might be less inclined to discuss their medical problems with their doctors if they knew that their discussion was not absolutely confidential. To allow doctors to reveal confidential information in a room full of lawyers during a deposition might undermine patients' trust in their doctors. Especially in cases such as this one, where the patients had suffered injuries in an automobile accident and were planning to sue for damages.

Houchens v. American Home Assurance Co.

(Widow) v. (Insurance Company)

927 F. 2d 163 (4th Cir. 1991)

M E M O R Y   G R A P H I C

 ## Instant Facts

A widow sues an insurance company for breach of contract when the insurance company refused to pay on her husband's accidental death claims after her husband had been declared legally dead.

Black Letter Rule

A legal presumption cannot be used to defeat a motion for summary judgment made on the grounds that a party does not have enough evidence to meet his burden of proof.

Case Vocabulary

INFERENCE: A permissible conclusion drawn from the evidence presented.

PRESUMPTION: A mandatory conclusion that has the effect of shifting to the opposing party the burden of disproving it.

Procedural Basis: Appeal of district court's granting motion for summary judgment.

Facts: In 1980, Coulter Houchens disappeared while on vacation in Thailand. According to Thai immigration records, Mr. Houchens arrived in Bangkok on August 15, 1980 and his entry permit was valid until August 29. No one has heard from Mr. Houchens since his arrival in Thailand. The State Department, FBI, ICAO, Red Cross, and Mrs. Houchens (P) all searched for Mr. Houchens, unsuccessfully. In 1988 a Virginia court issued an order declaring that Mr. Houchens was legally dead under Virginia law. Mrs. Houchens (P) then filed a claim with American Home Assurance Company ("American") (D), the provider of Mr. Houchens' two accidental death policies. American (D) refused to pay under these policies because there was no evidence that Mr. Houchens had died by accident. Mrs. Houchens (P) sued for breach of contract, and American (D) moved for summary judgment. The district court granted the motion on the grounds that Mrs. Houchens (P) did not have sufficient evidence that would allow a jury reasonably to find that Mr. Houchens was dead and that his death resulted from an accident.

Issue: Can a legal presumption be used to defeat a motion for summary judgment made on the grounds that the plaintiff cannot meet the burden of proof?

Decision and Rationale: (Ervin, C.J.) No. A legal presumption of death cannot be used to defeat a motion for summary judgment made on the grounds that the plaintiff cannot meet her burden of proving that there was a death by accident. Under Virginia law, a person who has been missing for seven years is presumed to be dead. But in order to recover under American's (D) insurance policies, Mrs. Houchens (P) must prove that Mr. Houchens' death was caused by accident. The district court applied the standard for granting summary judgment developed by the Supreme Court. Under the Supreme Court standard, the court should grant a motion for summary judgment against a party "who fails to make a showing sufficient to establish the existence of an element essential to that party's case." Under the 4th Circuit's summary judgment jurisprudence, the court will reverse a grant of summary judgment made by a district court if the record shows that there is "an unresolved issue of material fact." The 4th Circuit will examine the evidence presented in the light most favorable to the party opposing the motion. Mrs. Houchens (P) argued that the presumption that Mr. Houchens is dead was enough to meet her burden of proving that Mr. Houchens died accidentally. She based her argument on three cases decided outside the 4th Circuit. In one case, the court applied the rule that a jury is not allowed to reach a conclusion by piling inferences upon inferences. In other words, " a jury will not be permitted to extrapolate conjecturally beyond a legal conclusion which is itself arrived at circumstantially by inference from a proven fact." That court went on to find that the evidence that the deceased man had last been seen alive while asking for directions in the American River Ridge, where he had been hunting elk without the aid of a compass, was enough to give rise to two separate inferences: that the man had died, and that he had died by accident. Because a jury could reasonably have decided that the evidence supported either or both of those conclusions, the plaintiff in that case had not "piled inferences on inferences." In this case, however, there is only evidence of a disappearance, not of a death or an accident. A jury could conclude that Mr. Houchens disappeared, and presume that he died under Virginia law, but there is no evidence that would allow a jury to conclude that Mr. Houchens died as a result of an accident. To conclude that Mr. Houchens had died by accident based on Virginia's presumption that he was dead, which itself was based not on the fact that he had died but on the fact that he had disappeared, would be to pile inference upon inference. Affirmed.

Analysis:

This case shows how difficult it can be for a plaintiff to bring her case to trial. Even after an extensive period of discovery, a plaintiff can still see her case dismissed because she does not have enough evidence to create a genuine issue for a jury to decide on. Motions for summary judgment are made before the trial starts and before a jury is selected. Under Rule 56, the judge must decide on the basis of the documents presented to him whether a reasonable juror could conclude that the nonmoving party had enough evidence to meet his burden of proof and win the case. The jury's role is to decide between issues of conflicting material facts. If one party's assertions are unsupported by the evidence, then there is no issue for the jury to decide. However, if the parties are able to present witnesses that contradict each other, or documentary evidence that can be disputed, then the judge will not take the case away from the jury. Although the summary judgment standard makes it difficult for a party to get his case in front of a jury, there are some benefits to allowing a judge to dispose of a case before a trial. Summary judgment reduces the administrative burden that an excessive number of trials would impose on the court system. It prevents juries from hypothesizing a plausible set of circumstances to support assertions made in the absence of evidence, as in this case. And it prevents defendants from having to go to the expense of defending themselves from a frivolous claim that is not supported by evidence.

COURT TRIES UNSUCCESSFULLY TO GRANT A JUDGMENT NOTWITHSTANDING THE VERDICT AFTER DENYING A MOTION FOR A DIRECTED VERDICT

Norton v. Snapper Power Equipment

(Lawnmower Accident Victim) v. (Lawnmower Manufacturer)

806 F.2d 1545 (11th Cir. 1987)

M E M O R Y   G R A P H I C

Instant Facts

A judge granted a judgment notwithstanding the verdict in a strict liability case involving a man who lost four fingers after a lawnmower accident.

Black Letter Rule

A judgment notwithstanding the verdict cannot be granted after a motion for a directed verdict has been denied based on the same facts.

Case Vocabulary

DIRECTED VERDICT: A verdict that the jury issues after the court tells it exactly which verdict to issue.

Procedural Basis: Appeal from district court's entering of a judgment notwithstanding the verdict to the defendant in a strict liability action for damages.

Facts: James L. Norton (P) was in the commercial lawn mowing business. He bought a riding mower manufactured by Snapper Power Equipment ("Snapper") (D) in 1981. In 1983 Norton (P) was using the riding mower to clear leaves from a yard. He drove the mower up an incline away from a creek. When he reached the top of the incline, the mower began to reverse toward the creek. The mower did not respond when Norton (P) tried to brake, and eventually the mower crashed into the creek. Norton (P) caught his hand in the mower's blades and lost four of his fingers [yipes!]. After Norton (P) had presented his case, Snapper (D) moved for a directed verdict on all counts. The court dismissed all of Norton's claims but the strict liability claim. Norton's (P) strict liability claim was that Snapper's (D) failure to install a safety device called a "dead man" device in the mower rendered the mower defective and that this defect was the cause of his injury. The jury found for Norton (P) on the strict liability claim, and the court decided to enter a judgment notwithstanding the verdict. The court decided that the jury could not reasonably have found that a Snapper mower used in the normal course of use for which it had been designed could have had a defect that was the cause of Norton's (P) injury because Norton (P) did not present sufficient evidence that there was a defect in the mower at the time he bought it.

Issue: Can a court grant a judgment notwithstanding the verdict on an issue on which it has already decided not to grant a motion for a directed verdict based on the same facts?

Decision and Rationale: (Clark, J.) No. A court cannot grant a judgment notwithstanding the verdict on an issue on which it has already denied a motion for a directed verdict based on the same facts. The test for a judgment notwithstanding the verdict is the same as the test for a directed verdict. The court must consider the evidence presented in the light most favorable to the nonmoving party and should grant the judgment only when the evidence points so strongly in favor of the moving party that a reasonable jury could not arrive at a contrary verdict. Snapper (D) argued that because Norton (P) did not know exactly how his hand got caught in the mower's blades, the jury could not have determined that Snapper's (D) failure to install the "dead man" safety device was the cause of Norton's (P) injury. The 11th Circuit applies the rule that plaintiffs "are not entitled to a verdict based on speculation and conjecture." Juries are allowed to decide on the facts by drawing inference upon inference. In the 5th Circuit case of *Fenner v. General Motors Corp.*, the district court had granted a judgment notwithstanding the verdict in a case where the plaintiff argued that his injuries were caused when a defective steering mechanism caused his car to swerve off the highway after a stone lodged itself in the mechanism. In that case, the plaintiff had not allowed experts to examine his car to verify his claim. Because the experts could only testify that theoretically it was possible that a stone had been lodged in the plaintiff's steering mechanism, the court entered a judgment notwithstanding the verdict. In this case however, the causation evidence is much stronger. Norton (P) testified that his mower reversed into the creek and expert testimony verified that a "dead man" safety device would have stopped the blades in less than a second. The blades in Norton's (P) mower took two or three seconds to stop. A reasonable jury could have concluded that a "dead man" device could have prevented Norton's (P) injury.

Analysis:

After Norton (P) presented his case, Snapper (D) moved for a directed verdict. The court decided to allow the strict liability claim to be decided by the jury, but when the jury decided in Norton's (P) favor, the court reversed the jury's verdict, and did so on the same facts on which it had made its decision to deny Snapper's (D) motion for a directed verdict. When it reversed the jury's verdict, the trial court was saying that it thought this jury unreasonable, because no reasonable jury could have decided that Snapper (D) was liable for Norton's (P) injuries on the basis of the facts presented. But why allow the jury to enter a verdict at all? Why did the court not dispose of the case by granting Snapper's (D) motion for a directed verdict? The court wanted a jury verdict on record in case its decision to issue a judgment notwithstanding the verdict was reversed on appeal. Having a jury verdict on record prevented the court and the parties from re-trying the case with a new jury. This saved the parties money and the court time.

Rush v. City of Maple Heights

(Motorcycle Rider) v. (City)
167 Ohio St. 221, 147 N.E.2d 599 (1958)

M E M O R Y   G R A P H I C

Instant Facts
One judge limited Rush's recovery from the City for her injuries from an accident to $100, and another judge ordered the County to pay more.

Black Letter Rule
Whether or not injuries to both person and property resulting from the same wrongful act are to be treated as injuries to separate rights or as separate items of damage, a plaintiff may maintain only one action to enforce his rights existing at the time such action is commenced.

Case Vocabulary

VEXATIOUS: Distressing, troubling.

Procedural Basis: Appeal from judgment in negligence action for damages.

Facts: Rush (P) was injured in a motorcycle accident. She (P) sued the City of Maple Heights (D) in the Municipal Court of Cleveland. Rush (P) claimed the City (D) was negligent in maintaining the street and this negligence was the proximate cause of her (P's) damages. The trial court ruled for Rush (P), and damages were fixed at $100. The City (P) appealed, but the judgment was affirmed by the Ohio Court of Appeals and Supreme Court. Rush (P) also brought this action in the Court of Common Pleas of Cuyahoga. Rush (P) sought recovery for personal injuries she suffered in the same accident. She (P) moved to set trial on the issue of damages alone. The court granted this motion on the ground that the issue of negligence was res judicata because of the Municipal Court action. The Cuyahoga court entered judgment on a verdict for $12,000 for Rush (P). The Court of Appeals affirmed.

Issue: Can a plaintiff maintain more than one action for injuries to his or her rights resulting from one accident?

Decision and Rationale: (Herbert) No. Whether or not injuries to both person and property resulting from the same wrongful act are to be treated as injuries to separate rights or as separate items of damage, a plaintiff may maintain only one action to enforce his rights existing at the time such action is commenced. The rule presented in *Vasu v. Kohlers* [recovery or denial of recovery of compensation for damages to property is no bar to subsequent action for personal injury from same wrongful act unless an adverse judgment in first action would affect issue in second action] should not be followed because it is in conflict with the great weight of authority in this country. Generally, injuries to person and property amount to several effects of a single, wrongful act. A single tort can be the basis of but one action. Otherwise, multiple suits will arise, leading to significant delays and costs for all parties concerned. Allowing more than one action to arise from a single tort would allow, as Lord Coleridge stated in his dissent in *Brunsden v. Humphrey*, a man to bring two actions "if besides his arm and leg being injured, his trousers, which contain his leg, and his coat-sleeve, which contains his arm, have been torn." Judgment reversed, and final judgment for the City (D).

Concurrence: (Stewart) The discussion in *Vasu* as to whether a single or double cause of action arises from one tort nor the language of the syllabus of the lower court in *Vasu* were necessary to decide this case. Neither are appropriate to the question presented in this case.

Dissent: (Zimmerman) Without changing conditions to compel upsetting prior decisions of this court, established law should remain undisturbed. There should be some kind of stability that the lower courts and other members of the legal profession can rely on.

Analysis:

The limits on the scope of claim preclusion have developed greatly since the turn of the century. As the Restatement (Second) of Judgments explains, the courts used to associate the word "claim" with a plaintiff's single theory of recovery. This meant that a plaintiff would have as many claims as there were theories of substantive law that he could use to gain relief from the defendant. Thus, a plaintiff could raise several claims from just one injury-causing act or event. For instance, some courts would hold that a denial of relief in a claim for bodily injury did not preclude relief for injury to property. Also, some courts believed that a plaintiff had an amount of claims equal to the amount of his primary rights that were violated. Other courts would find that if certain evidence were used in an earlier claim, then a second action on the same evidence was precluded. At times, this evidence test was used as the sole test; at other times, courts used it as just one test out of many. Today, the courts generally see claims in factual terms and make the underlying transaction the basis of the litigation. In other words, the scope of claim preclusion was tied to the transaction as far as litigation was concerned, and not the number of theories, the number of primary rights, or the body of evidence.

Apex Hosiery Co. v. Leader

(Hosiery Company) v. (Labor Union)
102 F.2d 702 (3rd Cir. 1939)

M E M O R Y   G R A P H I C

 ### Instant Facts

A hosiery company sues a labor union for treble damages under the Sherman Antitrust Act and when the hosiery company requests information from the union during discovery, the union objects, is denied, and appeals.

 ### Black Letter Rule

An order to produce information under Rule 34 cannot be appealed.

Case Vocabulary

INTERLOCUTORY ORDER: an order that is related to the action, but whose resolution will not determine the final outcome of the action.

SUBPOENA DUCES TECUM: a subpoena that both requires a witness to appear in court to testify and requires the witness to produce documents or other evidence.

Procedural Basis: Appeal from a Rule 34 order to produce documents for discovery purposes in a case for treble damages arising under the Sherman Antitrust Act.

Facts: Apex Hosiery Co. ("Apex Hosiery") (P) is the plaintiff in an antitrust action. During discovery, Apex Hosiery (P) requested that Leader (D) (a labor union) produce documents for its inspection, copying, and photographing under Rule 34. Leader (D) objected, and the court issued an order requiring that Leader (D) produce the documents. Leader (D) appealed.

Issue: Can a party appeal a federal court order to produce documents under Rule 34?

Decision and Rationale: (Per Curiam) No. An order to produce documents for the inspection, copying, and photographing of the opposing party is an interlocutory order and cannot be appealed. This is the rule developed by the Supreme Court in *Cogen v. United States*. Only orders that have the effect of ending the case in favor of one party or the other can be appealed. The only exception is for orders that punish parties criminally for contempt: these orders do not effectively end the trial, but can be appealed. The order to produce documents will not cause the final disposition of the case in favor of Apex Hosiery (P) or Leader (D), and is therefore not appealable under *Cogen*. It is also clear that in this case the district court drafted the order carefully enough so that the document production will not unduly burden Leader (D).

Analysis:

This case deals with the final judgment rule, which is one method courts use to reduce the administrative burden too much litigation places on the judicial system. The rule has two important effects. First, prohibiting parties from appealing non-final orders such as the discovery order in this case prevents parties from exhausting each other (and the court) early on in the case by objecting to and appealing every request for discovery. Second, prohibiting appeals such as the one in this case encourages parties to settle. Defendants, who usually have been dragged into expensive litigation against their will, have an incentive to settle cases as soon as possible in order to avoid the expense of discovery and the further expense of a trial. The process of discovery influences settlement terms. If a plaintiff is unable to obtain the kind of information he feels would convince a jury to award him damages, and the court will not issue a discovery order, he may be tempted to settle with the defendant. A defendant will likely pay the plaintiff just to avoid going to trial. If the court does issue an order, the defendant may be encouraged to make a settlement offer to the plaintiff in order to avoid going to the expense of document production. Thus, the appellate court need only review a case once. Two things should be noted. First, just because a discovery order is not appealable when it is made, does not mean that it cannot be appealed after a final judgment is entered. After final judgment is entered, any error of the trial court can be appealed, including a discovery order. (But, of course, the discovery will have been already supplied and, therefore, there may be little to gain by the appeal.) Second, discovery orders are often reviewable by extraordinary writ (which is not the same as an appeal).

Chapter 2

The study of Civil Procedure, in some respects, overlaps the study of Constitutional Law. This book will examine two forms of jurisdiction, "personal jurisdiction" and "subject matter jurisdiction" of the federal courts, plus a doctrine known as the Erie Problem.

The main focus in this chapter will be on "personal jurisdiction." This raises the question of whether or not one state has the power to render a valid judgment against a defendant that does not reside or do business within the state, or that has not even come close to its boundaries. Constitutional issues arise in that the Due Process Clause requires that no state shall deprive one of life, liberty or property without due process of law. When a question of jurisdiction arises, there will always follow a due process issue with respect to its application.

The simplest form of personal jurisdiction arises when a person both resides and engages in conduct within the state which results in an action against him. No one would challenge the state's right to exercise jurisdiction over the person. However, what if the person resided in the neighboring state and engaged in conduct while in another state that resulted in a lawsuit being filed against him. Can this person be sued in the state where he engaged in the conduct or must he be sued in the state where he resides?

When the defendant is a corporation, many different jurisdictional issues may arise. Is it fair to allow a defendant that is a corporation to be sued in a state where it has no office nor any business? What if the corporation has some activity within the state, but the cause of action does not pertain to that specific activity in the state. Is it fair to sue the corporate defendant for conduct unrelated to its presence in the state?

As will be discussed in this chapter, consideration will be given to whether or not the corporate defendant has in some way benefitted from the protections or laws of the state. If it has, there is a strong likelihood that it can be sued in that state. What if a corporate defendant has no contact whatsoever with a state, but yet it knows that its products will be used within the state. Can the defendant be sued in the state?

We will also look at the issue of whether or not a defendant has *consented* to the jurisdiction of a state based upon its conduct.

Finally, this chapter will consider various restraints on the power of a state to exercise jurisdiction over a non-resident defendant. Examples of such restraints are statutes that limit when a state may exercise jurisdiction over a defendant, specify which court will entertain the lawsuit, or specify when a court may decline jurisdiction over a matter even though it is otherwise proper. These issues will be addressed in detail in the cases that follow.

Chapter 2

NOTE: THE PURPOSE OF THIS OUTLINE IS TO ORGANIZE THE CASES SO THAT ONE CAN QUICKLY UNDERSTAND THE RELEVANCE OF EACH CASE TO THE COURSE. NO ATTEMPT IS MADE IN THIS OVERVIEW TO ADDRESS EVERY CONCEPT THAT MUST BE STUDIED. BE SURE TO READ THE ENTIRE CASEBOOK AND/OR OTHER MATERIALS TO GAIN A FULL UNDERSTANDING OF ALL CONCEPTS.

I. The Constitutional Framework for U.S. Litigations
  A. Approaching Civil Procedure
    1. This book will first utilize the "top-down" approach to show how the Constitution affects or limits a lawsuit, by examining the history and interpretation of the Constitution.
    2. Later, the "bottom-up" approach will be utilized to discover how a lawsuit develops, with emphasis on the features and problems of the modern procedural system.
  B. Constitutional Limits in Litigation
    1. The word "jurisdiction" has a narrower meaning in the context of civil procedure than when used in a general context to signify a state or particular territory. In the civil procedure arena, it signifies the *power* of a court to render a judgment that other courts and government agencies will recognize and enforce. *The Idea of Jurisdiction.*
    2. "Personal" jurisdiction, the power of one court to render a binding judgment on someone who may have never been in the state, is the subject of this chapter. "Subject matter" jurisdiction, the power of federal courts to decide certain cases as opposed to state courts, is the subject of the following chapter. A court must have both personal and subject matter jurisdiction to render a binding and valid judgment. The courts look to the Constitution to decide many jurisdiction problems. There are three portions of the Constitution which pertain to jurisdiction issues:
      a. Article III, section 2, which sets forth the jurisdictional boundaries of the federal courts
      b. Article IV, section 1, the Full Faith and Credit Clause, which requires one state to recognize and enforce judgments of another state; and
      c. Section 1 of the Fourteenth Amendment, the Due Process Clause, which provides that no state shall deprive one of life, liberty or property without due process of law. *Jurisdiction and the Constitution.*
    3. In addition to personal and subject matter jurisdiction, the Constitution sometimes dictates which set of laws a court must apply. *Choice of law* is determined by the Supremacy Clause of Article VI which provides that the Constitution and the federal laws are the supreme law of the land, even if there is a contrary state law. *Choice of law* is also determined by the *Erie*

doctrine, which holds that in the absence of controlling federal law, the federal courts must look to the law of the state. *The Constitution and Choice of Law.*

II. Personal Jurisdiction (One of Two Tiers of State Court Jurisdiction)
  A. Origins
    1. *In personam* jurisdiction is based on the state having power over a person present in the state.
      a. Due process under the Constitution requires that in order to exercise jurisdiction over a person, reasonable methods must be employed to give the person notice of the action and afford him a reasonable opportunity to be heard.
      b. The type of notice required varies depending upon the type of jurisdiction. A state can obtain *in personam* jurisdiction over a non-resident only if that non-resident is personally served with process while within the state.
    2. *In rem* jurisdiction is based on the state having power over a person's property present in the state.
      a. *In rem* jurisdiction can be obtained if the non-resident owns property within the state, and that property is seized by way of "attachment" (pre-judgment seizure of property through court order to secure assets to satisfy future judgment).
    3. Service of process by publication in a newspaper is valid for *in rem* jurisdiction, but will not suffice for *in personam* jurisdiction. *Pennoyer v. Neff.*
      a. The court in *Pennoyer* held that service by publication on one not present within the state, and who owned no property in the state at the time the action was commenced, was not valid.
      b. *Pennoyer* involved the concept of power over the person and over the person's property. Where the property attached is to satisfy a claim unrelated to the property, it is referred to as *quasi in rem*. In one case, expansion of quasi in rem jurisdiction resulted in a state having jurisdiction based upon a defendant's debtors being located in the state and attaching the debts.
      c. *Pennoyer* recognized certain exceptions to its rule, such as the status of a citizen toward a non-resident. Thus, a deserted spouse could sue even if the absent spouse could not be served within the state.
      d. *Pennoyer* held that notice by publication was sufficient for in rem actions, but not for in personam actions.
      e. *Pennoyer* also involved the concepts of consent and presence. If a defendant consented to the state's assertion of power or if the defendant was present in the state, jurisdiction existed. Thereafter, issues arose concerning whether out-of-state corporations

or partnerships *consented* to the jurisdiction of the forum state or were *present* by doing business within the state. *Notes and Problems.*

B.   If one is sued in another state, and jurisdiction is disputed, the best procedure to follow is to raise the defense of lack of personal jurisdiction in a pre-answer motion, or in the answer.

1.   Some courts permit making a "special appearance" to raise only the issue of jurisdiction.

2.   If the defense is not raised early, the courts may hold that the defendant has waived the defense of lack of jurisdiction.

3.   If nothing is done, and a default judgment is obtained, one may challenge the judgment when enforcement proceedings take place. This is known as a collateral attack.

    a.   However, there is a risk that the jurisdiction defense will be denied, and if so, there is no longer an opportunity to defend the claim on the merits. *Note on the Mechanics of Jurisdiction: Challenge and Waiver.*

III.   The Modern Constitutional Formulation of Power

A.   Redefining Constitutional Power

1.   Shifting away from *Pennoyer's* requirement of service within the state to support in personam jurisdiction, the Supreme Court developed a new standard for asserting in personam jurisdiction with respect to corporate defendants.

2.   Relying upon the Due Process Clause of the Constitution, the court held that personal jurisdiction over a non-resident corporate defendant exists where the defendant has certain minimum contacts with the state and maintenance of the suit does not offend traditional notions of fair play and substantial justice.

3.   The court stated that consideration should be given to whether the corporation has presence in the state, such as systematic and continuous activities within the state, even if the cause of action does not arise from these activities, or whether the corporation enjoys the benefits and protections of the state's laws, and whether it would be reasonable to require the corporation to defend a suit in the state. *International Shoe Co. v. Washington.*

4.   The court in *International Shoe* held that a non-resident corporation that employed salesmen in a state to sell its products, shipped a large volume of its product to the state, and benefited from the laws of the state, was subject to jurisdiction in that state.

B.   Absorbing *In Rem* Jurisdiction

1.   *International Shoe* pertained to corporate non-resident defendants and did not address its applicability to individuals. It also pertained to in personam jurisdic-

tion, and did not address in rem jurisdiction.

2.   Subsequently, the Supreme Court held that *International Shoe's* minimum contacts standard applies to all forms of jurisdiction, including in rem and quasi in rem. Thus, even where there is property in the state that serves as a basis for jurisdiction, but is unrelated to the cause of action, there must be sufficient minimum contacts with the state to support jurisdiction over the defendant. *Shaffer v. Heitner.*

3.   The court in *Shaffer* held that neither the ownership of shares of stock of a corporation located in the forum state nor holding positions as directors and officers of the corporation, is sufficient minimum contacts to support jurisdiction over individual defendants.

C.   Specific Jurisdiction (There are two types of in personam jurisdiction, "general" and "specific.")

1.   For *specific jurisdiction*, the cause of action must arise out of the activities in the forum state, or the defendant must have purposely availed himself of the privilege of conducting activities in the state, thereby invoking the benefits and protections of its laws. The Modern Cases:

    a.   A single business transaction is enough to satisfy the minimum contacts test, provided the transaction is what gave rise to the claim, and was purposefully undertaken. *McGee v. International Life Insurance Co.*

    b.   The court in *McGee* held that a non-resident insurance company that refused to pay a life insurance claim may be sued in the state where the insured resided since the contract was delivered to the insured in the state, premiums were mailed from the insured's home to the defendant, and the insured was a resident of the state at the time of his death.

2.   Sufficient Minimum Contacts: There must be some act by which the defendant purposefully avails itself of the privilege of conducting activities within the forum state, thus invoking the benefits and protections of its laws. Sufficient minimum contacts do not exist if the only contacts with the state are sporadic and inadvertent, and do not give rise to the claim being asserted. *Hanson v. Denckla.*

    a.   The court in *Hanson* held that where a company has no office in the state, and neither transacts nor solicits any business there, it has not performed any acts within the state so as to establish jurisdiction. Merely sending income payments to a resident of the state does not constitute an act by which the company purposefully availed itself of the privilege of conducting activities within the state.

    b.   In order for there to be sufficient minimum contacts, a defendant must have purposefully availed itself of the forum state; if not, considerations of fairness, convenience and the interests of the state in overseeing the litigation are irrelevant. Foreseeability alone is insufficient. *World-Wide Volkswagen v. Woodson.*

    (1) The court in *World-Wide Volkswagen* held that where a car was sold and distributed in one state, and the buyers were involved in an accident while driving it through another state, the seller and distributor defendants did not purposefully avail themselves of the state where the accident occurred.

    (2) The court stated that it does not matter that it may be foreseeable that the car would be driven in other states.

    (3) The issue is foreseeability of litigation in the forum state. The court concluded that it was not foreseeable that the defendants would be haled into court in a state where they did not conduct business or intend to have the products reach that market.

3. Sufficient minimum contacts do not exist merely from intentionally putting a product into the stream of commerce with the expectation that it will reach the forum state. There must be some act showing that the company deliberately intended to take advantage of the state's market or laws. Even if sufficient minimum contacts exist, jurisdiction over the party must not offend the traditional notions of fair play and substantial justice. *Asahi Metal Industry Co. v. Superior Court.*

    a. The court in *Asahi* held that a manufacturer of a tire tube valve, who did no business with the forum state, and did not import any products thereto, lacked sufficient contacts with the state even though it was aware that its products might wind up in the state. Even if there were sufficient minimum contacts, the manufacturer was from a foreign country and it would not be fair or just to require it to defend in a distant forum with a foreign legal system.

4. Once sufficient minimum contacts with the forum state have been established, there is a presumption that it would be fair to require the defendant to defend a suit there. To overcome the presumption, the defendant has the burden of proving that it would be fundamentally unfair to defend in that state. *Burger King Corp. v. Rudzewicz.*

    a. The court in *Burger King Corp.* held that where a franchisee entered into a contract with the franchisor which expressly provided which state's law would govern, it was up to the non-resident franchisee to show that he would be unfairly prejudiced or harmed by having to defend in that state. Since he purposefully availed himself with a company from another state, sufficient minimum contacts

existed, even though he does not do any business within the state. Without any showing of unfairness or harm, the franchisee is subject to the jurisdiction of the forum state.

D. General Jurisdiction

  1. General jurisdiction arises when the activities in the forum state are so substantial and continuous that they need not have a connection to the cause of action alleged.

  2. To establish general jurisdiction over foreign corporations, the activities in the state must be substantial and continuous. A foreign corporation does not consent to general personal jurisdiction by merely complying with the state's mandatory requirements for doing business there. *Washington Equipment Mfg. Co. v. Concrete Placing Co.*

    a. The court in *Washington* held that a foreign corporation did not consent to general personal jurisdiction by obtaining a certificate of authority to do business and appointing a registered agent in the state in compliance with the state's law, all of which did not pertain to the claim sued upon.

  3. Transient jurisdiction (service of process on non-resident defendant while present in the state) by itself is sufficient for personal jurisdiction over an individual defendant. Such jurisdiction comports with due process and it is not necessary to establish minimum contacts with the state. *Burnham v. Superior Court.*

    a. The court in *Burnham* held that jurisdiction was properly obtained over a non-resident defendant who was visiting the forum state on business and was served with divorce papers while in the state.

E. The Outer Limits of Jurisdictional Power: Jurisdiction to Determine Jurisdiction

  1. Consent to jurisdiction may be implied by failure to comply with jurisdictional-related discovery. *Insurance Corp. of Ireland v. Compagnie des Bauxites de Guinee.*

IV. Consent as a Substitute for Power

A. Reasonable forum selection clauses are enforceable to establish consent to jurisdiction. Minimum contacts test is inapplicable when the clause is reasonable. *Carnival Cruise Lines v. Schutte.*

B. The court in *Carnival Cruise Lines* upheld jurisdiction based upon a forum selection clause contained on the back of a cruise ticket. According to the court, this amounted to consent to jurisdiction.

V. The Constitutional Requirement of Notice

A. In addition to jurisdiction, due process requires that a defendant be given notice that proceedings have been instituted against him. This requires that reasonable efforts be made to provide notice to persons affected.

B. Notice by publication fails to comply with due process where the names and addresses of the parties are known. *Mullane v. Central Hanover Bank & Trust Co.*

  1. In *Mullane*, the court required that notice be given by mail, rather than publication, to those individuals whose addresses were known.

C. State and federal rules provide regulation for the form of notice to be applied.

  1. In federal cases, notice may be given by personal service by the U.S. Marshal, or a person over eighteen years of age and not a party to the litigation.

  2. Mailing notice to a defendant and requesting the signing of a waiver of personal service is a proper method of informal service of notice.

    a. If a wavier is not obtained, other methods of giving notice are proscribed by the rules depending upon whether it is an individual or corporate defendant, domestic or foreign, or a state or federal governmental agency.

VI. Self-Imposed Restraints on Jurisdictional Power: Long-Arm Statutes, Venue, and Discretionary Refusal of Jurisdiction

A. Long-Arm Statutes as a Restraint on Jurisdiction

  1. Long-arm statutes authorize various methods of service of process on out-of-state defendants. They authorize states to extend their jurisdictional "arms" beyond their own borders.

  2. A state's long-arm statute may restrict personal jurisdiction even if the constitution would otherwise permit jurisdiction. *Gibbons v. Brown*.

    a. In *Gibbons*, a state long-arm statute provided that "a non-resident defendant who is engaged in substantial and not isolated activity within this state" is subject to the jurisdiction of the state.

    b. The court held that jurisdiction was not proper where the only contact the non-resident defendant had with the state was the filing of a lawsuit two years earlier against a defendant who was not a party to the current suit.

B. Venue as a Further Localizing Principle

  1. Venue determines where the litigation takes place. It is based upon statutory limitation on the geographic location of the litigation. Venue must be determined in addition to jurisdiction.

    a. Thus, if there are a number of federal district court's within a state, venue statutes will provide which district is proper.

    b. Depending upon the applicable statute, venue may be determined by the place of defendant's residence, or where the activity that is the subject of cause of action took place.

  2. Venue is determined solely from statutory rather than constitutional sources. This differs from jurisdiction which requires a statute, and then a constitutional analysis concerning due process of law. *Dee-K Enterprises, Inc. v. Heveafil Sdn. Bhd.*

    a. In *Dee-K Enterprises*, the court held that a general federal venue statute subjecting alien corporations to suit in any judicial district overrides other federal statutes that may contain specific venue provisions.

  3. If an action is brought in state court, federal venue statutes are irrelevant since they apply only to federal actions.

C. Declining Jurisdiction: Transfer and Forum Non Conveniens

  1. State and federal courts have the power to decline jurisdiction even though it exists. An example is a long-arm statute that is more limiting than that which is permitted by the Constitution. Other situations occur where there are transfers among federal district courts and transfers based upon forum non conveniens.

  2. Forum Non Conveniens

    a. In applying the doctrine of forum non conveniens, the fact that the substantive law is less favorable to a plaintiff in an alternative forum than the one in which the action was initially brought should not be given conclusive or substantial weight. *Piper Aircraft v. Reyno*.

    b. Transfer under 28 U.S.C. §§1404, 1406, and 1631: Federal statutory law permits transfer to a different judicial district for the convenience of parties and witnesses, in the interest of justice. This allows transfers within the federal court system without the need for dismissal and refiling, which would be required under the doctrine of forum non conveniens.

Pennoyer v. Neff

(Current Occupier of Land) v. (Rightful Owner of Land)
95 U.S. 714 (1877)

M E M O R Y   G R A P H I C

Instant Facts

Neff (P) sought to recover possession of land which had been seized and sold to pay off a default judgment against him, claiming that the judgment was invalid, as the court involved had not had personal jurisdiction over him.

Black Letter Rule

Every state possesses exclusive jurisdiction and sovereignty over persons and property within its territory; therefore, the courts of that state may enter a binding judgment against a non-resident only if he is personally served with process while within the state, or, if he has property within the state, if that property is attached before litigation begins.

Case Vocabulary

EX PARTE: With the presence of one party only.

Procedural Basis: Writ of Error to the Circuit Court of the United States for the District of Oregon, for its judgment in action to recover the possession of land.

Facts: In the years prior to the Civil War, as America pursued its Manifest Destiny ever Westward, a young man named Marcus Neff (P) set out for the Oregon frontier--thus setting in motion a chain of events that would eventually culminate in one of the most famous Supreme Court cases ever--as well as the bane of law students everywhere for more than a hundred years. Neff (P) staked a claim for land from the federal government and in 1862 sought advice from a well-known Portland attorney (and future U.S. Senator) named John Mitchell, who specialized in land litigation. Whatever Mitchell did for Neff (P), Neff (P) apparently never paid him for it. Mitchell waited until late 1865, and then brought suit against Neff (P) in Oregon state court to recover the unpaid legal fees. As was totally proper under Oregon law at the time, Mitchell did not serve Neff (P) personally with notice of the suit, but published notice in a local newspaper (so-called "service by publication"). Neff (P), not being an Oregon resident at the time, somehow failed to see this notice, and did not show up to defend his rights in court. Mitchell thus easily obtained a default judgment against Neff (P) in 1866. Coincidentally enough, this happened to be the same year that Neff's (P) land patent arrived, which enabled Mitchell to have the land seized and sold at auction by the local sheriff to satisfy the judgment. At the auction, Mitchell himself was the lucky bidder. One can only assume that he got a fair price from himself for the land! Anyway, a few days after the auction Mitchell assigned the land to Sylvester Pennoyer (D), future Mayor of Portland and Governor of Oregon. Pennoyer (D) spent nine years and quite a bit of money improving the property, only to have Neff (P) show back up, claiming the land was still his. Neff (P) then sued Pennoyer (D) in federal court for possession of the property, claiming that the original judgment against him had not been valid, because the Oregon court had not had jurisdiction over him or the land. The Federal Circuit Court agreed that the other judgment was invalid and that the land really did belong to Neff (P), although not for the reasons that the Supreme Court later found persuasive. Apparently, the Circuit Court's decision was based on some technicality related to how the notice had been published. Of course, it's possible to suspect ulterior motives for the Circuit Court's judgment, since Judge Deady, the judge involved, seemed to be just as immersed in local politics as Mitchell and Pennoyer (D). In fact, Deady was later instrumental in exposing Mitchell for the lying, bigamous, adulterer that he was. (Not that this had a negative impact on his career as a Senator!) Pennoyer (D) appealed Deady's decision to the Supreme Court, but lost there too. So Neff (P) got his land back, and the country got a new-and-improved theory of personal jurisdiction. Well, the personal jurisdiction theory lived on for years, but Mitchell's career was eventually brought to a halt, when he was indicted and convicted for-- of all things--land fraud in Alaska.

Issue: Can a state court exercise personal jurisdiction over a non-resident who has not been personally served with process while within the state, and whose property within the state was not attached before the litigation began?

Decision and Rationale: (Field) No. A state can obtain *in personam* jurisdiction over a non-resident only if that non-resident is personally served with process while within the territory of the state. *In rem* jurisdiction can be obtained if the non-resident owns property within the state, and that property is attached at the very outset of the trial. *In personam* jurisdiction means that the state has complete power over an individual, and stems from the notion that a state has exclusive control over all people within its borders; *in rem* jurisdiction stems from the idea that a state has exclusive control over all land within its territory, and means that the state can adjudicate disputes over the status of such property, but only up to the value of the property. In the case before us, the original action was initiated by publication of service. The Oregon state court which heard that case did not exercise either *in personam* or *in rem* jurisdiction -- nor could it have. Neff (P), the defendant in that action, was not within the state of Oregon at the time, and so could not be personally served with process. Service of process is basically a command by a court to appear before it, or suffer the consequences. It dates back to a time when lawsuits were initiated not by a command to appear before the court, but by the sheriff actually taking the defendant into custody and physically bringing him before the court. But an Oregon sheriff could not go into another state--say California--and start hauling California residents back to Oregon to appear before an Oregon court. This would be an infringement of California's sovereignty. Thus, those same California residents could not be commanded to appear before an Oregon court either--unless, of course, they came into Oregon, in which case they came under Oregon's power, and could be seized or served with process while there. As Neff (P) was not within Oregon, he was not within Oregon's power, and could not be made to appear before an Oregon court. Period. Certainly not by publication in some obscure local newspaper, but not even if he had been tracked down and served with process personally wherever he was at the time. If he had come into Oregon and been served with process while there, then the Oregon courts would have had *in personam* jurisdiction over him. But he did not, and they did not. End of *(in personam)* story. *In rem*, however, still remains to be dealt with. While Oregon courts cannot exercise power over non-residents not found within the state, they do have power over any property the non-residents might own within Oregon. Originally, "property" in this context meant land, and dated back to the idea that a state should and did have ultimate power over all land within its borders. If there is a dispute over land, it makes sense that the state where that land is located should be able to mediate and resolve the dispute. And it also makes some sense that

anyone who claims an interest in that particular piece of land should keep an eye on it--or at least check on it every so often. Ideally, an out-of-state landowner will appoint an agent of some kind to look after the land in his absence. It's not good public policy to encourage people to just abandon land for years at a time. Therefore, it is reasonable to assume that if land is attached by a court prior to a lawsuit, the owner of the land will--or should--find out about the lawsuit. (Attachment here simply means that the court forbids the land from being sold, etc., while the suit is pending. Practically speaking, the sheriff will go out to the land and post notices announcing the suit, so anyone living there or going by to check it out will see them and know what's going on.) If the owner of that land does not check on it at least occasionally, he doesn't really deserve to own it, and it will be forfeit to the other party. While this type of proceeding was originally limited to pure *in rem* actions actually relating to the land itself, the doctrine of *quasi in rem* jurisdiction developed to allow the attachment of land as a means of initiating an action that had absolutely nothing to do with the land. But the same theory was involved--anyone really taking care of his land would find out what was going on. However, this was not done in the case at issue. If Mitchell had attached Neff's (P) land at the very beginning of his suit, then the court would have been able to issue a valid judgment in the case. However, Mitchell did not attach Neff's (P) land at the beginning of the suit. In fact, there's no way that he could have done so, since Neff (P) did not own the land at the time Mitchell instituted the action. Neff's (P) land patent did not arrive until after Mitchell had already obtained a judgment. Thus the court had no basis for exercising jurisdiction over Neff (P) at all, so the default judgment must be declared invalid. Since the sheriff therefore had no power to auction the land, Neff (P) must still legally own it. Judgment affirmed.

Analysis:

Just about every Civil Procedure course starts out with the study of personal jurisdiction, and the study of personal jurisdiction usually starts with *Pennoyer v. Neff*. Learn it, love it, live it. Just don't get too upset when you realize it's long since been overturned. People still refer to it and talk about it, and all the personal jurisdiction cases that follow it can't be understood without it, so it's still really important to fully understand what it says. The sordid background histories of the various characters involved in the actual case liven it up a little bit, but the decision itself deals with concepts of territory and power that are central to our federal system of government. Actually, *Pennoyer* didn't invent anything new; it represents rather the first time that the U.S. Supreme Court had enunciated a coherent, national standard for the exercise of jurisdiction by states over non-residents. The idea that a sovereign state had exclusive and complete power over everything and everyone within its borders, but not outside them, wasn't new, and was similar to how the international law worked at the time. What was different, of course, was that the various states of the United States were not independent and fully sovereign nation-states. The states were bound by the Constitution to give "full faith and credit" to the judgments of the courts of its sister states, which put some limitations on state power. These limitations were increased by the passage of the 14th Amendment after the Civil War, which allowed the direct challenge of judgments that had been rendered without proper jurisdiction. More mobility of people could be expected between the states than between countries, which increased the chances that one state's citizen would come under the jurisdiction of another state. A standard needed to be found that would allow states some power over non-residents without offending the power of other states. *Pennoyer* was the Supreme Court's answer to this problem, but as it turned out it was probably well on its way to being obsolete even at the time it was announced. The following cases will demonstrate that the increasing interdependence of the national economy caused problems that the *Pennoyer* standard could not hope to solve, and called for new approach.

International Shoe Co. v. Washington

(Delinquent Taxpayer) v. (Tax Assessor)
326 U.S. 310 (1945)

M E M O R Y   G R A P H I C

Instant Facts

A shoe company with salesmen in Washington State claimed not to be subject to Washington's jurisdiction when the state tried to collect unemployment taxes.

Black Letter Rule

A corporation will be subject to the jurisdiction of any state with which it has "minimum contacts" that make the exercise of jurisdiction consistent with "traditional notions of fair play and substantial justice."

Case Vocabulary

CAPIAS AD RESPONDENDUM: Method of commencing a court action in which the defendant is physically seized by the sheriff, and kept in custody until he is brought before the court.
DISTRAINT: Seizure of property.

Procedural Basis: Appeal from sustaining of denial of motion to dismiss notice of assessment of unpaid unemployment contributions.

Facts: International Shoe Co. (D) was incorporated in Delaware, and had its primary place of business in St. Louis, Missouri. It made and sold shoes in several states. In Washington State it did not maintain any offices or manufacturing facilities, but did employ some 11 to 13 salesmen during the years at issue (1937-1940). These salesmen were under the direct supervision of sales managers in St. Louis but lived and worked entirely within the state of Washington. The salesmen received samples from the company and showed these samples to potential customers to solicit orders. Sometimes the salesmen rented showrooms for the samples. Orders were filled from St. Louis, and the merchandise was sent straight to the customer, not to the salesman. The salesmen operated on commission and averaged around $31,000 per year (not bad during the Great Depression!). The State of Washington (P), in accordance with its laws on unemployment insurance, assessed International Shoe Co. (D) for its contribution and served notice both personally on one of the salesmen within the state and by mail to the St. Louis headquarters. International Shoe (D) challenged the service, claiming that the salesman was not a proper agent for service of process, and that it was not "present" or "doing business" within the state of Washington so as to be subject to that state's jurisdiction. The unemployment office, the Commissioner, the Superior Court, and the Supreme Court of Washington all held that service had been proper, and that jurisdiction did exist. International Shoe (D) appealed to the U.S. Supreme Court, claiming that its due process rights had been violated.

Issue: Is a corporation not chartered within a state subject to that state's jurisdiction if it has certain "minimum contacts" with the state?

Decision and Rationale: (Stone) Yes. A corporation is subject to the jurisdiction of a state so long as it has certain "minimum contacts" with that state. Many previous decisions have based jurisdiction over corporations on whether they are "present" within the state. Since it is much harder to determine whether a corporation--which is after all merely a fiction--is to be found within a state's borders for exercise of its territorial power than it is with an actual human defendant, there has been a lot of debate over what it means for a corporation to be "present" within a state. Discussions of "presence" have centered around the extent of a corporation's activities within a state necessary to make subjecting it to jurisdiction there consistent with due process. Generally, systematic and continuous activities within a state have been held to be enough to subject a corporation to jurisdiction there--especially when the cause of action arises from those activities, but even in some cases where the cause of action does not arise from those activities. In some cases even a single, isolated contact with a state has been enough, when that contact gives rise to the cause of action. Obviously, a corporation that has no contacts at all with a state should not be subject to that state's jurisdiction. But a corporation that does conduct activities within a state also enjoys the benefits and protections of the state's laws and should therefore be held subject as well to those laws, and to actions brought to enforce those laws. There is no mechanical way to decide whether, in a particular case, a corporation's contacts with a state have reached the level necessary for the exercise of jurisdiction; instead, the nature and extent of those contacts must be evaluated under traditional concepts of fairness and justice to determine whether it would be reasonable to require the corporation to defend a suit in that state. In this case, International Shoe (D) has benefitted from the laws of Washington, which protected its numerous sales there. It has shipped a large volume of merchandise into Washington over the years, and has exercised continuous and systematic sales activities there. Also, the very nature of this suit arose from the company's activities there. The fact that International Shoe (D) employed salesmen within the state of Washington raised the issue of whether the company, as an employer, was required to make contributions to the state unemployment system. Therefore, the exercise of jurisdiction in this case by the courts of the state of Washington was not improper, and did not infringe International Shoe's (D) due process rights. Judgment affirmed.

Concurrence: Jurisdiction was proper in this case. The U.S. Constitution granted to each state the right to tax and subject to suit any corporation whose activities within a state affect that state's citizens and businesses. Period. This Court should not have the power to invalidate a state's assertion of jurisdiction merely because the members of this Court have a different opinion of what is "fair" or "reasonable."

Analysis:

This is another biggie. *International Shoe* essentially overturned the in personam half of *Pennoyer,* and provided the basis for the jurisdictional tests that are still used today. MINIMUM CONTACTS. FAIR PLAY AND SUBSTANTIAL JUSTICE. REMEMBER THESE WORDS! They will haunt you forever! (Well, hopefully at least through your final exam in Civil Procedure.) While *International Shoe* was originally geared to the burgeoning problem of establishing jurisdiction over corporations, which did not really fit within the *Pennoyer* categories, it did not take long at all for the ideas behind *Shoe* to spill over onto individuals. With regard to corporations, however, some guidance was badly needed. Since corporations are considered legal fictions that could not exist outside the state that created them, it was difficult for states to get jurisdiction over foreign corporations. And yet, corporations could obviously operate in more than one state at a time, and could have large impacts on the economy and society of states other than their own. Disputes with a corporation would often arise in a state where that corporation did not legally "exist." Somehow, states needed a way to obtain jurisdiction in these types of situations. Various theories, such as implied consent, were tried, but the time was ripe for change when *International Shoe* came along.

Shaffer v. Heitner

(Officer or Director) v. (Shareholder)
433 U.S. 186 (1977)

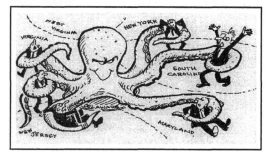

M E M O R Y   G R A P H I C

 ### Instant Facts
Heitner (P) brought a shareholder's derivative suit against several officers and directors of Greyhound, a Delaware corporation, gaining in rem jurisdiction by attaching their stock in Greyhound.

Black Letter Rule
Minimum contacts must exist in order for in rem jurisdiction to attach.

Case Vocabulary

SEQUESTRATION STATUTE: A law providing for the attachment of intangible personal property, such as stock, pending a litigation.

SHAREHOLDER'S DERIVATIVE SUIT: A suit by a shareholder raising a corporate cause of action, such as a suit against officers for a breach of fiduciary duty.

SPECIAL APPEARANCE: A submission to the jurisdiction of a court for limited purposes, including the contesting of jurisdiction.

Procedural Basis: Writ of certiorari reviewing affirmance of rejection of arguments contesting jurisdiction for shareholder's derivative suit.

Facts: Heitner (P), a nonresident of Delaware, owned one share of stock in Greyhound Corp., a business incorporated in Delaware. Heitner (P) filed a shareholder's derivative suit in Delaware state court, naming 28 officers or directors of Greyhound as defendants. Heitner (P) alleged that the officers and directors had breached their fiduciary duties. At the same time the complaint was filed, Heitner (P) filed a motion for sequestration of shares of approximately 82,000 shares of stock owned by 21 of the officers and directors, as allowed by Delaware law. Those 21 defendants entered a special appearance in Delaware, contending that the sequestration procedure violated due process and that the property was incapable of attachment in Delaware. In addition, the 21 defendants asserted that they did not have sufficient minimum contacts to justify Delaware jurisdiction. The Court of Chancery rejected these arguments, and the Delaware Supreme Court affirmed, holding that Delaware had a sufficient interest in the action to justify jurisdiction. The Supreme Court granted certiorari.

Issue: Is in rem jurisdiction subject to a minimum contacts analysis?

Decision and Rationale: (Marshall, J.) Yes. In rem jurisdiction is subject to a minimum contacts analysis. Traditionally, courts have ignored the lack of contacts between a defendant and a state in asserting quasi in rem jurisdiction. While the law governing in personam jurisdiction has expanded dramatically in recent years, no such change has occurred in the law governing in rem jurisdiction. In *Mullane v. Central Hanover Bank & Trust Co.* [Reasonable efforts must be made to give property owners actual notice of the action], we noted that, since an adverse judgment in rem directly affects the property owner by divesting him of his rights in property, certain Fourteenth Amendment rights must attach. Since jurisdiction over property involves jurisdiction over a person's interests in the property, the proper standard is the minimum contacts standard elucidated in *International Shoe Co. v. Washington* [Due process requires that minimum contacts exist for in personam jurisdiction]. We recognize that the presence of property in a State may impact this minimum contacts analysis, as a defendant having property in the state would normally have purposefully availed himself of the jurisdiction of the state. However, in this case, we focus on a different type of quasi in rem action, in which the property serving as the basis for state-court jurisdiction is completely unrelated to Heitner's (P) cause of action. Since the assertion of jurisdiction over property is really just an assertion of jurisdiction over the owner of the property, we conclude that all assertions of state-court jurisdiction must be evaluated according to the standards set forth in *International Shoe* and its progeny. In the case at hand, the officers' and directors' holdings in Greyhound do not provide contacts with Delaware sufficient to support Delaware jurisdiction. Indeed, Delaware has a strong interest in supervising the management of a Delaware corporation, but the Delaware Legislature has failed to assert this interest. Moreover, Delaware is not a fair forum for this litigation. As far as the record indicates, the officers and directors had never set foot in Delaware, and they had not purposefully availed themselves of the benefits and protections of that State. It strains reason to suggest that anyone buying securities in a corporation formed in Delaware impliedly consents to Delaware jurisdiction on any cause of action. Reversed.

Concurrence: (Powell, J.) While I reserve judgment on whether ownership of property in a State may provide the contacts necessary for jurisdiction, I favor the preservation of the common law concept of quasi in rem jurisdiction in the case of real property.

Concurrence: (Stevens, J.) I would find the Delaware sequestration statute unconstitutional, creating an unacceptable risk of judgment without notice.

Delaware denies a defendant the opportunity to defend the merits of a suit unless he subjects himself to the jurisdiction of the court. In effect, this creates a duty of inquiry upon every purchaser of securities to know the place of incorporation of the company and the unique requirements of Delaware law. However, I am uneasy with the reach of the opinion, and I concur with Justice Powell that the opinion should not be read so as to invalidate in rem jurisdiction over real property.

Dissent and Concurrence: (Brennan, J.) While I agree that the minimum-contacts analysis represents a sensible approach to the exertion of state court jurisdiction, I dissent from the ultimate holding of the case. The majority has treated Delaware's

statute as a long-arm statute requiring a minimum contacts analysis. However, the Delaware statute expressly denied such an approach. State court jurisdiction is proper only with notice and an applicable long-arm statute, and there was no such statute applicable in this case. Jurisdiction might indeed be in Delaware's best interest, and the problems with other states applying Delaware's laws argues against denying Delaware jurisdiction over this matter. Nothing noted in the majority opinion persuades me that it would be unfair to subject the officers and directors to suit in Delaware. They certainly associated themselves with the State of Delaware, thereby invoking the benefits and protections of its laws.

Analysis:

This is undoubtedly one of the most important of all of the cases pertaining to jurisdiction. In one broad opinion, Justice Marshall overturned the traditional approach to in rem jurisdiction, equating the in rem test with the minimum contacts test for personal jurisdiction. Thus, in rem jurisdiction is appropriate only where a defendant purposefully availed himself to the benefits and protections of the forum state, or where there is sufficient relatedness between the cause of action and the forum state. Arguably, neither were present in this case. Of course, Marshall could have simply chosen to invalidate the sequestration statute, but instead he took this opportunity to alter the constitutional in rem analysis substantially. The opinion makes a number of logically sound conclusions on the way to its revolutionary holding. First, it is indeed true that in rem jurisdiction can affect a person just as much as in personam jurisdiction. Both affect a person's rights in money or property. Second, considerations of fairness dictate requiring some minimum contacts between the forum state and any person whose interests may be adversely affected by litigation. In the case at hand, the only contact between the property at issue and the state of Delaware was the fact that the stock happened to be in a Delaware corporation. If ever there was a case to deny jurisdiction, this seems to be a very strong one. Note that this decision is likely to have the most profound effect on in rem cases where there was no pre-existing legal interest between the plaintiff and the property, and where the suit is unrelated to the property. Otherwise, there may well be sufficient minimum contacts to justify in rem jurisdiction. After this case, it may be questioned whether there is any continued need to distinguish between in rem and in personam jurisdiction. For two reasons, it is important to continue the distinction. First, where a state's long-arm statute does not extend to the full limits of due process, it may remain impossible to obtain in personam jurisdiction over nonresident defendants, even if minimum contacts could be demonstrated to obtain jurisdiction over their property in rem. Second, in some "true" in rem cases, it is impossible to know who the owners of the property are. The traditional rules for in rem jurisdiction continue in force for these cases. It is also important to note the discussion related to the "special appearance" which the officers and directors attempted to make in Delaware. While most states allow limited appearances for the purposes of contesting jurisdiction, Delaware expressly forbade such actions. Thus, by contesting jurisdiction, the officers and directors voluntarily submitted to unlimited jurisdiction of Delaware. In ruling that no such jurisdiction attached in this case, the court may have implicitly invalidated Delaware's harsh law and all others like it. Finally, the immediate aftermath of this suit is interesting. Within thirteen days after the decision, Delaware amended its laws to provide unlimited personal jurisdiction over every director of a Delaware corporation. Shortly thereafter, Greyhound reincorporated in Arizona so as to avoid the unreasonable burden the new Delaware statute would place on directors. Unfortunately for Delaware, its attempt to force Delaware jurisdiction backfired in at least this one instance.

McGee v. International Life Insurance Co.

(Beneficiary of Policy) v. (Holder of Policy)
355 U.S. 220 (1957)

M E M O R Y   G R A P H I C

Instant Facts

McGee (P), the beneficiary of a life insurance policy held by International Life (D), a Texas company, brought suit in California when International Life (D) refused to pay.

Black Letter Rule

A state may exercise jurisdiction over a defendant whose contacts with that state consist of only a single act, provided that that act is what gave rise to the claim for which jurisdiction is being sought, and was deliberately directed toward the state.

Procedural Basis: Appeal from Texas court's refusal to enforce California judgment in action to recover proceeds of life insurance policy.

Facts: Lowell Franklin, a resident of California, had a life insurance policy with the Empire Mutual Insurance Company, of Arizona. In 1948 International Life Insurance Company (D), of Texas, took over Empire Mutual's policies. International Life (D) sent statements to Franklin in California, and Franklin sent payments to International Life (D) in Texas. When Franklin died in 1950, International Life (D) refused to pay the proceeds of his policy to his designated beneficiary, McGee (P), claiming that Franklin had committed suicide. McGee (P) brought suit in California, under a state law that authorized service of process on out-of-state companies holding insurance contracts with in-state residents. McGee (P) won a judgment against International Life (D) in California, then tried to enforce it in Texas. The Texas courts, however, refused to enforce the judgment, claiming that California's exercise of jurisdiction was improper. McGee (P) appealed the Texas decision to the U.S. Supreme Court.

Issue: Can a state ever exercise jurisdiction over a defendant whose contacts with that state are limited to a single act or contract?

Decision and Rationale: Yes. A state can exercise jurisdiction over a defendant whose contacts with that state consist solely of a single act or contract, provided that that act is what gave rise to the claim, and was purposefully undertaken. Due to the fact that business has become increasingly nationalized in recent years, more and more contracts are between actors in different states. This trend has encouraged and necessitated an increasingly wide scope for the exercise of jurisdiction across state lines. California enacted this particular long-arm statute to protect the rights of its citizens against out-of-state insurance companies. Given the nature of the insurance business, it is much more likely that small policy holders would be denied justice if forced to file suit in a foreign jurisdiction, than that insurance companies would be more than slightly inconvenienced by having to defend a suit in California. True, in this particular case International Life (D) claims to have had only the one policy holder in California, and not to have been in the habit of conducting business there. But it did knowingly hold that one policy, and communicated with the policy holder in California, so it shouldn't come as a complete surprise to be required to defend suit there after refusing to pay that policy holder's beneficiary. Also, the inconvenience involved in defending a suit in California cannot be much greater than defending the same suit in Texas, and having to transport all the witnesses and evidence found in California to Texas for the trial. Whatever inconvenience does arise from being subject to suit in California certainly does not amount to a denial of due process. International Life (D) had actual notice of the suit and plenty of time to prepare a defense. Therefore, justice is best served by allowing the California courts to exercise jurisdiction in this case. Reversed.

Analysis:

The *McGee* case represented a rather expansive application of the *International Shoe* guidelines. The Court explicitly approved the idea that minimum contacts could be very minimal indeed, so long as the case came out of those contacts. Although the Court did not use the term, this is now referred to as "specific jurisdiction." That is to say, a defendant does not have extensive contacts with a state, but the nature of the contacts it does have is such as to justify the state's exercise of jurisdiction over cases arising from those contacts, but not over cases unrelated to those contacts. If a defendant's contacts are more extensive, they might give rise to "general jurisdiction," which would enable the state to exercise jurisdiction over any claim involving the defendant, whether or not it was related to the defendant's contacts with the state.

Hanson v. Denckla

(Not Stated) v. (Not Stated)

357 U.S. 235 (1958)

M E M O R Y   G R A P H I C

 ## Instant Facts

Various claimants to a Delaware trust filed suit against the trustee in Florida, claiming that the trust was invalid under Florida law.

Black Letter Rule

A state may not exercise jurisdiction over a defendant if the defendant's contacts with the state are negligible and non-deliberate, and the claim does not arise from those contacts.

Case Vocabulary

LEGATEE: Heir designated to receive property in a will.

Procedural Basis: Appeal from conflicting judgments in two separate but related actions for final disposition of a trust.

Facts: Dora Donner, a resident of Pennsylvania, established a trust with a Delaware bank as trustee. Donner was to collect the income from the trust during her lifetime; after her death the money would go to her beneficiary. She retained the power to change her beneficiary at any time. After establishing the trust, Donner moved to Florida, where she eventually drew up a will naming two of her daughters as her primary heirs. The same day, she named two of her grandchildren--the children of her third daughter, Elizabeth--as the beneficiaries of her trust. However, when Donner died several years later, the two daughters named in her will brought suit in Florida against the trust company (D), claiming that the appointment of beneficiaries had been invalid, and that the trust money should really go to the estate. [That is, to the two of them. How greedy can you get?! They were already getting more than half a million a piece. Are we talking, like, Cinderella here? Did they hate their sister *so much* that they would go to all this trouble to cheat her kids out of their grandmother's inheritance? To get another $200,000 each?] Anyway, while the Florida action was still pending, another action was filed in Delaware to determine the distribution of the trust money. The Florida court then decided that the trust was invalid, and that the money should go to the estate. The sisters tried to introduce this judgment in Delaware, as *res judicata*. The Delaware court held that the Florida court had not had jurisdiction over the trust company, however, and so refused to recognize the validity of that action. The Delaware court resolved that the trust had been valid, and that the grandchildren should get the money. Everybody appealed something, and the U.S. Supreme Court consolidated both actions for review.

Issue: May a state exercise jurisdiction over a non-resident defendant with only sporadic and inadvertent contacts with the state, when those contacts do not give rise to the claim for which jurisdiction is being sought?

Decision and Rationale: (Warren) No. A state may not exercise jurisdiction over a non-resident defendant with only sporadic and inadvertent contacts with the state, when those contacts do not give rise to the claim for which jurisdiction is being sought. Although the boundaries of a state's jurisdiction over non-residents have been expanding ever since the decision in *International Shoe*, that does not mean that there are no longer any limits on a state's exercise of personal jurisdiction. There are restrictions on a state's power to exercise jurisdiction over non-residents not just to protect those non-residents from the burden of defending a suit in a distant, inconvenient court, but also to protect other states. In this case, the laws of Delaware allowed the trust to be created, maintained, and administered. Allowing Florida courts using Florida law to invalidate that trust is, in a way, like allowing Florida to overturn Delaware's laws and to legislate for the people of Delaware instead. Without minimum contacts between the trustee (D) and Florida, Florida cannot exercise jurisdiction over the trustee (D). The trustee (D) conducts no business in Florida, has no office there, solicits no business there. The fact that the trustee's (D) client, Mrs. Donner, moved to Florida after the trust had been created does not indicate any desire of the trustee (D) to take advantage of Florida's laws or to start doing business there. Without some action "by which the defendant purposefully avails itself of the privilege of conducting activities within the forum State, thus invoking the benefits and protections of its laws," it cannot be said to have the necessary contacts with that state. The fact that another, independent actor with a relationship to the defendant chose to interact with the forum state does not establish contact between the state and the defendant. Therefore, Mrs. Donner's contacts with Florida did not establish contacts between her trustee (D) and Florida, and Florida thus cannot exercise jurisdiction over the trustee (D). Since the trustee (D) was an essential party to the Florida action, that action is invalid, and the Delaware court was correct in not awarding that judgment res judicata value. The judgment of the Delaware courts is affirmed; that of the Florida courts is reversed.

Dissent: (Black) Florida had a strong interest in overseeing this litigation, and would have been the most convenient forum. Donner lived in Florida, her heirs lived in Florida, her will was being administered in Florida. The trustee (D) chose to carry on business with a resident of Florida. The trust company (D) had sufficient contacts with Florida to justify Florida's exertion of jurisdiction over it, and there was nothing that unfair about subjecting it to suit there. Therefore, Florida's exercise of jurisdiction should have been upheld.

Analysis:

[First of all, who were these people?! If I inherited more than half a million dollars, you wouldn't catch me wasting most of it in legal fees trying to cheat my nieces and nephews out of another couple hundred thousand. But back to the legal arguments.] This case sort of put a limit on the expanding boundaries of personal jurisdiction. Where *McGee* had perhaps seemed to indicate that the idea of minimum contacts would continue to expand until it became almost meaningless, *Hanson* tried to reign in this enthusiasm. *Hanson* made clear that some exercises of jurisdiction would be struck down--if not to protect the due process interests of the defendants involved, then to protect the sovereignty of other states. *Hanson* also introduced the idea that a defendant must perform some purposeful, deliberate act in order to associate itself with the forum state. This was to prove a major sticking point between two separate factions of the Court, one of which endorsed the "purposeful availment" idea, and one of which, often led by Brennan, preferred to focus on the relationship between the defendant, the litigation, and the interests of the forum state. The next case, *World-Wide Volkswagen v. Woodson*, begins to demonstrate the depth of the Court's split.

World-Wide Volkswagen v. Woodson

(Regional Distributor of Defective Car) v. (Trial Court Judge)
444 U.S. 286 (1980)

MEMORY GRAPHIC

Instant Facts

A New York family passing through Oklahoma was in a car accident, and tried to bring suit there against the dealer who sold them the car in New York.

Black Letter Rule

In order to be subject to a state's jurisdiction, a defendant must have chosen to have some contact with that state; considerations of fairness, convenience, and the interests of the state in overseeing the litigation are otherwise irrelevant.

Case Vocabulary

CHATTEL: An item of personal property.

Procedural Basis: Writ of Certiorari to the Supreme Court of Oklahoma, for its denial of the defendants' writ of prohibition to restrain the trial court judge from exercising personal jurisdiction over them.

Facts: In 1976, the Robinson family--Harry, Kay, and their two kids--purchased a new Audi from Seaway Volkswagen, Inc. ("Seaway") (D), in Massena, New York. A year later, as the Robinsons were en route from their old home in New York to their new home in Arizona, disaster struck. While passing through Oklahoma, another car rear-ended the Robinsons' Audi, rupturing the gas tank and starting a fire that severely injured Kay and both children. Since the driver of the other car was unfortunately not wealthy, the Robinsons brought a product liability suit against the car's manufacturer, Audi NSU Auto Union Aktiengesellschaft ('Audi"), claiming that the gas tank and fuel system had been defective. They filed the action in Oklahoma state court, and named as additional defendants the car's importer, Volkswagen of America, Inc. ('Volkswagen"), its regional distributor, World-Wide Volkswagen Corporation ("World-Wide"), and Seaway, the retail dealer where they had purchased the car. World-Wide (D) and Seaway (D) challenged the Oklahoma court's exercise of jurisdiction, claiming that they did not have the necessary minimum contacts with Oklahoma. Seaway (D) claimed to do business in New York state only, and World-Wide (D) claimed to do business only within the tri-state area of New York, New Jersey, and Connecticut. Neither conducted any business in Oklahoma, employed anyone in Oklahoma, kept office space in Oklahoma, or directed advertising at the Oklahoma market. Both the trial court and the Supreme Court of Oklahoma rejected the claim that World-Wide (D) and Seaway (D) should not be subjected to jurisdiction there, based largely on the theory that they should have foreseen the possibility of litigation there, given the uniquely mobile nature of the product they sold. World-Wide (D) and Seaway (D) next appealed to the U.S. Supreme Court.

Issue: When a particular state would be the most convenient forum for a trial (i.e., all the witnesses are there, the plaintiffs are hospitalized there, the claim arose there, etc.), and the defendant would not find it at all inconvenient to defend itself there, can that state exercise jurisdiction even if the defendant has not deliberately sought contacts with that state?

Decision and Rationale: (White) No. A state cannot exercise jurisdiction over a defendant who has not deliberately sought some contact with the state. Minimum contacts must be based on some act committed by the defendant. This is a result, in part, of the requirement, first stated in *International Shoe*, that jurisdiction should not be exercised when it is inconsistent with "traditional notions of fair play and substantial justice." It is fundamentally unfair to hold a defendant responsible for the actions of others, such as the action of the Robinsons in driving their car through Oklahoma. However, the minimum contacts requirement also stems from the idea that each state's jurisdiction is limited, not just to protect defendants, but to protect the interests of other states. It has been becoming less and less difficult for defendants to defend themselves in other states, as technology progresses, but the interests of other states in not having their own sovereignty infringed remains constant, as provided for in the Constitution. Unless a defendant had chosen to avail itself somehow of another state, that state's exercise of jurisdiction might very well conflict with the sovereignty of the state which the defendant did choose. It has been argued that the defendants in this case should have foreseen that their product might wind up in Oklahoma, especially given the mobile nature of automobiles. However, it is not the foreseeability that a given product might travel to a distant forum that is important, but rather the foreseeability that the defendant might be "haled into court there." It is reasonable to believe that neither Seaway (D) nor World-Wide

(D) expected to be haled into court in Oklahoma. Since there is no evidence to support the view that either Seaway (D) or World-Wide (D) conducted business in Oklahoma, or intended their products to reach the Oklahoma market, there is basis for the Oklahoma court's exercise of jurisdiction over either defendant. Judgment reversed.

Dissent: (Brennan) Yes. A state may exercise jurisdiction over a defendant who has not deliberately sought contacts with that state. Of course, the defendant must have *some* contacts with the state. For instance, in this case, if the Robinsons' car had blown up in Texas, the Oklahoma courts would obviously not have jurisdiction over the case. But the fact the defendants did sell the Robinsons the actual car which did reach Oklahoma and did blow up there, should be enough. Perhaps the Court is right to mock the idea of all chattels being treated in this way, but surely an exception should be made for a car, which by its very nature is meant to travel. It would be difficult to believe that the defendants truly believed that none of the cars they sold would ever leave the New York area. It is true that the contacts between Seaway (D) and World-Wide (D) and Oklahoma were not extensive, but given the other factors that must be considered--fairness and convenience--it is certainly reasonable to subject them to Oklahoma's jurisdiction for this case. There is no doubt that Oklahoma is the most efficient forum in which to try the case. The witnesses are there. The evidence is there. The plaintiffs were hospitalized there when they filed suit. And the defendants would only suffer minimal inconvenience, if any, in being required to defend themselves there. The two parent companies, Volkswagen and Audi, will be required to defend the case there one way or another. Expanding that defense to encompass World-Wide (D) and Seaway (D) would not be very difficult. Given these reasons, and Oklahoma's strong interest in the litigation, both Seaway (D) and World-Wide should be held subject to Oklahoma's jurisdiction.

Analysis:

Whew. This is yet another ultra-huge case. And unfortunately, this is where personal jurisdiction starts to get really messy. If you think that the conflicting views in WWVW were confusing, just wait 'til you get to some of the cases coming up. WWVW is the first real indication of a serious split in the Court over what constitutes sufficient minimum contacts. Sometimes, as here, Brennan loses out. Sometimes he wins. And sometimes it's totally unclear if anyone came through the debate alive, let alone with a majority behind them. The split stems from two different views on what the most important concern should be in exercising personal jurisdiction: the due process rights of the defendant, or the interests of the forum state in the litigation. Here, the winning side focused more on the former, and Brennan, on the losing side, focused more on the latter. The great irony of this case, however, lies in the fact that neither side really cared whether or not Oklahoma had jurisdiction over Seaway (D) or World-Wide (D), or whether either of these defendants even stayed in the case--after all, Audi and Volkswagen were still in the case, and they were most likely capable of satisfying any judgment which the Robinsons might be able to recover. What everybody involved really cared about was not whether or not the case would be tried in Oklahoma, but whether the case would be tried in Oklahoma state court or Oklahoma federal court. Apparently, the relevant federal and state courts must have drawn from significantly different jury pools, since the state court juries had a noticeable tendency to award more money, more often, to plaintiffs, than their federal court counterparts. The Robinsons therefore strategically filed their lawsuit in state court. The defendants, for the same reasons, wanted to be able to remove the action to federal court. (Any action that could have been filed originally in federal court by the plaintiff can be "removed" to federal court by the defendant.) However, the Robinsons, although in the process of moving to Arizona on the fateful day, were still considered residents of New York for diversity purposes. As Seaway (D) and World-Wide (D) were also from New York, the action could not be removed while they remained as defendants in the case, due to a lack of complete diversity. [These concepts will be studied in more detail when you get subject matter jurisdiction, as opposed to personal jurisdiction.] Therefore, if Seaway (D) and World-Wide (D) could be kicked out of the case, then Audi and Volkswagen could remove to federal court and stand a better chance of winning. In short, this is exactly what happened. Justice? You decide.

Asahi Metal Industry Co. v. Superior Court

(Japanese Manufacturer) v. (California Trial Court)
480 U.S. 102 (1987)

M E M O R Y   G R A P H I C

Instant Facts

Victim of motorcycle accident brought suit in California court against Taiwanese tire-tube maker, who cross-claimed against Japanese manufacturer of the tire tube valve assembly.

Black Letter Rule

The plaintiff must purposefully avail himself of the forum by more than just putting a product into the stream of commerce with the expectation that it will reach the forum state, however, such conduct is enough to satisfy the minimum contacts requirement. Nonetheless, once it has been established that minimum contacts exist, the fairness requirement must still be met as well, which will be much harder to do in the case of a non-U.S. resident.

Procedural Basis: Writ of Certiorari to the Supreme Court of California for its reversal of the Court of Appeal's writ of mandate directing the Superior Court to quash service of summons on cross-complaint for indemnification in action for damages for negligence.

Facts: In September of 1978 Gary Zurcher and his wife, Ruth Ann Moreno, were in a serious motorcycle accident that left Ruth dead and Gary seriously injured. He claimed that the accident had been caused when the rear wheel of his motorcycle suddenly lost air and exploded, sending the motorcycle out of control and into a tractor. Zurcher filed suit in Solano County, California, where the accident had occurred, alleging that the tire, tube, and sealant of his motorcycle were defective. Accordingly, he named as one of the defendants Cheng Shin Rubber Industrial Co., Ltd., the tire tube's Taiwanese manufacturer. Cheng Shin in turn filed a cross-claim--for indemnification in the event it was found liable-- against the other defendants, and against Asahi Metal Industry Co., Ltd. (D), the Japanese manufacturer of the tire tube's valve assembly. Zurcher eventually settled out of court with Cheng Shin and all the other defendants, leaving Cheng Shin's cross-claim against Asahi (D) as the sole remaining issue to be tried. Asahi (D) argued that California could not exert jurisdiction over it, since it lacked sufficient contacts with the state. Asahi (D) did not do business in California and did not import any products into California itself. Rather, it sold its valve assemblies to Cheng Shin and various other tire manufacturers. The sales to Cheng Shin took place in Taiwan, and the valve assemblies were shipped to Taiwan. Cheng Shin bought valve assemblies from other manufacturers as well. Sales to Cheng Shin accounted for a very small fraction of Asahi's (D) annual income--usually less than 1-2%. In the years for which data were available, Cheng Shin used anywhere from 100,000 to 500,000 Asahi (D) valve assemblies per year, and sold finished tires all over the world. It is unknown what percentage of its sales are in the U.S., but of those U.S. sales roughly 20 percent are in California. Asahi (D) claimed that it had never contemplated that it might be subject to suit in California because of sales to Cheng Shin in Taiwan, but Cheng Shin claimed that Asahi (D) had been told and definitely knew that its products were being sold in California. The trial court found that Asahi (D), as an international company, could be subjected to California's jurisdiction. The Court of Appeal disagreed, however, and ordered the Superior Court to quash service of summons on Asahi (D). Unfortunately for Asahi (D), the Supreme Court of California overruled the Court of Appeal, finding that Asahi's (D) intentional act of putting its products into the "stream of commerce" with the awareness that they might wind up in California was enough to justify California's exercise of jurisdiction. Asahi (D) appealed to the U.S. Supreme Court.

Issue: Is it sufficient, in order to establish minimum contacts with a state, to put a product into the stream of commerce, with the expectation that it will reach the forum state?

Decision and Rationale: (O'Connor, joined by Rehnquist, Powell, and Scalia) No. It is not sufficient, for purposes of establishing that the defendant has minimum contacts with the forum state, to show that the defendant has intentionally placed its products into the stream of commerce--even if the defendant had the expectation in doing so that its products would reach the forum state. Something more, in addition to placing products in the stream of commerce, is necessary to establish minimum contacts between the defendant and the forum state. As the Court decided in *World-Wide Volkswagen*, foreseeability alone is insufficient as a basis for jurisdiction. It is not enough that Asahi (D) might have been able to guess that some one or more of its products might eventually find its way into the state of California. Asahi (D) must have performed some act showing that it deliberately intended to take advantage of that state's market or laws. This does not mean that Asahi (D) could only invoke California's jurisdiction by importing its products directly. Cheng Shin's actions in importing Asahi's (D) products could qualify, provided that Asahi (D) took additional actions indicating its intent, such as, for instance, advertising or marketing its product in California, or deliberately designing its product to conform to regulations or laws unique to California, or providing a means for California users of its products to receive technical help or advice. Since Asahi (D) has done nothing to indicate a deliberate wish on its part to see its products in California or to exploit the California market, it cannot be said to have the requisite minimum contacts with the state. However, in this particular case the minimum contacts analysis is not the only reason why California cannot exercise jurisdiction. There is still the matter of "traditional notions of fair play and substantial justice." Even if minimum contacts existed between Asahi (D) and California, it would be fundamentally unfair to require Asahi (D) to defend itself there. California's interest in this matter--the welfare of its citizens--was put to rest, for the most part, when Zurcher settled. The dispute is between, not just two non-residents of California, but two non-residents of the U.S. Given the rather extreme inconvenience necessitated by defending a suit in a distant forum and a *foreign* legal system, it would be unreasonable and unfair for California to exercise jurisdiction over Asahi (D) in this matter. Reversed and remanded.

Concurrence: (Brennan, joined by White, Marshall, and Blackmun, concurring in part and concurring in the judgment) Yes.

It is sufficient, for purposes of establishing that the defendant has minimum contacts with the forum state, to show that the defendant has intentionally placed its products into the stream of commerce. The "stream of commerce" referred to here indicates the regular and continuous flow of products from manufacture to consumption, not unanticipated and random single occurrences. Since Asahi's (D) products were regularly and steadily flowing into California, with Asahi's (D) knowledge, Asahi (D) was benefiting from the laws of California and should be held to have the necessary contacts with California to be subject to its jurisdiction. However, the Court is correct in its analysis of the fairness aspect of the test for jurisdiction, as it would be fundamentally unfair and unreasonable to require Asahi (D) to defend this suit in California. Therefore, the Court was correct in overturning the judgment of the California Supreme Court.

Concurrence: (Stevens, joined by White and Blackmun, concurring in part and concurring in the judgment) We don't need to decide for this case. It is quite obvious that it would not be fair to require the Japanese defendant to defend itself in California, especially when there are no American parties left in the case. But if we did need to formulate here a test requiring minimum contacts, the Court has not done so correctly. Asahi (D) did have sufficient knowledge that its product was being sold in California and should therefore be held to have had sufficient minimum contacts with that state.

Analysis:

So what does this case really say, you ask? Good question. It isn't very clear from the opinion what the Court's stance is. All that we really know from this case is that it will be more difficult to meet the fairness element of the test for minimum contacts when a foreign defendant is involved. Also, we know that the *International Shoe* test for personal jurisdiction is still the right one to use: "minimum contacts" and "fair play and substantial justice." Of course, how to apply it is a different story. Strangely enough, the *Asahi* court was actually unanimous in finding that no jurisdiction existed. They just couldn't decide why no jurisdiction existed. Was it because minimum contacts did not exist? Or because minimum contacts existed, but it would not be fair? The only real thing to do is to wait and see how *Asahi* is applied in future cases.

Burger King Corp. v. Rudzewicz

(Franchise Owner) v. (Franchisee)

471 U.S. 462 (1985)

M E M O R Y   G R A P H I C

Instant Facts

Rudzewicz (D) contracted with Burger King (D), a Florida corporation, to operate a Burger King restaurant in Michigan, then defaulted on payments, so Burger King (P) sued him in Florida.

Black Letter Rule

Once it has been established that the defendant has minimum contacts with a state, it is up to the defendant to prove that being required to defend a suit there would be "fundamentally unfair."

Procedural Basis: Appeal from reversal of judgment in action for damages and injunctive relief for breach of contract.

Facts: John Rudzewicz (D) and Brian MacShara, both Michigan residents, entered into a franchise agreement with Burger King Corporation (P), a Florida company. The contract licensed Rudzewicz (D) and MacShara to use Burger King's (P) trademarks and service marks for a period of 20 years, in connection with their operation of a Burger King restaurant in Michigan. The contract provided that the agreement would be governed by Florida law, and called for payment of all franchise fees and royalties to Burger King's (P) Miami headquarters. In connection with establishing the restaurant, MacShara attended a training course at Burger King University in Miami. After operating the restaurant for a while, Rudzewicz (D) and MacShara fell behind in their monthly payments to Burger King (P). Burger King (P) then instituted an action in federal court in Florida, based on diversity jurisdiction. Rudzewicz (D) and MacShara claimed that they did not have sufficient contacts with Florida to be subjected to jurisdiction there. The District Court found that Florida could exercise jurisdiction in this case, based on a long-arm statute which extends jurisdiction to anyone who breaches a contract within the state. The Court of Appeals reversed, however, finding that, although the defendants could be said to have the necessary contacts with Florida, such an exercise of jurisdiction would be fundamentally unfair, and an infringement of due process--and an especially dangerous precedent. Burger King (P) appealed to the U.S. Supreme Court.

Issue: In asserting jurisdiction against out-of-state defendants, does a state have to show both that the defendant has minimum contacts with the state, and that it would be fair and equitable to require the defendant to defend a suit there?

Decision and Rationale: (Brennan) No. The state does not have to show both that the defendant has minimum contacts with the state, and that it would be fair and equitable to require the defendant to defend a suit there. Once it has been established that the defendant has minimum contacts with a state, there is a presumption that it would be fair to require the defendant to defend a suit there. This presumption can of course be overcome, but it is the defendant who must show that it would be unfair to require him to defend there, and not the state which must show that it would be fair. In deciding the question of fairness, the court may look to and balance the forum state's interest in the litigation, the plaintiff's interest in efficient and convenient relief, the demands and best interests of the federal system as a whole, and the defendant's interest in not having to defend a suit in an extremely remote or disadvantageous forum. In the case at hand, Rudzewicz (D) deliberately and voluntarily entered into a 20-year-long contract with a Florida corporation, governed by Florida law. That contract required that someone associated with the new restaurant attend training in Florida at Burger King University. While Rudzewicz (D) himself did not go, and in fact has never been to Florida at all, it can hardly have come as a complete shock to him to learn that Burger King (P) might sue him there should he breach the agreement. Florida is certainly the most convenient forum for this case, and while this is not the determining factor, it is something to consider. Rudzewicz (D) has not shown that his case would be unfairly prejudiced or harmed by a trial in Florida. Of course he will be somewhat inconvenienced, but doesn't the mere fact of being sued cause some inconvenience in and of itself? We shouldn't therefore prohibit all lawsuits. And undoubtedly Burger King (P) was inconvenienced by not receiving the monthly payments. In short, Rudzewicz's (D) purposeful involvement with a Florida company provides the necessary minimum contacts for Florida to exercise jurisdiction, and he has failed to show that it would be fundamentally unfair to allow Florida to do so. Reversed and remanded.

Dissent: (Stevens) Rudzewicz (D) did no business in Florida. He sold no products there, did not anticipate that any of his products would ever wind up there, maintained no offices there, and had in fact never been there. His principal contact with Burger King (P) was through its Michigan branch office, not its Florida headquarters. There is no reason to believe that Rudzewicz (D) ever anticipated any involvement with the Florida office, and every reason to think that he would have expected to resolve any problems that arose with the Michigan office-- including any potential litigation. Also, the typical franchise is at best a very local operation, with far less capital or bargaining power than a huge national corporation like Burger King (P). Therefore, it would be fundamentally unfair to require local franchise operators like Rudzewicz (D) to defend themselves in a forum as distant and unfamiliar as Florida. The judgment of the Court of Appeals dismissing the Florida action should be upheld.

Analysis:

This time, apparently, Brennan's side won. This time it's the majority opinion that stresses the forum state's interest in the litigation, and the dissent that stresses the due process concerns of the defendant. The swing votes must have come over to Brennan's side this time because here, unlike in cases such as *World-Wide Volkswagen*, the defendant had taken some purposeful action to associate himself with the forum state. One interesting question to wonder about, however, is why Rudzewicz (D) took this case all the way up to the Supreme Court. It's not as if, had Burger King (P) been denied the right to sue him in Florida, the case would have ended. Burger King (P) would probably have just turned around and sued him in Michigan. Do you think that having the "home-court" advantage is worth that much effort? Sure, Rudzewicz (D) might have been able to try to portray himself as the virtuous local businessman victimized by a big, out-of-state corporation. But the action was in federal court, and one of the main reasons for establishing a federal court system in the first place was to provide a neutral forum where non-residents could see justice without the interference of local prejudice against out-of-staters. If this *isn't* working, then why do we have a separate federal court system?

Washington Equipment Mfg. Co. v. Concrete Placing Co.

(Equipment Seller) v. (Concrete Co.)

(1997) 85 Wash. App. 240, 931 P.2d 170

M E M O R Y   G R A P H I C

Instant Facts

A non-resident Concrete Co. (D) appointed a registered agent in accordance with state law but did not otherwise do business in the state.

Black Letter Rule

A foreign corporation does not consent to general personal jurisdiction by complying with the state's mandatory requirements for doing business there.

Case Vocabulary

FOREIGN CORPORATION: A corporation incorporated or having its principal place of business in another state.

FORUM NON CONVENIENS: Declining jurisdiction over a matter where, in the interest of justice, it would be more appropriately tried in another location based upon convenience to the parties and witnesses, and the bests interests of the public.

Procedural Basis: Appeal from dismissal of complaint seeking damages for sums due under purchase agreement on ground of no jurisdiction.

Facts: A Washington State statute required a foreign corporation to obtain a certificate of authority to do business and appoint a registered agent to transact business in the state. Concrete Placing Co. (Concrete) (D), an Idaho corporation, [not wanting to break any laws] obtained a certificate and appointed a registered agent in order to build roads in Washington. Approximately 8 years thereafter, Concrete (D) bought a concrete placing machine and a concrete paving plant from Washington Equipment Manufacturing Co. (Equipment Co.) (P) and refused to pay the full purchase price. Equipment Co. (P) sued Concrete (D) in Washington for the balance of the purchase price. The trial court dismissed the complaint for lack of jurisdiction and Equipment Co. (P) appealed. On appeal, Equipment Co. (P) contended that Concrete (D) consented to general personal jurisdiction by appointing a registered agent and having a registered office in the state.

Issue: Does a foreign corporation consent to general personal jurisdiction by complying with a state's mandatory requirements for doing business there?

Decision and Rationale: (Sweeney) No. Consent does not occur by merely complying with certain mandatory requirements of the state for doing business there. The issue of whether Concrete (D) consented to general personal jurisdiction by obtaining a certificate of authority to do business and appointing a registered agent requires us to focus on whether the foreign corporation's general business activities in the state are substantial and continuous. Unlike specific jurisdiction, general jurisdiction is unrelated to the corporation's specific activities in the state. Specific jurisdiction is appropriate when the cause of action arises out of, or relates to, the foreign corporation's activities in the state. The Washington Business Corporation Act does not state or imply that a foreign corporation consents to general jurisdiction in the state by complying with the requirements of appointing a registered agent and having a registered office in the state. Another statute applicable to foreign limited liability companies expressly provides that the company submits to personal jurisdiction of the state. Consent requires some knowing and voluntary act. A foreign corporation cannot be deemed to have knowingly consented to general jurisdiction by doing an act required by the state. [Trying to salvage its case, Equipment Co. (P) asserted more arguments.] With respect to the contention that there was a waiver of the defense of lack of jurisdiction because Concrete Co. (D) asserted forum non conveniens, there can be no waiver unless there is a claim for affirmative relief. The claim of forum non conveniens is not one for affirmative relief. Dismissal with prejudice was not error since Equipment Co. (P) can renew its claim in an appropriate forum.

Analysis:

This case examines the issue of consent in the context of general jurisdiction. The cases in the previous section pertained to specific jurisdiction, that is, where the defendant's dealings with the forum state actually give rise to a cause of action. In this case, and the next, general jurisdiction is studied. When may a defendant be subject to jurisdiction for all claims, including those without any connection to the forum state? The state where a corporation is incorporated or has its principal place of business, or the state of an individual's domicile, are clear examples of general jurisdiction. This case demonstrates the limits of general jurisdiction. Concrete Co. (D) was not incorporated in the forum state, and its activities in the state 8 years prior, *i.e.*, appointing a registered agent and obtaining a certificate of authority to do business, did not relate to the much later claim that it failed to pay the entire purchase price for equipment and the concrete paving plant. Note that the court identified the issue as one of "consent", and whether the activities in the state were substantial and continuous. However, in its decision, the court placed emphasis on the interpretation of the state statute to conclude that complying with the requirements of the law of the state did not equate to consent to jurisdiction. Compare the holding in this case with the next case, *Burnham v. Superior Court*, where general jurisdiction over a non-resident individual defendant visiting the state was upheld. It can be argued that it is not fair to subject an individual to general jurisdiction but not the corporation doing unrelated business in the state.

Burnham v. Superior Court

(Prospective Divorcee) v. (Court)
495 U.S. 604 (1990)

M E M O R Y   G R A P H I C

 Instant Facts

While visiting California for business and vacation, Dennis Burnham (D) was served with process for a divorce proceeding, and Burnham (D) contends that California jurisdiction violates due process.

Black Letter Rule

Jurisdiction based on physical presence comports with due process, regardless of the defendant's contacts with the forum State.

Case Vocabulary

MANDAMUS: A proceeding in some superior court, seeking an order for an inferior court to perform some duty, such as quashing a service of process.

TRANSIENT JURISDICTION: Jurisdiction over a nonresident defendant based on service of process on the defendant while present in the forum State.

Procedural Basis: Writ of certiorari reviewing denial of mandamus relief following denial of motion to quash service of process in divorce action.

Facts: Francie Burnham (P), a resident of California, brought suit for divorce against her husband, Dennis Burnham (Burnham) (D), in California state court. Mr. Burnham (D) was served with the summons and complaint while voluntarily visiting California for three days. Burnham's (D) presence in California did not relate to the divorce action, as he was initially on business and later traveled to San Francisco to visit his daughters [That's what he gets for trying to do something nice!]. Subsequently, Burnham (D) made a special appearance in California Superior Court, moving to quash the service of process. Burnham (D) argued that the court lacked personal jurisdiction because his only contacts with the state were a few short trips on business and to visit his daughters. The Superior Court denied the motion. Thereafter, the California Court of Appeal denied mandamus relief, holding that physical presence and personal service in the forum state constituted valid grounds for jurisdiction. The Supreme Court granted certiorari.

Issue: Does transient jurisdiction, obtained by a defendant's physical presence in the forum state, violate due process?

Decision and Rationale: (Scalia, J.) No. Transient jurisdiction, obtained by a defendant's physical presence in the forum state, does not violate due process. In order to decide whether the assertion of personal jurisdiction comports with due process, we have relied on well-established traditional principles of jurisdiction. Jurisdiction based on physical presence is one of these traditional forms of in personam jurisdiction. On occasion, we have held that deviations from the traditional 19th century rules are permissible, but only with respect to suits arising out of the absent defendant's contacts with the forum state. Thus, in *International Shoe Co. v. Washington* [Minimum contacts are required in order to satisfy the traditional notions of fair play and substantial justice], we established a minimum contacts test for such situations. In the instant action, Burnham (D) contends that the *International Shoe* minimum contacts test should also be applied to a situation where a nonresident defendant is physically present in the forum state. However, we find nothing in *International Shoe* or its progeny requiring an extension to situations of transient jurisdiction. We therefore hold that jurisdiction based on physical presence alone satisfies due process because it is one of the continuing traditions of our legal system and, therefore, is consistent with "traditional notions of fair play and substantial justice." Burnham's (D) argument, that our decision in *Shaffer v. Heitner* [Quasi in rem jurisdiction is subject to the same minimum contacts analysis as is in personam jurisdiction] requires reversal, is likewise unavailing. Burnham (D) misinterprets our statement in *Shaffer* that "all assertions of state-court jurisdiction must be evaluated according to the standards set forth in *International Shoe* and its progeny." The context of this statement reveals that only quasi in rem jurisdiction must be subjected to the minimum contacts analysis. *Shaffer* does not, therefore, compel the conclusion that physically present defendants must be treated identically to absent ones. Where a jurisdictional principal is firmly approved by tradition and still favored, such as the doctrine of jurisdiction by physical presence, due process is not violated by obtaining such jurisdiction. Thus, the California courts could exercise jurisdiction over Burnham (D) based on in-state service of process. Affirmed.

Concurrence: (White, J.) I concur in the affirmance and in Justice Scalia's conclusion that jurisdiction by personal service is so widely accepted that it should not be struck down as violative of the Fourteenth Amendment Due Process Clause.

Concurrence: (Brennan, J.) While I concur in the judgment, I do not agree with the unshakable reliance on tradition as supporting all forms of jurisdiction. Unlike Justice Scalia, I would undertake an independent inquiry into the fairness of the prevailing in-state service rule. Justice Scalia's historical approach is foreclosed by our decisions in *International Shoe* and *Shaffer v. Heitner*. Pursuant to *Shaffer*, I believe that all rules of jurisdiction, even ancient ones, must satisfy the contemporary notions of due process elucidated in *International Shoe's* minimum contacts analysis. However, as transient jurisdiction is consistent with the reasonable expectations of a nonresident defendant, it is entitled to a strong presumption that it comports with due process. By visiting the forum State, a nonresident defendant purposefully avails himself of the benefits and protections of the forum State. Moreover, the potential burdens on a transient defendant are slight. Thus, I believe

that, as a rule the exercise of personal jurisdiction over a defendant based on his voluntary presence in the forum state will satisfy the requirements of due process.

Concurrence: (Stevens, J.) I am concerned with the broad reach of Justice Scalia's majority opinion. However, the historical evidence identified by Justice Scalia, the considerations of fairness identified by Justice Brennan, and the common sense displayed by Justice White convince me that this is a very easy case. I agree that the judgment should be affirmed.

Analysis:

This is an extremely important case in ascertaining the correct application of *Shaffer v. Heitner* and *International Shoe*. Although *Shaffer* apparently stated that all jurisdictional issues must now be evaluated by the *International Shoe* minimum contacts test, Justice Scalia's opinion makes it clear that this is not the case. Rather, the traditional notion of jurisdiction based on physical presence can survive even absent sufficient minimum contacts between the defendant and the forum State. While Justice Scalia's unyielding rule has the advantages of certainty and judicial efficiency, his reliance on history should nevertheless be questioned. Indeed, it makes little sense to rely on historical notions of jurisdiction in this case, when prior cases like *Shaffer* and *International Shoe* expressly invalidated other historical approaches. Thus, Justice Brennan's concurrence may present a more sensible approach. Brennan argues that *all* forms of jurisdiction, including jurisdiction based on physical presence, must satisfy the minimum contacts test in order to comport with due process. However, after conducting the minimum contacts analysis as to transient jurisdiction, Brennan seemingly concludes that *every* exercise of personal jurisdiction based on *voluntary* presence comports with due process! Thus, it appears that Justices Scalia and Brennan reached essentially the same strict rule, although they took different approaches to get there. Indeed, it may be inferred that the only difference between Scalia's rule and Brennan's involves cases of involuntary physical presence. While Brennan focuses on the voluntary nature of the physical presence, Scalia's approach would seem to grant jurisdiction over a defendant who did not know he was in the forum State, or who was involuntarily dragged over the border into the forum State. Nevertheless, these situations of involuntary presence in a forum State are likely so rare that Scalia and Brennan have, in effect, adopted the same rule: Jurisdiction based on in-state service of process over a defendant physically present in the forum State comports with due process.

Insurance Corp. of Ireland v. Compagnie des Bauxites de Guinee

(Insurance Company) v. (Mining Company)
456 U.S. 694 (1982)

M E M O R Y   G R A P H I C

Instant Facts

Compagnie des Bauxites de Guinee (CBG) (P) sued for the non-payment of insurance benefits, and the insurers failed to comply with the court's discovery order.

Black Letter Rule

The failure to comply with jurisdictional-related discovery may constitute implied consent to jurisdiction.

Case Vocabulary

BUSINESS-INTERRUPTION INSURANCE: Insurance which protects a company from suffering losses due to reasonable interruptions in their business dealings.

Procedural Basis: Writ of certiorari reviewing District Court's sanction order for failure to comply with discovery.

Facts: Compagnie des Bauxites de Guinee (CBG) (P), a bauxite producer, had purchased business-interruption insurance from the Insurance Corp. of Ireland (D) and other insurers. When a mechanical failure forced a halt in CBG's (P) bauxite production, CBG (P) filed a multi-million dollar claim. However, the insurers refused to pay the claim. CBG (P) then brought suit in federal court in Pennsylvania. Most of the foreign insurance companies made special appearances to contest personal jurisdiction. In order to prove that jurisdiction existed, CBG (P) attempted to use discovery. However, the insurance companies failed to comply with discovery requests and with the court's orders for document production. The District Court then imposed a sanction, pursuant to Rule 37(b)(2)(A) [Court may impose reasonable sanctions for failure to comply with order compelling discovery], consisting of a presumptive finding that the insurers were subject to jurisdiction because of their business contacts with Pennsylvania. The Supreme Court granted certiorari.

Issue: May objections to personal jurisdiction be impliedly waived by failure to comply with a court's discovery orders?

Decision and Rationale: (Justice Not Stated) Yes. Objections to personal jurisdiction may be impliedly waived by failure to comply with a court's discovery orders. In voluntarily submitting to the jurisdiction of the District Court for the limited purpose of challenging jurisdiction, a defendant agrees to abide by the court's determination on the jurisdictional issue. Thus, the insurers did not have the option of blocking CBG's (P) attempts to prove the insurers had sufficient minimum contacts with Pennsylvania. The insurers' failure to supply the requested information as to their contacts with Pennsylvania supports the presumption that the insurers' jurisdictional defense was invalid. Thus, the sanction was reasonable, as it presumed the facts that CBG (P) was seeking to establish through discovery. Affirmed.

Analysis:

This case presents an extension of the traditional situation of jurisdiction-by-consent under the regime of *Pennoyer v. Neff* [A defendant may consent to personal jurisdiction either by expressly agreeing to jurisdiction or by performing certain acts that constitute a waiver of objections to personal jurisdiction]. In the case at hand, the insurance companies surely did not voluntarily submit to personal jurisdiction; in fact, they appeared specially in order to contest such jurisdiction. Furthermore, the insurers arguably did not perform acts which directly constituted a waiver of consent. Rather, by failing to comply with the court's discovery order, the insurers were simply liable for the appropriate discovery sanctions pursuant to Rule 37(b)(2)(A). This rule allows a court, in the face of noncompliance with a discovery order, to take the matter sought to be discovered as true. It just so happened that the matter sought to be discovered related to personal jurisdiction. Thus, according to the Supreme Court, the insurance companies indirectly and impliedly consented to a waiver of any objections to personal jurisdiction. If nothing else, this case demonstrates the extremely long reach of consent as a basis for jurisdiction. However, it should be noted that the Supreme Court likely did not even need to reach the issue of an implied waiver or consent. By failing to comply with the discovery rules, the insurers were simply liable for the appropriate discovery sanctions.

Carnival Cruise Lines v. Schutte

(Cruise Line) v. (Passenger)
111 S.Ct. 1522 (1991)

M E M O R Y   G R A P H I C

Instant Facts
In response to a suit for injuries occurring on one of its cruise ships, Carnival Cruise Lines (D) argued that the forum selection clause contained on the ticket should establish jurisdiction.

Black Letter Rule
Reasonable forum selection clauses are effective in imposing jurisdiction.

Case Vocabulary

EX ANTE: Beforehand; ahead of time.
FORA: The plural form of "forum."

Procedural Basis: Writ of certiorari reviewing reversal of dismissal of action for damages for negligence due to lack of jurisdiction.

Facts: Eulala and Russel Shutte (P) purchased tickets for a cruise on Carnival Cruise Lines (D). The tickets were purchased from a travel agent in Washington, who forwarded the payment to Carnival's (D) headquarters in Florida. A provision on the tickets stated that all disputes were required to be litigated in Florida. While sailing from Los Angeles to Mexico, Mrs. Shutte (P) slipped on a deck mat and was injured. The Shuttes (P) filed suit in a Washington district court, alleging damages for negligence on the part of Carnival (D) and its employees. However, the District Court ruled that Carnival's (D) contacts with Washington were insufficient to support jurisdiction. The Court of Appeals reversed, and the Supreme Court granted certiorari.

Issue: Is a reasonable forum selection clause enforceable to establish consent to jurisdiction?

Decision and Rationale: (Justice Not Stated) Yes. A reasonable forum selection clause is enforceable in order to establish consent to jurisdiction. The minimum contacts analysis is inapplicable in the instant action, as the forum selection clause contained on the ticket was reasonable for several reasons. First, a cruise line has a special interest in limiting the potentially vast number of forums in which it could be sued. Second, a forum selection clause has the beneficial effect of sparing litigants and courts the time and expense of pretrial motions to determine the correct forum [although it does not spare parties the cost of litigating in a distant jurisdiction!]. Third, passengers who purchase tickets containing a forum selection clause presumably benefit in the form of reduced fares, reflecting the savings that cruise lines enjoy by limiting the forums in which they may be sued.

Analysis:

This decision essentially reiterates the reasonableness requirement for forum selection clauses, established in *Bremen v. Zapata* [an express forum-selection clause in a contract suffices to establish jurisdiction by consent]. However, the Court's reasoning can be questioned on a number of fronts. First, while a cruise line certainly has an interest in limiting the number of forums in which it can be sued, the court fails to consider the interests and burdens suffered by passengers who must litigate in a distant state. Arguably, it would be less burdensome for a large corporate cruise line to defend suits in distant states than it would be for passengers to litigate in far-away locales. The Court's holding could have the effect of dissuading passengers from bringing valid claims due to the expense involved. Second, in reality it is unlikely that passengers such as the Shuttes (P) benefitted very much in the form of reduced fares by the insertion of the forum selection clause. Perhaps the court should have conducted a modified minimum-contacts test, weighing the benefits and burdens of each of the parties and determining whether passengers or the cruise line purposefully availed themselves of jurisdiction in a distant state. Finally, the forum selection clause in this case could arguably be construed as unconscionable. It is unlikely that a passenger would read the boilerplate language in fine print on the back of his ticket. Moreover, even if the Shuttes (P) had knowledge of the clause, the parties were of vastly unequal bargaining power, and the forum selection clause may be viewed as a take-it-or-leave-it contract of adhesion. Nevertheless, the Court seems to believe that the purported advantages of a forum selection clause outweigh the many potential disadvantages.

Mullane v. Central Hanover Bank & Trust Co.

(Special Guardian) v. (Common Trustee)
339 U.S. 306 (1950)

M E M O R Y   G R A P H I C

Instant Facts

Central Hanover Bank and Trust Company (P) petitioned for a judicial settlement of a trust and provided notice by publication to all of the beneficiaries.

Black Letter Rule

Notice by publication fails to comply with due process where the names and addresses of the parties are known.

Case Vocabulary

INTER VIVOS TRUST: A trust created by distribution of property to a trustee during the lifetime of the settlor (the entity creating the trust), in which the property is held for the benefit of the beneficiaries.
SURROGATE COURT: A court with jurisdiction over probate matters, including wills and trusts.
TESTAMENTARY TRUST: A trust created by will upon the death of the settlor.

Procedural Basis: Writ of certiorari reviewing affirmance of order overruling due-process objection to service of process in petition for settlement of trust.

Facts: Central Hanover Bank and Trust Company (P) established a common trust fund, in which 113 small trusts were pooled into one fund for investment administration. Central Hanover (P) petitioned the Surrogate's Court of New York for judicial settlement of this account as common trustee. If granted, the decree would settle all questions respecting the management of the common fund, terminating all rights of beneficiaries against the trustee for improper management. Pursuant to New York statute, all beneficiaries of this common trust were notified by publication in a local newspaper for four successive weeks. [After all, everyone reads the "legal notices" section of the newspaper, don't they?] Mullane (D), who was appointed special guardian for all beneficiaries not otherwise appearing in the action, entered a special appearance in New York in order to object to the notice. According to Mullane (D), the Trust Company (P) should have provided notice by mail, as the company had actual knowledge of the names and addresses of the beneficiaries. Therefore, Mullane (D) argued that the statutorily-endorsed notice was inadequate to afford due process under the Fourteenth Amendment, and therefore that the court was without jurisdiction to enter a final decree. The Surrogate overruled Mullane's (D) objections, and a final decree accepting the accounts was entered. The Appellate Division of the New York Supreme Court and the Court of Appeals of New York affirmed. The Supreme Court granted certiorari.

Issue: Where the names and addresses of parties are known, does notice by publication comply with due process?

Decision and Rationale: (Jackson, J.) No. Where the names and addresses of parties are known, notice by publication does not comply with due process. Due process requires that notice be provided prior to the deprivation of life, liberty or property by adjudication. In the situation at hand, the proceeding had the possibility of depriving the beneficiaries of property, as a decree would cut off their rights to hold the common trustee liable for negligence. Further, we hold that due process requires that this notice be reasonably calculated, under the circumstances, to apprise interested parties of the pendency of the action and afford them and an opportunity to be heard. Personal service of written notice always complies with due process. However, parties residing outside of the forum state do not necessarily have to be provided with written notice, as this would place impossible obstacles in the instant action where the number of interested beneficiaries is numerous. Indeed, in many circumstances, notice by mail complies with due process, even though there is a risk that notice may not actually reach all interested parties. Where a large number of parties share a common interest, it can be assumed that those beneficiaries present will defend the rights of the absent parties. However, in the instant action, Central Hanover (P) only provided notice by publication. Such notice was not reasonably calculated to provide notice to those parties whose names and addresses were known. Notice by publication is certainly not a reliable method of apprising interested parties of the pending adjudication of their rights. The record indicates that, upon the foundation of the common trust, Central Hanover (P) had mailed information to a number of the beneficiaries. Likewise, Central Hanover (P) should have mailed notice of the legal proceeding to all of these beneficiaries, as this would not seriously burden the trust. Thus, the New York statute providing for service by publication in such circumstances is unconstitutional, as it fails to comply with the Fourteenth Amendment. However, with regard to those beneficiaries whose addresses were not known, or whose interests in the trust were uncertain, we hold that notice by publication did comply with due process. Reversed in part.

Analysis:

This case states the essential due process requirements for notice, which typically includes a summons and a copy of the complaint. Whenever legal proceedings affect the life, liberty or property interests of parties, these parties must be provided with notice reasonably calculated under the circumstances to apprise them of the proceedings and give them an opportunity to be heard. The focus of the case is on the phrase "reasonably calculated under the circumstances." There is a wide spectrum of potential notice devices, ranging from personal service (the best form of notice) to notice by publication (the least reliable method). Whenever possible, personal service should be provided, although this may be impossible when the number of parties are numerous or when the parties reside in distant states. In such circumstances, it is easy to see that mailed notice is sufficient, even though some of the parties might not receive the notice. However, courts generally disfavor notice by publication. Indeed, notice by publication is really just a legal fiction, since no reasonable person would regularly read the legal notices of a newspaper (published in a distant state!). Thus, it is interesting that the court allows notice by publication in some situations. However, there really is no other way to provide notice to some parties, such as those parties whose address was not known or easily ascertainable. In addition, as the Court notes, notice by publication is sufficient in some in rem proceedings, since the notice is typically coupled with seizure of property. Even if an interested party failed to read the legal notices in the paper, the seizure of property would certainly afford constructive notice of the proceedings. Overall, however, the court declines distinguishing between in rem and in personam situations, establishing the same "reasonably calculated" requirements for notice in both types of actions.

Gibbons v. Brown

(Direction Giving Passenger) v. (Passenger)
(1998) 716 So.2d 868

M E M O R Y   G R A P H I C

Instant Facts

Passenger versus passenger lawsuit where personal jurisdiction was asserted based upon non-resident Brown (D) having filed a lawsuit in the state two years prior against a non-party driver.

Black Letter Rule

Jurisdiction over a non-resident defendant is not proper where the only contact with the state was filing a lawsuit two years earlier against a defendant not a party to the current suit.

Case Vocabulary

MOTION TO DISMISS COMPLAINT: Challenging the right of the court to entertain the lawsuit based on various legal theories.

MOTION TO QUASH SERVICE OF PROCESS: To void the act of legally serving documents, such as the summons and complaint.

PER CURIAM: An opinion by the whole court, rather than one judge.

Procedural Basis: Appeal from order denying motion to quash service of process and, alternatively, motion to dismiss complaint for damages for personal injuries.

Facts: Gibbons (D), a passenger in the car driven by Mr. Brown, was sued by Mrs. Brown (P), also a passenger, for injuries sustained in an automobile accident that occurred in Canada. Gibbons (D) had given wrong directions to Mr. Brown, the driver of the car, which caused him to turn onto a one-way street, resulting in a head-on collision. Gibbons (D) resided in Texas and Brown (P) resided in Florida. Brown (P) brought the action in Florida [asserting a theory of bad direction giving]. However, a prior lawsuit had been brought in Florida by Gibbons as a plaintiff against Mr. Brown, the driver, two years earlier. [Gibbons felt that Mr. Brown caused the accident notwithstanding her bad directions.] In the current lawsuit, Brown (P) contended that non-resident Gibbons (D) subjected herself to the personal jurisdiction of Florida because she had brought the prior lawsuit against Mr. Brown in Florida. However, she did not name Mrs. Brown as a defendant in that suit. Florida's long-arm statute provides that "a defendant who is engaged in substantial and not isolated activity within this state, whether such activity is wholly intrastate, interstate, or otherwise, is subject to the jurisdiction of the courts of this state, whether or not the claim arises from that activity." Gibbons (D) challenges Florida's jurisdiction over her because her prior lawsuit, although involving the same accident, did not include Brown (P) as a defendant, and there were two years between that lawsuit and this action.

Issue: Is jurisdiction over a non-resident defendant proper where the only contact with the state was filing a lawsuit two years earlier against a defendant not a party to the current suit?

Decision and Rationale: (Per Curiam) No. To come within Florida's jurisdiction under its long-arm statute, a defendant must be "engaged in substantial and not isolated activity" within the state. Even if we were to assume [by stretching it to the extreme] that bringing an action in Florida can constitute "substantial and not isolated activity", there is nevertheless no showing by Brown (P) that Gibbons (D) "is engaged" in any activity in the state other than defending this lawsuit. Because of the length of time between the two lawsuits and the fact that the prior suit did not name Brown (P) as a defendant, we conclude that Brown (P) has not alleged a satisfactory ground for personal jurisdiction pursuant to Florida's long-arm statute. The trial court is directed to dismiss Brown's (P) complaint.

Analysis:

This case is an example of a state's long-arm statute limiting jurisdiction even where the Constitution would permit such jurisdiction absent the statutory restrictions. This is a Florida court of appeal case, and the decision states that Florida's long-arm statute requires more activities or contacts than are currently required by the decisions of the United States Supreme Court. Thus, the statute at issue in this case limits jurisdiction to specified occurrences, whereas other states, such as California, permit jurisdiction on any basis not inconsistent with the Constitution. For example, in *Adam v. Saenger*, the Supreme Court upheld California's jurisdiction over a non-resident whose only contact with the state was commencing a lawsuit that resulted in the defendant filing a counterclaim against him. In Gibbons, the court was unwilling to hold that a person's bringing of a prior lawsuit in the state should indefinitely prevent challenging jurisdiction in a separate suit, even one arising from the same subject matter. The court relied upon the length of time between the two actions and the fact that a non-party to the instant action was named as a defendant in the prior action. Note that the issue in this case concerned whether or not Gibbons (D) "engaged" in activity assumed to be "substantial" and not "isolated". If the court had determined that she had engaged in such activity, the next consideration would be whether or not the long-arm statute complied with the Due Process Clause.

Dee-K Enterprises, Inc. v. Heveafil Sdn. Bhd.

(Rubber Thread Purchaser) v. (Distributors)

(1997) 982 F.Supp. 1138

M E M O R Y   G R A P H I C

Instant Facts

Manufacturers of rubber thread outside of the United States challenge jurisdiction and venue to sue them in federal district court.

Black Letter Rule

General federal venue statute subjecting alien corporations to suit in any judicial district overrides other federal statutes that may contain specific venue provisions.

Case Vocabulary

ALIENS: Foreign persons or companies that are citizens or subjects of a foreign nation.

ANTITRUST ACTION: Lawsuit alleging unlawful monopolies or restraints on trade and commerce.

Procedural Basis: Decision by federal district court judge ordering plaintiff to amend antitrust complaint to allege, with specificity, venue in the district in which complaint was filed.

Facts: Dee-K Enterprises, Inc. (Dee-K) (P) and other American purchasers of rubber thread used in the making of bungee cords brought suit against various foreign governments and distributors of the thread alleging an international conspiracy to restrain trade in, and fix prices of, the thread in the United States. [The defendants must have foreseen big business in bungee jumping and wanted to make lots of money from their rubber threads.] Heveafil Sdn. Bhd. (Heveafil) (D) and other defendants moved to dismiss on the grounds of 1) lack of personal jurisdiction over a manufacturer from a foreign country where it consummates sales of the thread in the foreign country, and 2) improper venue in the Eastern District of Virginia.

Issue: Does the general federal venue statute subjecting alien corporations to suit in any judicial district override other federal statutes that may contain specific venue provisions?

Decision and Rationale: (Ellis) Yes. The federal venue statute, 28 U.S.C. §1391(d), provides that aliens may be sued in any district. This statute overrides any special venue provision contained in other federal statutes. We first address the issue of jurisdiction. Jurisdiction is based upon a federal antitrust statute and a federal rule of civil procedure which provide for worldwide service of process when the antitrust defendant is a corporation. We initially must determine whether under the federal statute or rule, due process is complied with pursuant to the "fair play and substantial justice" test of *International Shoe* [personal jurisdiction over a non-resident defendant corporation exists where the defendant has certain minimum contacts with the state and maintenance of the suit does not offend traditional notions of fair play and substantial justice]. We find that due process was satisfied [hands down] by Heveafil's (D) appointment of exclusive U.S. sales agents and the customizing of its products for the U.S. markets. We next must consider venue. The antitrust statute provides that venue is proper in any district where the defendant is "found" or where it "transacts business." Although Heveafil (D) and the other foreign defendants conduct their business abroad, [no need to worry,] this is not fatal. The Supreme Court has held that the general federal venue statute, 28 U.S.C. §1391(d), which provides that aliens may be sued in any district, overrides any special venue provision contained in other federal statutes such as the one pertaining to antitrust actions. With respect to the American defendants, subsection (b) of 28 U.S.C. §1391 provides that venue is proper, among other things, in a "judicial district in which any defendant may be found, if there is no district in which the action may otherwise be brought." Although (Dee-K) (P) has alleged that some defendants have contact with Virginia, additional allegations are necessary to show that the contacts or businesses are located in the Eastern District so that venue here is proper.

Analysis:

This case briefly examines the issue of personal jurisdiction but quickly concludes that jurisdiction has been met because of appointment of an agent and customizing of the products for the U.S. markets. The real significance of the case is the venue portion. The court shows how the issue of venue is one determined by statute rather than upon a constitutional review. Understand that when jurisdiction is the issue, a statute must be found and then there is a constitutional analysis concerning due process of law. This case is somewhat complicated in that there are multiple defendants. The court found proper venue with respect to the foreign corporations, but required (Dee-K) (P) to amend its complaint with respect to allegations of venue for the American defendants. Note that venue further defines the location where the trial will occur. Whereas jurisdiction may place the matter in a particular state, venue determines which district within the state is proper. Also, the case demonstrates statutory interpretation and illustrates the overriding of the antitrust statute by the general federal venue statute. Finally, notice that there is a very broad venue statute applicable to alien corporations.

Piper Aircraft Co. v. Reyno

(Plane Manufacturer) v. (Estate Representative)
454 U.S. 235, 102 S.Ct. 252, 70 L.Ed.2d 419 (1981)

M E M O R Y   G R A P H I C

Instant Facts

The Scottish heirs of plane crash victims in Scotland try to sue for wrongful death in an American court because American courts recognize wrongful death as a cause of action and are known generally to be more favorable to plaintiffs than the courts in Scotland.

Black Letter Rule

The fact of a substantive law being less favorable to plaintiffs in an alternative forum should not be given conclusive or even substantial weight in applying the doctrine of forum non conveniens.

Case Vocabulary

ADMINISTRATRIX: One (female) appointed to handle the affairs of one who has died intestate, or who has left no executor.

CHOICE-OF-LAW RULES: Rule applied in a court to determine whether federal or state law is applicable and/or whether the law of the forum or some other state applies.

FORUM NON CONVENIENS: Discretionary doctrine whereby a court which has jurisdiction over a case may decline to exercise it, as there is no substantive reason for the case to be brought there, or if in presenting the case in that court it would create a hardship on the defendants or witnesses.

IMPLEAD: To bring a third party, who is allegedly liable, into a lawsuit for purposes of indemnity or contribution.

INDEMNITY: The obligation of one person to make good on a loss of another; an assurance to compensate for the damage caused by another.

Procedural Basis: Appeal from order of the Court of Appeals granting jurisdiction in Pennsylvania District Court.

Facts: A commercial aircraft manufactured in Pennsylvania by Piper (D) crashed in the Scottish highlands. Reports suggested either that the airplane suffered mechanical failure or pilot error. (Legend says only the Lochness monster witnessed it.) At the time of the crash, the plane was registered in Great Britain, operated by a Scottish air taxi service, subject to Scottish air traffic patrol, and full of Scottish residents. Naturally, then, Gaynell Reyno (P), the estate administratrix and legal secretary to the attorney who filed the wrongful death suit on behalf of the Scottish families, brought the action in California state court. Claiming negligence and strict liability, Reyno (P) admits that the choice of forum was determined by the fact that the laws regarding liability, capacity to sue, and damages are more favorable in America than in Scotland. Oddly enough, Piper (D) didn't see this as a boon and moved to transfer the case to a Pennsylvania District Court and subsequently motioned to dismiss it under the doctrine of forum non conveniens. The District Court granted the motion but the Circuit Court overruled it and remanded for trial in Pennsylvania because the plaintiffs would be disadvantaged more by the law in Scotland than the law in Pennsylvania.

Issue: Should a motion to dismiss for forum non conveniens be denied merely because the substantive law of an alternative forum is less favorable to plaintiffs?

Decision and Rationale: (Marshall, J.) No. In analyzing a motion to dismiss for forum non conveniens, courts should not give dispositive or even substantial weight to the fact that the alternative forum is less favorable to plaintiffs than the one in which the action was initially brought. At present, the doctrine of forum non conveniens is designed to avoid conducting complex exercises in comparative law. Giving substantial weight to such a consideration, however, would render the doctrine effectively moot. On the one hand, if courts give much weight to change in substantive law, they will be forced to interpret the law of foreign jurisdictions to make the determination of which is the more favorable forum. On the other hand, it is clear that plaintiffs initially select the most favorable forum to them so courts won't even have to consider a motion to dismiss for forum non conveniens because any alternative forum will be less favorable to plaintiffs than the one they selected for themselves. Of course, substantial weight may be given to the disadvantaging law of an alternative forum if the remedy would be so clearly inadequate that dismissal would not be "in the interests of justice." This is not the case for the Scottish plaintiffs, though. Other considerations are more important in this case. First, the strong presumption in *Gulf Oil Corp. v. Gilbert* [creating a balancing test of public and private interests between plaintiffs and defendants to determine the appropriateness of a forum non conveniens dismissal] in favor of the plaintiff's choice of forum applies with less force when, as in this case, the plaintiffs are foreign. It is unreasonable to assume that a foreign plaintiff's choice of an American forum is for the sake of convenience. Great deference to a foreign plaintiff would also encourage an onslaught of litigation to be brought in the United States which could and should have been brought in a foreign forum. Second, private policy interests dictate that the result of the District Court should have been upheld. Because witnesses and much relevant evidence are more easily located in Great Britain, there would be fewer evidentiary problems in Scotland. Furthermore, because it is far more convenient to resolve all claims in one trial and because Piper (D) would have a hard time impleading potential third party defendants in the United States, the trial should be held in Scotland. Third, public policy interests recommend toward trial in Scotland because Piper (D) and Hartzell, the other defendant, would have two

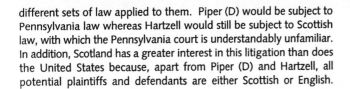

different sets of law applied to them. Piper (D) would be subject to Pennsylvania law whereas Hartzell would still be subject to Scottish law, with which the Pennsylvania court is understandably unfamiliar. In addition, Scotland has a greater interest in this litigation than does the United States because, apart from Piper (D) and Hartzell, all potential plaintiffs and defendants are either Scottish or English.

Finally, the important base consideration is that reversal of a dismissal for forum non conveniens should only be granted if the District Court abused its discretion. In the instant case, it is apparent that the District Court did no such thing, but the Circuit Court simply disagreed with their analysis. Reversed.

Analysis:

This case is one of the jewels in the crown of civil procedure law. *Piper* represents the current approach to the forum non conveniens doctrine after it was set put in *Gulf Oil Corp. v. Gilbert* [a court which has proper jurisdiction may refuse to exercise it when the suit can be more properly brought in another forum.] An underlying tenet of *Piper* is that forum non conveniens doctrine applies only when venue is proper in the initial forum and there is an alternative forum available. In *Piper*, for example, the choice was clearly between the United States and Scotland, both the litigants and the courts were aware of this. The crucial progressive step that *Piper* takes is to establish a balancing test of the conveniences to all parties, without allowing any one factor to be dispositive. The result of such a balancing test is rarely removal to another country. Most courts would not grant such a drastic forum non conveniens motion until all other jurisdictional possibilities have been exhausted. This is an important policy to keep in mind when you remember (and remember you will) that a forum non conveniens dismissal is not equivalent or analogous to a §1404 transfer of venue. Transfer is usually much easier for a court to execute and more predictable for the parties involved since the transferor court's substantive law will be applied regardless of the location of the transferee court. Dismissal is obviously a more final, more difficult decision for a court to make and, therefore, it requires a greater showing of inconvenience than transfer. Once the case is out of the dismissing court's hands, the burden falls on the plaintiffs to re-submit the case in the alternate forum. Another burden on plaintiff may be to become familiar with the substantive law of the new forum before the statute of limitations for filing runs out because, unlike in transfer of venue, the substantive law of the initial forum does not follow to the next one. Finally, there is a notable distinction to be made between the application of forum non conveniens dismissal in federal and state courts. Federal courts rarely utilize the dismissal option because if another federal court is available as a proper forum, they need only resort to transfer. Only when the more convenient forum is foreign, which is a rare occurrence, will the federal courts have to dismiss. State courts, on the other hand, end up exercising their right to dismiss for forum non conveniens because the more convenient forum is often another state and state courts can't transfer a case to a court in another state. The only options are dismissal or increasing their own caseload and you can imagine which they prefer.

Chapter 3

Subject matter jurisdiction can be thought of as the authority of a court to hear a certain type of case or claim. The court system in the United States has both federal and state components. Each system, federal and state, has the authority to hear cases the other cannot. Sometimes their authority overlaps, and a case could be heard in either system.

The decision of which court to bring a case in is critical. A court must have authority over both the parties and the type of case that is being brought. If a court has no power to hear a particular type of case, the best legal claim in the world will be useless. The decision of where to file suit is sometimes easy, but at times it is very difficult. Of course, because this is Civil Procedure, you will study only the difficult situations. Through this study, however, you will come away with a better understanding of the types of cases the federal courts have been given the power to adjudicate.

Chapter 3

NOTE: THE PURPOSE OF THIS OUTLINE IS TO ORGANIZE THE CASES SO THAT ONE CAN QUICKLY UNDERSTAND THE RELEVANCE OF EACH CASE TO THE COURSE. NO ATTEMPT IS MADE IN THIS OVERVIEW TO ADDRESS EVERY CONCEPT THAT MUST BE STUDIED. BE SURE TO READ THE ENTIRE CASEBOOK AND/OR OTHER MATERIALS TO GAIN A FULL UNDERSTANDING OF ALL CONCEPTS.

I. Introduction
   A. Subject matter jurisdiction deals with the type of cases a court can hear, whereas the law of personal jurisdiction limits courts in relation to a particular defendant. A court must have both personal jurisdiction over the defendant and subject matter jurisdiction over the claim to proceed with a case.
      1. Article III, Section 1 of the U. S. Constitution gives congress the power to create federal courts.
      2. Article III, Section 2 establishes the scope of the federal judicial power. Within these boundaries, Congress is free to grant jurisdiction to the federal courts.
   B. The relationship between state courts and federal courts.
      1. Cases arising under federal law can be brought in either state or federal courts. Such shared jurisdiction is called concurrent jurisdiction.
      2. Congress has made federal court the exclusive forum for certain types of actions such as bankruptcy and antitrust cases. Over these cases, federal courts are said to have exclusive jurisdiction.
      3. Why would an attorney prefer federal court to state court or state court to federal court?
         a. Some federal courts have shorter waiting times for trial than many state courts.
         b. A jury from one area may be more desirable than from another.
         c. A local state judge may be more or less sympathetic to a local case than a federal judge.

II. Federal Question Jurisdiction
   A. Article III, Section 2 of the U. S. Constitution and its statutory codification, 28 U.S.C. §1331, provide that the federal judicial power shall extend to cases arising under the Constitution and laws of the United States. The difficulty is in determining when a case "arises under" federal law.

   B. The well-pleaded complaint rule: The plaintiff's federal question must appear in the allegations of the complaint. *Louisville & Nashville Railroad v. Mottley.*
      1. An allegation that an anticipated defense will be based on federal law is not sufficient to raise a federal question.
      2. The justification for the well-pleaded complaint rule is that it is impossible to be certain what defenses a defendant will raise in the answer. Whether a case actually involves a federal question can be quickly determined before too much time and expense is wasted in the wrong court.

   C. What should be done if a case is filed in federal court and the defense believes there is no basis for federal subject matter jurisdiction?
      1. In diversity cases, a motion under Rule 12(b)(1) asserting lack of subject matter jurisdiction is proper.
      2. In federal question cases, however, jurisdiction depends on the substance of the plaintiff's claim. Therefore, if there is any arguable basis for a federal claim, the court should examine the federal question on a Rule 12(b)(6) motion to dismiss the substantive claim.
      3. Even if a defendant fails to move for dismissal under either Rule 12(b)(1) or Rule 12(b)(6), jurisdiction is not waived.
         a. Subject matter jurisdiction is considered so fundamental that a court must raise the issue on its own and dismiss the case if it finds a lack of jurisdiction. *Louisville & Nashville Railroad v. Mottley.*
         b. Even if the lack of jurisdiction is discovered for the first time on appeal, the case must be dismissed.
         c. Contrast this with the defense of lack of personal jurisdiction which may be waived by failing to raise it at the beginning of the litigation.
      4. If a defendant challenges both personal and subject matter jurisdiction and the case is dismissed, the results are different depending on the basis for dismissal.
         a. If the case is dismissed for lack of subject matter jurisdiction, the plaintiff may refile in state court.

b. If the case is dismissed for lack of personal jurisdiction, the plaintiff may not refile in state court because the federal court's decision that personal jurisdiction was absent will bind the state court under the rules of issue preclusion.

III. Diversity Jurisdiction

A. Diversity jurisdiction is made possible by Article III, Section 2 of the U.S. Constitution which permits federal court jurisdiction over "controversies between citizens of different states" and between citizens of a state and foreign citizens or subjects.

1. This jurisdiction is not mandated by the Constitution. Congress may establish inferior federal courts and grant them diversity jurisdiction, but it is not required to do so.

2. Diversity jurisdiction is codified at 28 U.S.C. §1332.

3. Diversity jurisdiction was likely established to combat the fear that State courts would be biased against litigants from out of State.

B. Citizenship for diversity jurisdiction purposes is the equivalent of domicile. *Mas v. Perry.*

1. A person's domicile is the place of his true and fixed home to which he intends to return. One's domicile can be changed by meeting both of the following requirements:

a. Taking up residence in a different domicile

b. With the intention to remain there.

2. A person retains his old domicile until he obtains a new one.

C. While the constitution does not require it, the U.S. Supreme Court has interpreted the diversity statute to require complete diversity. This means that no party on one side of the suit may be a citizen of the same state as any party on the other side. *Strawbridge v. Curtiss.*

D. A corporation can have dual citizenship for diversity jurisdiction purposes.

1. A corporation is deemed to be a citizen of every state in which it is incorporated and the state where it has its chief place of business.

2. A corporation can have only one chief place of business. Courts use two different tests to determine the chief place of business. Some courts look to both tests:

a. The corporate "nerve center" where most managerial and executive functions are controlled.

b. Some courts may also look at where the every-day business activities or "muscle" of the corporation exists.

E. U.S. Supreme Court has found there is no federal diversity jurisdiction over suits for divorce, child custody, and alimony, even if spouses are citizens of different states. *Ankenbrandt v. Richards.*

F. Congress amended 28 U.S.C. §1332(a) in 1988 to provide that an alien admitted to the U.S. for permanent residence is deemed a resident of the state in which the alien is domiciled.

1. This eliminated diversity jurisdiction between a state citizen and a permanent resident alien living in the same state.

2. The amendment, however, has been interpreted to not extend diversity jurisdiction over an action between an alien and another alien who has achieved permanent resident immigration status in the U.S. *Saadeh v. Farouki.*

G. In addition to diversity, 28 U.S.C. §1332 also requires an amount greater than $75,000 to be in controversy for federal jurisdiction to be present.

1. The courts generally view the allegations in the pleading as controlling, and do not guess about the likelihood of the plaintiff collecting what is asked for.

a. It must appear to a legal certainty that the claim is really for less than the statutory amount to justify dismissal. *St. Paul Mercury Indemnity Co. v. Red Cab Co.*

2. Different claims may be aggregated to meet the statutory amount under some circumstances.

a. A single plaintiff with two or more unrelated claims against a single defendant may aggregate the claims to meet the statutory amount

b. Two plaintiffs with claims against a single defendant cannot aggregate if their claims are separate and distinct.

c. Where there are multiple plaintiffs or multiple defendants with a common interest and a single title or right, the value of the total interest is the amount in controversy.

3. For counterclaims, when a plaintiff's claim exceeds $75,000, a compulsory counterclaim may be heard regardless of the amount, but a permissive counterclaim requires an independent basis for jurisdiction.

IV. Supplemental Jurisdiction

A. The common law concepts of pendant and ancillary jurisdiction were combined and codified in 28

U.S.C. §1367 as supplemental jurisdiction.
B. When a federal court has proper original jurisdiction over a claim, it may hear all other claims that form part of the same case or controversy.
C. The federal claim must be substantial enough to support federal question jurisdiction, and the federal and nonfederal claims must arise from a common nucleus of operative fact such that they should be tried in one proceeding. *United Mine Workers v. Gibbs.*
  a. The court may decline to exercise supplemental jurisdiction in its discretion. Factors which a court will consider in making this determination include:
    (1) If the issues of state law substantially predominate over the issues of federal law.
    (2) If the state claim is closely tied to questions of federal policy, such as pre-emption, the court may want to hear both claims.
    (3) If the federal law claims are dismissed, the court may dismiss the other nonfederal law claims.
    (4) Judicial economy and fairness to the litigants are also important considerations.

V. Removal
  A. Removal allows a defendant to shift a case from state court to federal court. The text of 28 U.S.C. §1441 generally allows a defendant to remove a case if the plaintiff could have originally filed the case in federal court.
  B. If the district court lacks jurisdiction, or there is a defect in the removal procedure, the federal district court is to remand the case back to the state court.

    1. If the district court fails to remand a case which was improperly removed, the ensuing adjudication will be upheld if the federal jurisdictional requirements are met at the time the judgment is entered. *Caterpillar, Inc. v. Lewis.*
    2. Considerations of finality, efficiency, and judicial economy dictate that the judgment be upheld if the jurisdictional defects are ultimately cured. *Caterpillar, Inc. v. Lewis.*

Louisville & Nashville Railroad v. Mottley

(Railroad) v. (Victim)
211 U.S. 149 (1908)

M E M O R Y   G R A P H I C

Instant Facts

Injured railroad customers sought to enforce the use of their free passes in the wrong court.

Black Letter Rule

The plaintiff's federal question must appear in the allegations of the complaint, and anticipated defense, involving federal law are inadequate for federal question jurisdiction.

Case Vocabulary

BILL: The first pleading by the plaintiff. It is now called a complaint.

DEMURRER: A motion arguing that even if the facts as alleged are true, they are legally insufficient to make a claim. It is now called a motion to dismiss.

SUA SPONTE: This means to take action on its own will without the suggestion of another.

Procedural Basis: Appeal by the Railroad (D) when a demurrer in their favor was overruled.

Facts: The Mottleys (P) were injured in a railway accident on Louisville & Nashville Railroad (D) and given lifetime passes on the railroad to settle their claims. Many years later, Congress made free passes unlawful, believing that railroads were using free passes to bribe public officials. When the railroad (D) refused to honor the Mottleys' (P) passes, they sued in federal court asking for specific performance. The Mottleys (P) alleged that the Railroad (D) would raise the federal law as a defense, and that applying this law to them would be unconstitutional.

Issue: Is a plaintiff's allegation that a defense to his complaint will raise an issue of federal or constitutional law adequate to give a federal court jurisdiction over the suit?

Decision and Rationale: (Moody, J.) No, the plaintiff's federal question must appear in the complaint. Louisville & Nashville Railroad (D) filed a demurrer to the bill and raised two questions of law which are presented here on appeal. The first is whether the act of Congress at issue prohibits the giving of passes under the circumstances of this case, and secondly, if the act does apply to this case, whether the statute is in violation of the Fifth Amendment of the Constitution of the United States. We are not going to consider these issues because the court below was without jurisdiction. Neither party questioned that jurisdiction, but we may on our own see to it that the jurisdiction of the Circuit Court is not exceeded. There is no diversity of citizenship here so the only possible ground for jurisdiction is that the case was a suit "arising under the Constitution and laws of the United States" as the jurisdiction statute provides. The settled meaning of this statute is that a suit arises under the Constitution and laws of the United States when the plaintiff's statement of his own cause of action shows that it is based upon those laws or the Constitution. It is not enough that the plaintiff alleges that some anticipated defense to his suit will be unconstitutional. While some question under the Constitution will likely arise at some point in the litigation, this does not mean that the original suit arises under the Constitution. The plaintiff should be confined to his own statement in the complaint. The defendant should be left to set up the defense. We find that the application of this rule to the present case shows that the Circuit Court had no subject matter jurisdiction. Reversed and remanded with instructions to dismiss for lack of jurisdiction.

Analysis:

This case presents the well-pleaded complaint rule under which the plaintiff's federal question must appear in the allegations of the complaint. This rule allows for an early determination of whether the federal court has jurisdiction. It is difficult, if not impossible, to predict what defenses a defendant may raise in the answer or at a later point in the litigation. Therefore, it is reasonable to disallow the consideration of possible defenses in determining whether a federal question exists. Note how the court raised the issue of jurisdiction on its own, or sua sponte. Unlike personal jurisdiction, subject matter jurisdiction cannot be waived by the parties. A defect in subject matter jurisdiction can be raised at any time by the court. Note: it is probably not smart to settle a client's case for "free passes" or a lifetime supply of coffee.

Mas v. Perry

(Married Couple) v. (Peeping Tom)
489 F.2d 1396 (5th Cir. 1974)

M E M O R Y   G R A P H I C

Instant Facts

A French citizen and his wife sued a Louisiana resident for torts committed in Louisiana seeking federal diversity jurisdiction.

Black Letter Rule

To change domicile for diversity jurisdiction purposes, one must take up residence in a different domicile with the intent to remain there.

Procedural Basis: Appeal from denial of motion to dismiss for lack of jurisdiction.

Facts: Jean Paul Mas (P) and Judy Mas (P) were married at Judy's home in Mississippi. Jean Paul Mas (P) is a citizen of France. Both Jean Paul and Judy Mas (P) were graduate students in Louisiana where they lived for approximately two years after their marriage. They subsequently moved to Illinois. At the time of trial, they intended to return to Louisiana until Mr. Mas (P) finished his studies. They were undecided as to where they would live after that. While Mr. and Mrs. Mas (P) lived in Baton Rouge, they rented an apartment from Perry (D), a citizen of Louisiana. Mr. and Mrs. Mas (P) obtained a judgment against Perry (D) in federal court for damages sustained by them when they discovered that they had been watched by Perry (D) through two-way mirrors in their bedroom and bathroom. At trial in the district court, Perry (D) made an oral motion to dismiss for lack of diversity jurisdiction which was denied.

Issue: For diversity jurisdiction purposes, must a person change her domicile by taking up residence in another domicile with the intent to remain there?

Decision and Rationale: (Ainsworth, J.) Yes. Perry (D) challenges the judgment below on jurisdictional grounds. Diversity jurisdiction requires the complete diversity of the parties. This means that no party on one side may be a citizen of the same State as any party on the other side. Citizenship for diversity purposes is controlled by federal law and must exist at the time the complaint is filed. For diversity purposes, citizenship means domicile, and mere residence in the State is not sufficient. A person's domicile is the place of his true, fixed and permanent home, and to which he has the intention of returning. A change of domicile can only occur when two conditions are met: 1) taking up residence in a different domicile with 2) the intention to remain there. Also, one cannot lose one's domicile until one obtains a new one. Mrs. Mas (P) was clearly a domiciliary of Mississippi at the time of her marriage. Simply because she married a French citizen does not change her domicile or citizenship to French. Her domicile was not disturbed by her marriage or the time she spent in Louisiana as a graduate student. She did not affect a change in domicile since she and Mr. Mas (P) were in Louisiana only as students and lacked intent to stay there. Even though she had no intention of returning to her parent's home in Mississippi, her domicile has not changed because until she acquires a new one, she remains a domiciliary of Mississippi. Diversity jurisdiction was established on two grounds in this case: a suit by an alien against a State citizen, and an action between citizens of different states. It is also wise to allow both these claims to be heard together because they arise from the same operative facts. Because the district court had jurisdiction over Mr. Mas's claim, sound judicial administration weighs in favor of federal jurisdiction over Mrs. Mas's (P) claim. Affirmed.

Analysis:

This case hinges on the "rule of complete diversity" under which no party on one side can be a citizen of the same state as any party on the other side. This interpretation was attached to the predecessor statute of 28 U.S.C. §1332 in the case of *Strawbridge v. Curtiss*. Note that citizenship means domicile for purposes of determining federal diversity jurisdiction. What if the court had found that Mrs. Mas (P) was a domiciliary of Louisiana and thus there was not complete diversity? Would the case have to be dismissed? It would likely be allowed to proceed with only Mr. Mas (P) if Mrs. Mas (P) was not found to be an indispensable party.

Saadeh v. Farouki

(Greek Citizen) v. (Permanent Resident)
107 F.3d 52 (D.C. Cir. 1997)

M E M O R Y   G R A P H I C

Instant Facts

Saadeh (P), a Greek citizen, sued Farouki (D), a Jordanian living in Maryland, in federal court on a defaulted loan.

Black Letter Rule

There is no federal diversity jurisdiction over an action between an alien and another alien who has achieved permanent resident immigration status in the United States.

Procedural Basis: Appeal after judgment in favor of Saadeh (P).

Facts: Mr. Saadeh (P), a Greek citizen, sued Mr. Farouki (D) on a defaulted loan in federal court claiming diversity jurisdiction. Mr. Farouki (D) was a Jordanian citizen residing in Maryland who had achieved "permanent resident" immigration status in the United States by the time the suit was filed. After the litigation was underway, Mr. Farouki (D) became a citizen of the United States. Mr. Farouki (D) lost the suit and appealed on the merits.

Issue: Is there federal diversity jurisdiction over a suit between an alien and another alien who has achieved permanent resident status in the United States?

Decision and Rationale: (Rogers, J.) No. We do not reach the merits of the case because we find a lack of subject matter jurisdiction. The United States Supreme Court has never addressed the scope of the complete diversity rule in cases involving alien parties. However, in 1988 Congress amended the diversity statute to add the last sentence of 28 U.S.C.§ 1332(a) to provide that "an alien admitted to the United States for permanent residence shall be deemed a citizen of the State in which such alien is domiciled." Under this amendment, diversity no longer exists between a citizen of State A and an alien admitted to the United States for permanent residence who lives in State A. Read literally, the amendment would create diversity between Saadeh (P), a Greek citizen, and Farouki (D), who would be deemed a resident of Maryland. Citizenship at the time the suit was filed is the relevant test, so Mr. Farouki (D) subsequently becoming a U.S. citizen does not create diversity. The question remains whether Mr. Farouki (D) was a "citizen of the State" when the complaint was filed. A literal reading of the amendment would create an odd and possibly unconstitutional result. It would create federal diversity jurisdiction over a lawsuit between two aliens, without a citizen of a state on either side of the action. The judicial power of the United States under the Diversity Clause of Article III does not extend to such an action. Under the circumstances, we must examine the legislative history of the amendment. The Congressional Record makes clear that the purpose of the amendment was to reduce diversity jurisdiction to relieve caseload pressures in the federal courts. Despite its language, the amendment was intended only to eliminate diversity jurisdiction between a citizen and an alien living in the same state. There is no reason to believe the amendment was intended to create diversity jurisdiction where it did not previously exist. The literal language of the statue is at odds with the Congressional intent, therefore our construction is necessary to avoid constitutional difficulties. Dismissed for lack of jurisdiction.

Analysis:

Was it proper for the court to go beyond the plain language of the amendment to inquire into legislative intent? Apparently it had to do so because a literal reading would have made Farouki (D) a citizen of Maryland, even though he was actually still an alien. It would be unconstitutional for a United States District Court to exercise jurisdiction over a suit between two aliens. This case also raises the question of the purpose of diversity jurisdiction. The original purpose of diversity jurisdiction was to give residents of two different states a neutral federal forum in which to resolve their disputes without any prejudice based on their state citizenship. Some have argued that prejudice based on state citizenship is no longer a factor in modern society. Based on this, should diversity jurisdiction be abolished?

United Mine Workers v. Gibbs

(Union) v. (Strike Breaker)
383 U.S. 715 (1966)

M E M O R Y   G R A P H I C

Instant Facts

Gibbs (P), involved in a labor dispute, lost his job and several subsequent trucking contracts; he believed these losses were a result of a concerted union plan against him.

Black Letter Rule

Where a federal court has proper jurisdiction over a federal law claim, it may also hear related state law claims where both claims arise from a common nucleus of operative fact.

Case Vocabulary

FEDERAL PRE-EMPTION: The doctrine holding that certain matters are of such national concern that federal laws take precedence over state laws, and the states may not make laws inconsistent with the federal law.

PENDANT JURISDICTION: A principle which allows a federal court which has proper jurisdiction over a federal law claim to also exercise jurisdiction over a related state law claim where both claims arise from a common nucleus of operative fact.

Procedural Basis: Writ of certiorari granted after district court heard both state and federal claims.

Facts: Paul Gibbs (P) was hired as superintendent to run a mine and haul coal. Members of a local chapter of the United Mine Workers (D) who were involved in a labor dispute threatened Gibbs (P) and forcibly prevented the opening of the mine. Gibbs (P) subsequently lost his job as superintendent and began losing other trucking contracts and mine leases in nearby areas. He claimed these losses were a result of a concerted union plan against him and brought suit against the United Mine Workers (D) in a Tennessee district court. Jurisdiction was based on a claim under the federal Labor Management Relations Act and a pendant state law claim asserting a conspiracy and boycott against him to maliciously interfere with his contracts. The district court heard both claims, but found that there was no claim under the federal labor laws.

Issue: May a federal court properly exercise jurisdiction over both a federal and a related state claim if they arise from a common nucleus of operative fact?

Decision and Rationale: (Brennan, J.) Yes. State law claims are appropriate for federal court determination if they form a separate but parallel ground for relief along with a substantial claim based on federal law. Under the Federal Rules of Civil Procedure, the impulse is toward allowing the broadest possible scope of action consistent with fairness to the parties. Pendant jurisdiction exists whenever the relationship between the federal claim and the state claim can be said to comprise but one "case." The state and federal claims must derive from a common nucleus of operative fact. A court is not required to hear both the state and federal claim in every case where the power to do so exists. A court may use its discretion in making the determination. Considerations of judicial economy, convenience, and fairness to the litigants are important. Also, if it appears that the state issues substantially predominate in terms of proof or scope, the state claims may be dismissed without prejudice. There may also be circumstances where the state claim is so closely tied to questions of federal policy that the need to exercise pendant jurisdiction is particularly strong. For example, in the present case, the allowable scope of the state claim implicates the federal doctrine of pre-emption. There may be other reasons such as the likelihood of jury confusion in considering different theories of legal relief which may justify separating the state and federal claims. The question whether pendant jurisdiction was proper will remain open throughout the litigation as new issues may arise. Once it appears the state claim is the real body of the case, and the federal claim is only an appendage, the state claim can be dismissed. In the present case, the district court did not exceed its discretion in proceeding to judgment on the state claim. The federal and state claims arose from the same nucleus of operative fact. Even though the federal claim ultimately failed, it was not a mere appendage of the federal claim. The district court may have dismissed the state claim, but there was no error in refusing to do so. Affirmed.

Analysis:

This was the leading case regarding supplemental jurisdiction before the concept was codified in 28 U.S.C. §1367. As you can see from the case, supplemental jurisdiction broadens the jurisdiction of the federal courts to include related claims it could not otherwise hear. The rationale of supplemental jurisdiction, as the court in *Gibbs* explained, is to promote judicial economy by allowing related claims to be decided in one proceeding. *Gibbs* deals with a particular type of supplemental jurisdiction called pendant jurisdiction which arises when federal and nonfederal claims arise from the same event. As the court phrased it, whether the claims arose from "a common nucleus of operative fact."

A FEDERAL TRIAL COURT'S ERROR IN FAILING TO REMAND A CASE IMPROPERLY REMOVED IS NOT FATAL TO THE FINAL JUDGMENT IF THE JURISDICTIONAL REQUIREMENTS ARE MET AT THE TIME THE JUDGMENT IS ENTERED

Caterpillar, Inc. v. Lewis

(Manufacturer) v. (Injured Operator)

519 U.S. 61 (1996)

M E M O R Y   G R A P H I C

Instant Facts

Lewis's (P) state case was improperly removed to federal court because there was not completed diversity of the parties. The jurisdictional defect was cured before judgment.

Black Letter Rule

A district court's error in failing to remand a case improperly removed is not fatal to the ensuing judgment if federal jurisdictional requirements are met at the time judgment is entered.

Case Vocabulary

REMAND: When an appellate court sends a case back to the trial court. In the case of removal, the federal district court sends the case back to the state court.

REMOVAL OF CAUSES: The transfer of a case from one court to another.

SUBROGATION: The right of one who has paid an obligation on behalf of another to be compensated for these payments. Insurance companies often have the right to take the place of their insured and sue any party their insured could have sued to recover insurance payouts.

Procedural Basis: Appeal from vacation of district court judgment for lack of jurisdiction.

Facts: James David Lewis (P), a resident of Kentucky, was injured while operating a bulldozer. He brought state law claims in Kentucky state court for breach of warranty, defective manufacture, negligent maintenance, and failure to warn against Caterpillar (D), a Delaware corporation with its principal place of business in Illinois. Lewis (P) also made claims against Whayne Supply Company, a Kentucky corporation with its principal place of business in Kentucky, who serviced the bulldozer. Later, the insurance carrier for Lewis' (P) employer, Liberty Mutual, intervened in the lawsuit as a plaintiff seeking subrogation against both Caterpillar (D) and Whayne Supply Company for workers' compensation benefits Liberty Mutual had paid to Lewis (P). Lewis (P) subsequently settled with Whayne Supply. Caterpillar (D) then asked for removal to the District Court for the Eastern District of Kentucky on the basis of diversity of citizenship. Caterpillar (D) satisfied with only one day to spare the statutory requirement that diversity removal take place within one year of the lawsuit's commencement as required by 28 U.S.C. §1446(b). The case was not removable at the lawsuit's commencement because complete diversity was absent as Lewis (P) and Whayne Supply were both citizens of Kentucky. Caterpillar (D) assumed that the settlement agreement between Lewis (P) and Whayne Supply would result in Wayne Supply being dismissed from the lawsuit. However, Lewis (P) argued the case should be remanded to state court because Liberty Mutual had not yet settled its subrogation claim against Whayne Supply, and Whayne Supply's presence in the lawsuit defeated diversity jurisdiction. The district court rejected Lewis' (P) argument. Three years later, before a verdict was rendered in favor of Caterpillar (D), Liberty Mutual and Whayne Supply settled.

Issue: Is the absence of complete diversity at the time of removal fatal to federal court jurisdiction where the jurisdictional requirements are ultimately met at the time the judgment is entered?

Decision and Rationale: (Ginsburg, J.) No. The District Court erred in failing to remand the case to state court because it was improperly removed. It incorrectly treated Whayne Supply, the nondiverse defendant, as effectively dropped from the suit. Whayne Supply, however, remained in the suit as a defendant of Liberty Mutual. However, this error is not fatal to federal jurisdiction because the jurisdictional requirements were ultimately met before judgment when Liberty Mutual and Whayne Supply settled. Lewis (P) did all that was required to preserve his objection to removal by filing a motion to remand to state court. Lewis (P) argues that the ultimate satisfaction of the complete diversity requirements should not swallow up previous statutory jurisdictional violations. Lewis (P) also emphasizes that Caterpillar (D) was only able to get into federal court by removing prematurely. If Caterpillar (D) had waited until Whayne Supply had been dismissed from the case, the 1-year limitation of §1446(b) would have barred removal, and the case would have remained in state court. These arguments are not without merit. However, they run up against the overriding considerations of finality, efficiency, and economy. If a federal court judge denies a motion to remand, and the jurisdictional defect remains uncured, the judgment must be vacated. In the present case, however, no jurisdictional defect lingered through judgment. To wipe out the judgment at this point and return to state court a case now satisfying all federal jurisdictional requirements would impose a huge cost on our court system that is incompatible with the fair administration of justice. Lewis (P) argues that if we allow the judgment against him to stand, defendants will have an incentive to attempt wrongful removals. We do not believe these dire consequences are likely. Federal trial court judges will still

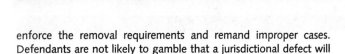

enforce the removal requirements and remand improper cases. Defendants are not likely to gamble that a jurisdictional defect will escape detection and then disappear prior to judgment. The judgment of the court of appeals is reversed.

Analysis:

This case illustrates the difficult situations which can arise with removal issues. When federal and state court jurisdiction overlap, the plaintiff has the initial choice of forum. However, removal gives the defendant the power to challenge this choice and move the case to federal court. Caterpillar (D) eventually won the suit in federal court, and the judgment was upheld. It could be said that Caterpillar (D) benefitted from the District Court erroneously refusing to remand the case. Is it fair to allow Caterpillar (D) to benefit from its own mistake and that of the District Court? Generally, complete diversity must exist at the time the case is filed for a federal court to have proper diversity jurisdiction. Can this rule be reconciled with the Court's ruling in *Caterpillar* that a jurisdictional defect can be corrected sometime before judgment? Does the fact that *Caterpillar* was a removal case make a difference?

Chapter 4

This Chapter examines the question of whether federal or state law will apply when a matter is being tried in federal court. It specifically looks at those situations where a federal court is hearing a matter based upon diversity jurisdiction. (You learned what diversity means in the previous chapter—It's where a party on one side of a lawsuit is a citizen of one state and the party on the other side is a citizen of another state.) Should the federal court apply the law of the state where the matter is being tried, or should it apply federal law? The answer depends, in part, upon how the particular law is characterized.

As discussed at length in this Chapter, a law is generally viewed as "procedural" or "substantive," and defining the law as one or the other will determine whether state or federal law should be applied. Deciding which law to apply is important to litigants, because in some situations varying results can occur depending upon which law is applied. For example, assume that Mr. Smith is visiting friends in State A and is hit by a train while walking along the tracks. He returns home to State B and sues the train company in the federal district court located in State B, based upon diversity jurisdiction. (Mr. Smith is a resident of State B and the train company is headquartered in State A, and Mr. Smith is seeking big bucks!) The law of State A provides that Mr. Smith is a trespasser because he was on the train tracks, and thus the train company is liable only for wanton negligence. The federal judge in State B decides that the train company should be liable for ordinary negligence, and disregards the law of State A. Mr. Smith wins because of application of the judge-made law, but he would have lost if State A's law had been applied.

Assume that after filing his lawsuit, Mr. Smith served the complaint on the wife of the owner of the train as allowed under federal law, but State A law requires Mr. Smith to hand the complaint directly to the owner of the train. The federal judge applies the federal law and holds that the service of the complaint on the wife of the owner is valid. Assume that State A's law allows the judge to decide the factual disputes involved in Mr. Smith's lawsuit, but the federal law allows the jury to decide the issues. The federal judge in State B applies the federal law and allows the jury to decide the case. Assume that the jury found in Mr. Smith's favor and awarded him a lot of money for his injuries. The train owner appeals but is not successful. Mr. Smith, knowing that State A law would give him extra money because the train owner lost on appeal, tries to obtain the additional money. The federal judge doesn't give Mr. Smith the extra money because federal law requires the appeal to be "frivolous", and the judge rules that the train owner's appeal is not frivolous.

Finally, assume that Mr. Smith brought his lawsuit more than one year after he was hit by the train. State A law provides that lawsuits brought more than one year after the injury are barred, but the federal law allows such lawsuits if there was a good explanation for the delay in bringing the suit. The federal judge in State B decides that State A's one year statute of limitations should apply, and dismisses Mr. Smith's lawsuit. These issues are examples of the problems that can arise when contrary state and federal laws exist. Knowing which law to apply is thus critical. The Chapter is entitled *The Erie Problem* because, as will be seen, determining whether a law is "substantive" or "procedural" is not so easily accomplished.

Chapter 4

NOTE: THE PURPOSE OF THIS OUTLINE IS TO ORGANIZE THE CASES SO THAT ONE CAN QUICKLY UNDERSTAND THE RELEVANCE OF EACH CASE TO THE COURSE. NO ATTEMPT IS MADE IN THIS OVERVIEW TO ADDRESS EVERY CONCEPT THAT MUST BE STUDIED. BE SURE TO READ THE ENTIRE CASEBOOK AND/OR OTHER MATERIALS TO GAIN A FULL UNDERSTANDING OF ALL CONCEPTS.

I. State Courts as Lawmakers in a Federal System
   A. The first law of the Republic, adopted in 1789, provided that "the laws of the several states" shall be followed in federal diversity cases. *Rules of Decision Act.*
      1. In 1841, the Supreme Court interpreted the meaning of "laws", as used in the Rules of Decision Act, and held that it did *not* include so-called "unwritten" decisional law by a state's highest court, unless it was of a local nature such as land title. Statutory "written" laws, did fall within the meaning of "laws." *Swift v. Tyson.*
      2. The federal courts were free to ignore state unwritten law, even when the matters before them were not explicitly governed by federal law. *The Issue in Historical Context.*
   B. Constitutionalizing the Issue
      1. In 1938, the Supreme Court reversed *Swift v. Tyson* in the landmark case of *Erie Railroad v. Tompkins.*
         a. The court interpreted the meaning of the phrase "laws of the several states" in the Rules of Decision Act to include state "common law," consisting of the decisional law from the state's highest court.
         b. The court held that a state's substantive law must be applied in federal diversity cases, except in matters governed by the Federal Constitution or by Acts of Congress.
         c. It rejected the existence of a federal common law in favor of individual state's substantive common law.
         d. The court specifically held that Congress has no power to declare substantive rules of common law applicable in a State.
         e. Thus, in diversity cases, the federal courts follow state substantive law and federal procedural law. *Erie Railroad v. Tompkins.*
      2. The Supreme Court did permit the development of a federal common law in a non-diversity case under the Taft-Hartley Act [organized labor act]. It held that Congress must have intended to give the courts substantive rulemaking power since the act was silent regarding any governing substantive rules. *Textile Workers Union of America v. Lincoln Mills.*
      3. In diversity cases, federal courts must apply the conflict of laws rules of the forum state. *Klaxon Co. v.*

Stentor Manufacturing Co.
      4. The Court's pronouncement in Erie that there is no federal general common law is not entirely accurate. Certain federal statutes exist that allow the federal courts to create common law for cases pertaining to such statutes. Thus, Erie prohibits a general federal common law from displacing the states' common laws in areas where the states have lawmaking powers under the Constitution. *Note: Erie and the Persistence of Federal Common Law.*

II. The Limits of State Power in Federal Courts
   A. Interpreting the Constitutional Command of Erie
      1. The Supreme Court developed what is known as the "Outcome-Determinative Test" for deciding whether or not state law is substantive. Applying this test, the court held that a state statute of limitations applies in a federal diversity case if disregarding the statute would significantly affect the result of the litigation, as compared with the outcome had it been tried in state court. *Guaranty Trust Co. v. York.*
         a. When state practices conflict with a federal statute or rule of civil procedure, the state practices apply.
         b. Examples include the following:
            (1) State law, rather than federal, determines when an action was *commenced* for purposes of state statute of limitations.
            (2) State law requiring plaintiff to post bond when filing a shareholder's derivative suit applied although no similar federal statute exists.
            (3) State law, rather than federal, determines the enforceability of arbitration agreements.
            (4) State law denying out-of-state corporations not qualified to do business in the state the right to sue, applies to federal courts within the state. *Notes and Problems.*
      2. The Supreme Court expanded on the "outcome-determinative test" and developed an "interest balancing" approach for determining whether or not state law is substantive. *Byrd v. Blue Ridge Rural Electric Cooperative.*
         a. In using this approach, there are several factors that must be balanced.
         b. These include considering the relation between the state rule and the underlying state right, examining the strength of the federal policy before holding that it must yield to a counter state policy, and finally giving consideration to the outcome-determinative test.
         c. A state decisional law was held not to apply in a federal diversity case where it allowed a judge, and not the jury, to determine a factual issue.

B. De-Constitutionalizing *Erie*
1. Under both the "out-come determinative" test and the "interest balancing" approach, the question of whether to follow the state practice is a constitutional question. However, the issue may, in certain circumstances, be determined based upon statutory rather than constitutional interpretation.
2. Where federal rules of procedure conflict with state rules *Erie* constitutional questions are not appropriate to determine which rules to apply.
   a. Instead, the scope of the Rules Enabling Act [gives Supreme Court the power to prescribe procedural rules as long as they do not abridge, enlarge or modify substantive right and preserve the right to jury trial] is considered as well as the constitutionality of the specific federal rules.
   b. If federal rules of procedure conflict with state rules, the federal procedural rule will prevail unless it violates the Constitution or the terms of the Rules Enabling Act.
   c. Thus, as long as the rules are procedural in nature and do not abridge, enlarge or modify any substantive right, they will be upheld. Federal Rules of Civil Procedure governing service of process apply to federal diversity cases, notwithstanding conflicting state rule. *Hanna v. Plumer*.
C. Determining the Scope of Federal Law: Avoiding and Accommodating *Erie*
1. Where federal appellate rules govern the situation, an *Erie* analysis is unnecessary. Thus, a governing federal rule of appellate procedure applying to all appeals controls over a contrary state statute, even if it is silent with respect to a certain subject covered by the state rule. *Burlington Northern Railroad v. Woods*.
2. Where a federal procedural statute has been passed by an Act of Congress, it displaces contrary substantive state decisional law.
   a. In this situation, there is no need to balance the interests concerning the federal and state statutes. Congress, by passing the law, has already balanced the state and federal interests involved.
   b. Thus, a federal court in a diversity case is not required to apply state decisional law concerning forum selection clauses if a federal procedural statute exists and governs the subject. *Stewart Organization, Inc. v. Ricoh*.

3. Where the Federal Constitution controls, a substantive state statute is displaced.
   a. Thus, in a federal diversity case, the Reexamination Clause of the Seventh Amendment displaced a substantive state statute regarding excessive jury verdicts.
   b. However, the federal trial court may initially apply the state statute and then the court of appeals can review the trial court's application of the statute for abuse of discretion.
   c. By allowing the federal trial court to perform the functions of the state statute, i.e., review of verdicts for purpose of setting aside those that are unreasonable, it permits the state's dominant interest to be respected, but without disrupting the federal system. *Gasperini v. Center for Humanities, Inc.*
D. Determining the Scope of State Law: an Entailment of *Erie*
1. Federal courts are faced with a difficult situation if they must apply state law when the law is unclear, not declared by the highest court of the state, or very old and outdated, or when the issue has never been raised before.
   a. Lower courts have faced these difficult situations but the Supreme Court has not ruled directly on the issue.
   b. Often times the federal court will review the state decisional law, and other relevant sources, to determine what it believes the state courts would do if faced with the issue.
2. The federal appellate courts are not permitted to defer to the interpretation of the state law by federal trial judges.
   a. Instead, they must themselves make an independent review of the district court's interpretation of state law.
   b. Some states have adopted certification laws where the federal court asks the state supreme court for an answer to a question about state law.
   c. If certification is not available, the federal court under special circumstances may abstain from deciding the case, if it determines that the effect of misinterpreting state law might be drastic.

Erie Railroad v. Tompkins

(Railroad) v. (Injured person)

(1938) 304 U.S. 64, 58 S.Ct. 817, 82 L.Ed. 1188

M E M O R Y   G R A P H I C

Instant Facts

Lower federal court refused to apply state decisional law concerning duty of due care owed by railroad to injured person in federal diversity case.

Black Letter Rule

In federal diversity cases, the substantive laws of the state must be applied.

Case Vocabulary

COMMON LAW: Law which originated in England and developed over the years from case law decisions, as opposed to statutory laws.

DIVERSITY OF CITIZENSHIP: It creates federal jurisdiction when party on one side of a lawsuit is a citizen of one state and the party on the other side is a citizen of another state.

EQUITY: A claim or remedy based upon the underlying principles of fairness and justice, and not part of legal or common law claims and remedies.

GENERAL LAW: A law that affects all, and is not local or unique to one group.

Procedural Basis: Writ of certiorari granted by Supreme Court to interpret meaning of federal statute and constitutionality of its application in negligence action following judgment.

Facts: Tompkins (P) was injured by an Erie Railroad (D) train. Suit was brought in federal court based upon diversity of citizenship. Erie Railroad (D) contended that its liability for injuries sustained by Tompkins (P) should be determined in accordance with Pennsylvania case law, as decided by Pennsylvania's highest court. Pennsylvania law provided that the duty of due care of a railroad to someone on its land is no greater than that owed to a trespasser, e.g., to refrain from willful or wanton injury. [In other words, it's okay to negligently hit a trespasser with a train.] Erie Railroad (D) contended that the federal Rules of Decision Act [which says that laws of the states shall be regarded as rules of decision in federal civil cases, unless otherwise provided by the Constitution or federal statute] required the application of the state case law to the federal case. The lower court did not apply Pennsylvania common law, and instead held that the issue of liability should be based upon federal general common law. The lower court held that Pennsylvania's case law was not within the meaning of the "laws of the states" as used in the Rules of Decision Act. The state's substantive law concerning the duty of due care was thus not applied by the federal court.

Issue: In federal diversity cases, must the substantive laws of the state be applied?

Decision and Rationale: (Brandeis) Yes. We hold that in federal diversity cases the law to be applied is the law of the State, except in matters governed by the Federal Constitution or by Acts of Congress. In so doing, we disapprove of *Swift v. Tyson* [federal courts hearing diversity of citizenship cases are not required to apply the unwritten state laws, i.e., the decisions by the state courts, but may exercise an independent judgment as to what is the common law of the state]. Criticism of the *Swift v. Tyson* doctrine has become widespread following a [really terrible] decision where a company was permitted to reincorporate under the laws of another state and sue under its laws for the purpose of avoiding the laws of the first state of incorporation. [This is known as forum-shopping at its worst!] Application of the *Swift v. Tyson* doctrine has revealed defects, and no benefits derived therefrom. There is no uniformity of common law and no certainty regarding what is general law and local law. The purpose of diversity of citizenship is to prevent discrimination in State courts against non-citizens. However, discrimination by non-citizens against citizens has resulted. The rights under the unwritten law vary depending upon whether they are being enforced in state or federal court, and the choice of court is with the non-citizen. Therefore, the doctrine of *Swift v. Tyson* must be disapproved. We hold that the law to be applied is the law of the State, except in matters governed by the Federal Constitution or by Acts of Congress. It does not matter if the State law is pursuant to statute or case law. There is no federal general common law. Congress has no power to declare substantive rules of common law applicable in a State whether they be local in their nature or general, be they commercial law or a part of the law of torts. No clause in the Constitution purports to confer such a power upon the federal courts. The doctrine of *Swift v. Tyson* is an unconstitutional assumption of powers by the courts of the United States. By applying this doctrine, the lower courts have invaded rights reserved by the Constitution to the states. The issue of liability must therefore be decided based upon state law. Judgment is reversed and case remanded.

Concurrence: (Reed) I concur with the majority decision disapproving of *Swift v. Tyson*. However, it is unnecessary to declare that the "course pursued" therein was "unconstitutional," instead of merely erroneous. The unconstitutional course is apparently the ruling in *Swift v. Tyson* that the supposed omission of Congress to legislate as to the effect of decisions leaves federal courts free to interpret general law for themselves. I am not sure whether federal courts would be compelled to follow state decisions.

Analysis:

Before this case was decided, *Swift v. Tyson's* interpretation of the Rules of Decision Act was that federal courts could interpret what the common law was, in general. This meant that a state's common law, i.e., the decisions by the state's courts, was not always applied, and federal judges were free to use their own interpretation concerning general common law. Unfortunately, it became apparent that there was no true uniform common law, and, as such, there were different rules among different states depending upon whether the litigation took place in federal or state court. This generated forum-shopping, and caused discrimination against citizens by non-citizens. The *Erie* case is a landmark decision in that it held that the state's substantive law must be applied in federal diversity cases, except in matters governed by the Federal Constitution or by Acts of Congress. In so holding, the Supreme Court interpreted the meaning of the phrase "laws of the several states" in the Rules of Decision Act to include state common law. Thus, this case reflects the rejection of a federal common law in favor of individual state's substantive common law. The court specifically stated that Congress has no power to declare substantive rules of common law applicable in a State. In the cases following *Erie*, the issues turned toward whether or not the law was substantive or procedural. Note that one of the criticisms of the *Swift v. Tyson* doctrine mentioned in this case as a basis for disapproving the doctrine was forum-shopping. However, often times forum-shopping among states exists and is permissible. There is no explanation why it would be so wrong to permit forum-shopping between states and federal courts. Finally, although the court declared in the decision that there is no federal general common law, this is not entirely accurate. There are certain federal statutes that allow the federal courts to create common law for cases pertaining to such statutes. Thus, *Erie* prohibits a general federal common law from displacing the states' common laws in areas where the states have lawmaking powers under the Constitution.

Guaranty Trust Co. v. York

(Bond Trustee) v. (Victim of Misrepresentations)
(1945) 326 U.S. 99, 65 S.Ct. 1464, 89 L.Ed. 2079

M E M O R Y   G R A P H I C

Instant Facts

State statute of limitations applied to bar federal diversity case, rather than more lenient equitable federal rules concerning delay in bringing suit.

Black Letter Rule

State statute of limitations applies in federal diversity case where, disregarding it, would significantly affect the result of the litigation, as compared with the outcome had it been tried in state court.

Case Vocabulary

STATUTE OF LIMITATIONS: A statute used as a defense to bar untimely filed claims.

Procedural Basis: Appeal to Supreme Court following judgment on equitable causes of action for misrepresentation and breach of trust.

Facts: York (P) sued Guaranty Trust Co. (D) in a federal diversity action alleging misrepresentation and breach of trust. One of the defenses invoked by Guaranty Trust (D) was the New York statute of limitations. York (P) contended that the statute of limitations did not bar the suit because the suit was one based on equity and, although federal courts in equity consider the delay in bringing suit, they are not strictly bound by the statute of limitations. The lower court [to the joy of York(P)] held that York's (P) suit was not barred. [Unfortunately for York (P)] the Supreme Court disagreed and reversed.]

Issue: In a federal diversity case, must the federal court apply the state statute of limitations?

Decision and Rationale: (Frankfurter) Yes. New York's statute of limitations governs the matter. In determining whether or not to apply the state statute of limitations, characterization of the statute as "substance" or "procedure" is not altogether determinative because these same key words are used throughout law for very different issues. Each implies different variables depending on the particular problem for which it is used. The intent of the *Erie Railroad v. Tompkins* decision [state substantive laws apply to federal diversity cases] was to insure that in federal diversity cases, the outcome of the litigation in federal court should be substantially the same as it would be if tried in a state court. [Remember forum-shopping is a *no no* under Erie.] Thus, the proper method of determining if the state statute of limitations will be applied in federal diversity cases is to ask if the federal court were to disregard it, would so doing significantly affect the result of the litigation. If this matter had been tried in state court, no recovery could be had because the action was barred by the statute of limitations. However, by using the federal method of merely considering the delay in bringing suit and disregarding the state statute of limitations, if desired, the claims could proceed. Thus, the outcome of the litigation would have different results, although upon the same claim by the same parties, if litigated in federal instead of state court. If permitted, this would be contrary to the intent of Erie. Judgment reversed and case remanded.

Analysis:

This case addresses the issue of whether or not a state statute of limitations is, in effect, substantive, and therefore controlling in federal litigation. However, the court attacked the use of the terms "substantive" and "procedural" because of their differing meanings depending upon the particular problems for which they are used. Rather, the court developed an "outcome-determinative test". Thus, a state rule that was outcome-determinative should be followed no matter whether it is labeled procedural or substantive. In its holding, the court referenced other diversity cases where it held that federal courts must follow the law of the state including burden of proof, conflict of laws and contributory negligence. The court commented that state law must not be disregarded in federal diversity cases, and that a policy so important to federalism, "must be kept free from entanglements with analytical or terminological niceties." Consider the argument that almost any procedural rule could affect the outcome of the case. Even certain codified federal procedural rules could possibly not be permitted when state law differs. However, most of these far-reaching analyses of the York decision have been rejected. The "outcome-determinative" test became just one factor, among several, for determining whether to apply state or federal rules. The case that follows, *Byrd v. Blue Ridge Rural Electric Cooperative*, created an "interest balancing" approach, of which the *York* outcome-determinative test is just one of three main factors to consider in choosing between state or federal rules.

Byrd v. Blue Ridge Rural Electric Cooperative

(Injured Worker) v. (Employer)
(1958) 356 U.S. 525, 78 S.Ct. 893, 2 L.Ed.2d 953

M E M O R Y   G R A P H I C

Instant Facts

Injured worker sued employer for personal injuries in federal court and state law required the judge, not jury, to decide issue of application of workman's compensation law.

Black Letter Rule

State decisional law did not apply in federal diversity case where it allowed a judge, and not jury, to determine a factual issue.

Case Vocabulary

INDEPENDENT CONTRACTOR: Employment relationship where one works pursuant to his own rules and control.

REMAND: Sending the case back to the same court from which it came, such as after reversal on appeal and further proceedings ordered.

Procedural Basis: Appeal to Supreme Court from judgment in personal injury case seeking damages.

Facts: Byrd (P), an independent contractor, was employed by Blue Ridge Rural Electric Cooperative (Blue Ridge) (D) as a construction worker. He was injured on the job and sued Blue Ridge (D) in federal court under diversity jurisdiction for the personal injuries he sustained. As a defense, Blue Ridge (D) contended that Byrd (P) was a "statutory" employee whose exclusive remedy was under the state's Workmen's [or, better stated, "workers'"] Compensation Act. If this were true, the tort action would be barred. Blue Ridge (D) argued that a state Supreme Court decision should be controlling on remand in the federal court. The decision provided that the judge, rather than the jury, is to decide the issue of whether the workman's personal injury claim is within the workman's compensation jurisdiction. If so, Blue Ridge (D) would be immune to the tort action.

Issue: In a federal diversity case, must the federal court apply state decisional law that allows a judge, and not a jury, to determine a factual issue?

Decision and Rationale: (Brennan) No. We hold that the decision of the State Supreme Court that a judge, and not a jury, shall determine factual issues, shall not be applied in this federal case. There are several factors that bear on our decision. The state court decision must be examined to determine whether its holding must be applied in the federal case. Using the [very limited] outcome-determinative test, consideration must be given to whether disregarding the state rule would significantly affect the result of the litigation, as compared with the outcome had the matter been tried in state court. The state court decision which provides that the judge, rather than the jury, shall decide the issue of immunity appears to be merely a form and mode of enforcing the immunity against tort actions. It does not appear to be a rule bound up with the definition of the rights and obligations of the parties. In other words, it is not an integral part of a state substantive right. However, the outcome of Byrd's (P) case may be substantially affected by whether the issue of immunity is decided by a judge or jury. Therefore, if the [very limited] outcome-determinative test were the only consideration, a strong case might be had for requiring the federal court to follow state practice. Other countervailing considerations should be reviewed [so that we can expand on the very limited outcome-determinative test and create our own balancing test]. There is a strong federal policy against allowing state rules to interfere with the federal court's distribution of functions between the judge and the jury. The function assigned to the jury by the federal courts should not yield to the state rule in order to further the objective of the same outcome in federal and state courts. Finally, it cannot be assumed that the outcome may, with certainty, be different if decided by a judge or a jury. There are factors here which reduce the possibility of differing results. Federal judges have powers denied to many state judges to comment on the weight of evidence and credibility of witnesses, and to exercise discretion in granting new trials. The likelihood of a different result is not so strong as to require the federal practice of allowing a jury to determine the issues to yield to the state rule. Reversed and remanded.

Analysis:

This case expands on *Guaranty Trust Co. v. York's* outcome-determinative test and develops an "interest balancing" approach to *Erie* problems [the substantive laws of the state must be applied in federal diversity cases]. The court held that there are several factors that must be balanced in deciding whether to apply federal or state rules to federal diversity cases. Consideration must be given to the relation between the state rule and the underlying state right. The strength of the federal policy must be examined before holding that it must yield to a counter state policy. In this case, there was obviously a strong federal policy, based on the Constitution, to allow juries to decide factual issues. Finally, the *York* outcome-determinative test must still be considered. The court concluded that it was far from certain that a different result would occur if decided by a judge or a jury. The interest balancing approach of Byrd was significant in that it recognized the relevance of both federal and state concerns in determining which rules to apply. It also reduced the threat that the Federal Rules of Civil Procedure would frequently have to yield to state rules. In later years, the interest balancing approach has been virtually ignored by the Supreme Court in favor of the principles articulated in the following case, *Hanna v. Plumer.*

SUPREME COURT HOLDS THAT *ERIE* IS NOT THE APPROPRIATE TEST TO DETERMINE THE VALIDITY AND APPLICATION OF FEDERAL RULES OF CIVIL PROCEDURE

Hanna v. Plumer

(Injured Person) v. (Executor of Estate)
(1965) 380 U.S. 460, 85 S.Ct. 1136, 14 L.Ed.2d 8

THIS IS FOR YOUR HUSBAND UNDER FEDERAL LAW!!

COMPLAINT

M E M O R Y   G R A P H I C

Instant Facts
Executor of estate of automobile driver was sued, and summons and complaint were served on spouse in accordance with federal rule, but contrary to state rule requiring in-hand service.

Black Letter Rule
Federal Rules of Civil Procedure governing service of process apply to federal diversity cases, notwithstanding conflicting state rule.

Case Vocabulary

INTER ALIA: Latin for among other things.
MOTION FOR SUMMARY JUDGMENT: A legal motion requesting the judge to enter judgment, before trial, on the ground that the action has no merit or there is no defense to the action.
SERVICE OF PROCESS: Transmitting to another legal documents such as summons and complaints in a manner provided by rules which thereby constitutes serving the documents.
SYLLOGISM: An argument which has two premises resulting in a conclusion.

Procedural Basis: Writ of certiorari granted by Supreme Court following the affirming of summary judgment in action for negligence seeking damages.

Facts: Hanna (P) filed a federal court lawsuit for personal injuries against Plumer (D), the executor of the estate of an alleged negligent automobile driver. Service of the summons and complaint was made pursuant to the Federal Rules of Civil Procedure by leaving copies with Plumer's (D) wife at his residence. Plumer (D) contended that the lawsuit could not proceed because the service of the summons and complaint was not in compliance with the statutory *state* law requiring actual in-hand service on the person being sued. The federal district court granted Plumer's (D) motion for summary judgment [and promptly threw the matter out of court]. On appeal, Hanna (P) contended that the Federal Rules of Civil Procedure governed the method of service of process in diversity actions [and begged to have the lawsuit reinstated]. The Court of Appeals affirmed, finding that the state law involved a substantive rather than a procedural matter and thus should have been applied.

Issue: In a federal diversity case, must the federal court apply state rules concerning service of process?

Decision and Rationale: (Warren) No. The Federal Rules of Civil Procedure govern the method of service of process in diversity actions, and the federal rule shall apply notwithstanding a conflicting state rule. The federal statute, known as the Rules Enabling Act, provides that the Supreme Court shall have the power, among other things, to prescribe, by general rules, the forms of process, and the practice and procedure of the federal courts in civil actions. It further provides that such rules shall not abridge, enlarge or modify any substantive right and shall preserve the right of trial by jury. It is clear from existing case law that the federal rule regarding service of process at issue herein clearly complies with the Rules Enabling Act. Thus, without a conflicting state law, the federal rule would certainly control. Plumer (D) contends that federal courts must apply state law whenever the application of federal law, in place of the state law, would alter the outcome of the case. In this case, if the state law concerning service of process was applied, Plumer (D) would win. If federal law was applied, litigation would continue and he could lose. Thus, Plumer (D) [seeing an easy way out of the lawsuit] asserts that state law must apply. However, this argument cannot stand for several reasons. First, even if there was no federal rule allowing for service on a spouse at home, it is doubtful that the federal court would have been required to follow the state law. The outcome-determinative test cannot be read without reference to the "twin aims" of the *Erie* rule: discouragement of forum-shopping and avoidance of inequitable administration of the laws. If the test were taken to its extreme, every procedural variation would be outcome-determinative. Although the choice between federal and state rules in this matter will affect the outcome of the case, the difference between the two rules would be of scant relevance to the choice of a forum. In other words, when Hanna (P) decided where to file the complaint, she was not presented with a situation where applicability of the state rule would wholly bar recovery; rather, the state rule merely would alter the way in which process was served. In addition, it cannot be said that serving the spouse in lieu of personal in-hand service substantially alters the mode of enforcement of state rights so as to result in inequitable administration of the laws. *Erie* [substantive state laws must be applied] is not the proper test for determining the validity and applicability of a Federal Rule of Civil Procedure. Instead, we consider the scope of the Enabling Act and the constitutionality of the specific federal rules. Congress has the power to prescribe housekeeping rules for federal courts even though they may differ [in a big way] from comparable state rules. The federal rule considered herein is valid. Judgment reversed.

Concurrence: (Harlan) The proper approach in determining whether to apply a state or federal rule, whether substantive or procedural, is to ask if the choice of rule would substantially affect those primary decisions respecting human conduct which our constitutional system leaves to state regulation. If so, the state rule should prevail, even when there is a conflicting federal rule. The majority's opinion can be understood to mean that so long as a reasonable man could characterize a federal rule as procedural, it would have to apply even if the rule frustrated a state's substantive rule. The majority's test goes too far. However, the facts of the present case cause me to concur in the opinion.

Analysis:

This case has two important holdings. First, it modified the outcome-determinative test so it is applied only in those situations where the rule would encourage forum shopping or cause inequitable administration of the laws. The court referred to this as the "twin aims" policies of the Erie rule. Second, it held that where federal rules of procedure conflict with state rules, the federal procedural rule will prevail unless it violates the Constitution or the terms of the Rules Enabling Act. Thus, as long as the rules are procedural in nature and do not abridge, enlarge or modify any substantive right, they will be upheld. Note that Justice Harlan felt that the court was going too far in favor of procedural rules. Congress has the power to regulate procedure in federal courts, and this power has been delegated to the Supreme Court through the Rules Enabling Act. Note that the court indicated a very strong presumption in favor of the validity of the Federal Rule. This case reflects a method of determining which rule to apply, federal or state, but only when the rule in question is one of federal procedure. The cases examined so far in this Chapter have established various tests or methods concerning whether a state or federal law should prevail. The Hanna case demonstrates that the source of the federal practice must be considered. If it is a federal rule of civil procedure there is a very strong chance that it will prevail. Note that this is so even if the out-come of the litigation would be the opposite result of the state litigation if the state rule was applied. The application of the Hanna ruling is considered in the following three cases, all with varied results.

Burlington Northern Railroad v. Woods

(Penalized Loser) v. (Winner)

(1987) 480 U.S. 1, 107 S.Ct. 967, 94 L.Ed.2d 1

M E M O R Y   G R A P H I C

Instant Facts

Following unsuccessful party's losing of appeal in federal diversity case, successful party sought mandatory penalty under *state* statute, but a federal appellate rule provided for discretionary penalty upon finding appeal was frivolous.

Black Letter Rule

A governing federal rule of appellate procedure controls over a contrary state statute.

Case Vocabulary

APPELLANT: Party who initiates the appeal.
APPELLEE: Party who is responding to an appeal, rather than initiating it.
FRIVOLOUS: Having no merit and done in bad faith or for an improper purpose.

Procedural Basis: Appeal to Supreme Court challenging constitutionality of state statute following affirming of judgment for damages.

Facts: A state statute provided that the successful party on appeal must be awarded ten percent damages on the amount of the judgment affirmed plus costs. In other words, the statute penalizes a losing party even for non-frivolous appeals. The federal courts have no such rule, except for Federal Rule of Appellate Procedure 38 which provides for discretionary damages and costs if the appeal is frivolous. Thus, the federal appellate rules are silent with respect to non-frivolous appeals. Burlington Northern Railroad (Burlington) (D) lost its appeal in a federal diversity case. [The very greedy] Woods (P) sought the ten percent damages under the state statute and Burlington (D) objected on the grounds that a penalty, without regard to the merits of the appeal, violates the Due Process and Equal Protection clauses.

Issue: Does a governing federal rule of appellate procedure control over a contrary state statute?

Decision and Rationale: [Name of Justice Not Given] Yes. We hold that Federal Rule of Appellate Procedure 38 conflicts with the state statute and it controls. We base our holding on the decision in Hanna [consideration must be given to the Rules Enabling Act and the constitutionality of the specific federal rule]. We reject Woods' (P) interpretation that the federal rule does not conflict with the state statute because a court could award the mandatory ten percent penalty for an unsuccessful appeal and, as a matter of discretion, additional damages and costs if it believed the appeal was frivolous.

Analysis:

The court did not address the constitutional challenges raised by Woods (P), nor did it embark on an Erie analysis. Instead, the court determined that there was a conflict between the state statute and the federal appellate rule, and the federal appellate rule controlled. The state statute had a pro-plaintiff effect, by imposing a penalty on unsuccessful defendants' appeals. The court read the particular federal appellate rule as if it also addressed unsuccessful appeals that were non-frivolous. Since the rule applied to all appeals, the silence regarding non-frivolous appeals displaced the contrary state statute. Consider that if the state statute had been applied, it would have penalized non-frivolous appeals, and this would be contrary to the federal judgment that an appeal should be relatively inexpensive. The court, after determining that the federal appellate rule governed the situation, chose not to consider the issue by way of a constitutional Erie analysis.

Stewart Organization, Inc. v. Ricoh Corp.

(Dealer) v. (Manufacturer)
487 U.S. 22 (1988)

MEMORY GRAPHIC

 Instant Facts

Relying on a forum selection clause in their dealership agreement, Ricoh (D) attempted to transfer a case from Alabama to New York district court.

Black Letter Rule

A federal rule, established within the limits of the constitution, prevails over conflicting state law provided the federal rule is sufficiently broad to cover the issue.

Case Vocabulary

EN BANC: A session (usually of a Court of Appeal) in which all of the members participate in a decision.
INTERLOCUTORY APPEAL: An appeal taken during the course of trial on some decision reached in the case.

Procedural Basis: Writ of certiorari from reversal of denial of motion to transfer venue in a contractual action.

Facts: Stewart Organization (P) entered into a dealership agreement to market the copier products of Ricoh (D). The agreement contained a forum-selection clause, requiring all disputes arising out of the contract to be litigated in Manhattan court. However, when relations soured between the companies, Stewart (P) sued Ricoh (D) in an Alabama district court. Ricoh moved to transfer the case to a New York district court, pursuant to 28 U.S.C. § 1404(a) and in reliance on the forum selection clause. Holding that Alabama law controls the transfer motion, and noting that Alabama looks unfavorably upon contractual forum-selection clauses, the District Court denied the motion. However, the Eleventh Circuit reversed, concluding that the venue question was governed by federal law, under which the forum selection clause was enforceable. The Supreme Court granted certiorari.

Issue: When a constitutional federal rule directly conflicts with state law, does the federal rule prevail?

Decision and Rationale: (Marshall, J.) Yes. A simple two-part analysis covers cases in which federal statutes conflict with state law. First, the court must determine whether the statute is sufficiently broad to control the issue before the court. In the case at hand, § 1404(a) is broad enough to cover the issue of whether to transfer the case to a Manhattan court in accordance with the forum selection clause. Section 1404(a) allows a district court, in its discretion, to weigh a number of factors in determining whether transfer is appropriate. The forum selection clause is a significant factor in this analysis, and the district court must analyze the convenience of the forum, the parties' preferences, the fairness of the transfer, and the parties' relative bargaining power in agreeing to the clause. A state policy--such as Alabama's--that focuses on only a subset of these considerations by specifically disfavoring forum selection clauses, cannot co-exist with § 1404(a). Thus, there is a direct conflict between § 1404(a) and the Alabama approach, and we arrive at the second step in the analysis. Section 1404(a) must be applied only if it represents a valid exercise of Congress' authority under the constitution. This is an easy determination, as the constitutional provision for a federal court system carries with it the congressional power to prescribe rules under which these courts operate. Section 1404(a) was a valid exercise of Congress' power under the Necessary and Proper Clause of the Constitution. Remanded for a determination of the forum selection clause on Ricoh's (D) § 1404(a) motion.

Analysis:

Justice Marshall finally manages to consolidate and simplify the analysis for situations where federal statutes conflict with state law. There is really only one step to this analysis, as the constitutional question in all of these cases can be settled by a cursory reference to Congress' power. The more-difficult step has been stated in various ways in cases from *Hanna* to *Walker* to *Stewart*. The previous explanation, that the federal statute must be in direct conflict with a state law, has been changed slightly by Marshall, who now declares that the federal statute must be sufficiently broad enough to control the issue before the court. These two tests are really saying the same thing. The "issue before the court" is, of course, one for which state law supplies an answer. [Things only get complicated when parties try to avoid this state law and obtain presumably more favorable treatment in federal court.] Thus, state law is necessarily broad enough to control the issue. Furthermore, where a federal rule is also sufficiently broad, there exists a definite conflict between the rule and state law. This new approach perhaps helps explain the questionable earlier ruling in *Walker*, where Rule 3 and an Oklahoma statute appeared to be in direct conflict. Under the new test, Rule 3 was clearly not sufficiently broad enough to control the issue, as it was not in itself a statute of limitations. If Justice Marshall had only reformulated the test in *Walker* perhaps that opinion would have been a bit more clear.

Gasperini v. Center for Humanities, Inc.

(Photographer) v. (Producer)
116 S.Ct. 2211 (1996)

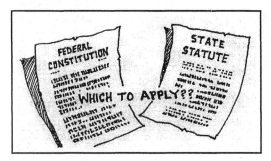

M E M O R Y   G R A P H I C

Instant Facts

A federal court applied a state law standard in reviewing whether a jury's verdict was excessive, despite the contrary mandate of the Seventh Amendment.

Black Letter Rule

A state statute governing reexamination of jury awards can be given effect by federal appellate courts without violating the Seventh Amendment's reexamination clause.

Case Vocabulary

REMITTITUR: The procedure for reducing an excessive jury verdict.
TALISMAN: Something with apparent magical power.

Procedural Basis: Writ of certiorari reviewing vacation of judgment denying motion for new trial for excessiveness of jury verdict.

Facts: William Gasperini (P) was a journalist who photographed events in Central America beginning in 1984. He supplied 300 slides to The Center for Humanities, Inc. ("Center") (D). The Center (D) lost the slides and could not return them to Gasperini (P). Gasperini (P) sued in federal district court, invoking diversity jurisdiction. The Center (D) conceded liability, and the issue of damages was tried before a jury. Gasperini's (P) expert witnesses testified to the "industry standard" and valued a lost slide at $1,500. Accordingly, the jury awarded Gasperini (P) $450,000 in compensatory damages. The Center (D) moved for a new trial, arguing that the verdict was excessive. The district court denied the motion, but the Second Circuit Court of Appeals vacated the judgment. The Second Circuit applied New York law, which required that a state appellate division must determine whether an award deviates materially from what would be reasonable compensation. Based on state holdings, the Second Circuit viewed the award as excessive because other factors (such as the uniqueness of the slides and the photographer's earning level) should be considered. Thus, the Second Circuit set aside the verdict and ordered a new trial, unless Gasperini (P) would accept $100,000. Gasperini (P) contended that the Second Circuit erred in applying New York law. He argued that the Seventh Amendment controls and provides that no fact tried by a jury should be reexamined in a federal court except under federal common law. Federal common law refuses to overturn jury verdicts unless they "shock the conscience." The United States Supreme Court granted certiorari.

Issue: Can a state statute governing reexamination of jury awards be given effect by federal appellate courts without violating the Seventh Amendment's reexamination clause?

Decision and Rationale: (Ginsburg, J.) Yes. A state statute governing reexamination of jury awards can be given effect by federal appellate courts without violating the Seventh Amendment's reexamination clause. The New York statute's "deviates materially" standard is both procedural and substantive. It is substantive in that the standard controls how much a plaintiff can be awarded, and it is procedural in that it assigns decision-making authority to New York appellate courts. We feel that federal courts can adequately apply the "deviates materially" standard. The standard is "outcome-affective" because failure to apply it would unfairly discriminate against citizens of the forum state or be likely to cause a plaintiff to choose the federal court. In the case at hand, the Second Circuit utilized the "deviates materially" standard. We agree with Gasperini (P) that the Second Circuit did not attend to an essential characteristic of the federal court system when it applied the New York statute. The federal appeals court must overturn a trial judge's decision only if it constitutes an abuse of discretion. It is not clear that the Second Circuit utilized this standard, or that the district court checked the relevant New York decisions demanding more than analysis of the "industry standard" in awarding damages. Accordingly, we vacate the judgment of the Second Circuit and remand the case to the district court so that the trial judge may test the verdict under New York's "deviates materially" standard.

Dissent: (Stevens, J.) While I agree with the majority's reasoning, I would affirm the judgment of the Second Circuit. The district court had the power to consider the propriety of the jury's award, and it erred. Nothing prohibits the reviewing court from correcting the judge's error. I do not agree that the "abuse of discretion" standard is relevant. *Erie* simply requires federal appellate courts to apply the damage control standard state law supplies.

Dissent: (Scalia, J.) The majority holds that a state practice, relating to the division of duties between state judges and juries, must be followed by federal courts. This is contrary to our prior cases. The Seventh Amendment was designed specifically to preclude federal appellate reexamination of facts found by a jury. It puts to rest apprehensions of new trials by appellate courts. Federal appellate courts cannot review the factual issues such as the measure of damages. At common law, reexamination of facts found by a jury could only be undertaken by trial courts. And it is not possible to review the denial of a new trial without engaging in a reexamination of the facts tried by the jury. Changing the standard by which trial judges review jury verdicts does, contrary to the majority's statement, disrupt the federal system and is plainly inconsistent with federal policy. The majority commits the classic *Erie* mistake of regarding whatever changes the outcome as substantive; furthermore, it exaggerates the difference that the state standard will make. Moreover, in my view, the *Erie* question should not even be reached in this case. The Federal Rules of Civil Procedure provide the standard to be applied by a district court in ruling on a motion for new trial. A new trial may be granted for any reason which new trials have been granted in actions in federal courts. This is undeniably a federal standard, and the standard is sufficiently broad to cause a direct collision with state law. Thus, the federal court must apply the Federal Rule.

Analysis:

This complicated case illustrates how courts can shape the determination of whether federal or state law applies. By characterizing the New York statute as "substantive," the majority justifies its tenuous holding that the reviewing appellate court (the Second Circuit) should have applied New York's "deviates materially" standard of review of a jury verdict. The majority further justifies its position by returning to the outdated *York* outcome-determinative test. All in all, the holding seems to be in clear violation of the clear mandate of the Seventh Amendment. But the majority thinks that the holding is not inconsistent with the Seventh Amendment and that the federal and state interests can be accommodated. Justice Scalia's dissent is well-reasoned and merits close attention. The review of jury verdicts does, as Scalia points out, necessarily require a reexamination of the facts of the case. Federal courts are constitutionally forbidden to undertake such factual inquiries. Finally, Scalia makes a good point in mentioning Federal Rule 59. This federal procedural standard limits new trials only based upon federal law, and it certainly appears to be in direct conflict with the New York statute. As we have seen in other cases, federal courts are required to apply federal law in such a situation.

Perspective
Incentives to Litigate

Chapter 5

Why do people file lawsuits? Simple, they want a court to redress a wrong cased by another party. Courts provide plaintiffs with a variety of *remedies*. These remedies are divided into two groups. Those that seek to provide the plaintiff with a substitute for his loss are known as substitutionary remedies. On the other hand, courts offer specific remedies that are aimed at directly and specifically addressing the plaintiff's injury.

Subsitutionary remedies often take the form of money damages. Courts offer substitutionary remedies because they are unable to give the plaintiff exactly what he has lost. For example, a plaintiff who sues his doctor for negligently amputating his leg can never recover his leg, so courts offer money damages as compensation [even if the plaintiff doesn't have a leg to stand on]. However, a plaintiff's recovery of money damages is curtailed by: (1) his ability to prove the extent of his injury; (2) statutes providing for maximum or minimum awards; and (3) the Constitution's prohibition against the arbitrary deprivation of a defendant's property.

In contrast to the inherent weakness of money damages, specific remedies provide a plaintiff with exactly what he is looking for. These remedies involve a court's order that a party do or refrain from doing something. Although courts have a variety of specific remedies, the most common type is the injunction. There is also an important sub-class of specific remedies, known as provisional remedies. The most common of which are the Temporary Restraining Order and the Preliminary Injunction. These seek to provide a party with some form of temporary protection before the court decides the merits of the case.

One should not think that courts remedy every harm that is occasioned. If a party is unable to afford litigation, the remedies offered by a court are a mere illusion. Litigation can be expensive; and the general rule is that a party – whether successful on the merits or not – must pay for his own legal expenses. Luckily there are a few exceptions to this rule. First, some statutes provide that a party who prevails on the merits may recover his expenses from the defendant. These "fee shifting" provisions are usually intended to encourage some specific type of lawsuit. Second, parties to a contract often agree that in case of a breach, the winner will pay the loser's expenses. Third, some attorneys represent people on a contingent basis. In other words, the lawyer gets paid only if the plaintiff recovers money from the defendant. Finally, representation is often available through public funds or private charities.

Chapter 5

NOTE: THE PURPOSE OF THIS OUTLINE IS TO ORGANIZE THE CASES SO THAT ONE CAN QUICKLY UNDERSTAND THE RELEVANCE OF EACH CASE TO THE COURSE. NO ATTEMPT IS MADE IN THIS OVERVIEW TO ADDRESS EVERY CONCEPT THAT MUST BE STUDIED. BE SURE TO READ THE ENTIRE CASEBOOK AND/OR OTHER MATERIALS TO GAIN A FULL UNDERSTANDING OF ALL CONCEPTS.

I. Approaching Civil Procedure
    A. American civil procedure can be studied in one of two ways.
        1. The first method begins with an examination of an individual lawsuit and the procedures for instituting and resolving the case, and then reviewing how procedural rules are constrained by the Constitution.
        2. Civil procedure can also be studied by first examining the constitutional framework surrounding a lawsuit, and then focusing on particular choices available to litigants.
    B. Choosing Procedure
        1. Procedural rules involve a choice between the efficiency of the system and the accuracy of the result.
        2. As the speed of the system increases, so does the likelihood for error.

II. Litigation in the United States at the End of the Twentieth Century
    A. How Much Litigation?
        1. There is a current debate as to whether the United States is experiencing a litigation boom.
        2. Some data suggests that the increase in court cases has occurred mainly in the areas of criminal prosecutions and family disputes, while tort and contract cases have leveled off.
        3. Whatever the increase may be attributable to, courts are experiencing difficulty in keeping up with the growth of litigation.
    B. Why Litigate?
        1. Plaintiffs file law suits to *remedy* a "harm" caused by the defendant.
        2. Courts have two types of remedies, specific and substitutionary.
        a. Substitutionary remedies are those that seek to provide a reasonable substitute for whatever the defendant has taken from the plaintiff.
        b. Specific remedies restore directly and specifi-

cally whatever the plaintiff has lost.

III. Substitutionary Remedies
    A. Generally
        1. The predominant form of substitutionary remedies are money damages.
        2. Because damages are a substitute, courts encounter difficulties in measuring the precise amount to be awarded.
        3. Courts often resort to the fair market value of whatever the plaintiff has lost.
    B. Compensatory Damages
        1. The purpose of compensatory damages is to restore the plaintiff, as nearly as possible, to the position he would have been in had it not been for the wrong of the other party. *United States v. Hatahley*.
        2. Courts require the plaintiff to prove his damages before ordering an award. *United States v. Hatahley*.
        a. Calculating damages often proves difficult because the calculation depends on the existence of a market
        3. A defendant's liability is not endless and the plaintiff is usually under a duty to take reasonable steps to mitigate his loss. *United States v. Hatahley*.
    C. Liquidated, Statutory, and Punitive Damages
        1. Liquidated Damages
        a. In order to combat the difficulty associated with calculating damages, parties to a contract will agree to a set amount in case of a breach.
        b. Parties may contract for liquidated damages only if actual damages are too difficult to calculate and the agreed amount is reasonable.
        2. Statutory Damages: Some legislation provides for a maximum or minimum (or both) amount that a plaintiff may recover in a certain type of case.
        3. Punitive Damages
        a. Punitive damages are aimed and punishing the conduct of the defendant.
        (1) Usually, the defendant's behavior must be egregious before punitive damages can be imposed, negligence is not enough.
        b. The Due Process Clause of the Fourteenth Amendment places limits on a State's ability

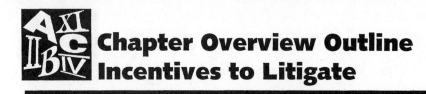

to award punitive damages. *Browning Ferris Indus. v. Kelco Disposal*.

   (1) The Due Process Clause requires states to provide some form of judicial review of punitive damages awards. *Honda Motor Co. v. Oberg*.

   (2) Punitive damages awards that are "grossly excessive" violate the Due Process Clause. *BMW of North America v. Gore*.

   (3) In determining when an award is "grossly excessive" courts should look to: the reprehensibility of the defendant's conduct; the disparity between the actual harm suffered and the punitive damages award; and the difference between the punitive damages award and the civil penalties authorized or imposed in similar cases. *BMW of North America v. Gore*.

IV. Specific Remedies

  A. The Idea of Specific Relief: When providing specific relief, courts often order a party to do, or refrain from doing something.

  B. An Excursus on Equity and Specific Relief

    1. Specific relief is usually the type granted by courts of equity.

    2. Types of equitable relief include: injunctions; constructive trusts; rescission, reformation, or cancellation of contracts; accountings; quieting title; replevin; writs of mandamus; and habeas corpus among others.

  C. Is There a Remedial Hierarchy?

    1. Courts often refer to the requirement that, before obtaining equitable relief, a plaintiff must show that there is no adequate remedy at law (i.e., money damages are inadequate).

    2. There is some debate as to whether this requirement is ever enforced; those that argue it is, admit enforcement is lax.

    3. Injunctions: Before granting an injunction, a court should balance the hardship on the plaintiff if relief is denied against the hardship to the defendant if it is granted. *Sigma Chemical Co. v. Harris*.

V. Declaratory Relief

  A. Declaratory relief is used to determine the rights of parties, before those rights have actually been affected (e.g., determining that a law is unconsti-

tutional before a public official enforces it).

  B. Because Article III of the Constitution only gives courts the power to decide actual cases and controversies, the use of declaratory judgments in federal courts is limited.

VI. Financing Litigation

  A. The American Rule

    1. A system that requires a party to pay his legal fees regardless of success on the merits is known as the *American Rule*.

    2. This rule is justified on the basis that it permits plaintiffs who have uncertain cases to invoke the help of courts without a fear of bearing double the expense.

  B. The *English Rule* requires that the losing party pay its fees and those of the prevailing party.

  C. Insurance and the Contingent Fee

    1. Many forms of insurance require the insurance company to pay for legal fees arising out of a certain event.

     a. For example, vehicle liability insurance requires the insurance company to pay for the defense if the insured is sued for negligence.

    2. The Contingent Fee

     a. A plaintiff who cannot afford to pay an attorney's fees may resort to obtaining representation on a contingent basis.

     b. In this case, the attorney agrees to take the case and his fees will come out of any money that is recovered from the defendant.

      (1) Standard contingent arrangements range anywhere from 25 to 50 percent of the recovery.

  D. Public Subsidies and Professional Charity

    1. Parties who cannot afford an attorney, and whose legal problem cannot be remedied by contingent representation or insurance, must depend on the availability of free legal services provided by public and private entities.

    2. Maintenance of the judicial system is costly, and in this sense all litigation is publicly subsidized.

  E. From Fee Spreading to Fee Shifting

    1. Asymmetrical and Symmetrical Fee Shifting

     a. Asymmetrical fee shifting provides that a prevailing plaintiff may recover legal fees, but that a prevailing defendant may not collect fees unless the plaintiff has sued in bad faith.

b. Symmetrical fee shifting on the other hand, requires the loser – whoever that may be – to pay the winner's legal fees.

2. The Common Fund

a. One form of shifting fees is the *common fund*, a court created doctrine whereby a plaintiff may recover his legal fees if his efforts have created a recovery fund for subsequent plaintiffs.

b. The common fund is important in financing class actions, where only a handful of parties represent a class of thousands.

3. By Contract: Parties to a contract may provide that in case of litigation, the loser will pay the winner's legal fees.

4. By Common Law: An exception to the American Rule is an action *for malicious prosecution*, which allows a defendant to recover his legal expenses from a plaintiff who has sued in bad faith.

5. By Statute

a. Many statutes creating a cause of action also provide for the recovery of reasonable legal expenses.

b. One of the most important fee shifting statutes is the Civil Rights Attorney's Fees Awards Act, which provides that a court, in its discretion, may allow the prevailing party in a civil rights case to recover legal expenses. *42 U.S.C. §1988(b).*

(1) Although it speaks of recovery for the "prevailing party," the statute has been interpreted to allow only a prevailing plaintiff to recover attorney's fees (*asymmetrical fee shifting*). *Christianburg Garment Co. v. EEOC.*

F. Fee Shifting and Settlement

1. Rule 68

a. The Federal Rules of Civil Procedure permit a defendant to make a formal settlement offer and create an incentive for plaintiffs to accept.

b. If a defendant makes a formal offer and the plaintiff rejects the offer and then recovers less than the offered amount, not only is the plaintiff prohibited from recovering costs incurred after the formal offer, but he must pay the defendant's costs incurred after the offer. *Fed.R.Civ.P. 68.*

c. A successful Rule 68 offer will not cause an unsuccessful plaintiff to pay the defendant's attorney's fees. *Marek v. Chesney.*

2. Separating Lawyer and Client

a. Fee shifting statutes can cause a conflict of interest between a lawyer's ethical duty to his client and the lawyer's interest in being compensated.

b. In one case the Supreme Court held that the civil rights fee shifting provision did not prohibit settlements conditioned on the waiver of fees. *Evans v. Jeff D.*

c. The problem with allowing such waivers is that an attorney will always be forced to accept a settlement that is beneficial to his client regardless of his inability to obtain payment, giving defendants an incentive to offer a "good" settlement with the condition that the attorney waive his fee.

VII. Provisional Remedies

A. Generally: Provisional remedies are those granted by a court in order to avoid an immediate harm, pending the final outcome of the legal dispute.

B. Preliminary Injunctions and Temporary Restraining Orders

1. A party moving for a preliminary injunction must demonstrate either: a combination of probable success and the possibility of irreparable injury; or that serious questions are raised and the balance of hardships tips sharply in his favor. *William Inglis & Sons Baking Co. v. ITT Continental Baking Co.*

C. Provisional Remedies and Due Process

1. A State may deprive a party of a protected property interest before a final adjudication of his rights, but the Due Process Clause of the Fourteenth Amendment requires that before it deprives a person of a protected property interest, the State must provide him with adequate notice and an opportunity to be heard. *Fuentes v. Shevin.*

United States v. Hatahley

(Government) v. (Navaho Indian)
257 F.2d 920 (10th Cir. 1958)

M E M O R Y   G R A P H I C

Instant Facts

After its agents were found liable for rounding up and selling livestock belonging to a group of Navajo Indians, the District Court rejected any evidence on the availability of like animals and ordered the United States to pay compensatory damages totaling $186,017.50 on theory that the livestock taken were unique and not replaceable.

Black Letter Rule

The fundamental principle of damages is to restore the injured party, as nearly as possible, to the position he would have been in had it not been for the wrong of the other party.

Procedural Basis: Decision of the Court of Appeals reversing the District Court's calculation of damages, a calculation ordered by the Supreme Court after it had determined the issue of liability.

Facts: Hatahley (P) and other members of a Navajo Tribe sued the federal government under the Federal Tort Claims Act (statute authorizing plaintiffs to recover against the United States (D) for committing a tort under state law). Hatahley (P) claimed that the United States' (D) agents rounded up the group's burros and horses that had been grazing on federal range land and sold the animals to a glue factory. The Supreme Court determined the government was liable and remanded for a calculation of damages. The District Court entered a judgment against the United States (D) for the sum of $186,017.50. The value of each animal was fixed at $395; each plaintiff was awarded $3,500 for pain and suffering; and damages were given for one-half the value of the diminution of the individual herds of livestock caused by the loss of use of the horses and burros. The District Court accepted Hatahley's (P) theory that replacement could not be proved because the animals were unique due to their peculiar nature and training; the court rejected any evidence of the availability and value of like animals in the area. The court also found that a portion of the total judgment represented damage for the loss of use of the animal and pain and suffering, neither of which was proved. The Court of Appeals reversed.

Issue: Must a plaintiff prove the issue of damages in order to recover?

Decision and Rationale: (Pickett, J.) Yes. The fundamental principle of damages is to restore the injured party, as nearly as possible, to the position he would have been in had it not been for the wrong of the other party. Applying this rule, Hatahley (P) and the others were entitled to the market value, or replacement cost of their animals as of the time of the taking, plus the use value of the animals during the interim between the taking and the time a reasonable person would have replaced the animals. The court erred in rejecting evidence of the availability and value of like animals in the area. The fact that the animals were peculiar and specially trained does not make them invaluable, it only increases their market value. In arriving at market value, the court should consider the availability of like animals, together with all other elements which go to make up market value. The court also erred in its calculation of damages occasioned as a result of the deprivation of the animals' use. The measure of such damages should be the loss of profits occasioned by the deprivation of use. Hatahley (P) and the others testified the loss of the use of their burros and horses led to a reduction in the size of their herds. In one instance, the judge calculated loss of use damages by referring to the reduction in the size of the herd between the taking and the last hearing (a period of five years), and multiplying that number by the cost of the each animal. The court then found that approximately one half this amount represented loss of use damages. This was pure conjecture. The right to such damages does not extend forever, and it is limited to the time in which a prudent person would replace the destroyed horses and burros. The Court should have determined at what point a reasonably prudent person would have replaced the animals. Any loss thereafter cannot be said to be the proximate cause of the taking. The District Court also awarded each plaintiff $3,500 for pain and suffering. An award for pain and suffering was proper considering the evidence, but the court failed to determine the grief and hardship experienced by each plaintiff, it only guessed that each suffered a loss of $3,500. This was error. Pain and suffering are an individual matter, and must be treated as such. Reversed and remanded.

Analysis:

The court here provides an excellent elucidation on the calculation of damages and a party's duty to mitigate damages. The court holds that "the fundamental principle of damages is to restore the injured party, as nearly as possible, to the position he would have been in had it not been for the wrong of the other party." This court refers to this as a rule, but in reality it provides little guidance in calculating damages. The thrust of the court's opinion is that damages must be proved. How a court goes about calculating damages depends on the injury caused. The court orders that, for loss of property, damages should be calculated by reference to the fair market or replacement value. The court rejects Hatahley's (P) theory that animals could not be valued because of their unique nature. In the court's opinion uniqueness only increases the market value. The fact that some property truly is invaluable (e.g. the *Mona Lisa*, moon rocks, the Shroud of Turin, etc.) only points out the inability of courts to actually make a plaintiff whole. This weakness notwithstanding, this court was – as most courts are – satisfied with compensating Hatahley (P) as nearly as possible, so that the United States' (D) liability is not subjected to conjecture. Accordingly, the court requires some proof of damage, even if the calculation is imprecise. The court extends this requirement to the award for pain and suffering. The court thought that the District Court's award of $3,500 to each plaintiff for pain suffering indicated that pain and suffering was not proved for each individual plaintiff. The court goes on to hold that the loss of use damages were circumscribed by a duty to mitigate. The United States' liability (or that of any defendant) should not extend ad infinitum. Hatahley (P) and the others should have bought replacement horses whenever it became feasible to do so. At that point, the United States (D) ceases to be liable for any loss occurring thereafter.

Honda Motor Co. v. Oberg

(ATV Manufacturer) v. (Injured Rider)

512 U.S. 415 (1944)

M E M O R Y   G R A P H I C

Instant Facts

The jury found the manufacturer of an all-terrain vehicle liable for its design of the vehicle, and awarded punitive damages of $5,000,000, an award which was not reviewable under state law.

Black Letter Rule

A denial of judicial review of the size of punitive damage awards violates the Due Process Clause of the Fourteenth Amendment.

Facts: Mr. Oberg (P) sued Honda Motor Co. (Honda) (D), claiming that the company's design of its all-terrain vehicle (ATV) was the cause of the accident that led to his severe and permanent injuries. A jury found Honda (D) liable and awarded compensatory damages nearing $1,000,000 and punitive damages totaling $5,000,000. An amendment to the Oregon Constitution prohibited judicial review of the amount of punitive damages awarded by a jury unless there was no evidence to support the verdict. Honda appealed claiming the constitutional provision violated the Due Process Clause of the Fourteenth Amendment.

Issue: Does the Due Process Clause of the Fourteenth Amendment require states to provide some form of judicial review of the size of punitive damage awards?

Decision and Rationale: (Stevens, J.) Yes. We have recognized that the Constitution imposes a substantial limit on the size of punitive damage awards. Our previous decisions suggest that our analysis in this context should focus on Oregon's departure from traditional procedures. We first contrast the relevant common law practice with Oregon's procedure. We then examine the constitutional implications of the Oregon's departure from common law procedures. Judicial review of the size of punitive damages has been a safeguard against excessive verdicts for as long as punitive damages have been awarded. This procedure was continued in the common law courts of the United States. Oregon's procedure is a dramatic departure from the practice established at common law, for Oregon provides no relief from excessive punitive damages. Indeed, review of punitive damages in Oregon can only be had if the jury was improperly instructed, if error occurred during trial, or if there is no evidence at trial to support the award. Oregon's departure from the common law protection raises a presumption that its procedure violates due process. Although most of our Due Process Clause decisions involve arguments that the traditional procedures provide too little protection, there have been some cases where a party has been deprived of due process without the safeguards of the common law. Punitive damages pose a danger that the defendant will arbitrarily be deprived of property. Juries are give wide latitude in this area and there exists the danger that their awards will express bias against big business. Judicial review of awarded amounts was one of the few protections which the common law provided against that danger. But Oregon has removed this safeguard without providing a substitute. For these reasons, we hold that Oregon's denial of judicial review of the size of punitive damage awards violates the Due Process Clause of the Fourteenth Amendment. Reversed.

Dissent: (Ginsburg, J.) In product liability cases, Oregon guides and limits the factfinder's discretion to award punitive damages. The plaintiff must establish entitlement to punitive damages, under specific criteria, by clear and convincing evidence. The decision to award damages is subject to judicial review to this extent. Absent trial error, the Oregon Constitution provides that a properly instructed jury's verdict shall not be reexamined. This procedure satisfies due process. Therefore, I dissent.

Analysis:

The Court enunciates a new rule that the Due Process Clause of the Fourteenth Amendment requires a state to provide for judicial review of punitive damages. The Court bases its holding on the fact that punitive damages were reviewable at common law. The Court goes on to hold that Oregon's departure from the common law tradition amounted to violation of due process. In this case common law process is equated with due process. Its apparent distrust of juries leads the Court to base its rule on an arguably faulty assumption – that judicial review of the size of punitive damage awards is necessary to protect against arbitrary jury action. One can argue that a decision is not arbitrary if it must be made based on evidence presented. If an Oregon jury decided to ignore the evidence and award punitive damages, the State's Constitution would not prohibit judicial review of that award. If a jury is required to base its award on the evidence presented, and if appellate courts can overturn awards that have no basis in the evidence or are awarded by an improperly instructed jury, it is hard to say that the defendant has been "arbitrarily" deprived of property. In the Court's view, jury instructions and rules of evidence are not a sufficient protection against arbitrary action.

BMW of North America v. Gore

(Auto Distributor) v. (Car Buyer)
517 U.S. 559 (1996)

MEMORY GRAPHIC

Instant Facts

An Alabama jury ordered BMW to pay compensatory damages of $4,000 per vehicle and punitive damages of $4,000,000 for repainting severely rain-damaged vehicles and then selling them as new throughout the country.

Black Letter Rule

Punitive damage awards that are "grossly excessive" violate the Due Process Clause of the Fourteenth Amendment.

Procedural Basis: Appeal to the Supreme Court challenging the decision of the Alabama Supreme Court awarding punitive damages of $2,000,000.

Facts: While en route to the United States, some of BMW's (D) vehicles suffered paint damage from acid-rain. On arrival BMW (D) repainted the vehicles and sold them as new. Upon making this discovery, Gore (P) sued BMW on behalf of himself and 1000 other BMW owners throughout the nation. A jury found the diminution in value was $4,000 per car. The jury also awarded $4,000,000 in punitive damages. The Supreme Court of Alabama reduced the punitive damage award to $2,000,000. BMW appealed to the Supreme Court.

Issue: Does the Constitution prohibit the awarding of excessive punitive damages?

Decision and Rationale: (Stevens, J.) Yes. The Due Process Clause of the Fourteenth Amendment prohibits a State from imposing a "grossly excessive" punishment on a tortfeasor. A state may impose punitive damages to further its legitimate interest in punishing unlawful conduct and preventing its recurrence. Only when an award can be categorized as "grossly excessive" in relation to these interests does it enter into the zone of arbitrariness that violates the Due Process Clause of the Fourteenth Amendment. Alabama can have no interest in altering BMW's (D) nationwide policy, for that would infringe on the policy choices of other states. To the extent that the punitive damage award was for BMW's conduct in states other than Alabama, it was unconstitutional. Elementary notions of fairness dictate that a person receive fair notice not only of the conduct that will subject him to penalty, but also of the severity of the penalty. The guideposts, each indicating BMW (D) was inadequately notified, lead us to conclude the $2,000,000 award is grossly excessive: (1) the degree of reprehensibility of the nondisclosure; (2) the disparity between the harm suffered and the punitive award; (3) the difference between this remedy and the civil penalties authorized or imposed in comparable cases. In this case, the conduct was not very reprehensible. The harm was purely economic, and minor at that. Because the punitive award was also 500 times the amount of the actual harm caused, it was too disparate. Comparing the punitive award with the civil and criminal penalties authorized for such conduct also lead us to conclude the award was excessive. Alabama authorizes a maximum civil penalty of $2,000 for deceptive trade practices. We do not adopt a bright line marking the limits of a constitutionally acceptable punitive damages award, but we are convinced that the award in this case transcends that limit. Reversed.

Analysis:

The Court first holds that the State of Alabama could not impose an award for punitive damages based on BMW's conduct outside the state. The Court then takes one step beyond its holding in *Honda Motor Co. v. Oberg* [Supreme Court held that states must provide for judicial review of punitive damages awards] and holds that, in addition to requiring judicial review of punitive damage awards, the Due Process Clause of the Fourteenth Amendment also limits the size of such awards. Punitive damage awards that are "grossly excessive" are violative of due process. But the Court's holding has nothing to do with unfair procedures. In the Court's view, large punitive damages awards are unconstitutional, not because awarded in an unfair manner, but rather "grossly excessive" awards indicate that the defendant was not adequately notified that his conduct was subject to a severe penalty. The Court's rule, therefore, turns on its definition of "grossly excessive." According to the Court, a punitive damages award is "grossly excessive" not merely because it is large, but because the size of the award is disproportionate to three factors: the reprehensibility of the conduct; the actual harm caused; and the civil penalties imposed in similar cases. In applying the three factors to the present case the Court holds that the Alabama award was unconstitutional. First, BMW's conduct was not particularly reprehensible because the damage caused was purely economic. Second, the actual damage caused was merely $4,000. Finally, the court points out that state laws authorize a maximum penalty of only $2,000 for deceptive trade practices. When compared to the size of the punitive damage award the Court holds that these factors indicate the award to be "grossly excessive."

A DECISION TO ISSUE AN INJUNCTION INVOLVES A BALANCING OF INTERESTS – THE BENEFIT TO THE MOVING PARTY AGAINST THE HARM TO THE OPPOSING PARTY

Sigma Chemical Co. v. Harris

(Employer) v. (Former Employee)

605 F. Supp. 1253 (E.D. Mo. 1985)

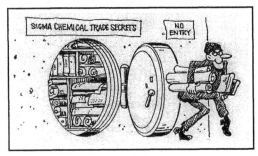

M E M O R Y   G R A P H I C

Instant Facts

A company sought to enforce a restrictive covenant by enjoining one of its former employees from continuing to work for one of the company's major competition.

Black Letter Rule

The determination whether to issue an injunction involves a balancing of the interests of the parties who might be affected by the court's decision.

Procedural Basis: Decision of the Federal District Court enjoining a salesman from competing with his former employer.

Facts: Sigma Chemical Co. (Sigma) (P) is a company that sells chemicals used in research, production, and analysis. Sigma's (P) knowledge of which supplier sells a particular chemical of a certain quality that satisfied a particular purpose at the right price is a trade secret. Foster Harris (D) went to work for Sigma (P) in 1979, after signing an agreement that he would not work for a competitor for two years after leaving Sigma (P) and that he would never disclose confidential information acquired from Sigma (P). In 1983, Harris (D) went to work for ICN, one of Sigma's (P) five major competitors. Sigma (P) sought to enjoin Harris (D) from working for ICN.

Issue: Does a company's interest in keeping a trade secret sufficiently outweigh a former employee's interest in seeking other employment, so that the latter may be enjoined from competing against the former?

Decision and Rationale: (Nangle, C.J.) Yes. The restrictive covenant at issue here is valid because it is necessary to protect Sigma's (P) legitimate interest in keeping a trade secret and because it is reasonable in both temporal and geographic scope. The determination whether to issue an injunction involves a balancing of the interests of the parties who might be affected by the Court's decision. The main prerequisite to obtaining injunctive relief is a finding that the plaintiff is being threatened by some injury for which he has no adequate legal remedy. First, it is clear that Harris (D) is violating the terms of the covenant. Harris (D) is contributing knowledge to the sale of a product that is in competition with that of Sigma (P). Harris (D) is also in a position that makes it likely he will use or disclose trade secret information that Harris (D) learned from Sigma's (P) product files. Under these circumstances there is a serious threat of irreparable harm to Sigma (P), for the company stands to lose its competitive edge. Harris (D) also faces substantial harm. He will be prevented from working for ICN for two years and likely will forever be prevented from using his knowledge of Sigma's (P) trade secrets. But the threat to Harris (D) is diminished by the fact that other former Sigma (P) employees have obtained employment with companies not in competition with Sigma (P). The balance of the equities do not favor Harris (D) because he was aware of the restrictions when he took employment with Sigma (P). On balance, the threat to Sigma (P) outweighs the detriment to Harris (D). It is ordered that Harris (D) be enjoined from: [1] rendering services to ICN as a purchasing agent involved in the purchase of products also sold by Sigma (P) for a period of two years; and [2] using or disclosing any trade secret that is the property of Sigma (P) and which Harris (D) acquired by reason of his employment with Sigma (P).

Analysis:

This opinion provides an example of the usual process courts undertake in determining whether to issue an injunction. The court mentions that before issuing an injunction, it must balance the interests of the parties involved. In balancing these interests the court takes a two step approach. First, the court determines the relative harm to each party. Sigma (P) stands to lose valuable trade secrets if the injunction is not issued. Harris (D), however, will be prevented from working for his new employer for two years and using his knowledge in the field. But the court notes that this harm is reduced by the fact that other former employees have sought employment outside Sigma's (P) product market. The second step in the process is the balancing of the equities – a sort of fairness determination. The court here holds that, since Harris (D) knew what he was getting into when he took the job with Sigma (P), it is only fair that he be held to the terms of his employment, including the restrictive covenant. In sum, the court holds that an injunction should issue because (a) the benefit to Sigma (P) outweighs the harm to Harris (D), and (b) fairness demands that Harris (D) be held to the terms of a contract he freely entered. One other point is notable. The court states that before Sigma (P) can obtain an injunction it must show that there is no available remedy at law. Yet, the court makes no mention of any such showing, nor does the court explain why damages are inadequate. This casts doubt on the continuing validity of this age-old requirement.

Evans v. Jeff D.

(State Governor) v. (Group of Handicapped
Children)
475 U.S. 717 (1986)

M E M O R Y   G R A P H I C

Instant Facts

While negotiating a settlement for his
clients, a class of handicapped children, a Legal Aid
attorney was forced to waive his claim for legal fees
provided by statute in order to obtain all of the
injunctive relief his clients sought from the state.

Black Letter Rule

The civil rights fee shifting provision does
not prohibit settlements conditioned on the waiver of
fees.

Facts: A class of mentally and emotionally handicapped children (plaintiff
class) (P) sued the State of Idaho (D) seeking injunctive relief for improved
treatment under the federal civil rights statute, 42 U.S.C. § 1983. The attorney
for the plaintiff class was employed by the Legal Aid Society; and his
representation agreement contained no provision for legal fees. Before trial, the
State of Idaho (D) offered a settlement proposal which granted the plaintiff class
(P) virtually all of the relief it was seeking.   The settlement, however, was
conditioned on the waiver of any claim of legal fees provided by 42 U.S.C.
§1988(b), the Civil Rights Attorney's Fees Award Act (Fees Act). This provision
permits a District Court to allow a prevailing party in a civil rights action to
recover reasonable attorney's fees. Although the waiver was unacceptable to the
Legal Aid Society, the attorney felt compelled by his ethical obligations to his
clients and accepted the settlement. The District Court rejected the attorney's
ethical argument and approved of the settlement conditioned upon the waiver
of fees.

Issue: Does the federal civil rights fee shifting provision prohibit a court
from accepting a settlement conditioned upon the waiver of fees?

Decision and Rationale: (Stevens, J.) No. The Fees Act does
not embody a general rule prohibiting settlements conditioned on the waiver of
fees in order to be faithful to the purposes of that Act. Although we believe that
the Legal Aid attorney was faced with a conflict of interest between pursuing
relief for his clients and obtaining a fee for the Legal Aid Society, we do not view
this as an "ethical dilemma." The attorney had no ethical duty to recover a fee
[it is perfectly okay for the attorney's family to starve]; his only ethical duty was
to obtain relief for the plaintiff class.   Since the settlement offer was more
favorable than any probable outcome at trial, the attorney's decision to settle was
consistent with the highest standards of our profession. Any defect in the
negotiated fee waiver must stem from a prohibition in the Fees Act, and not the
rules of ethics. We, however, can deduce no such prohibition from the fees Act.
The statute and its legislative history do not suggest that Congress intended to
prohibit all waivers of attorney's fees. In fact, we believe that such a prohibition
may impede the vindication of civil rights by reducing the attractiveness of
settlement. We must then decide whether the District Court abused its discretion
in this case when it approved the settlement and fee waiver. We believe the
District Court acted within its discretion. It is argued that a court's authority to
approve of class-action settlements must be exercised in accordance with the Fees
Act to ensure the availability of attorneys in civil rights cases. We disagree. The
question a court must ask is whether the settlement is fair; and in doing so, the
court may consider the waiver. We do not decide whether the availability of fee
waivers will actually diminish the availability of attorneys in civil rights cases.
That question is best left to Congress. Thus far, the Legislature has failed to
prohibit such waivers.

Analysis:

The Court here refuses to hold that a District Court – when exercising its settlement review authority under Federal Rule of Civil Procedure
23(e) – must reject any settlement conditioned on the waiver of attorney's fees made available by the civil rights statute. The Court bases
its holding on two factors. First, the court held such settlements do not create an ethical dilemma that requires a prohibition against fee
waivers. The Court notes the attorney in this case was pressured into waiving his fee in order to secure a favorable result for his client, but
in the Court's opinion, this conflict was not an "ethical" one since the rules of the profession do not require an attorney to seek a fee, they
only require an attorney to protect the interests of the client. Second, the Court goes on to hold that neither the statute authorizing a court
to award attorney's fees in civil rights cases, nor its legislative history, indicate an intent on the part of Congress to prohibit a ban on
settlements conditioned on a fee waiver. The Court noted that such a rule may actually interfere with the purposes of the statute by making
settlement less attractive. But the purpose of the fee shifting statute is not to make settlement more attractive, rather, it is to make attorneys
available in civil rights cases. Ethical rules will always require an attorney in this situation to take the settlement and waive his fee. If
attorneys fear their ethical duties will prevent the recovery of fees, they will refuse to take up civil rights cases. The Court states that it is
not equipped to determine the merits of this argument. If this is true, why is the Court equipped to determine that prohibiting waivers will
discourage settlements, frustrating the vindication of civil rights? Encouraging settlements may help vindicate civil rights, but favorable
settlements are rarely offered to those not represented by counsel. In its eagerness to encourage settlements, the Court downplays the role
played by attorneys in civil rights cases.

TO OBTAIN A PRELIMINARY INJUNCTION, IT IS NOT NECESSARY THAT THE MOVING PARTY BE REASONABLY CERTAIN OF SUCCESS ON THE MERITS

William Inglis & Sons Baking Co. v. ITT Continental Baking Co.

(Wholesale Baker) v. (Wholesale Baker)

526 F.2d 86 (9th Cir. 1976)

M E M O R Y   G R A P H I C

Instant Facts

A District Court denied a plaintiff's motion for a preliminary injunction against its competitors because the plaintiff failed to show the probability of success in its antitrust suit.

Black Letter Rule

A party moving for a preliminary injunction meets his burden if he shows that there is a combination of probable success and the possibility of irreparable injury or that serious questions are raised and the balance of the hardships tips sharply in his favor.

Procedural Basis: Appeal the Ninth Circuit challenging the District Court's denial of a motion for a preliminary injunction.

Facts: William Inglis & Sons Baking Co. (Inglis) (P) and other baking companies filed an antitrust suit against ITT Continental Baking Co. (ITT) (D) and four other defendants. Inglis (P) moved for a preliminary injunction to prevent ITT's below-cost pricing. ITT (D) claimed that its pricing scheme was a good faith effort to meet competition, a valid defense under the antitrust statutes. The District Court held a hearing and denied the motion. The court held serious reservations about Inglis' (P) probability of success on the merits. Furthermore, the court found that ITT (D) had adequately negated a violation by providing a defense. The Court of Appeals vacated the decision and remanded for a new hearing.

Issue: Is it necessary that party moving for a preliminary injunction show that there is a reasonable certainty the party will succeed on the merits?

Decision and Rationale: (Skopil, J.) No. To obtain a preliminary injunction, it is not necessary that the moving party be reasonably certain to succeed on the merits. The district court stated that a plaintiff is entitled to a preliminary injunction only if: (1) the plaintiff will suffer irreparable injury if relief is not granted; (2) the plaintiff will probably prevail on the merits; (3) in balancing the equities, the defendants will not be harmed more than plaintiff is helped by the injunction; and (4) granting the injunction is in the public interest. The court denied the injunction because it had serious doubts as to whether Inglis (P) would probably succeed. Our review of the grant or denial of a preliminary injunction is extremely limited. The decision of the court is subject to reversal only if it was based on an erroneous legal premise, or if the court abused its discretion. We are unable to conclude that the District Court abused its discretion in its conclusion that the plaintiff failed to satisfy the standard applied by the court. The court, however, failed to apply the alternative test. A party moving for a preliminary injunction meets his burden if he shows that there is a combination of probable success and the possibility of irreparable injury or that serious questions are raised and the balance of the hardships tips sharply in his favor. Since the District Court did not consider whether the injunction should be issued under this standard, we remand the question for further consideration. We, however, intimate no position as to whether the preliminary injunction should be issued. Reversed.

Analysis:

This case came to the federal appellate court under the statutory exemption that allows for interlocutory appeals from orders granting or denying injunctions (28 U.S.C. §1291). The Ninth Circuit creates a second basis upon which a party may obtain a preliminary injunction. Under either standard, a moving party must show that the benefit to him outweighs the harm to the opposing party. The question raised here is: When there is a doubt as to success on the merits, by how much must the benefit to the moving party outweigh the harm to the opposing party. Under the standard adopted by the District Court, a moving party must show a probability of success and that the benefit to the plaintiff outweighs the harm to the defendant. Under the rule adopted by the Court of Appeals, a party who is unable to show a reasonable certainty of success may obtain a preliminary injunction if his case raises some doubt and he faces severe hardship. In conjunction, the two standards provide a sliding scale which parties may use to obtain a preliminary injunction. In other words, as the probability of success on the merits increases, the need to show severe harm decreases, and vice versa.

Fuentes v. Shevin

(Debtor) v. (Not Stated)
407 U.S. 67 (1972)

M E M O R Y　　G R A P H I C

 ## Instant Facts

Margarita Fuentes (P) and other debtors challenge the constitutionality of Florida and Pennsylvania statutes allowing seizure of goods covered by an installment sales contract without providing an opportunity for the debtor to be heard prior to seizure.

Black Letter Rule

In order to comply with procedural due process, notice and an opportunity to be heard must be provided prior to seizure of any protected property interest.

Case Vocabulary

CHATTEL: An item of personal property.
DETINUE: Common law action allowing creditor to recover goods wrongfully detained.
REPLEVIN: Modern action allowing the title holder to repossess goods or chattels from a person who has wrongfully obtained or retained them.

Procedural Basis: Writ of certiorari reviewing affirmance of rejection of constitutional claims concerning replevin of chattels.

Facts: In this case, the Supreme Court reviews two separate appellate rulings regarding the constitutionality of state replevin statutes. One ruling involved Margarita Fuentes (P), who had purchased a stove and stereo system under a conditional sales contract. The supplier, Firestone Tire and Rubber Company, was to retain title to the merchandise until Mrs. Fuentes (P) made all of her payments, although Mrs. Fuentes (P) was allowed to possess the items in the interim. After more than a year of progress payments, a dispute developed regarding servicing of the stove. Firestone instituted an action in small claims court for repossession of the items, claiming that Mrs. Fuentes (P) had refused to make her payments. Firestone simultaneously obtained a writ of replevin, pursuant to Florida statute, ordering a sheriff to seize the goods without providing Mrs. Fuentes (P) with a pre-seizure hearing. Thereafter, Mrs. Fuentes (P) instituted the present action in federal district court, challenging the constitutionality of Florida's replevin statute. A similar action was brought in Pennsylvania by four other consumers who had entered into similar conditional sales contracts. In each suit, the district courts rejected the constitutional claims, and three-judge district courts considered the appeal and upheld the constitutionality of the statutes. The Supreme Court granted certiorari to review both appellate rulings.

Issue: Absent extraordinary circumstances, must notice and an opportunity to be heard be provided prior to depriving a party of a protected property interest?

Decision and Rationale: (Stewart, J.) Yes. Absent extraordinary circumstances, notice and an opportunity to be heard must be provided *prior* to depriving a party of a protected property interest. Consistent with procedural due process, we have repeatedly held that, prior to depriving a party of a property interest, an opportunity to be heard must be granted at a meaningful time. We now hold that, if notice and a hearing is to serve its full purpose, then the hearing must be granted at a time when the deprivation still can be prevented. Indeed, the Florida statute requires a post-seizure hearing in which the aggrieved party can argue her right to the goods. And in Pennsylvania, the aggrieved party can institute a lawsuit for the return of wrongfully-seized goods. Furthermore, pursuant to both statutes, the creditor seeking replevin must post a bond and may be forced to pay damages for wrongful repossession. However, no later hearing and no damage award can undo the fact that the arbitrary taking that was subject to procedural due process has already occurred. We have never embraced the position that a wrong may be done if it can be undone. Thus, we now hold that, in order to comply with due process, notice and an opportunity to be heard must be provided *prior* to any deprivation of a property interest protected by the Fourteenth Amendment. In the present cases, the Florida and Pennsylvania statutes are unconstitutional, as they provide for the replevin of chattels without the benefit of a hearing. Although Mrs. Fuentes (P) and the Pennsylvania appellants lacked full title to the replevied goods, the Fourteenth Amendment's property protection covers both possession and ownership. There are, however, extraordinary situations that justify postponing notice and opportunity for a hearing. In each such case, the seizure must be directly necessary to secure an important governmental or general public interest, there must be a special need for prompt action, and the statute must be narrowly drawn. For example, the Court has allowed summary seizure of property to collect the internal revenue of the United States, to meet the needs of a national war effort, to protect against the economic disaster of a bank failure, and to protect the public from mislabeled drugs and contaminated food. Since the Florida and Pennsylvania statutes serve no such important interests, and since the facts of the cases at hand are not these unusual situations, we hold that the statutes are unconstitutional. Vacated and remanded.

Dissent: (White, J.) I believe that the Florida and Pennsylvania statutes represent fair, constitutionally valid methods of reconciling the conflicting interests of the debtor and creditor in an installment sales contract. Both statutes immobilize the property during the pendency of the action, allowing the aggrieved debtor to reclaim the goods and recover damages if the seizure was invalid. The majority wrongfully ignores the creditor's interest in preventing further use and deterioration of a property in which he has a substantial interest.

Finally, the majority's result will have little impact on seizure in the installment sales context. A creditor could withstand attack under the majority's opinion by simply making clear in the original credit documents that they may retake possession without a hearing. Alternatively, they need only give a few days' notice of a hearing, and they need only establish probable cause for the default at the hearing. It is doubtful that such a hearing would result in protections for the debtor substantially different from those the present laws provide.

Analysis:

In this case, the majority presents compelling arguments for providing notice and an opportunity to be heard prior to seizure of goods via a writ of replevin. As we have already seen in *Mullane v. Central Hanover Bank & Trust Co.* [notice by publication fails to comply with due process where the names and addresses of the parties are known], due process requires that notice be provided prior to the deprivation of life, liberty or property by adjudication. The case at hand substantially broadens a party's due process rights, providing an almost universal *opportunity to be heard* prior to the deprivation of property. However, it should be noted that the unconstitutional "seizure" in this case was really only an *attachment*, as the debtor retained an ability to contest the "seizure" after it occurred. Thus, the case stands for the proposition that a pre-attachment opportunity to be heard is consistent with procedural due process. Nevertheless, the dissent raises some good points in questioning the holding. A creditor in an installment sales contract maintains a substantial property interest in the goods until the payments have been made in full. If notice and an opportunity to be heard are necessary prior to attachment, a very real danger exists that the debtor could destroy or conceal the goods, or that the goods would depreciate in value in the interim. An analogous concern surfaces in the context of quasi in rem jurisdiction, in which property which is not attached before an action is commenced may be removed from the forum state, destroying the court's jurisdiction. Perhaps, as later cases hold, a possessor of property should not be entitled to such sweeping constitutional protections.

Chapter 6

Think of pleading as the kick-off in a football game. There may have been a lot of practice and posturing and mental preparation done beforehand, but the kick-off is the first action in the game that anyone will see. Similarly, in a lawsuit, there is usually a good deal of negotiating and posturing and research and investigation done before a complaint is ever drafted. However, the pleading is the time a spectator (the court) gets to see how the "teams" will perform. The complaint and answer are important because they set the tone for the rest of the suit. If they are not done carefully and skillfully, it may result in added delay and expense. Inadequate pleadings may result in either dismissal of the lawsuit, loss of an otherwise viable claim, or loss of a valid defense.

Modern pleading schemes are more and more doing away with formal technicalities, and moving toward exulting substance over form. Still, a pleading must meet certain technical requirements. A complaint must give the defendant notice of why he is being sued, and it must say under what theory of law. An answer must tell the plaintiff if the defendant plans to assert any affirmative defenses that would relieve the defendant of liability. Some claims, such as fraud, need to be pled with more specificity than normal. Pleadings are not necessarily permanent. Courts may, at their discretion, allow a party to change a pleading. However, there is a tension between freely allowing an amendment, and prejudicing the other side by adding new stuff all of the time.

Under the Federal Rules, lawyers act as gatekeepers, and are often made responsible to see to it that pleadings are filed in good faith. This means that courts can hold lawyers responsible if their pleadings are filed for the sole purpose of harassing the other party or causing the other party needless expense or delay.

Chapter 6

NOTE: THE PURPOSE OF THIS OUTLINE IS TO ORGANIZE THE CASES SO THAT ONE CAN QUICKLY UNDERSTAND THE RELEVANCE OF EACH CASE TO THE COURSE. NO ATTEMPT IS MADE IN THIS OVERVIEW TO ADDRESS EVERY CONCEPT THAT MUST BE STUDIED. BE SURE TO READ THE ENTIRE CASEBOOK AND/OR OTHER MATERIALS TO GAIN A FULL UNDERSTANDING OF ALL CONCEPTS.

I. Defendants will sometimes move to dismiss a complaint immediately after receiving it, before any other work is done on the case. They say that the complaint fails to state a claim for which relief may be granted (known as a demurrer or a Rule 12(b)(6) motion).

   A. A complaint must say enough to tell the defendant why he is being sued, even though it need not describe every last detail. It must give the defendant sufficient notice of the case against him to enable him to prepare a defense. *People ex rel. Department of Transportation v. Superior Court.*

   B. The facts and law set forth in the complaint must constitute a viable cause of action. A complaint may be dismissed only if there is no set of facts in support of the plaintiff's claim that would entitle him to relief. *Haddle v. Garrison.*

II. Rule 11 imposes ethical limitations on pleading by requiring lawyers to investigate the legal and factual sufficiency of a claim before pleading it.

   A. Lawyers and parties have a duty to investigate claims before filing a complaint to make sure there is a factual basis for the claims. *Business Guides v. Chromatic Communications Enterprises.*

   B. Lawyers have a duty to make sure that claims are not frivolous – that their client's claims are well-grounded in the law before continuing to press the claim. *Religious Technology Center v. Gerbode.*

III. While Rule 8 normally provides for notice pleading – requiring that the plaintiff plead only enough information to give defendant a fair chance to respond – there are some claims, often called "disfavored claims" that require more specificity in pleading.

   A. Under Rule 9(b), fraud is a claim that must be pled with particularity. *Olsen v. Pratt & Whitney Aircraft.*

   B. The Rules do not require civil rights claims to be pled with particularity. Therefore, notice pleading of these claims is all that is required. *Leatherman v. Tarrant County Narcotics Intelligence & Coordination Unit.*

IV. In our system, where the parties take the initiative in a lawsuit, each party bears some responsibility for bringing its claims to the attention of the court and the other side.

   A. It is the burden of the defendant to assert an affirmative defense; it is not the burden of the plaintiff to anticipate affirmative defenses. *Gomez v. Toledo.*

V. A defendant responds to the complaint by admitting, denying, or claiming insufficient information to admit or deny the allegations in the complaint. The defendant may also impose a counter-claim or plead affirmative defenses.

   A. A general denial of all of plaintiff's claims may be done, but it must be done carefully. An inaccurate general denial may be deemed by the court to constitute an admittance if a more accurate answer would have put the plaintiff on notice that it was suing the wrong party.

   B. An affirmative defense must be pled in the answer or the defense is lost – the defendant will not be able to present evidence of the defense at trial. The harshness of this rule is compounded by the fact that it is not always clear whether certain evidence constitutes an affirmative defense or merely supports a denial. *Layman v. Southwestern Bell Telephone Co.*

VI. The court usually has discretion in determining whether or not to allow a party to amend a pleading.

   A. The court may allow a defendant to amend its answer to change an admission to a denial. *Beeck v. Aquaslide 'N' Dive Corp.*

   B. Relation back is desirable if the statute of limitations would otherwise bar the amendment. An amendment to a complaint will relate back to the date of the original complaint if the operational facts in the original complaint were enough to give the defendant notice of the claim complained of in the original complaint. *Moore v. Baker; Bonerb v. Richard J. Caron Foundation.*

People ex rel. Department of Transportation v. Superior Court

(Government Agency) v. (Car Accident Victims)
(1992) 5 Cal. App. 4th 1480

M E M O R Y   G R A P H I C

Instant Facts

Superior court overruled CalTrans' (D) demurrer to the complaint on the ground that pleadings on Judicial Council forms are non-demurrable.

Black Letter Rule

Complaints filed on Judicial Council pleading forms are vulnerable to attack if they do not sufficiently spell out the basis for the claim.

Case Vocabulary

DEMURRER: Similar to a motion under Federal Rule 12(b)(6), where the defendant claims that even if everything in the complaint is true, the plaintiff is still not entitled to relief.

SUFFICIENCY: Whether the complaint contains a set of facts and law that, if proven true and accurate, would entitle the plaintiff to relief.

WRIT OF MANDATE: A procedural devise that permits a party to appeal a lower court's decision, even though the decision is not a final judgment and would therefore ordinarily not be appealable.

Procedural Basis: Writ of mandate seeking review of lower court's ruling.

Facts: Accident victims (P) were injured on a California highway and sued the Department of Transportation ("CalTrans") (D). The Judicial Council, under state statute, has the authority to prescribe forms for use in the state courts. The accident victims (P) used a pleading form that the Judicial Council had prescribed for personal injury complaints. The complaint form alleged only that the accident victims' (P) Datsun was heading north when another vehicle, which was going south, crossed over the dirt center divider and struck the Datsun. CalTrans (D) filed a demurrer, claiming that the complaint did not set forth adequate circumstances of injury and reasons for liability. The superior court below overruled the demurrer, reasoning that the pleadings were non-demurrable because they were on the statutorily prescribed form.

Issue: Do the normal standards for sufficiency of pleading apply when the parties are using a statutorily approved complaint form?

Decision and Rationale: (Gilbert) Yes. Judicial Council pleading forms have significantly simplified the art of pleading. Nevertheless, a plaintiff must sometimes do more than simply put an "X" in a box – he must set forth enough facts to state a cause of action. Even though the allegations in a complaint are to be liberally construed to state a cause of action wherever possible, they must not be so liberally construed as to deny a defendant adequate notice and thereby impair his ability to properly prepare his case. Too many details in a complaint can obscure the true nature of the case, while too few details will confound and obfuscate. In either case, the environment is cloudy and justice cannot shine. In this case, the accident victims (P) have only alleged that a motorist crossed a dirt median and struck their vehicle. The complaint does not inform CalTrans (D) of its role in this accident. CalTrans (D) has no idea of the theory under which the accident victims (P) are claiming relief, which deprives CalTrans (D) of certain possible defenses. Sometimes checking a box on a pleading form will be enough, but other times the pleader will have to add more detail. A form complaint is no more immune to a demurrer than any other complaint that does not meet essential pleading requirements to state a cause of action. The superior court is overruled and the demurrer is sustained with leave to amend. Reversed.

Analysis:

This case involves one common problem with the pleading of complaints: sufficiency. Sufficiency of a complaint means how much the complaint needs to say about the relevant events. There is a difference of sufficiency between the old system of "code pleading" and the new system of "notice pleading." Under code pleading, which is still the system in some states, the complaint had to set out in a fair amount of detail the factual basis for the plaintiff's claim. The disadvantage of this was that sometimes the plaintiff did not know all of the relevant facts with such particularity. Often new facts come out later, in discovery, that the plaintiff could not have known about until after the suit is initiated. We don't want a legitimate claim to fail merely because the technicalities of pleading were not strictly followed. Under the newer system of notice pleading, the plaintiff need only give a defendant notice of the problem. The details are to come out and take shape later in the process. The disadvantage with notice pleading is that sometimes, as in this case, the defendant can not tell exactly what he is being sued for, making it hard for him to put up an adequate defense. For example, in this case the accident victims (P) did not tell CalTrans (D) what it did wrong or what it should have done differently. CalTrans (D) could not explain why it did not do what it should have done, or why it did not need to do what the accident victims (P) claim it should have done. Thus, the concept of sufficiency is in place to help insure that, on the one hand, the plaintiff is not overburdened by the technicalities of pleading and, on the other hand, the defendant is afforded fair notice of the claim against him. Also note that the court gave the accident victims (P) leave to amend their complaint to get it right. This is done as a matter of fairness – the court does not want a claim that seems to have merit to be dismissed for a minor procedural error. The problem with the complaint is a technical problem, not a problem with the merits of the case. Also, as some of the later cases show, there may be a situation where the statute of limitations would bar a claim if the case were to be dismissed with the court's permission to re-file (this is called dismissing a case without prejudice). With leave to amend, the accident victims (P) do not have to file their case all over again, they can just fix the problems with the original complaint.

Haddle v. Garrison (I)

(Whistleblower Employee) v. (Employer)

(1996) Unpublished Opinion. Docket No. 96-00029-CV-1

M E M O R Y   G R A P H I C

Instant Facts

Whistleblower (P), who is an at-will employee, alleges an injury from being fired as part of a conspiracy to deter him from testifying in federal court.

Black Letter Rule

As a matter of law, an at-will employee who was fired is not "injured," and therefore a claim for injury cannot be sustained.

Case Vocabulary

AT-WILL EMPLOYMENT: Absent a contract or statutory protection, an employer may fire an employee for any reason or for no reason at all.

Procedural Basis: District court sustains a motion to dismiss a complaint for failure to state a claim upon which relief may be granted.

Facts: Haddle (P) is a former employee of Healthmaster Home Health Care, Inc. (Healthmaster). Haddle (P) alleges that he was fired because he was planning to be a witness against Garrison (D) and others in a Federal criminal trial, that the firing was in retaliation for his planned testimony, and that the firing has caused Haddle (P) an actual injury. Haddle (P) concedes that he was an at-will employee at all relevant times. Haddle is suing his former employers for a violation of his civil rights under 42 U.S.C. § 1985(2) [making it a crime to conspire to cause an injury to any witness in order to deter the witness from testifying in federal court.]

Issue: Does an at-will employee state a cause of action by alleging that his termination from employment is an "injury?"

Decision and Rationale: (Alaimo) No. Rule 12(b)(6) permits a defendant to move to dismiss a complaint on the ground that the complaint fails to state a claim upon which relief can be granted. In other words, a defendant is saying to a plaintiff, "Even if everything you allege is true, the law affords you no relief." In deciding a 12(b)(6) motion, a court must assume that all of the factual allegations in the complaint are true. In the present case, Haddle (P) claims that his allegations will sustain a cause of action under § 1985(2) despite his status as an at-will employee. However, Haddle's (P) claim is contrary to binding 11th Circuit precedent in *Morast v. Lance* [a plaintiff must have been actually injured in order to sustain a claim under § 1985(2), and the discharge of an at-will employee is not an actual injury.] Under *Morast*, Haddle (P) has not been "injured." Therefore he has not stated a claim upon which relief can be granted. Dismissed.

Analysis:

This case illustrates another common problem in pleading in a complaint: if all of the facts in the case are taken as true, there is no law under which plaintiff can get relief. Notice that the court does not do any fact finding here. Rather, the court is testing the complaint to see if there is a need to take the case any further. The court is not worried at this stage whether the plaintiff will be able to prove the facts that are alleged in the complaint. The court will worry about that at the summary judgment stage later in the litigation. Notice that in this case Haddle (P) alleged that he had been "injured." Under the statute, an injury is a necessary element – if there is no injury, then there is no claim. Whether or not a person has been injured is a legal conclusion, not a factual question. So, the case turns on whether there has been an injury. The court reasoned that at-will employees have no guarantee of work the next day. Therefore, an at-will employee who is fired has not been injured, because he was not entitled to be working in the first place. Since Haddle (P) was an at-will employee, he was not injured, and thus could not make out a claim under the law invoked in the complaint. Even if every fact that Haddle (P) alleged was true, and he really did get fired in retaliation for cooperating with the feds, since there was no injury, the law allows for no recovery. Notice also that the district court here did not make an independent determination of whether there had been an injury. Rather, it applied a case from the Eleventh Circuit, which said that there is no injury in this situation. Since the Georgia district court is in the Eleventh Circuit, the court was bound by their determination of the question. That is, the district court could not independently decide that there had been an injury. The district court was obligated to follow the decision of the Eleventh Circuit Court.

Haddle v. Garrison (II)

(Whistleblower Employee) v. (Employer)

(1998) 119 S. Ct. 489

M E M O R Y   G R A P H I C

Instant Facts

An at-will employee was fired for cooperating (including willingness to testify in front of a federal grand jury) with the federal criminal investigation of his employer for welfare fraud.

Black Letter Rule

Firing an at-will employee causes injury because it is an interference with employment relationship, which is a tort under state law.

Case Vocabulary

CERTIORARI: When the Supreme Court agrees to hear a case.

INTERFERENCE WITH CONTRACT: A common law tort where one party causes another party damage by creating a situation where the second party, due to some action of the first party, cannot receive the benefits of a contract that it has made.

Procedural Basis: Appeal from dismissal of claim.

Facts: Haddle (P) is an at-will employee at Healthmaster, Inc. Haddle (P) was cooperating with a federal investigation of Healthmaster and its officers (including Garrison (D)) for allegations of Medicare fraud. Garrison (D) personally could not participate in the affairs of Healthmaster while he was under investigation, but he conspired with another officer of the corporation to have Haddle (P) fired. Haddle (P) alleged that he was fired in retaliation for his cooperation in the federal investigation, and that the termination was to discourage him from cooperating further with the authorities. Haddle (P) included in his complaint claims for relief under 42 U.S.C. § 1985 (2) [making it a crime to conspire to cause an injury to any witness in order to deter the witness from testifying in federal court.] The district court dismissed the action for failure to state a claim upon which relief may be granted. *Rule 12(b)(6).* It reasoned that because Haddle (P) was an at-will employee, he could not have suffered an "injury" by being fired. Injury is an essential element under the statute. The Eleventh Circuit Court of Appeals affirmed, relying on its precedent in *Morast* [holding that firing an at-will employee does not cause an "injury"].

Issue: Can an at-will employee suffer a legal "injury" if his employer fires him?

Decision and Rationale: (Rehnquist) Yes. Since the Eleventh Circuit's rule in *Morast* conflicts with rulings of the First and Ninth Circuits, we granted certiorari to resolve the question of whether an at-will employee is "injured in his person or property" under § 1985(2) if his employer fires him. Since this case was dismissed under Rule 12(b)(6), we must take all of the facts as alleged in Haddle's (P) complaint as true. We disagree with the Eleventh Circuit and hold that the firing of an at-will employee in this context does constitute a harm under § 1985(2). The harm alleged by Haddle (P) is a third-party interference with an at-will employment relationship. This is analogous to the long-standing tort of interference with contract. Wrongful interference with employment relations is a tort under the state law of Georgia, which is where the action here took place. Therefore, we find ample support for our holding that the harm occasioned by the conspiracy to fire Haddle (P) may give rise to a claim for damages under § 1985(2). Reversed and Remanded.

Analysis:

Here the Supreme Court reversed the district court's determination that there was no injury. It did that by reversing the Eleventh Circuit's holding that discharge from at-will employment does not cause injury. Both the district court and the Eleventh Circuit must now follow the Supreme Court's determination that an injury can follow from discharge of an at-will employee. Remember, this is still a case about whether the law will allow recovery under the facts as alleged by Haddle (P). This case is still at the pre-discovery stage, so the court is not requiring Haddle (P) to prove anything yet. It just assumes that all of the allegations in the complaint are true for purposes of deciding whether or not it should allow the dismissal to stand. Notice that the ultimate disposition is that the case is remanded for further action consistent with the Supreme Court's decision. This means that the case will be allowed to go forward, but it does not mean that Haddle (P) is guaranteed to win. Haddle (P) must still gather enough evidence to survive summary judgment, and to convince a jury that he had proven all of the elements of his claims. After going all the way to the Supreme Court, Haddle (P) has won nothing but the opportunity for more litigation.

Business Guides, Inc. v. Chromatic Communications Enterprises, Inc.

("Retail Directory" Publisher) v. ("Unfair" Competitor)
Supreme Court of the United States, 498 U.S. 533, 111 S.Ct. 922, 112 L.Ed. 1140 (1991)

M E M O R Y   G R A P H I C

Instant Facts

Defendant granted full dismissal of case and sanctions against plaintiff who filed a completely unsubstantiated and frivolous copyright infringement action without investigating its own charges of copying.

Black Letter Rule

A represented party may be sanctioned in addition to or instead of its attorney for violating the Rule 11 requirement that all information in signed documents submitted to the court be reasonably accurate.

Case Vocabulary

"SEEDS": Deliberately incorrect information, from grammatical error to outright fictitiousness, intended to locate copyright infringement by their presence in a competitor's publication.

Procedural Basis: Appeal from dismissal of case with prejudice and award of sanctions against the plaintiff.

Facts: Business Guides, Inc. (BGI) publishes 18 various retail directories and ensures the against copyright infringement by planting "seeds." (A "seed" is a false list which, if used by a competitor, implies that the name was taken from the plaintiff's directory.) When BGI (P) apparently found 10 such "seeds" in Chromatic's (D) directory, BGI (P) asked its counsel Finley, Kumble, etc., to file for an emergency temporary restraining order (TRO) on grounds of copyright infringement and unfair competition [yes, that's actually illegal] . The affidavits in support of the application charged Chromatic (D) with copying BGI's (P) directory directly. Another affidavit was of a sales representative who claimed she personally identified 10 listing seeds, but did not specify what these were. Three days before the hearing on the TRO, the district judge's law clerk phoned Finley, Kumble and asked what was wrong with each listing and the law firm, for the first time, turned to its clients to ask them the same. BGI's (P) Director replied by retracting 3 of the seeds and Finley, Kumble prepared supplemental affidavits to that effect. Unbeknownst to them, the busy law clerk conducted his own investigation by calling every listing in Chromatic's guide and discovered that 9 of the 10 "seeds" contained no incorrect information at all. At the hearing, then, the court denied the TRO, stayed further proceedings and at a later hearing decided sanctions were appropriate against both BGI (P) and Finley, Kumble. At a third hearing, BGI (P) explained that the discovery of 10 "seeds" was not in bad faith but a mistake which resulted from using an incorrect master source to uncover the "seeds" in the first place. While the judge accepted this, he found sanctions were still appropriate because (1) BGI failed to conduct a proper inquiry before filing the initial TRO, (2) both BGI and Finley, Kumble failed to investigate the "seeds" even after the Director discovered 3 of the "seeds" were incorrect, and (3) both BGI and Finley, Kumble were unreasonable for offering coincidence as their defense at the first two hearings. Consequently, Chromatic (D) brought a motion for sanctions, but only against BGI (P). The court granted $13,865 to cover legal expenses and costs, and dismissed the entire action with prejudice.

Issue: May violation of the FRCP 11 requirement for reasonable representation in signed documents be sanctioned even against a represented party?

Decision and Rationale: (O'Connor, J.) Yes. Even a represented party may be sanctioned for violating the Rule 11 requirement that all information in signed documents submitted to the court be reasonably accurate. The standard of conduct, "objective reasonableness," also applies to represented parties with the same force as it would to their attorneys. Thus, a represented party, if a document signer, is responsible for conducting a reasonable inquiry into the truthfulness of their information or face sanctions. To hold otherwise would unfairly force a higher objective standard on pro se litigants who can't afford counsel than on represented parties. Additionally, in emergency actions such as BGI's (P) TRO application, only Finley, Kumble would have been sanctioned for reasonably relying on their client's careless misrepresentation. As in this case, represented parties may often be better positioned to investigate their information, especially if they are insiders. However, since this may not always be the case, the determination of what constitutes "reasonable" inquiry will vary from case to case. Furthermore, the standard of what is reasonable for a client may be different from what is reasonable for an attorney. Thus, the "object reasonableness" standard is actually one of "reasonableness under the circumstances." An affirmative duty to conduct a reasonable inquiry into the facts before filing any documents is consistent with Rule 11 whether imposed on an attorney or the represented party. Signing is no longer a meaningless act. Judgment affirmed.

Dissent: (Kennedy, J.) The purpose of FRCP 11 is to control the irresponsible practice of attorneys. Extending the Rule to represented parties not only breaks with legal tradition but results in many unfair consequences. Many times clients are told by the attorney to just sign the papers and, when they do so in good faith, it is an abuse of judicial discretion to sanction them. Furthermore, the Rule does not require represented parties to sign papers, but allows it voluntarily. Thus, those parties who are aware of this Court's decision will resist voluntarily signing anything and those parties who are not aware of this decision will doubtfully change their behavior when signing. Thus the deterrent purpose of this Rule is not served if applied to represented parties. Citizens in general cannot be expected to be familiar with the FRCP and should, therefore, not be held primarily liable for pleading errors to the same degree as attorneys.

Analysis:

FRCP 11 enjoys a long and sordid history. Originally meant to control attorney conduct (or misconduct), the Rule was largely ineffective in its earlier form because the standard for applying it was subjective good faith. By 1983 the Legislatures caught on that this was nearly impossible to enforce or disprove and the standard of Rule 11 was changed to objective reasonableness. By signing a document, an attorney effectively promises that he read it, conducted a reasonable inquiry into its factual contents, and is acting in good faith by submitting it. If a judge finds that Rule 11 has been violated, he is required to impose sanctions. It is not left to his discretion. However, the amount and nature of the sanctions are left within the judge's discretion. Thus, a problem discovered with the Rule is that its application is completely arbitrary and results in rather inconsistent sanctions for comparable acts. Furthermore, the merits of applying sanctions at all have been hotly contested as well. Proponents of Rule 11 argue that it deters much frivolous and irresponsible litigation, upgrades lawyers, conduct, and compensates the objects of vexatious litigations. Critics of the Rule contend, however, that it is over deterrent, that it stifles creative advocacy, and that it generates too many minitrials separate from the core litigation. Consequently, the future of Rule 11, especially after the controversial *BGI v. Chromatic* decision, remains rather uncertain.

Religious Technology Center v. Gerbode

(Not Stated) v. (Not Stated)
(1994) 1994 U.S. Dist. LEXIS 6432

M E M O R Y   G R A P H I C

 ### Instant Facts

Gerbode and others (D) bring a Rule 11 motion for costs and attorneys' fees against Religious Technology Center (P) and its attorneys for filing a frivolous lawsuit.

Black Letter Rule

Under Rule 11 the court has discretion to award attorneys' fees or impose other sanctions in order to deter parties from filing meritless lawsuits.

Case Vocabulary

COURT'S INHERENT POWERS: The court has the inherent power to control the proceedings that come in front of it, including the power to sanction and the power of contempt.

LODESTAR METHOD: The method of computing attorney's fees based on the attorneys' usual and reasonable hourly rates and the usual and reasonable hours spent on that type of case, adjusted up or down depending on factors such as the novelty of the case, the complexity of the case, the attorney's familiarity with the case, and other circumstances of that particular case.

Procedural Basis: Defendants to a lawsuit bring a motion for costs and attorneys' fees under Rule 11.

Facts: Religious Technology Center ("RTC") (P) alleged that Gerbode and others (D) violated the Racketeer Influenced and Corrupt Organization Act (RICO). RTC (P) alleged that Gerbode (D) engaged in mail fraud and wire fraud in connection with the formation and operation of purported non-profit corporations. The complaint was dismissed on the merits. Gerbode (D) now moves for attorneys' fees from RTC (P) and RTC's (P) attorneys, Bowles & Moxon ("Bowles") and Cooley, Manion, Moore & Jones ("Cooley"). The court considers Gerbode's (D) motion for sanctions for a violation of Fed. R. Civ. P. 11 [prohibiting frivolous pleadings]. Gerbode (D) also moves for sanctions under 28 U.S.C. § 1927 [permitting judges to impose costs and attorneys' fees on a lawyer who in bad faith multiplies the proceedings so as to increase costs unreasonably and vexatiously] and the court's inherent powers. However, the court determines that § 1927 and the court's inherent powers add nothing to the outcome of this motion, and thus will not consider them.

Issue: Did RTC violate Rule 11 by bringing this action?

Decision and Rationale: (Tashima) Yes. RTC (P) first argues that Gerbode's (D) Rule 11 motion must fail because it was filed in violation of Rule 11's "safe harbor" provisions [Rule 11(c)(1)(A) provides that a Rule 11 motion for sanctions cannot be filed until the opposing party has had 21 days to either correct or withdraw the challenged pleading]. RTC's argument fails: The Amendment to Rule 11 requiring a waiting period became effective on the same date that this action was dismissed, thus it would be futile to now require Gerbode (D) to comply with the "safe harbor" provision. Turning to the merits of Gerbode's (D) motion, I find that reasonable inquiry into established law would have revealed that RTC's (P) RICO theory was clearly not viable. In addition, RTC (P) is not arguing for a modification of existing law that would support its RICO theory. Therefore, I conclude that it was frivolous to file the amended complaint. Next I consider Gerbode's (D) request for sanctions. The purpose of Rule 11 sanctions is to deter the filing of improper pleadings. The court should explore both monetary and non-monetary sanctions as effective deterrents. In this case, the long and acrimonious history of repeated litigation between the parties necessitates the partial award of attorneys' fees to deter further frivolous legal action. In addition, since this case has already been dismissed, other sanctions, which might be effective in the context of ongoing litigation, are unavailable. In determining the amount of sanctions, I will only hold RTC's (P) attorney and her firm (Bowles) responsible for the costs of defending this action after they became attorneys of record for RTC (P). This amount will include the costs to Gerbode (D) of bringing this Rule 11 motion. I find that Gerbode's (D) attorneys have spent a reasonable amount of time working on this case. I also find that the rates for all but one of Gerbode's (D) attorneys to be reasonable. For that one attorney, I find that his reasonable hourly rate is $200 per hour, rather than the $225 that was requested. Using the lodestar method, I determine that Gerbode's (D) reasonable expenses in defending this action were $17,775.00 in legal fees. I award one-half of the lodestar amount ($8,887.50) to Gerbode (D) as partial reimbursement for defending against the frivolous complaint. The same amount ($8,887.50) is also to be paid as a monetary penalty to the Clerk of the Court. Finally, I consider the question of who to sanction. Since this motion is based on the bringing of a frivolous complaint, Amended Rule 11 does not allow me to impose monetary sanctions against RTC (P). [The amendment restricts the scope of the ruling in *Business Guides, Inc. v. Chromatic Communications Enterprises, Inc.*] The Rule allows the court to sanction the lawyer signing the complaint as well as any law firm that took part in causing the violation. In this case, there is not sufficient evidence to find that any law firm aside from Bowles should share responsibility for drafting and filing the challenged pleading.

Therefore, the motion against Cooley will be denied. Motion granted.

Analysis:

The lawyers here were sanctioned for filing claims that they should have known were frivolous. Thus, Rule 11 sanctions are the system's way of trying to prevent lawyers from making up pleadings in order to get cases past dismissal and into the discovery stage. Remember that under Rule 12(b)(6), a court accepts the pleadings in the complaint as true for the limited purpose of determining whether to dismiss the case. A lawyer could say anything in the complaint and the court would have to accept it as true. Without Rule 11, lawyers would have incentive to make things up and put them into the complaint. Once discovery was obtained, the plaintiffs could always withdraw the pleadings or could find something in discovery and amend to form a viable complaint. Rule 11 is meant as a strong disincentive to keep things honest. It imposes a duty on lawyers to investigate, to plead only claims that are likely to have a basis in law and fact, and to file claims that are not frivolous. This does not mean that a lawyer must believe that he or she will ultimately prevail before filing a complaint. It just means that the lawyer has done honest work and can make a good argument on behalf of the client. [It is often said that an argument is not frivolous if it survives the straight-face test: if you can stand in front of a judge and make the argument with a straight face, then your argument is not frivolous.] Examine how the court got around the safe harbor provision of Rule 11(c)(1)(A) – it created a futility exception. The safe harbor provision gives the party who filed the challenged pleading 21 days to reconsider and withdraw or fix the pleading. The court claims that since the case had already been dismissed, it would be futile to give RTC (P) a chance to fix the pleading, therefore it would go straight to the sanction. This seems to defeat the purpose of having the safe harbor in the first place – to give parties and lawyers a chance to fix or withdraw the pleading before they get sanctioned for it. Notice also that the court could not sanction the client, as did the court in *Business Guides v. Chromatic Communications Enterprises*. Under Rule 11(c), clients may be sanctioned for everything except making frivolous arguments. This would seem to make sense, because it is the lawyers' job to determine the law and appear in court to make argument. Lawyers are also supposed to exercise independent legal judgment and, as officers of the court, it is their duty to be honest and not bring the practice of law into disrepute.

Olsen v. Pratt & Whitney Aircraft

(Employee) v. (Employer)

(1998) 136 F.3d 273

M E M O R Y   G R A P H I C

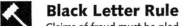 **Instant Facts**

An employee was fired after his employer convinced him to drop his participation in the company's early retirement plan.

Black Letter Rule

Claims of fraud must be pled with sufficient particularity.

 Case Vocabulary

PREEMPT BY FEDERAL LAW: Under the Constitution's supremacy clause, a federal statute that covers one area of law, such as employee retirement benefits, may take up the entire area and will replace or overrule state law that is inconsistent with the federal statute.

Procedural Basis: Appeal from dismissal of a complaint.

Facts: Olsen (P) was employed at Pratt & Whitney Aircraft ("P&W") (D) from 1956 to 1992. On December 18, 1991, Olsen (P) enrolled in P&W's (D) Voluntary Retirement Incentive Program ("VRIP"). VRIP granted special retirement benefits to eligible employees who agreed to take early retirement and to waive certain claims against the company. Olsen (P) signed the required forms and agreed to retire on March 31, 1992. Olsen (P) alleges that soon after he enrolled in VRIP, certain P&W (D) employees represented to him that his job was secure, and that he should revoke his participation in VRIP. Olsen (P) alleges that in reliance on these representations he revoked his participation in VRIP on January 2, 1992. On September 7, 1992, P&W (D) fired Olsen (P). P&W (D) claims that Olsen (P) was fired as a result of a reduction in P&W's (D) work force. Olsen (P) sued P&W (D), alleging, among other things, common law fraud. Specifically, Olsen (P) alleges that he relied to his detriment on P&W's (D) inducements of job security when he agreed to continue to work for P&W and give up the VRIP benefits. The district court dismissed Olsen's (P) common law fraud claim, finding that it was preempted by federal law. On appeal, Olsen (P) challenges the dismissal of his common law fraud claim. P&W (D) argues that Olsen's (P) fraud allegations fail to comply with the heightened pleading requirements of Fed. R. Civ. P. 9(b) [requiring that allegations of fraud be stated with particularity].

Issue: Does the complaint meet the requirements of Rule 9(b)?

Decision and Rationale: (Jacobs) No. We may affirm the decision of the district court on any ground that has support in the record, even if it is not the same ground that the district court relied on in making its decision. We agree with P&W (D) that Olsen's (P) fraud allegations do not comply with the heightened pleading requirements of Rule 9(b). Olsen's (P) allegations are conclusory and lacking in particulars. He does not allege what was said (he only gives the gist of what was said), when and where it was said, who specifically said it, how the words of the employees can bind the company, and why the prediction that there would be employment for Olsen (P) was a fraudulent misrepresentation or merely wishful thinking that did not come true. These deficiencies obscure the viability of Olsen's (P) fraud claim and whether it is truly preempted by federal law. Given the complexity of the federal law of retirement benefits, we cannot even attempt to resolve the preemption issue without a properly pleaded complaint. Since plaintiffs whose complaints are dismissed under Rule 9(b) are typically given the opportunity to amend their complaint, we vacate the judgment and remand with directions to the district court to afford Olsen (P) an opportunity to file an amended complaint that complies with Rule 9(b). Vacated and Remanded.

Analysis:

Here the court of appeals reversed the district court on grounds the district court did not ever consider in dismissing the complaint. The district court said that the state law fraud claim was preempted by the federal law of employee retirement benefits. The fraud claim was dismissed because of preemption, and the employee benefits claim was dismissed as well. Olsen (P) did not appeal the dismissal of the employee benefits claim. This is significant, because Olsen (P) now loses the right to bring that claim again. The matter is considered *res judicata* (to have been fully adjudicated). In other words, Olsen (P) has accepted the dismissal, and he cannot bring the employee benefits claim again on remand. With respect to the common law fraud claim, Olsen (P) gets a chance to fix the pleading. The court even tells Olsen (P) how to do so. It tells him that fraud must be pled with particularity and that he must include the whos, wheres, whens, whats, and whys of the fraud claim. The Federal Rules' treatment of Fraud as requiring a higher pleading threshold is not new. Fraud has traditionally required to be pleaded with increased particularity. There have been several reasons advanced as to why fraud should need special pleading requirements. It has been suggested that fraud involved allegations of immoral behavior, so the greater pleading requirements reflect the gravity of the accusation. In the context of contracts or real estate, fraud, if proven, will work to completely nullify (rather than modify or simply enforce) documents that would not otherwise be lightly set aside. As always, for the defendant discovery is time consuming, and fair notice may demand that fraud be alleged particularly so that defendant has a fair method of defending himself. Also, consider that fraud may need to be pled more particularly because of the nature of the claim. In essence, the plaintiff is saying, "He lied to me." Often the only defense is to say, "No, I didn't." If nothing more were required to bring a fraud claim, the court could almost never dismiss the fraud claim and the defendant would have to go through the expense of discovery for nothing in many cases. Also, it is very difficult for an attorney to investigate more thoroughly in a scenario where it's one party's word against another's. Therefore, the protections of Rule 11 would not really work to protect parties from bringing frivolous or insufficient fraud claims.

Leatherman v. Tarrant County Narcotics Intelligence & Coordination Unit

(Homeowners) v. (Municipal Police)
(1993) 507 U.S. 163

M E M O R Y   G R A P H I C

Instant Facts

Two homeowners sued the municipalities whose police officers entered and searched their houses in violation of the Constitution.

Black Letter Rule

Notice pleading is satisfactory except for claims that are specifically required by the Federal Rules to be pled with particularity.

Case Vocabulary

EXPRESSIO UNIUS: A cannon of statutory construction that if the legislature said one thing in a law (e.g., that fraud and mistake must be pled with particularity), by doing so it meant to exclude all other things from the scope of that law (e.g., that other suits may be pled generally).

Procedural Basis: Appeal from dismissal of a civil rights claim.

Facts: This case arose from two incidents of forcible entry into homes where the manufacture of narcotics was suspected. One homeowner (P) claims that the officers assaulted him, and another homeowner (P) claims that the officers went into her home while she was away and killed her two dogs. The homeowners (P) sued several local officials (D), the county (D), and two municipal corporations (D) that employed the officers involved. The homeowners (P) alleged that the police conduct violated the Fourth Amendment [against unreasonable searches and seizures]. The homeowners (P) sued under 42 U.S.C. § 1983 [permitting suit against those who act under color of law to deprive persons of their constitutional rights]. The basis for municipal liability was the failure of the municipalities (D) to adequately train their officers. The United States District Court for the Northern District of Texas dismissed the complaint because Fifth Circuit case law required heightened pleading standards to apply in § 1983 actions alleging municipal liability.

Issue: May a federal court apply a pleading standard that is more stringent than the usual pleading requirements of Rule 8(a) in cases alleging municipal liability under § 1983?

Decision and Rationale: (Rehnquist) No. The municipalities (D) attempt to defend the Fifth Circuit's heightened pleading requirement on two grounds – both of which we find unpersuasive. First, they claim that municipalities have immunity from suit, and therefore the more relaxed pleading requirement of Rule 8(a) [requiring only a short and plain statement of the claim] would subject municipalities to needless discovery. We disagree. Limited liability should not be confused with immunity from suit. Municipalities are not immune from suit. However, they cannot be held liable under § 1983 unless a municipal policy or custom caused the constitutional injury. Second, the municipalities (D) claim that the Fifth Circuit's standard is not really a heightened pleading standard at all. Rather, it is a reflection of the complexity of establishing liability under § 1983. We disagree. We think it obvious that the Fifth Circuit's "heightened pleading standard" is just what it claims to be: a more demanding rule for pleading a complaint under § 1983 than for pleading other types of claims. It is impossible to reconcile the Fifth Circuit's heightened pleading standard with the liberal system of notice pleading of the Federal Rules. We have already said that all the rules require is a short and plain statement of the claim that will give a defendant fair notice of the claim. *Conley v. Gibson.* Federal Rule 9(b) does impose a heightened pleading standard in two specific instances: fraud and mistake. A suit under § 1983 is not one of those instances. The doctrine of *Expressio unius* supports our conclusion that suits under § 1983 cannot be required to be pled with more particularity than the requirements of Rule 8(a). Reversed.

Analysis:

Here the court of appeals tried to impose a heightened pleading standard on § 1983 civil rights claims. Consider why the court would do this, since the federal rules obviously only require notice pleading. One unique element of this type of claim is that the municipalities (D) have partial immunity – they cannot be liable for the officer's actions unless the officers were following some policy or custom of the municipality when the constitutional violation occurred. Thus, in order to determine whether a claim should be allowed to go forward, the court would need to know the policy or custom of the municipality. From mere notice pleading, it is not likely that the court would be able to make this determination. The courts have the practical concern about subjecting defendants to unnecessary discovery. One way to prevent this would be to make plaintiffs plead with particularity. The problem for the plaintiffs is that they are usually not insiders and therefore they cannot know what the custom or policy of the municipality was – that information would be most likely to come out in discovery. They are put in the position where they cannot find out about the custom or policy unless they plead with specificity what exactly the custom or policy was. Obviously, this would be pretty difficult to do. In resolving this tension, the Supreme Court said that lower courts should just follow the rules, allow notice pleading, until the rules are changed. Notice that lower courts exercise a lot of discretion in applying the rules. Here, for instance, the lower courts had been forcing civil rights plaintiffs to plead with specificity, even though the rules did not require it. Recall also, in the *Religious Technology Center* case, the district court applied a "futility exception" to the 21 day safe harbor provision of Rule 11, even though no such exception exists in the rules. This may illustrate the need for courts to be flexible when dealing with the various proceedings that come before it, but it also gives judges tremendous power to get rid of cases they do not like at the expense of denying justice to an otherwise deserving litigant.

Gomez v. Toledo

(Police Officer) v. (Police Superintendent)
(1980) 446 U.S. 635

M E M O R Y   G R A P H I C

Instant Facts

A police officer who was summarily fired after testifying against fellow officers was subsequently reinstated and sued for a violation of his due process rights, but he did not allege that the police superintendent acted in bad faith.

Black Letter Rule

Qualified Immunity based on good faith is an affirmative defense and thus the defendant has the burden of pleading it – the plaintiff is not required to plead bad faith.

Case Vocabulary

BURDEN OF PERSUASION: One party has the burden of persuading the trier of fact that its claims are true.
BURDEN OF PLEADING: One party has the burden of bringing a claim or defense to the attention of the court and the other side.
GOOD FAITH: At the time a pleading is filed, there must be a belief by the pleader that the contents of the pleading are true and that the pleading is imposed for only for the purpose of presenting the pleader's side of the case, not for illegitimate purposes such as delay or imposing additional expense on the other side.

Procedural Basis: Appeal from dismissal of a complaint.

Facts: Gomez (P) has been employed by the Puerto Rican police since 1968. In April 1975, Gomez (P) submitted a sworn statement to his supervisor that two other officers had offered false evidence for use in a criminal case under their investigation. Gomez's (P) claims were investigated and found to be true. In April 1976, a criminal trial was held on the basis of Gomez's (P) allegations, and he testified consistently with his sworn statement that two officers had offered false evidence. In May 1976, Toledo (D) brought criminal charges against Gomez (P) for unlawfully wiretapping the officer's phones. Gomez (P) was suspended from the police department in May 1976 and was discharged without a hearing in July 1976. In October 1976, the Puerto Rican courts found that there was no probable cause to believe that Gomez (P) was guilty of wiretapping. Gomez (P) then sought review of his discharge, and was reinstated with back pay. Gomez (P) then brought this suit for damages under 42 U.S.C. § 1983 [permitting suit against those who act under color of law to deprive persons of their constitutional rights], alleging that he was discharged in violation of his right to procedural due process, which caused him anxiety, embarrassment, and injury to his reputation. Toledo (D) moved to dismiss the complaint for failure to state a cause upon which relief may be granted. *Rule 12(b)(6).* Toledo (D) claimed that he was entitled to qualified immunity for acts done in good faith, and that Gomez (P) failed to allege that Toledo (D) was motivated by bad faith.

Issue: Where Toledo (D) is entitled to qualified immunity if he acted in good faith, is Gomez (P) required to plead bad faith in order to state a claim for relief?

Decision and Rationale: (Marshall) No. Public officers are entitled to qualified immunity from damages liability under § 1983 if they acted in good faith. However, this is not to say that Gomez (P) must allege bad faith in order to state a claim. § 1983 requires only two allegations: 1) deprivation of some federal right; and 2) that the person doing the depriving acted under state or territorial law. Gomez (P) has sufficiently alleged these two elements. We find that qualified immunity based on good faith is a defense, and the burden of pleading it rests on the defendant. There is no reason to require that a plaintiff must anticipate every defense and include it in his complaint. Furthermore, as in this case, good faith rests upon the subjective belief of the defendant. A plaintiff could not reasonably be expected to know a defendant's state of mind at the pleading stage of the lawsuit. Gomez (P) has stated a claim for which relief can be granted. Reversed and Remanded.

Concurrence: (Rehnquist) I join the opinion of the Court, reading it to leave open the issue of the burden of persuasion, as opposed to the burden of pleading, with respect to a defense of qualified immunity.

Analysis:

This case talked about affirmative defenses and burdens of pleading. It is sometimes hard to tell when a fact is a defense and when it is a part of the claim. In this case, the statute itself required only two elements, both of which had been pled. The defendant was bringing something new into the mix by talking about good faith. Therefore, it seems right that defendant should have the burden to plead it. As the court points out, you can not expect the plaintiff to think of and to plead every affirmative defense. Consider how this case got to the Supreme Court. First the district court dismissed the claim for failure to allege bad faith. Why do you suppose the plaintiffs did not just move to amend the complaint to allege bad faith? Consider that if plaintiffs had pled bad faith, the judge might have forced them to prove bad faith – the normal rule is that the person that pleads it must prove it. Thus, the lawyers may have wanted to take care of the problem in the beginning, rather than have to litigate more difficult questions later on.

Zielinski v. Philadelphia Piers, Inc.

(Injured Victim) v. (Alleged Tortfeasor)
United States District Court, Eastern District of Pennsylvania,
139 F.Supp. 408 (1956)

M E M O R Y G R A P H I C

Instant Facts
A man who was hit by a forklift claims that it was owned by large company which denies owning it at the time of the accident

Black Letter Rule
A general denial will not be valid if any of the allegations being denied have been admitted by both parties as true.

Case Vocabulary

DEPOSITION: Legally admissible witness testimony taken outside court either in the form of oral questioning or written questionnaire.
EQUITABLE ESTOPPEL: The concept of justice which precludes a party from exercising what he would be entitled to if not for some voluntary act of his own which would make it unjust to grant him those rights.

Facts: Zielinski (P) suffered physical injuries on February 9, 1953 when his forklift was struck by another forklift. In his complaint for injuries, filed on April 23, 1953, Zielinski named Philadelphia Piers, Inc. (D) as the defendant because the forklift which collided with his had "PPI" written on its side. Thus, Zielinski (P) presumed an agency relationship existed between Johnson, the driver (who would have no money to go after), and Philadelphia Piers (D) (who would have money) as his employer at the time. After the complaint was served, Philadelphia Piers (D) answered it and referred to themselves as "defendant" within the answer. Furthermore, the complaint was also forwarded to Philadelphia Piers, (D) insurance company and they acknowledged responsibility as well. However, at a pretrial conference, information surfaced which made it clear that the business of moving freight on the pier had been sold by Philadelphia Piers (D) to Carload Contractors and Johnson and was switched over to the latter's payroll. In other words, Philadelphia Piers (D) does not believe it shared an agency relationship with Johnson and should, therefore, not be held accountable for any injury caused by him. Thus, Philadelphia Piers (D) generally denied the allegations of Zielinski's complaint. Zielinski (P) responded by filing this motion for a ruling by the court that an agency relationship did exist between Johnson and Philadelphia Piers (D) and that Zielinski (P) was therefore suing the correct defendant.

Issue: Is a general denial valid when at least some of the allegations being denied have been admitted by both parties as true?

Decision and Rationale: (Van Dusen, J.) No. A general denial is ineffective when at least some of the claims being denied are clearly true and not at issue. In such a circumstance, the defendant must make a more specific answer. Thus, when Zielinski (P) stated in the pleadings that he was hit and injured by a forklift operated by an agent of Philadelphia Piers (D), a general denial is plainly erroneous. It implies not only the intended denial that the forklift was operated by an agent of Philadelphia Piers (D) but also that Zielinski was injured, which cannot be denied because it was previously admitted as true fact. This finding is supported by two major policy considerations. First, Philadelphia Piers (D) knows that the statute of limitations to file another complaint on a different defendant has already run for Zielinski. Thus, dismissing this complaint would effectively deprive him of any opportunity at redress in violation of established principles of equitable estoppel. Second, when an improper and ineffective answer has been filed knowingly after the plaintiff's statute of limitations has run, an allegation of agency will be instructed to the jury as presumptively admitted by both parties for the purpose of the litigation. Therefore, plaintiff's motion to instruct the jury of the agency relationship between Johnson and Philadelphia Piers (D) is granted.

Analysis:

A defendant has three options when answering a complaint. He can either admit, deny, or plead insufficient information to answer at all. The admissions and denials can either be general, referring to every claim in the complaint, or specific, referring to particular claims as admitted and others as denied. A defendant who chooses to deny any of the claims must be very careful to understand everything that is actually being claimed. Otherwise, the defendant will find himself like Philadelphia Piers (D), where he is denying parts that are debatable as to their truth and parts which have clearly been established as truth. As a result of such an ineffective and erroneous denial (which may have resulted from a lazy or incompetent attorney), defendant may be presumed to admit even those facts which he could have effectively denied. While courts are not especially eager to punish defendants purely for procedural errors and will often allow them to amend the mistakes, there are times when such "punishment" is in the interests of justice. Such is the case in *Zielinski*. The information as to who was the actual employer of the forklift operator was always at the hands of Philadelphia Piers (D). However, by filing their answer in such a sloppy manner, the statute of limitations for Zielinski (P) to file a complaint against another defendant had already run out. Sustaining such behavior would create a devious manipulation tool to future defendants to hold off from making honest answers until it is too late for the plaintiff to do anything about it. A less obvious reason for granting Zielinski's motion for the instruction is that the correct defendant, Carload Contractors, is represented by the same insurance company as Philadelphia Piers (D) and would have to cover any possible judgment award regardless of which one was the defendant. Thus, the court is not only legal arbiter, but financial planner as well!

A DENIAL SAYS THAT THE ALLEGATIONS ARE NOT TRUE; AN AFFIRMATIVE DEFENSE SAYS THAT EVEN IF THE ALLEGATIONS ARE TRUE, THERE IS NO LIABILITY

Layman v. Southwestern Bell Telephone Co.

(Landowner) v. (Trespassers)

(1977) 554 S.W.2d 477

M E M O R Y   G R A P H I C

Instant Facts

A property owner sued the phone company for trespass after it buried some phone wires under her property.

Black Letter Rule

An easement is an affirmative defense to trespass and as such must be set forth in the answer, or evidence of the easement will not be allowed at trial.

Case Vocabulary

COURT TRIAL: A trial where the judge, rather than a jury, acts as the trier of fact.

EASEMENT: The right of one person to use a portion of another person's land for a limited purpose.

Procedural Basis: Appeal from a judgment after a court trial.

Facts: Layman (P) received 10.3 acres of land in 1956. In 1973, Layman (P) saw some men and equipment digging a trench on her land and destroying trees. Telephone wires were later laid in the trench and covered up. Layman (P) learned that Southwestern Bell Telephone Company ("Bell") (D) had hired Wright Tree Service ("Wright") (D) to install the telephone wires on Layman's (P) property. Layman (P) sued, alleging trespass because the telephone wires had been installed without her consent, and that Bell (D) and Wright (D) continued to enter upon her land to maintain the wires without her consent. Bell (D) answered Layman's (P) complaint with a general denial. At a court trial, the theory of Bell's (D) defense was that it had a right of entry by easement. Bell (D) introduced evidence that a recorded easement had been given by the property's previous owners to Union Electric Company in 1946 and the that the easement had been subsequently assigned to Bell (D). Layman (P) objected to the introduction of the easement on the ground that an easement is an affirmative defense and therefore must be affirmatively pled in the answer. The trial court overruled the objection and allowed the easement to come into evidence.

Issue: Is an easement an affirmative defense to trespass that will be waived if it is not affirmatively pled in the answer?

Decision and Rationale: (Weier) Yes. The state rules of civil procedure [similar to Federal Rule 8(c)] state that certain named affirmative defenses must be pled to a pleading that precedes the complaint, as well as any other matter constituting an avoidance or affirmative defense. A general denial challenges all of the material allegations in the complaint, and a defendant is entitled to prove any fact showing that the plaintiff's cause of action never had any legal existence. An affirmative defense, on the other hand, admits the facts in the complaint, but avers that a defendant still has no legal responsibility for its actions because of some additional element. Such a defense must be set forth in the answer. Here, Bell (D) must prove that it had the right to enter upon Layman's (P) land. Bell(D) must show that despite Layman's (P) rights in the land, Bell (D) had a positive right to enter and disturb Layman's (P) possessory rights. It should also be noted that another form of authority to go upon land, a license, is specifically listed in the rules as an affirmative defense. Thus, Bell's (D) easement should have been pled as an affirmative defense, and since it was not, the easement should not have been allowed into evidence at trial. Reversed and Remanded.

Analysis:

Notice in this case just how important the technical and procedural aspects of pleading became. The rule is that unless an affirmative defense is pled in the answer (to give the plaintiff notice that this defense exists), the defendant will not be able to prove the defense later. Essentially, Bell (D) lost what would have probably been a total defense because its lawyer did not plead it in the answer. As in this case, it is sometimes difficult to tell exactly when a fact is a denial of the plaintiff's claim, or when it rises to the level of an affirmative defense. One rule of thumb is that when the defendant raises a new matter, some matter that is not yet an issue in the case, that this matter should be pled as an affirmative defense. But, in this case, that rule is difficult to apply. Layman (P) claimed that Bell (D) entered onto her land without any claim of right. Bell (D) produced the easement to show that it had the right to enter onto the land. Thus, the easement *did* go to disprove one element of Layman's (P) claim. One might argue that the easement is new since Layman (P) did not know about it. However, the easement existed prior to Layman's (P) purchase of the land and it also was recorded in the county recording office. Thus, the law of real estate says that Layman (P) did have constructive notice of the easement by virtue of its being recorded, and may have had actual notice of the easement, as Layman (P) should have checked the real estate recordings before buying the property. Thus, it is not as obvious as the court claims that Bell's (D) introduction of the easement really introduces something new to the case.

AN ADMISSION IN A PLEADING CAN BE CHANGED TO A DENIAL IN THE COURT'S DISCRETION

Beeck v. Aquaslide 'N' Dive Corp.

(Slide Victim) v. (Alleged Slide Manufacturer)
United States Court of Appeals, Eighth Circuit, 562 F.2d 537 (1977)

M E M O R Y   G R A P H I C

Instant Facts
Defendant admits manufacturing the defective water slide at issue in the case but a year later moves the court to amend the answer to deny manufacture.

Black Letter Rule
A court does not abuse its discretion by allowing an amendment to an answer which initially admitted responsibility for the manufacture of the product at issue but now seeks to deny manufacturing it.

Case Vocabulary

NEGLIGENCE: Tort term for the failure to use such standard of care as a reasonable person would in the same circumstances.
STRICT LIABILITY: Tort doctrine of imposing liability for any adverse consequences of a product or act, even when it was not negligent (applies to inherently dangerous products).

Facts: During a company sponsored gathering, Beeck (P) was severely injured at Kimberly Village while using a water slide he claims was negligently manufactured by Aquaslide (D). Kimberly investigated the accident and soon thereafter sent a notice to Aquaslide (D) informing them that one of their Queen Model slides was involved [a kind term for "implicated"]. Aquaslide (D) forwarded this notice to its insurer and an adjuster came out to investigate the slide and question persons who ordered and assembled the slide. The insurance adjuster, as well as investigators for Kimberly Village, indicated that the slide was definitely manufactured by Aquaslide (D). Beeck (P) filed the personal injury complaint which Aquaslide (D) answered, admitting that it "designed, manufactured, assembled and sold" the slide. About six months after the statute of limitations for Beeck's claim had run out (he was on time, though) and a total of one year after the filing of the complaint and answer, the president and owner of Aquaslide visited the sight of the accident himself. From his inspection, he determined that the slide was not Aquaslide's (D) product and then moved the court for leave to amend the answer to deny the slide's manufacture. The court granted the motion and Beeck (P) appealed. Then the court granted a separate jury trial to decide the issue of manufacture which Beeck (P) lost and Beeck (P) appealed this too.

Issue: Is it an abuse of trial court discretion to allow an amendment to an answer from admitting to denying responsibility for the manufacture of the product at issue?

Decision and Rationale: (Benson, J.) No. A court does not abuse its discretion by allowing an amendment to an answer which initially admitted responsibility for the manufacture of the product at issue but now seeks to deny manufacturing it. There is substantial authority for this decision both in case law and in the Federal Rules. In *Foman v. Davis* the Supreme Court held that, in the absence of bad faith or dilatory motive on the part of the movant, leave to amend is fully within the discretion of the District court. This holding is rooted in FRCP 15(a) which declares that leave to amend should be "freely given when justice so requires." Applying these principles to the case at hand, the trial court did not abuse its discretion by allowing either the amendment or the trial on the issue. The trial court searched the record for evidence of bad faith and rightfully found none. After all, Aquaslide (D) legitimately relied on the findings of separate insurance adjustors until its president made his own belated investigation and arrived at a contrary conclusion. As to Beeck's (P) contention of prejudice because the statute of limitations had already run prior to the motion to amend, it is unfounded. This presumes that the trial court should have known that Beeck (P) would have lost on the issue at trial or at the mini trial on this particular issue. That is an unreasonable expectation. If anything, to prevent the defendant from denying a disputed factual issue would be prejudicial to it more than to Beeck (P). (Aquaslide would be forced into the ludicrous position of arguing that the slide was not manufactured negligently when it did not manufacture the slide at all!) The blame for this gross error should be shared equally. Thus, the district court ruling is affirmed.

Analysis:

The sympathetic reader may be inclined to feel sorry for the poor injured plaintiff who, as a result of the leave to amend, has lost the opportunity to refile his claim against a different defendant because the statute of limitation has run out. The issue of manufacture, however, would have to be resolved by the trier of fact in any case, so Beeck (P) was not really deprived of a fair trial. He was just deprived of a trial on the issue of negligence. This is not necessarily a bad thing because going to trial on all the issues when manufacture was really the essential one would have been a waste of judicial resources. Not to mention, Aquaslide would have been forced to expend much time and money to defend itself against a claim for which it could not have been responsible. While a day in court belongs to everyone who has a legitimate complaint, it should not be afforded at the expense of other parties. In this case, any decision the court would have made would have resulted in gross external injustice. However, as great as the need may be to insure accountability for negligence, the greater injustice must be to hold the wrong party accountable for it. Many states allow a plaintiff to allege a cause of action against fictitiously named defendants (such as "Doe 1") and later to amend the complaint to substitute a true name. If a fictitious defendant had been named in this case, there probably would be no problem.

Moore v. Baker

(Patient) v. (Doctor)

(1993) 989 F.3d 1129

M E M O R Y   G R A P H I C

 Instant Facts

A patient who was disabled after an operation sued the doctor for violation of the informed consent law, and later tried to amend the complaint to include allegations of negligence.

Black Letter Rule

In order to relate back to the time of the original complaint, a proposed amendment must have its basis in the same facts that are alleged in the original complaint.

Case Vocabulary

INFORMED CONSENT: The duty of a doctor to fully warn the patient about all of the risks involved in a surgery and get the patient's consent before performing an operation.

PROFESSIONAL NEGLIGENCE: When a professional, such as a doctor or lawyer, does not perform his or her professional duties with the same amount of care that a reasonable, prudent professional would use in that particular case.

RELATION BACK: When the amendment to a pleading is treated as if it were filed on the same date as the original pleading was filed.

Procedural Basis: Appeal from a denial of a motion to amend a complaint.

Facts: Dr. Baker (D) performed surgery on Judith Moore (P) to remove a blockage of her carotid artery. Baker (D) warned Moore (P) about the surgery and its risks, and Moore (P) signed a consent form. The operation went badly and Moore (P) was permanently and severely disabled. Moore (P) filed her complaint on the last day permitted by the state's statute of limitations, alleging that Baker (D) had violated the state's informed consent law by failing to advise Moore (P) of alternative therapy. Moore (P) later moved to amend her complaint to include allegations of negligence against Baker (D). The district court denied the motion.

Issue: Will the amendment to the complaint relate back to the date of filing the original complaint?

Decision and Rationale: (Morgan) No. The statute of limitations will bar Moore's (P) claim of negligence asserted in her amended complaint unless it can be made to relate back to the time of the original complaint, which was filed just before the statute of limitations was about to run. Rule 15(c) permits an amended pleading to relate back to the date of the original pleading whenever the claim or defense asserted in the amended pleading arose out of the conduct, transaction, or occurrence set forth or attempted to be set forth in the original pleading. Thus, *the question is whether the original complaint gave notice to the defendant of the claim that is now being asserted*. We find that it does not. The original complaint focused on Baker's (D) actions before the surgery, whereas the amendment seeks to focus on his actions during and after the surgery. There is nothing in the original complaint that would put Baker (D) on notice that Moore (P) might claim that he was negligent. In order to recover on her negligence claim, Moore would have to prove completely different facts than would otherwise have been required for the informed consent claim of the original complaint. We conclude that Moore's (P) negligence claim does not arise out of the same conduct, transaction, or occurrence as the claims in the original complaint. Therefore, the proposed new claims are barred by the statute of limitations. Affirmed.

Analysis:

Notice that here and in the next case, the plaintiff is attempting to get the amendment to relate back to the date of the filing of the original pleading in order to beat the statute of limitations. If the statute of limitations had not run, the plaintiff would be able to simply amend the complaint without a problem. Why didn't Moore (P) just file sooner to avoid the whole problem? Sometimes the applicable statute of limitations is very short, and it will start to run before the plaintiff even discovers the problem. Another reason is that some people hesitate to contact a lawyer or don't even realize until too late that they have a legal right to compensation for damages that they've suffered. Even after a lawyer has been contacted, if there is some time until the statute of limitations will run, the lawyer will try to settle the case without filing suit. For example, in a medical malpractice case the attorney will talk directly to the doctor's insurer to try to negotiate a settlement without going to court. The client saves both time and money in court costs and attorney's fees, and the insurance company saves attorney's fees, the uncertainty of a large jury verdict, and avoids getting the reputation as a company that doesn't pay out its claims. Under Rule 15(c)(2), the amendment is supposed to relate back to the original complaint if it seeks to assert a claim arising out of the conduct, transaction, or occurrence set forth in the original complaint. In the present case, it seems that Moore's (P) negligence claim and her informed consent claim both would arise out of the operation. Yet the court requires more – it requires notice of the claim. If notice were so important, then it seems that the rule should provide for it. After all, the doctor has notice that something went terribly wrong with the operation. This may be another case where the judge is taking liberty with the rules to get the result that the court thinks is most fair. (See analysis in *Bonerb* for more on relation back.)

Bonerb v. Richard J. Caron Foundation

(Patient) v. (Rehab Center)
(1994) 159 F.R.D. 16

M E M O R Y   G R A P H I C

Instant Facts

Patient originally sued the Rehab Center for negligent maintenance of its basketball court, and later tried to amend the complaint to include a claim for counseling malpractice.

Black Letter Rule

A claim will relate back if the operational facts set out in the original complaint are sufficient to put the defendant on notice that the amended claim could be brought.

Case Vocabulary

OPERATIONAL FACTS: Facts that, if different or absent, would affect the outcome of the case; facts giving rise to the claim.

Procedural Basis: Motion to amend the complaint.

Facts: Bonerb (P) was a patient in the Richard J. Caron Foundation's ("the Foundation") (D) drug and alcohol rehabilitation facility. Bonerb was injured when he slipped and fell while playing basketball as part of the Foundation's (D) mandatory exercise program. Bonerb (P) claimed that the Foundation (D) negligently maintained that basketball court. A year after the complaint was filed, and after the statute of limitations had run, Bonerb (P) has filed a motion to amend his complaint to include a cause of action for counseling malpractice. The Foundation (D) objects, claiming that the counseling malpractice claim does not relate back to the original pleading and will therefore be barred by the statute of limitations.

Issue: Does the malpractice claim relate back to the original negligence claim?

Decision and Rationale: (Heckman) Yes. Rule 15(a) provides that leave to amend a complaint should be freely granted absent undue prejudice to the other party, undue delay by the moving party, or bad faith. However, amendment to add a time-barred claim would be futile unless it will relate back to the date of the original complaint. A claim will relate back if the operational facts set out in the original complaint are sufficient to put the defendant on notice that the amended claim could be brought. The principle for this is that one who has been given notice of litigation concerning a given transaction or occurrence has been provided with all the protection that statutes of limitation are designed to afford. In this case, the allegations in the original and amended complaints derive from the same operative facts involving injury suffered by Bonerb (P). The original complaint alleged that participation in the exercise program was mandatory and that Bonerb's (P) injury was caused by the Foundation's (D) failure to properly supervise and instruct Bonerb (P). These allegations are sufficient to alert the Foundation (D) to the possibility of a claim based on negligent performance of professional duties. That is all that is required for relation back under Rule 15(c). Motion granted.

Analysis:

Here again the court is concerned with notice to the defendant that the amended claims could have been brought. Why is it that notice is so important? This has to do with the fact that the statute of limitations is involved. A statute of limitations is a harsh incentive for bringing actions in a timely fashion – claims are barred if the statute of limitations has run. The purpose of the statute of limitations is to prevent the burden of litigating stale claims, forcing a defendant to defend long after memories have faded, witnesses have died or disappeared, and evidence has been destroyed. In the case of a proposed amendment, since the case is ongoing anyway, the purpose of preventing a stale claim has been satisfied. However, a defendant still needs to have notice so that he can build a defense. Also, consider the tension between Rule 15(a) [freely granting leave to amend] and Rule 15(c) [relation back only under certain circumstances]. These rules could be seen as inconsistent – one being liberal in granting leave to amend and the other being very stingy in granting leave to amend. Consider whether the timing of the motions will explain their seeming inconsistency. Under Rule 15(a), amendment is usually done very early in the proceeding – before the answer or sometime during discovery. On the other hand, under 15(c), the real problem arises after some discovery has been done, a new claim has been discovered, but the statute of limitations has run. It may be that Rule 15(c) is less favorable to plaintiffs because it is also less favorable to defendants by allowing otherwise time-barred claims to be brought. The court here allowed amendment. This may have been because of the circumstances under which amendment was sought. The amendment to add a professional negligence claim was brought only after Bonerb (P) brought a new attorney onto the case. There might be an element of fairness in allowing the amendment, that the plaintiff should not be punished because the old attorney was not as aggressive in pleading as he or she should have been.

Chapter 7

The discovery process is the stage between pleading and trial where the parties to a suit obtain and preserve information regarding their case. The modern discovery process is a relatively new part of the litigation process and is unique to American law.

Historically, the trial itself was the primary fact-finding part of the litigation process. Any pre-trial fact-finding occurred by parties employing their own investigations without conferring with the opposing party. As a result, parties would often show up at the first day of trial not knowing exactly what legal theory or evidence the opponent would use during the trial.

The modern American discovery process virtually ensures that the trial itself will have no surprises. At the end of the process, both parties will have collected from each other or third parties all or most of the evidence they will need to support their side of the case. Furthermore, each side will have a good idea of exactly how their opponent will present their case. In most cases, the discovery stage lasts much longer than the trial itself. In simple cases, discovery can last weeks. More complicated cases can last years before the trial stage begins.

Modern discovery has four basic purposes. First, parties are compelled to negotiate and confer with one another, so they can obtain information held by the other and agree about how the case should proceed. This is often accomplished by parties sending each other a list of questions, or interrogatories, about facts relevant to the case. In addition, a party may depose, or interview, the other party or other witnesses. Parties may later ask the opposing side to turnover, or produce, relevant documents or other evidence in their possession. A court will intervene only where the parties are unable to agree on a particular discovery request.

Second, discovery also allows parties to resolve or eliminate some, if not all, of the factual disputes presented in the parties' pleadings. Interrogatories, depositions, and requests to produce or admit may uncover information that was disputed in the pleadings, making the trial more efficient or even unnecessary. In some cases, discovery may reveal strengths and weaknesses about a case and force the parties to withdraw or settle a suit.

Third, the discovery process can also dredge up information that may not be directly on point, but may lead to the discovery of information relevant to the case. For example, the plaintiff in a design defect case may request the manufacturer to produce documents about safety testing that may contain information indicating a possible defect. The safety testing documents may or may not actually reveal evidence of a defect, but it's a good place to look for evidence of one.

Finally, discovery preserves evidence that may otherwise not be available at trial. For example, discovery may allow the parties to interview a witness by deposition who is too ill to attend trial. This deposition, as a record of the witness's testimony, can then be used at trial, instead of the witness personally testifying in court.

Unfortunately, discovery may also have a fifth, unintended purpose- to wear down your opponent. Since discovery has evolved to entail a considerable amount of time and expense, a party with more resources can easily harass the opponent through objections to discovery, intrusive discovery requests, or refusals to cooperate. The laws governing discovery have attempted to mitigate the problems by providing protection against requests that are intrusive, over broad, or not complied with. Still, discovery has often degraded into a war of motions, dilatory tactics, and mountains of incomprehensible documents. Recently, the system has responded to the problem by requiring the parties to make initial, required disclosures as the discovery process begins. These required disclosures prevent the parties, to some extent, from delaying the process through objections or delay. However, the bigger the case, the higher the stakes, and the more likely that the parties will abuse the discovery process to overwhelm and intimidate the opponent.

The following cases provide a sketch of how the discovery process operates in terms of the role of the court and the parties. Most of the cases deal with defining the limitations of discovery in the interests of privacy, relevance, efficiency, and privilege.

Chapter 7

I. Scope of Discovery
   A. Determining What is Relevant
      1. Parties have a right to discover any matter, not privileged, which is relevant to the subject matter involved in the pending action. *Federal Rules of Civil Procedure*, Rule 26(b)(1).
      2. A party is entitled to discovery of relevant information that may include evidence admissible at trial and evidence that appears reasonably calculated to lead to the discovery of admissible evidence. *Blank v. Sullivan & Cromwell.*
      3. Evidence is not relevant if it does not relate to a matter pertinent to the decision of the case. *Steffan v. Cheney.*
   B. The Boundaries of Privilege
      1. The attorney-client privilege may extend to communications between the lawyer and all employees of the corporate client, not just corporate managers. *Upjohn Co. v. United States.*

II. Procedures and Methods of Discovery
   A. Meetings and Required Disclosures
      1. Within 90 days after a defendant's appearance and 120 days after service, the judge must hold a scheduling conference to discuss the discovery process and other pretrial matters. *Federal Rules of Civil Procedure,* Rule 16(b).
      2. At least 14 days before this scheduling conference the parties must meet without the judge to discuss the case. *Federal Rules of Civil Procedure,* Rule 26(f).
      3. At this meeting or within 10 days after it, each party must offer the opposing party: calculations of damages, copies of insurance agreements, and the names of witnesses and descriptions of documents relevant to the disputed facts alleged with particularity. *Federal Rules of Civil Procedure,* Rule 26(a)(1).
   B. Procedures for Interrogatories
      1. A party must seek permission from the court to send the opposing party more than 25 questions.

Federal Rules of Civil Procedure, Rule 33.
      2. Interrogatories may only be sent to a party, not non-party witnesses. *Federal Rules of Civil Procedure*, Rule 33.
   C. Procedures for Depositions
      1. A party must obtain the court's permission to obtain more than 10 depositions or to depose a person twice. *Federal Rules of Civil Procedure,* Rule 30(a)(2)(A).
      2. Non-party witnesses may be deposed. *Federal Rules of Civil Procedure*, Rule 30(c).
   D. Examining People and Things
      1. Examining Things
         a. Discovery includes the inspection of land, objects, and documents. *Federal Rules of Civil Procedure*, Rule 34.
         b. "Documents" includes any medium for recording data or information. *Federal Rules of Civil Procedure*, Rule 34.
         c. There is no limit on the number of document requests. *Federal Rules of Civil Procedure*, Rule 34.
         d. Document requests sent to non-party must be done by a subpoena. *Federal Rules of Civil Procedure,* Rule 45(a)(1)(C).
         e. The producing party must produce the documents "as they are kept in the usual course of business or shall organize and label them to correspond with the categories in the request." *Federal Rules of Civil Procedure,* Rule 34(b).
      2. Examining People
         a. A physical or mental examination of a party requires a special application to the court. *Federal Rules of Civil Procedure,* Rule 35.
   E. Requests for Admission
      1. Courts are split on what to do where a party served with a request for admission fails to admit a fact that is central to the case. *Federal Rules of Civil Procedure,* Rule 36.
      2. The failure to admit is considered an admission and the fact is admitted. *Morast v. Auble.*
         a. If a defendant refuses to admit and loses the ensuing trial, the court may award the plaintiff attorney's fees for all the legal fees incurred after the refusal to admit. *Marchand v. Mercy Medical Center.*
      2. Other courts hold that requests for admission do not concern central issues in a case; therefore,

the failure to admit is not tantamount to an admission. *Pickens v. Equitable Life Assurance Society.*

F. Procedures for Ensuring Compliance with Discovery Orders

1. Parties may be subject to a wide range of sanctions for failing to comply with the court's discovery order. *Federal Rules of Civil Procedure*, Rule 37(b).

2. Parties may be subject to more limited sanctions for failing to sign disclosures, discovery requests, and objections or for unjustified requests and refusals that do not violate a court order. *Federal Rules of Civil Procedure,* Rule 26(g).

3. Before filing a motion to compel discovery, the moving party must make a good faith effort to meet and confer with the opposing party in order to avoid compliance through a court order. *Shuffle Master, Inc. v. Progressive Games, Inc.*

III. Discovery and Privacy Issues

A. A judge may enter any order in which justice requires protecting a party or person from annoyance, embarrassment, oppression, or undue burden or expense. *Federal Rules of Civil Procedure,* Rule 26(c).

B. A party seeking a protective order must establish good cause for the order by submitting a particular and specific demonstration of fact. *Stalnaker v. Kmart Corp.*

1. Deceased persons may have a diminished privacy interest. *Long v. American Red Cross.*

2. Protective orders may be issued to protect the confidential tenure files of non-party tenured professors. *Blum v. Schlegel.*

3. Coca-Cola's secret formula was relevant to the case and unprotected by any privilege, but efforts should be made to prevent the trade secret from disclosure to third parties. *Coca-Cola Bottling Co. v. Coca-Cola Co.*

4. A protective order is limited to the protection of trade secrets, but not for information relevant to other lawsuits on the same topic. *Jochims v. Isuzu Motors Ltd.*

5. The Full Faith and Credit Clause does not apply to protective orders. *Baker v. General Motors.*

B. Appeal of Discovery Rulings

1. A district court's non-final ruling cannot be appealed. 28 U.S.C. §1291.

2. A magistrate judge's discovery rulings are appeal-able if clearly erroneous or contrary to law. 28 U.S.C. §636.

3. A magistrate may only hear non-dispositive motions, motions that do not have the potential to end a case. 28 U.S.C. §636(b)(1)(A).

C. A physical or mental examination may be ordered when good cause exists, and when a party's physical or mental condition is in controversy. *Schlagenhauf v. Holder.*

1. Courts are split about whether the person being examined can have his or her attorney present during the examination. *Langefeldt-Haaland v. Saupe Enterprises* (presence of attorney ordered); *Wheat v. Biesecker* (attorney had no right); and *Di Bari v. Incaica Cia Armadora, S.A.* (attorney had no right, but stenographer allowed).

IV. Discovery in an Adversary System

A. The Scope of Privilege

1. A party is not entitled, without a showing of good cause, to obtain copies of an opposing attorney's notes and memoranda acquired from interviews with witnesses. *Hickman v. Taylor.*

2. Employees' accident reports to claims departments are discoverable. *Rakus v.Erie-Lackawanna Railroad.*

3. Reports made, without an attorney's legal expertise, in the regular course of business when insurers were trying to find out about an unusual accident are discoverable. *Spaulding v. Denton.*

4. Work Product of Defense-hired Surveillance Investigators

a. A showing of substantial need and undue hardship is enough to overcome the work product protection for an investigator's videotape, but not his report. *Freiman v. USAIR Group, Inc.*

b. An investigator's surveillance report is discoverable only if the defendant plans to offer it in evidence, but the defense must disclose a reasonable time before trial whether it plans to offer the surveillance in evidence. *Gibson v. National Rail Pass. Corp.*

5. Interrogatories or Deposition Questions that Implicate the Opposing Lawyer's Mental Impressions or Legal Theories.

a. The court may delay an answer to such an interrogatory until after discovery, a pre-trial conference, or other time. *Federal Rules of Civil Procedure*, Rule 33(c).

b. In action between attorneys regarding fee disputes, it is proper to seek by interrogatory a list of documents supporting affirmative defenses, but it is not proper to ask the same question by deposition. *Rifkind v. Good.*

B. Disclosing Expert Information

1. As part of the initial disclosures, a party must reveal information about experts who may testify, the basis of their testimony, and give the opposing party a written report signed by the witnesses containing a complete statement of all opinions expressed and reasons therefor. *Federal Rules of Civil Procedure,* Rule 26(a)(2).

2. A party cannot compel discovery of the opinions or findings of a non-testifying expert hired by the opposing party in preparation of litigation unless there are no other practical means to obtain the facts and opinions contained in that report. *Thompson v. The Haskell Co.*

3. Discovery of an opposing party's non-testifying expert cannot be permitted under the exceptional circumstances exception where the party seeking discovery had an opportunity to examine the subject of the expert's opinion. *Chiquita International Ltd. v. M/V Bolero Reefer.*

4. The law concerning attempts to compel the testimony of the opposing party's non-testifying expert is confusing but is balanced between notions of fairness and four additional considerations:

   a. The need to facilitate the ability of counsel to seek expert opinions without fear of producing information useful to the adversary;

b. The need to prevent a party from benefiting from the other side's effort and expense;

c. Concerns that compelling testimony may decrease the willingness of experts to serve as consultants; and

d. The likelihood of prejudice created from the fact that the opposing party hired the expert but choose not to utilize the expert for their case. Wright et al., *Federal Practice and Procedure*: Civil §2032.

V. Ensuring Compliance and Controlling Abuse of Discovery

A. *Sanctions*: A court abuses its discretion when it imposes severe discovery sanctions on a party whose rights were materially prejudiced by the court's mismanagement of the case. *Chudasama v. Mazada Motor Corp.*

B. *Interlocutory Review of Sanctions*: Appellate review is possible only where the district court certifies the order for interlocutory rule. 28 U.S.C. SS1292(b).

C. *Failure to Disclose a Document*: A case decided for the defendant may be reopened under Rule 60(b)(3) where the defendant denied the existence of a document during discovery but, after the trial's conclusion, the document is subsequently found because it reveals the defendant's fraud, misrepresentation, or other misconduct. *Rozier v. Ford Motor Co.*

Blank v. Sullivan & Cromwell

(Lawyers) v. (Law Firm)
(1976) 16 Fair Empl. Prac. Cas. (BNA) 87

M E M O R Y   G R A P H I C

Instant Facts

Several female attorneys, suing a law firm alleging sexual discrimination in their hiring practices, sought information about the firm's promotion practices.

Black Letter Rule

A party is entitled to discovery of relevant information that may include evidence admissible at trial and evidence which appears reasonably calculated to lead to the discovery of admissible evidence.

Case Vocabulary

AMICUS CURIAE: Literally "friend of the court"; A brief filed not by a party to the action but by a person who has a strong interest in the outcome of the action. Sometimes shortened to "amicus".

INTERROGATORY: A question, among a list of written questions, submitted to an opposing party usually during discovery in a lawsuit.

MAGISTRATE: A judicial officer with limited jurisdiction and authority.

Procedural Basis: Plaintiffs moved for a rehearing and modification of an order denying their request to compel the defendant to answer certain interrogatories.

Facts: Several female attorneys (P) formed a class action against a law firm after they had unsuccessfully applied for associate positions at Sullivan and Cromwell (D). They sued Sullivan and Cromwell (D) alleging sexual discrimination in their hiring practices. During discovery, the plaintiffs sent interrogatories to Sullivan and Cromwell (D). These interrogatories sought information about the firm's practices regarding the promotion of female and male associates to partnerships. These interrogatories asked how many female and male permanent associates were offered partnerships, became partners, and the average length of service before becoming a partner. Sullivan & Cromwell (D) refused to answer these interrogatories, and the female attorneys (P) filed a Rule 37 motion to force the firm to answer the questions. A magistrate, Harold J. Raby, [who imposed a glass ceiling of his own] recommended that Sullivan and Cromwell (D) did not need to respond to these interrogatories because they were not relevant to the female attorneys' (P) case. The court adopted the magistrate's recommendation. The female attorneys (P) then moved for a rehearing and modification of the court order following the magistrate's recommendation.

Issue: Is the requested information so unrelated to the plaintiff's case that the information cannot be said to be relevant within the meaning of a Rule 26?

Decision and Rationale: (Motley) No. We decide to order Sullivan and Cromwell (D) to respond to the interrogatories at issue here. While we reverse the prior ruling, the court emphasizes that the female attorneys' (P) class action is of a narrow class, therefore they cannot represent in this action individuals who have been harmed by the law firm's partner selection criteria. However, the female attorneys (P) are entitled to discovery on the issue of the partner selection criteria. Under Rule 26 of the Federal Rules of Civil Procedure, a party is entitled to discovery of information that "appears reasonably calculated to lead to the discovery of admissible evidence". In addition, since Title VII cases deal with discriminatory hiring practices, both the Supreme Court and the Second Circuit have ruled that an employer's general information on their "labor hierarchy" may illustrate discriminatory hiring practices under Title VII. See *McDonnell Douglas Corp. v. Green*, 411 U.S. 792, 804-805 (1973) and *Kohn v. Royall, Koegel, & Wells*, 496 F.2d 1094, 1101 (1974) [both allowing the admission of evidence regarding the defendant's "labor hierarchy" because it may reflect discriminatory hiring practices]. This court has ruled that the class at issue here in this case "is defined to include all women qualified to hold legal positions at the law firm of Sullivan & Cromwell who have been or would be denied employment because of their sex." Judge Lasker, in *Kohn v. Royall, Koegel, & Wells*, dealt with a similar class and granted discovery for the plaintiffs regarding the firm's partnership advancement practices. Judge Lasker adopted the recommendation of the magistrate who noted that the partnership advancement practices regarding female associates would be highly reflective on the firm's hiring practices. While we acknowledge that there are numerous factors involved in the partnership advancement process, it cannot be said that these practices have no relation or "no probative bearing upon allegations of improper discrimination in hiring associates." Even assuming that Title VII does not prohibit the use of sex as a criterion for partnership advancement, this legal issue does not prevent the inference that evidence of sexual bias at the partnership level may be reflective of a similar pattern in the hiring of associates where Title VII is unquestionably applicable. Sullivan and Cromwell (D) is ordered to answer the interrogatories referred to above.

Analysis:

This opinion deals with interpreting the meaning of Rule 26 of the Federal Rules of Civil Procedure. Rule 26 gives parties broad discretion to discover any material that is relevant to the subject matter of the case. As the opinion points out, the discovery test of the relevancy of evidence is whether the information "appears reasonably calculated to lead to the discovery of admissible evidence." Consequently, parties have room to argue the introduction of evidence which is not only relevant, but also evidence which, while not relevant by itself, may lead to relevant information. Therefore, in this case, the information regarding the firm's partnership promotion practices, while not relevant to the issue of whether the firm discriminated against women in their hiring of associates, may lead to the discovery a pattern of sexual bias in the firm. This sexual bias, if present in the area of partnership promotion, may extend to the hiring of associates. As a result, the partnership promotion practices were deemed relevant because it could lead to the discovery of admissible evidence directly on the point of sexual bias in hiring, which is at issue in this case. Thus, the initial order denying the plaintiff's request to compel the law firm to answer the interrogatories was correct in stating that the partnership information was not relevant to the hiring issue; however, the initial order failed to realize that the partnership information may lead to the discovery of relevant information.

Steffan v. Cheney

(Naval Officer) v. (United States Secretary of Defense)

(1990) 920 F.2d 74

M E M O R Y   G R A P H I C

Instant Facts

A naval officer refused to answer deposition questions about his sexual conduct in his suit challenging an administrative board's recommendation that he be discharged based on his admission that he was a homosexual.

Black Letter Rule

Evidence is not relevant if it does not relate to a matter pertinent to the decision of the case.

Case Vocabulary

CONSTRUCTIVE DISCHARGE: A discharge not necessarily in fact, but by law.

VEL NON: Literally "or not"; or the absence of it. "This case does not hinge on the issue of sexual conduct vel non (or the absence of it)."

Procedural Basis: An appeal of a district court ruling dismissing the plaintiff's cause of action for failure to comply with a discovery order.

Facts: Joseph C. Steffan (P) was a naval officer who resigned from the military in 1987 after an administrative board recommended his discharge after Steffan's (P) admission that he was a homosexual. He was not discharged for any homosexual conduct. In 1988, Steffan (P) filed an action against the government (D), represented by then Secretary of Defense, Dick Cheney, to challenge the constitutionality of the regulations that required the discharge of admitted homosexuals. During the discovery phase, Steffan (P) [who decided to resort to his own "don't ask, don't tell" policy] refused to answer deposition questions regarding whether he engaged in homosexual conduct while in the Navy and asserted his Fifth Amendment privilege against self-incrimination. The district court, after issuing a prior warning, dismissed Steffan's (P) case for failure to comply with the discovery order. Steffan (P) appealed to the appellate court.

Issue: Is evidence relevant if it does not speak to a matter pertinent to the decision of the case?

Decision and R

ationale: (Court) No. The district court acknowledged that "the record is clear that [Steffan] was separated from the naval academy based on his admission that he is a homosexual rather than on any evidence of his conduct". However, the district court found that questions about his homosexual conduct were "highly relevant" because the navy could discharge individuals engaged in homosexual conduct. The district court held that "in seeking reinstatement and award of his diploma, [Steffan] through his claims has placed in issue whether he is qualified for such relief." [Any judicial review of an administrative action, including administrative actions by the military, is confined to "the grounds upon which the record discloses that [the] action was based"]. *SEC v. Chenery Corp.* 318 U.S. 80, 87 (1943). In this case, Steffan (P) is challenging the Navy's administrative action finding him unfit for military service because he stated he was a homosexual. Since this was the basis for his discharge, the issue of whether he engaged in potentially disqualifying conduct is not relevant. Evidence is not relevant if it does not relate to a matter pertinent to the decision of the case. Therefore, the district court erred in finding the issue of homosexual conduct to be relevant in this case. The judgment of the district court is reversed and remanded for further proceedings consistent with this opinion.

Analysis:

This opinion, unlike the previous case, does not hinge on whether the disputed evidence would lead to the discovery of admissible evidence, but rests on whether the disputed evidence is relevant to a fact of consequence in the case. If a person is being sued for employment discrimination, evidence of the employer's propensities for pedophilia would not be relevant. This is because the pedophilia is not a fact of consequence in the case. The important issue is whether the employer discriminated against the plaintiff in the hiring process. Similarly, in this case, Steffan (P) was recommended for discharge for admitting he was a homosexual, not for homosexual conduct. The record clearly stated that his admission was the basis of the government's (D) decision. His admission was a fact of consequence. Therefore, while evidence of homosexual conduct may prove that Steffan (P) was a homosexual, this was not at issue because he was not discharged for such conduct. Homosexual conduct may also mandate a discharge, but the administrative board's decision had nothing to do with an inquiry into such conduct. As a result, his homosexual conduct, if any, was irrelevant to the facts at issue.

Stalnaker v. Kmart Corp.

(Employee) v. (Corporation and Co-Worker)

(1996) 71 Fair Empl. Prac. Cas. (BNA) 705

M E M O R Y   G R A P H I C

Instant Facts

An employee, who was sued by a former co-worker for sexual harassment, sought a protective order preventing the co-worker from deposing four non-party witnesses in order to determine whether they had any romantic conduct or sexually related activities with the co-worker.

Black Letter Rule

A party seeking a protective order must establish good cause for the order by submitting a particular and specific demonstration of fact.

Case Vocabulary

PROBATIVE VALUE: The value of a piece of evidence in terms of proving or disproving a fact.

Procedural Basis: Consideration of a protective order filed by the defendant to prohibit the plaintiff from deposing certain non-party witnesses.

Facts: Stalnaker (P) was an employee of Kmart (D1) corporation. She filed suit against both Kmart (D1) and a fellow employee, Donald Graves (D2), alleging that he created a hostile working environment and sexually harassed her by engaging in inappropriate touching. [Apparently Stalnaker (P) wasn't the only woman whom Graves (D2) tried to work his charms on], so Stalnaker (P) issued depositions for four non-party witnesses who had relationships with Graves (D2). Graves (D2) moved for a protective order protecting these witnesses from discovery, especially regarding any voluntary romantic conduct or any sexually related activities with Graves (D2). Stalnaker (P) opposed Graves' (D2) motion.

Issue: Can the discovery of information potentially embarrassing and annoying to a party or non-party be limited?

Decision and Rationale: (Judge) Yes. While Rule 26 of the *Federal Rules of Civil Procedure* "permits a broad scope of discovery", a court may issue protective orders to either totally prohibit or limit the scope of discovery on certain matters. According to *Federal Rules of Civil Procedure* Rule 26(c), a court has the discretion to issue a protective order upon good cause where "justice requires to protect a party or person from annoyance, embarrassment, oppression, or undue burden or expense" or where the inquiry reaches "into areas that are clearly outside the scope of appropriate discovery". *Caldwell v. Life Ins. Co. of N. Am.*, 165 F.R.D. 633, 637 (D. Kan. 1996). The party seeking a protective order must establish good cause showing "a particular and specific demonstration of fact, as distinguished from stereotyped and conclusory statements." *Gulf Oil Co. v. Bernard*, 452 U.S. 89, 102 n. 16 (1981). In addition, the *Federal Rules of Evidence*, Rule 412, provides that ["[e]vidence offered to prove that any alleged victim has engaged in other sexual behavior" or "to prove the any alleged victim's sexual predisposition" is not admissible in criminal or civil actions involving sexual misconduct]. Rule 412 was designed to protect the victim of sexual abuse against invasion of privacy, embarrassment, and stereotyping that can be associated with the public disclosure of intimate sexual practices and encourages victims to initiate and participate in legal proceedings against the their abusers. However, Rule 412 does not apply in this case because Graves (D2) is not the victim of sexual misconduct. Nevertheless, Graves (D2) has shown good cause to limit discovery of voluntary romances and sexual activities of the non-party witnesses to the extent they have no relationship to the allegations against Kmart (D1). Graves (D2) asserts that the witnesses were not involved in the creation of the hostile work environment, the sexual harassment claim, or otherwise wronged Stalnaker (P). In addition, none of these witnesses have complained about sexual harassment. Furthermore, inquiry into such activities will also constitute an invasion of their privacy. Stalnaker (P) argues that these witnesses may possess relevant information about sexual harassment at Kmart (D1); however, she would agree to a protective order preventing disclosure to any third party. Consequently, discovery is limited to inquiry about "any voluntary romantic or sexual activities with Mr. Graves (D2) to the extent they show any conduct on his part to encourage, solicit, or influence any employee of Graves (D2) to engage or continue in such activities." The parties will utilize such discovery only for the purposes of litigation and the information will not be disclosed any third parties. The court grants in part and overrules in part the Graves' (D2) motion for a protective order.

Analysis:

This opinion shows that, while certain issues may have relevance, their value is outweighed by the embarrassment, annoyance, or invasion of privacy the disclosure may cause. This limit exists for two reasons. First, we want to encourage witnesses and parties to be able to bring actions or participate in actions without fear of embarrassment, annoyance, oppression, or invasion of privacy. A witness in a sexual harassment claim may not be willing to testify if her entire sexual history is brought out in the open. Therefore, the protective order under Rule 26 encourages the introduction of evidence by attempting to eliminate relevant, but tangential issues that may be sensitive to the witness or party. Second, protective orders also prevent the opposing party from harassing the other side. Since discovery is a powerful tool, courts have realized a need to prevent overzealous attorneys from intimidating their opponents by seeking to disclose every conceivably relevant issue. In this case, the opinion struck a balance by closing the door on the voluntary sexual activities between the defendant and the witnesses, but leaving open those sexual activities that may have some bearing on the sexual harassment claim. Furthermore, the opinion prohibited the disclosure outside of the litigation. This ruling protected the privacy interests of the witnesses and the defendant, while not shutting out any highly relevant evidence. In addition, it took the extra precaution of limiting disclosure to the proceedings and not to any third party.

Schlagenhauf v. Holder

(Bus Driver) v. (District Court Judge)
379 U.S. 104 (1964)

M E M O R Y   G R A P H I C

Instant Facts

Robert Schlagenhauf (D), a defendant who allegedly caused a collision while driving a bus, objected to an order requiring him to submit to a number of physical and mental examinations.

Black Letter Rule

A physical or mental examination may be ordered when good cause exists, and when a party's physical or mental condition is in controversy,

Case Vocabulary

AFFIANT: A party who makes an affidavit or undergoes a deposition or examination for discovery purposes.
VIS-A-VIS: Literally "face to face"; in relation to another person or thing.
WRIT OF MANDAMUS: An order from a superior jurisdiction commanding an action by an inferior tribunal.

Procedural Basis: Writ of certiorari considering denial of writ of mandamus seeking to set aside order to undergo mental and physical examinations.

Facts: An action was brought in district court seeking damages arising from the collision of a tractor-trailer, owned by Contract Carriers (D) and National Lead Company (D), and a Greyhound (D) bus. Robert Schlagenhauf (D) was the driver of the bus at the time of the accident. Numerous cross-claims were filed among the defendants. First, Greyhound (D) cross-claimed against Contract Carriers (D) and National Lead Company (D) for negligence in the operation of the tractor-trailer. Then Contract Carriers (D) and National Lead Company (D) petitioned the District Court for an order directing Schlagenhauf (D) to submit to four mental and/or physical examinations, alleging that the mental and physical condition of Schlagenhauf (D) was "in controversy." National Lead (D) then cross-claimed against Greyhound (D) and Schlagenhauf (D) for damage to its trailer. The District Court ordered Schlagenhauf (D) to submit to nine examinations [Although only four were requested!]. Schlagenhauf (D) applied for a writ of mandamus in the Court of Appeals against Holder (P), the district court judge, seeking to have the examination order set aside. The Court of Appeals denied mandamus, and the Supreme Court granted certiorari.

Issue: (1) May Rule 35 examinations be made on any party, including a defendant to a lawsuit? (2) Do physical or mental examinations require an affirmative showing that the condition sought to be examined is genuinely in controversy and that good cause exists for ordering each examination?

Decision and Rationale: (Goldberg, J.) (1) Yes. Rule 35 physical or mental examinations may be made on any party to a lawsuit. On its face, Rule 35 applies to all parties, which would normally include a defendant. However, Schlagenhauf (D) contends that the application of the Rule to him would constitute an unconstitutional invasion of his privacy. Previous cases have held that plaintiffs must submit to physical examinations, as noted in *Sibbach v. Wilson* [plaintiff in negligence action who asserted physical injury as basis for recovery must submit to physical examinations]. However, the application of Rule 35 discovery only to plaintiffs would deprive a plaintiff from obtaining redress for his injuries. Thus, Rule 35 examinations may be conducted on defendants as well. It makes no difference that Schlagenhauf (D) was not a defendant to any cross-claims at the time of the examination order. Schlagenhauf (D) was always a party to the lawsuit, and Rule 35 allows examinations to be conducted on any parties. Insistence that the party seeking examination must file claims against all parties sought to be examined would unnecessarily proliferate cross-claims and would defeat the liberal application of the Federal Rules. (2) Yes. In order to force a physical or mental examination pursuant to Rule 35, the party seeking the discovery must make an affirmative showing that the condition sought to be examined is genuinely in controversy and that good cause exists for ordering each examination. Contract Carriers (D) and National Lead Company (D) failed to make the required showing. The "in controversy" and "good cause" requirements may be automatically satisfied in some situations, such as when a party places his mental or physical condition at issue by asserting the condition either in support of or in defense of a claim. However, Schlagenhauf (D) did not place his conditions at issue. Rather, his condition was sought to be placed in issue by other parties. Nothing in the pleadings affords a basis for the belief that Schlagenhauf (D) was suffering a neurological illness warranting mental examinations. In fact the only allegation made in support of examinations was the contention that Schlagenhauf's (D) eyes and vision were impaired. Thus, if Contract Carriers (D) and National Lead Company (D) had sought to obtain only a visual examination, they might have made the required showing. Nevertheless, there is an insufficient

Schlagenhauf v. Holder (Continued)

basis for finding that Schlagenhauf's (D) health was in controversy so as to require the battery of tests ordered by the District Court. The judgment of the Court of Appeals denying the writ of mandamus is vacated and remanded.

Concurrence and Dissent: (Black, J.) In a lawsuit based on a traffic collision, the mental or physical health of the drivers is of the highest relevance. Allegations showed that the tractor-trailer was in plain sight of Schlagenhauf (D), and there was allegedly ample time to avoid the collision. Schlagenhauf's (D) failure to avoid the collision certainly calls into question his mental or physical health, sufficient to put the question "in controversy."

Dissent: (Douglas, J.) Until today, neither Congress nor this Court has required every party to a lawsuit to surrender his right to keep his person inviolate. Of course, *Sibbach* held that a plaintiff must choose between his privacy and his recovery, but this has not been extended to non-voluntary defendants. Furthermore, plaintiff's doctors would naturally go on a fishing expedition in search of anything that would tend to prove that the defendant was unfit to perform certain acts. Any doctor for a fee can discover something wrong with a patient, and a defendant would be at the doctor's mercy, subject to numerous invasive procedures. The doctor's report may either overawe or confuse the jury and prevent a fair trial. Although Congress and this Court can authorize a rule allowing examinations of defendants, such a rule must be carefully drawn in order to prevent blackmail.

Analysis:

This case demonstrates the complexities in dealing with orders that could force a party to surrender his right to bodily autonomy. Even the most basic notions of privacy argue against anyone being forced to submit to an unpleasant, invasive physical or mental examination. These concerns are easily overcome in some cases, such as when a plaintiff puts his conditions at issue in a suit for bodily injuries. However, the case at hand is very different. Schlagenhauf (D) did nothing, other than colliding with a tractor-trailer, which should force him to submit to doctors' examinations. He did not choose to be a party to the lawsuit, and he never defended on the grounds of being mentally or physically fit. In this light, it seems somewhat unfair that Schlagenhauf (D) could be forced to submit to examinations, as the court held in the first part of the opinion. And as Douglas' dissent notes, doctors examining defendants would likely run numerous tests and strive to find anything wrong with a defendant. Contrast this to examinations of plaintiffs, where the defendants do not want to discover any injuries and where the examining physician would not, therefore, subject the plaintiff to similarly invasive treatment. On the other hand, it would present a great hardship to the plaintiff if Schlagenhauf (D) was physically or mentally impaired, and if these impairments caused the accident, if the plaintiff could not independently examine Schlagenhauf (D). Other defendants could suffer similar hardships, being forced to pay for injuries caused by a bus driver who may not have had the physical or mental capacity to drive the vehicle. In this light, the Court's holding in the first part of the opinion makes some sense. Furthermore, the second part of the opinion dismisses any worries about privacy invasions by requiring strict showings by the party seeking the examinations. If a party's condition is not actually in controversy, and if good cause does not exist, then the party's physical autonomy should not be sacrificed. Black's dissent seems to suggest that the mere fact that Schlagenhauf's (D) condition was relevant should satisfy these Rule 35 requirements. However, the majority takes a more cautious, and more sensible, approach.

Hickman v. Taylor

(Representative of Decedent) v. (Tugboat Owners)
329 U.S. 495 (1947)

M E M O R Y   G R A P H I C

Instant Facts

Hickman (P) sought to obtain copies of written statements and descriptions of oral interviews acquired by Fortenbaugh, the opposing counsel.

Black Letter Rule

A party is not entitled, without a showing of good cause, to obtain copies of an opposing attorney's notes and memoranda acquired from interviews with witnesses.

Case Vocabulary

WORK PRODUCT: Materials prepared and statements obtained in preparation of a lawsuit for trial.

Procedural Basis: Writ of certiorari reviewing reversal of order for contempt and order to respond to discovery request.

Facts: This suit arises out of the mysterious sinking of the tugboat "J.M. Taylor," an accident which killed five crew members. Hickman (P), the representative of a deceased crew member, brought suit against the tug owners and the Baltimore & Ohio Railroad, whose cars were being tugged at the time of the accident. The tug owners were represented by Fortenbaugh, an attorney who privately interviewed the survivors and other witnesses prior to the institution of the lawsuit. Hickman (P) submitted interrogatories to the tug owners seeking the production of written statements and other memoranda acquired by Fortenbaugh, as well as detailed accounts of any oral statements made to Fortenbaugh. The tug owners, through Fortenbaugh, declined to answer some interrogatories or produce the documents, claiming that the requests called for privileged matter and constituted an attempt to obtain Fortenbaugh's private files. The District Court, sitting en banc, held that the requested matters were not privileged. Accordingly, the Court ordered the tug owners and Fortenbaugh to answer the interrogatories and produce the documents.

Issue: Are all of an attorney's files related to an incident open to discovery by the opposing party?

Decision and Rationale: (Murphy, J.) No. Even with liberal discovery rules, not all of an attorney's files are open to discovery by the opposing party. Rule 26(b) provides necessary limitations on discovery when the inquiry encroaches upon the recognized domains of privilege. In the case at hand, the memoranda, statements and mental impressions in issue and in Fortenbaugh's possession fall outside the scope of the attorney-client privilege. Nevertheless, they are not freely discoverable by Hickman (P). Hickman (P) had an adequate opportunity to seek discovery of the same basic facts, through inquiries and production requests propounded on Fortenbaugh and on the parties to the lawsuit, and through direct interviews with the witnesses themselves. Hickman (P) showed no compelling reason why he should be entitled to the information in Fortenbaugh's files, and he did not indicate that the denial of such production would unduly prejudice the preparation of his case. An attorney's work product may be discovered where relevant and non-privileged facts remain hidden in an attorney's file and where production of those facts is essential to the preparation of the opposing party's case. However, the policy against invading the privacy of an attorney's work product is so essential that the party seeking the production must bear the burden. Hickman (P) failed to make the requisite showing. Further, as to the oral statements made by witnesses to Fortenbaugh, no showing of necessity is sufficient to justify production. It should be noted that procedural irregularities existed in Hickman's (P) discovery requests, although these irregularities are insufficient in themselves to deny production. Hickman was incorrect in propounding Rule 33 interrogatories and seeking the production of documents, and Rule 34 could not have been used to obtain documents from a non-party such as Fortenbaugh. Hickman (P) should have taken Fortenbaugh's deposition under Rule 26 and attempted to force Fortenbaugh to produce the materials by way of a subpoena duces tecum in accordance with Rule 45. Regardless, Hickman (P) would have had no unqualified right to discovery of Fortenbaugh's private files. Affirmed.

Concurrence: (Jackson, J.) Hickman (P) has no right to receive a detailed account of any oral statements made to Fortenbaugh. In arguing that such discovery is permissible, Hickman (P) erroneously maintains that the Rules were created to do away with the "battle of wits" between counsel, effectively placing all counsel on equal footing. Discovery was never intended to diminish the adversarial nature of common law trials. Requiring an attorney to recount every

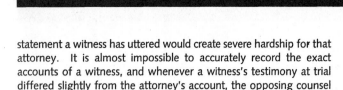

statement a witness has uttered would create severe hardship for that attorney. It is almost impossible to accurately record the exact accounts of a witness, and whenever a witness's testimony at trial differed slightly from the attorney's account, the opposing counsel could impeach the witness using the attorney's account. Moreover, in the situation at hand, Hickman (P) gives no reason why he cannot interview the witnesses himself. In addition, Hickman (P) has no right to use the signed statements acquired by Fortenbaugh in the case at hand. Production of such statements is governed by Rule 34, which requires the party seeking discovery to show good cause. Hickman (P) did not make such an application here. Thus, I agree to the affirmance of the Court of Appeals.

Analysis:

This case analyzes the extent to which a party has access to an opposing attorney's "work product," information obtained by counsel in preparation for trial. The literal language of the initial Federal Rules allowed virtually unlimited access to the discovery of such information. However, this case creates an exception to the unlimited access approach, requiring the party to show a need for obtaining an opposing counsel's work product. And as the opinion states, this need must be substantial. A party who can question the same witnesses, and obtain much the same information in other ways, has no right to reap the benefits of another party's or another attorney's hard work. This holding is sensible, since an alternative view would discourage attorneys from actively investigating the issues. Notice that this work-product exemption applies only to materials prepared in anticipation of trial. Thus, statements of witnesses taken in the ordinary course of business, outside of a pending litigation, remain open to discovery. Following this famous case, several states nevertheless continued to allow unlimited access to work products. In response, Federal Rule 26(b)(3) was promulgated, which now codifies the work-product exception to discovery. It is important to note the differences between the work-product exception and the exception for privileged matter. Privileged information is completely immune from discovery, whereas an attorney's work product is discoverable on a showing of substantial need. In line with the *Hickman* case, Rule 26(b)(3) affords the highest protection to mental impressions of an attorney, although even these may be obtained upon a sufficient showing.

Thompson v. The Haskell Co.

(Employee) v. (Employer)

(1994) 65 F. Empl. Prac. Cas. (BNA) 1088

M E M O R Y   G R A P H I C

Instant Facts

An employee suing an employer for sexual harassment seeks to protect a psychologist's report regarding the employee.

Black Letter Rule

A party cannot compel discovery of the opinions or findings of a non-testifying expert hired by the opposing party in preparation of litigation unless there are no other practical means to obtain the facts and opinions contained in that report.

Case Vocabulary

ARGUENDO: For the sake of argument.

Procedural Basis: A motion to shield from discovery documents relating to a psychological report.

Facts: Thompson (P) sued her employer, Haskell Company (D1), and her supervisor, Zona (D2), for sexual harassment after being fired on June 5, 1992. Thompson (P) alleged she was fired because she did not "acquiesce to the advances of [Zona]" and her termination reduced her "to a severely depressed emotional state". Thompson (P) hired an attorney who retained a psychologist, Dr. Lucas, to perform a diagnostic review and personality profile of Thompson (P). On June 15, 1992, Dr. Lucas prepared a psychological report. Haskell Company (D1) sought discovery of Dr. Lucas' report. On May 13, 1994, Thompson (P) filed a motion for a protective order to prevent Haskell Company (D1) from discovering the report. Thompson (P) argued that Rules 26(b)(3)-(4) of the Federal Rules of Civil Procedure protected the psychological report from discovery. Rule 26(b)(4)(B) provides that opinions and facts held by a non-testifying expert who has been retained or employed by the opposing party in anticipation of litigation cannot be discovered except as provided for under Rule 35(b) or if there is a showing of exceptional circumstances where it is impracticable for the party seeking discovery to obtain the same facts or opinions on the same subject by other means.

Issue: Can a party compel discovery of the opinions or findings of a non-testifying expert's report, retained by the opposing party in preparation of litigation, where there are no other means to obtain the facts and opinions contained in that report?

Decision and Rationale: (Snyder) Yes. Dr. Lucas' psychological report was made just ten days after her termination from the Haskell Company (D1) and is "highly probative" of Thompson's (P) depressed emotional state. This report is still discoverable under Rule 26(b)(4) because the information contained in the report cannot be obtained by other means. Under Rule 26(b)(4), an opposing party's expert's opinions or facts retained in anticipation of litigation cannot be discovered unless exceptional circumstances make it impracticable for the party to discover the facts or opinions by other means. In this case, there exists no other report regarding Thompson's (P) state of mind made during the weeks immediately following her termination. In a similar case, the court found that "independent examinations. . . pursuant to Rule 35 would not contain equivalent information". *Dixon v. Capellini*, 88 F.R.D. 1,3 (M.D. Pa. 1980). Therefore, with these facts, there exist exceptional circumstances allowing for the disclosure of Dr. Lucas' report. The motion is denied.

Analysis:

This opinion illustrates another balance between protecting work product and the need to discover relevant information. Experts hired by parties are not independent experts, but are usually sought and retained by attorneys to prove certain facts or opinions that are essential to their case. Thus, these experts are acting, in a sense, as an agent of the attorney. Therefore, it would seem logical to expand the work product rule to these experts because often they are a mere extension of the attorney's legal theory regarding the case. This is especially true if the attorney decides the expert should not testify. This usually happens where the expert has made a finding or opinion that is unfavorable to the attorney's case. The disclosure in court of such an adverse finding could destroy the case of the party who employed that expert. However, if an expert retained by the party does not testify at trial, the opposing party does not have the opportunity to discover relevant information from the expert. The opposing party may find the information that this expert holds by other means, but a difficult situation arises if the information sought is simply not discoverable by other means. Thus, in such a situation, Rule 26(b)(4) opens the door and makes the expert's work product discoverable. It does so in the interest of fairness to the opposing party. For example, if one party retains the only available expert on the matter, the opposing party would be out of luck if the retaining party decides not to put the expert on the stand. Also, a situation may arise where one party hires an expert who had an opportunity to examine evidence that is later lost or destroyed before the opposing party has a chance to examine it. The case at hand is just such an example. Thompson's (P) emotional state was at issue in the case, and the severe emotional impact of her harassment and firing was evident at the time of her firing but not two years later. Since there were no other examinations of Thompson (P), the court realized that the opposing party had no other way of ascertaining her emotional state. Thus, discovery was granted.

THE EXCEPTIONAL CIRCUMSTANCES EXCEPTION DOES NOT APPLY WHERE THE PARTY SEEKING DISCOVERY HAD AN OPPORTUNITY TO EXAMINE THE SUBJECT OF THE EXPERT'S OPINION

Chiquita International Ltd. v. M/V Bolero Reefer

(Shipper) v. (Carrier)
(1994) 1994 U.S. Dist. LEXIS 5820

M E M O R Y   G R A P H I C

Instant Facts

A carrier, sued by a shipper for loss and damage to a cargo of bananas, sought to depose and discover any documents held by a non-testifying expert witness hired by the shipper to examine the cause of the damage.

Black Letter Rule

Discovery of an opposing party's non-testifying expert cannot be permitted under the exceptional circumstances exception where the party seeking discovery had an opportunity to examine the subject of the expert's opinion.

Case Vocabulary

FORECLOSED: Stopped or prevented from doing something.

Procedural Basis: A hearing on a motion to prohibit a discovery request.

Facts: Chiquita International (P) employed International Reefer Services (D) ("International Reefer") to ship 154,660 boxes of bananas from Ecuador to Germany aboard the ship Bolero Reefer. However, Chiquita International (P) alleged that the ship's loading cranes and side-ports were defective and allowed only 111,660 boxes to be loaded. The remaining 43,000 boxes of bananas were left in Ecuador and were thrown away. The cargo that did arrive in Germany arrived in poor condition. Shortly after the ship arrived in Germany, Chiquita International (P) hired Joseph Winer, a marine surveyor, to inspect the ship and the loading gear. After the inspection, Chiquita International (P) [went bananas] and sued International Reefer (D). International Reefer (D) sought to depose Mr. Winer as a witness and compelled disclosure of documents he prepared in connection to his inspection. Chiquita objected on the ground that Mr. Winer is a non-testifying expert who is protected from discovery under Rule 26(b)(4)(B). International Reefer (D) claims that Mr. Winer is not an expert but a witness, and, even if he is an expert, discovery is warranted because he was the only surveyor who inspected the vessel shortly after it arrived in Germany.

Issue: Can discovery of an opposing party's non-testifying expert be permitted under the exceptional circumstances exception where the party seeking discovery had an opportunity to examine the subject of the expert's opinion?

Decision and Rationale: (Francis) No. A non-testifying expert is immune from discovery except where there are exceptional circumstances that make it impossible or highly impracticable for the party seeking the information to obtain facts or opinions on the same subject by other means. Mr. Winer qualifies as a non-testifying expert because he is a marine engineer who was hired by Chiquita (P) to inspect the vessel in question, and Chiquita (P) is not calling him as a witness. He is an expert because he used his technical knowledge and background to offer an opinion to Chiquita (P). While Mr. Winer learned "facts" firsthand and not from the observations of others, this does not disqualify him as an expert. The Federal Rules understand that experts may base their opinions on their own firsthand investigations. In addition, the Federal Rules specifically protect the "facts known or opinions held" by a non-testifying expert. Therefore, distinguishing between fact and opinion is irrelevant and Rule 26(b)(4)(B) applies. International Reefer (D) further argues that discovery still should be permitted under the exceptional circumstances clause of Rule 26(b)(4)(B). However, this argument has no merit since International Reefer (D) had an opportunity to send its own expert to the scene when the ship arrived in Germany. There were no forces beyond its control that would have prevented such an inspection by International Reefer (D). Furthermore, during the three week trip to Germany, International Reefer's (D) employees had the exclusive opportunity to inspect the ship and its cranes. Therefore, permitting discovery where International Reefer (D) failed to hire, in a timely manner, its own marine surveyor to investigate "would permit the exceptional circumstances exception to swallow Rule 26(b)(4)(B)". Finally, International Reefer (D) argues that if it is prohibited from deposing Mr. Winer, it should be given access to the documents he prepared as result of its inspection. However, Rule 26(b)(4)(B) also applies to document discovery of non-testifying experts as well. Nevertheless, International Reefer (D) may discover information provided to Mr. Winer by others provided that this information does not reflect Mr. Winer's own observations or opinions. International Reefer's (D) request to take the deposition of Joseph Winer is denied and Chiquita (P) will produce information from Mr. Winer's files that do not contain his observations and opinions or are otherwise privileged.

Analysis:

This opinion illustrates the scope of the protections provided for in Rule 26(b)(4)(B) in two different ways. The first relates to the scope of the exceptional circumstances clause of the Rule. The exceptional circumstances clause was included in Rule 26(b)(4)(B) in fairness to parties who were unable to examine a critical piece of evidence before it is lost, destroyed, or altered. However, this exception carries with it a notion of responsibility on the party seeking discovery. If the party seeking discovery did in fact have an opportunity to inspect the evidence in question and failed to do so in a timely fashion, then permitting the exception to apply would effectively allow the party seeking discovery to obtain expert testimony and information [on the dime of the opposing party]. Thus, if the party seeking discovery passed on an opportunity that it could have used to examine the evidence in question, it cannot later conveniently benefit by stealing the fruits of the opposing party's efforts. In this case, the opinion takes special note that International Reefer, in fact, had the exclusive opportunity to examine the ship and its loading cranes. Unlike the previous case, where the evidence at issue was a person's state of mind and beyond the control of the opposing party, International Reefer (D) had full access to the evidence in question. Thus, International Reefer (D) was not allowed to freeload on the efforts of the opposing party. The second relates to the scope of information protected under Rule 26(b)(4)(B). A non-testifying expert's opinions and facts personally observed are protected under the rule. However, if the expert uses the observations or opinions of others in his or her own investigation, these observations or opinions of others are not protected by the rule and may be discovered. This is justified by the fact that a party who hires an expert is hiring that expert for his or her expertise and specialized judgment, not the judgment or observations of others. Furthermore, the opinions and observations of third parties should not be subject to protection because these third parties are not agents of the party, unlike the hired expert. Still, this creates the need and difficulty of going through the information produced by an expert and filtering out the personal observations and opinions of the expert. This could be a problem because often the personal observations and opinions of the expert are closely intertwined with the observations and opinions of third parties. In the case at hand, the court ordered Chiquita (P) to disclose documents that did not include the personal observations and opinions of their hired expert. Presumably, this means that a document that contains *any* reference to the expert's finding or opinions may not be disclosed. This may be somewhat underinclusive since some documents may only partially contain the opinion or findings of the expert; however, it does err on the side of caution to avoid violating Rule 26(b)(4)(B).

Chudasama v. Mazda Motor Corp.

(Automobile Owner) v. (Auto Manufacturer)

(1997) F.3d 1355

M E M O R Y   G R A P H I C

 Instant Facts

An automobile manufacturer sought to reverse sanctions issued against it for failing to comply with a burdensome discovery order for a suit involving a couple injured in a car built by the automobile manufacturer.

Black Letter Rule

A court abuses its discretion when it imposes severe discovery sanctions on a party whose rights were materially prejudiced by the court's mismanagement of the case.

Case Vocabulary

DEFAULT JUDGMENT: A judgment entered against a party where the party failed to comply with a discovery order, plead, defend against the claim, or appear at trial.

DILATORY: Causing delay.

DRACONIAN: Severe, harsh.

EXCORIATE: To denounce harshly

INTERLOCUTORY APPEAL: An appeal of an issue before the trial court has made a final ruling on the whole case.

VACATUR: Literally "let it be vacated"; an order or ruling which sets aside a proceeding.

Procedural Basis: An interlocutory appeal of a district court decision imposing sanctions for violations of discovery orders.

Facts: On May 16, 1991, Mr. and Mrs. Chudasama (P) purchased a used 1989 Mazda (D) MPV minivan from a Columbus, Georgia used car dealer. On October 15, 1991 Mrs. Chudasama was injured when Mr. Chudasama (P) lost control of the minivan and collided with a utility pole. Mrs. Chudasama (P) suffered a broken pelvis and facial bones, spent $13,000.00 in medical bills, and lost $5,000.00 in wages. The minivan, worth approximately $11,000.00, was damaged beyond repair. The Chudasamas (P) filed suit against Mazda (D) based on two alleged defects in the minivan: 1) Defective brakes, and 2) A defective side structure that was "unreasonably likely to crush and deform into the passenger compartment." The Chudasamas' (P) complaint raised four counts of strict liability, breach of implied warranty, negligent design and manufacture, and fraud. Each count sought compensatory damages including pain and suffering, loss of consortium, medical bills, and the loss of the vehicle. In addition, on three counts, the Chudasamas (P) also sought punitive damages. Over the next two years, the parties engaged in a long and drawn out discovery process in which the Chudasamas (P) overwhelmed Mazda (D) with discovery requests asking "for almost every tangible piece of information or property possessed." During these two years, the district court never moved to resolve any of the parties' discovery disputes and allowed the Chudasamas (P) to continue to overwhelm Mazda (D) with broad discovery requests [of biblical proportions]. The Chudasamas' (P) interrogatories served on July 28, 1993 contained 121 numbered requests with extensive sub parts effectively expanding the number of interrogatories to 635. "The production requests all but asked for every document Mazda had ever had in its possession and then some." Among other things, the Chudasamas (P) sought detailed information about Mazda's (D) marketing practices and strategies worldwide, manufacturing and design process, and safety testing. Between September 1993 and November 1994, Mazda (D) objected ten different times to virtually every discovery request on some grounds that bordered on being frivolous, but many grounds which raised bona fide questions of law. In every case, the district court refused to rule on Mazda's (D) objections. During this period, Mazda (D) asked the court to rule on its objections 25 times, but the district court refused to rule. Mazda (D) also filed a motion to dismiss the count of fraud for failure to plead fraud with particularity. Mazda (D) attacked this fraud count because much of the Chudasamas' (P) discovery requests focused on this issue. Again, the district court refused to rule on the dismissal of the fraud count. Mazda (D) also sought a protective order. Mazda (D) claimed that the information requested regarding the marketing, developing, and design of the minivan and other vehicles was confidential and would harm Mazda (D) if competitors or other potential plaintiffs gained access to it. In protest of the court's inaction, Mazda (D) withheld a "substantial amount of information" which it later admitted was properly discoverable. Three different discovery conferences were held, and the court refused to respond to Mazda's (D) objections to the Chudasamas' (P) discovery requests. In each of these conferences, the Chudasamas (P) made additional requests for discovery. In December 1994, the district court granted the Chudasamas' (P) motion compelling Mazda (D) to give more complete responses to their discovery requests. The court entered a compel order admonishing Mazda (D) and ordered compliance within 15 days or risk the entrance of a default judgment against them. Overwhelmed by the broad and vague discovery requests, Mazda (D) "made a near-Herculean effort to comply", but was unable to meet a 5 o'clock deadline. The Chudasamas (P) filed a motion for sanctions the same day. In June 1995, the court issued its opinion and granted the Chudasamas' (P) motion for sanctions. The court struck down Mazda's (D) answer and entered a default judgment against Mazda (D) on all claims, granted costs and attorney fees to the Chudasamas (P), and left only damages as an issue to be tried on the merits. It also vacated Mazda's (D) protective order. Mazda (D) now seeks an interlocutory appeal of the order for sanctions and the entrance of the default judgment.

Issue: Does a court abuse its discretion when it imposes severe sanctions on a party whose rights are materially prejudiced by the court's mismanagement of the case?

Decision and Rationale: (Tjoflat) Yes. Our jurisdiction in this case is proper because the district court certified this appeal. While the court did not distinguish between the two rules, it imposed sanctions based on Rule 37(b)(2) and 26(g). [Rule 37 allows a court to impose sanctions "as are just" against a party that has violated a discovery order.] While courts enjoy substantial discretion in deciding when and how to impose sanctions, the review of an order striking the defendant's pleadings "should be particularly scrupulous" because this extreme sanction does not give the defendant an opportunity to be heard on the merits. The validity of the sanctions order depends on the validity of the earlier compel order. Orders compelling discovery are reviewed under the same abuse of discretion standard. Therefore we must determine whether the compel order itself was an abuse of discretion. The court's failure to address Mazda's (D) motion to dismiss the fraud claim and Mazda's (D) repeated requests to limit discovery indicate an abuse of discretion. First, the failure to rule on important pretrial motions before beginning discovery can be an abuse of discretion. Issues regarding the legal sufficiency of a claim should be resolved before discovery begins in order to narrow discovery to the relevant issues and to reduce unnecessary costs to the parties and the court. In this case, even a casual review of the Chudasamas' (P) complaint reveals a questionable fraud count. Without the fraud count, the scope of discovery would have been much more limited. As a result, Mazda (D) faced "significant uncertainty" in certifying the completeness and appropriateness of its responses. Second, while the Federal Rules are designed to minimize the need for a court to intervene in discovery matters, a court must resolve objections raising discovery disputes. The filtering out of broad and vague discovery requests also saves cost to the parties and the court and results in a more efficient discovery process. Our review indicates that Mazda (D) asserted a number of "good faith objections based on persuasive grounds", and we are disturbed that the court failed to rule on them. Therefore, the court's failure to rule on both issues "strongly suggests" that the order to compel discovery was an abuse of the court's discretion. As a result, we find that the court's sanctions were an abuse of discretion as well, especially considering that the reversal of the protective order exposed Mazda's (D) sensitive information to its commercial competitors. "The sanctions were so unduly severe under the circumstances as to constitute a clear abuse of discretion". In addition, the district court also based its decision to order sanctions on Rule 26(g). [This rule requires that discovery-related filings are "made for a proper purpose, and does not impose undue burdens on the opposing party in light of the circumstances of the case."] If a court finds such a violation, it must impose "an appropriate sanction". However, the appropriateness of the sanction is within the court's discretion. While the record does reveal that Mazda (D) may have abused some discovery procedures and engaged in delay tactics, this kind of conduct is not enough to support the severe sanctions imposed in this case. First, much of Mazda's (D) failure to comply was due to the court's failure to make rulings on its objections. Second, in order to assess an appropriate sanction under Rule 26(g)(3), the court must "analyze the needs of the case". As noted earlier, the court did not do this. As a result, while sanctions may have been appropriate, they were far too excessive and an abuse of discretion. We vacate the district court's order to compel discovery and the order granting the Chudasamas' (P) motion for sanctions and remand the case to the district court what the instruction that it be reassigned to a different district judge for further proceedings consistent with this ruling.

Analysis:

This opinion is not so much illustrative of how a court may issue discovery sanctions as it is about what a court's role should be in managing discovery. The laws governing the discovery process place discovery in the hands of the parties. A court will only intervene where the parties disagree as to how to proceed. However, once a party approaches the court by filing a motion regarding discovery disputes, the court is expected to rule on that matter. Furthermore, the opinion also illustrates the logical connection between pleadings and the discovery process. The pleadings determine the appropriate scope of discovery. If a pleading validly asserts a claim of a product defect, then information about the product's design should be discoverable. However, if the pleading also validly alleges fraud alongside the product defect, then the scope of discovery would not be limited to information regarding product design. Therefore, it is logical for the court and the parties to first determine the legal sufficiency of the pleadings before entering the discovery stage. Should aspects of the pleadings be thrown out or narrowed, then, accordingly, the scope of discovery would be truncated as well. As the opinion points out, a court has fairly broad discretion in determining the appropriate sanctions for a non-complying party. These sanctions may include: the exclusion of the undisclosed information from the entire trial, awarding the cost of seeking the order to the party seeking discovery, establishing the disputed fact as true, prohibit the non-complying party from supporting a claim or defense, striking the pleadings, dismissal of the case, or entering a default judgment against a non-complying defendant. In this case, the court issued a sanction that was the most severe possible - the entrance of a default judgment, in addition to other sanctions. Note, however, that Mazda (D) admitted that it did not comply with some of the Chudasamas' (P) valid discovery requests. The opinion acknowledges this but concludes that Mazda's (D) actions, given the court's unwillingness to address its concerns, did not merit such severe sanctions. This suggests that the sanction issued should bear some proportionality to the discovery violation. Sanctions against Mazda (D) may have been warranted, but withholding relevant information and using dilatory tactics was not enough misconduct to merit a default judgment. In a footnote, the opinion suggests that a sanction against Mazda imposing the costs of attorney's fees would not have been an abuse of discretion.

Chapter 8

Litigation does not always end in a jury verdict. Disputes between parties may be resolved in within the judicial system, or outside that system, all without a trial. With courts facing caseloads that threaten the efficient operation of the judicial system, alternatives to trial are a must. Moreover, the resources and time expended on litigation often drives parties to seek other avenues to settle their dispute.

Lawsuits are begun when a party files a complaint. The filing of a complaint requires the defendant to respond after being served. If the defendant fails to do so within the time allotted, the plaintiff may seek a default judgment; as the name implies, the plaintiff is then declared "winner" by default. Conversely, a defendant who has answered a complaint, but has not otherwise heard from the plaintiff, may petition a court to order an involuntary dismissal of the case.

Assuming the parties pursue the litigation and the case is not disposed of by the court, the parties may try and resolve their dispute without resorting to trial. The oldest and most common method of resolution without adjudication is settlement. Generally speaking, settlements are contracts where the plaintiff agrees to either not file a lawsuit or drop one already filed. In return, the defendant offers the plaintiff money or some other consideration. Settlements usually do not require any action by the court, but sometimes, parties petition the court to approve the settlement in order to give it the effect of law. Courts have differing rules as to what they will and will not order as part of a settlement. In order to deal with burdensome caseloads courts are given the power to force parties to negotiate a settlement, but courts may not force parties to reach a settlement.

Another alternative to trial is arbitration. Arbitration is an extra-judicial proceeding conducted by private parties. Parties often contract to have their disputes submitted to arbitration. A party is usually restricted from filing a suit in court to settle a dispute that the party previously agreed to submit to arbitration. Indeed, absent some compelling circumstance, courts will require a party to submit their dispute to arbitration if that is what the party contracted for. Although conducted as private proceedings, arbitration decisions are generally enforced by courts, and treated as *res judicata* between the parties.

These alternatives notwithstanding, simply because a case survives default judgment and is not otherwise resolved by the parties, does not mean that the case will go to trial. Prior to trial, either party may move for summary judgment. Summary judgment is an adjudication of the case without trial. Courts grant summary judgment when either the plaintiff has no provable case or defendant lacks a defense on the merits.

If a case survives summary judgment and is set for trial, the court will order the parties to attend a pre-trial conference. The purpose of the conference is to identify and narrow the issues to be litigated. Once the conference is completed, the court issues an order which frames the issues to be litigated, supplanting the pleadings. Soon after, the trial begins.

Chapter 8

NOTE: THE PURPOSE OF THIS OUTLINE IS TO ORGANIZE THE CASES SO THAT ONE CAN QUICKLY UNDERSTAND THE RELEVANCE OF EACH CASE TO THE COURSE. NO ATTEMPT IS MADE IN THIS OVERVIEW TO ADDRESS EVERY CONCEPT THAT MUST BE STUDIED. BE SURE TO READ THE ENTIRE CASEBOOK AND/OR OTHER MATERIALS TO GAIN A FULL UNDERSTANDING OF ALL CONCEPTS.

I. The Pressure to Choose Adjudication or an Alternative
  A. Default and Default Judgments
    1. The threat of a default judgment is designed to compel the defendant to respond to the action.
      a. A court may enter a default against a party who has failed to plead or otherwise defend. *Fed.R.Civ.P. 55.*
    2. Regardless of any absence of a defense on the merits, a default judgment may not be entered if the defendant has not received notice satisfying the Due Process Clause. *Peralta v. Heights Medical Center.*
      a. A defendant against whom a default judgment has been entered can often reopen the case if he failed to receive notice. *Fed.R.Civ.P. 60.*
  B. Failure to Prosecute: Involuntary Dismissal
    1. Defendants may move to dismiss a case on the grounds that the plaintiff has failed to pursue the lawsuit. *Fed.R.Civ.P. 41(b).*
      a. Judges are often given discretion in determining when a plaintiff has "abandoned" his law suit.
    2. Some states set timetables for determining when a case should be dismissed for failure to prosecute. *Cal.C.Civ.P. §583.310.*
  C. Voluntary Dismissal
    1. Plaintiffs are permitted to dismiss a law suit if all the parties agree. *Fed.R.Civ.P. 41(a).*
      a. Voluntary dismissal does not bar a later refiling.
    2. The plaintiff may unilaterally dismiss the suit at any time before the defendant has answered. *Fed.R.Civ.P. 41(a)(1).*
      a. After the defendant has answered, voluntary dismissal may be granted at the discretion of the court. *Fed.R.Civ.P. 41(a)(2).*

II. Avoiding Adjudication
  A. Negotiation and Settlement
    1. Although settlements are cheaper and faster than litigation, there remains a debate as to whether they are better.
      a. While some argue that settlement is better because the outcome is not an "all or nothing" basis, others contend that settlement leaves both parties less than satisfied and is most advantageous to those with greater bargaining power.
    2. Contracting to Dismiss
      a. Most settlements consist of a contract where the plaintiff, in return for some benefit (usually money), agrees not to bring a lawsuit or drop one already filed.
      b. Typically, settlements do not need the approval of the court.
        (1) But settlements in class action cases do need court approval. *Fed.R.Civ.P. 23(e).*
      c. Litigants may also have their settlements embodied in a judgment of dismissal.
        (1) As judgments, these settlements have the force of law, and a breach constitutes a violation of court order.
          (a) These judgments must be given Full Faith and Credit by state and federal courts. *U.S. Constitution Art. IV, Sec. 1; 28 U.S.C. §1738.*
        (2) Federal courts must give full faith and credit to state judgments approving settlements, even if the settlement releases claims within the exclusive jurisdiction of the federal courts. *Matsushita Elec. Industrial Co. v. Epstein.*
    3. Contracting for Confidentiality
      a. As a part of the settlement, defendants often demand that the plaintiff keep the details of the litigation, and its underlying facts, confidential.
      b. Even when entered as part of a court order, confidentiality agreements may not prevent another litigant from using the rules of discovery to depose the party who agreed to keep silent. *Kalinauskas v. Wong.*
      c. A court may withhold full faith and credit from a court order that embodies a confidentiality agreement if the order effects control of litigation in other states *Baker v. General Motors.*
    4. Contracting for a Judgment
      a. Settlement sometimes occurs after the court renders its judgment; as part of these settlements, parties may try to stipulate to a reversal of the judgment.
      b. Some states allow parties to stipulate to a reversal. *Neary v. University of California.*
      c. In federal court, parties are generally not entitled to demand a stipulated reversal. *U.S. Bancorp Mortgage Co. v. Bonner Mall.*
  B. Guided Negotiation: Mediation and Coercion
    1. In an effort to reduce caseloads, some courts, particularly those in the federal system, have taken a proactive approach in guiding parties to a resolution.
      a. Judges often act as mediators, attempting to bring the two sides to some agreement.
    2. Courts have the power to manage litigation by estab-

lishing time limits, encouraging settlement, and scheduling conferences. *Fed.R.Civ.P. 16.*

   a. Federal courts are also required to develop alternative dispute resolution programs. *28 U.S.C. 651 et seq.*

   b. Courts have the power to order parties to attend settlement conferences, and may impose severe sanctions for a failure to do so. *Fed.R.Civ.P. 16(c)*; *Lockhart v. Patel.*

C. Contracting for Arbitration

   1. As a means of avoiding litigation, parties may contract for their disputes to be submitted for arbitration.

   a. Under the Federal Arbitration Act, federal courts are permitted to enforce arbitration agreements, and are restricted from hearing cases where parties have agreed to submit to arbitration. *9 U.S.C. §§2 et seq.*

   2. Possibilities of Aribtration

   a. Arbitration may be conducted according to any set of procedural rules the contracting parties agree to; judicial review of those procedures is severely limited. *Ferguson v. Writers Guild of America, West.*

   3. Limits of Arbitration

   a. Some issues are of such vital interest to the public (e.g., divorce, child custody, etc.) that courts will not enforce agreements to arbitrate them. *Faherty v. Faherty.*

   b. A party to an arbitration agreement may avoid arbitration by objecting to the agreement on contractual grounds such as fraud, unconscionability, and duress among others. *Engalla v. Permanente Medical Group, Inc..*

III. Curtailed Adjudication: Summary Judgment

A. When the record shows that there is no genuine issue as to any material fact a moving party is entitled to judgments as a matter of law. *Fed.R.Civ.P. 56(c).*

   1. Courts decide summary judgment motions based on affidavits, depositions, transcripts, and other documents.

   2. There is no testimony and no jury.

B. Burden of Persuasion in a Motion for Summary Judgment

   1. A party moving for summary judgment must either show that the opposing party cannot prevail at trial, or show the plaintiff has failed to supply sufficient evidence establishing a genuine issue of material fact. *Adickes v. S.H. Kress & Co.; Celotex Corp. v. Catrett.*

   2. After the moving party has met his burden, the party opposing the motion for summary judgment must provide evidence showing that a reasonable jury could find in its favor. *Visser v. Packer Engineering.*

IV. Judicial Management of Litigation

A. Managing Litigation

   1. In an effort to streamline the judicial process, courts often set deadlines for making motions, completing discovery, attending conferences, and going to trial. *Fed.R.Civ.P. 16.*

   2. Failure to abide by these deadlines carries with it severe consequences, including – but not limited to – dismissal of the case. *Sanders v. Union Pacific Railroad.*

B. Managing Litigation Bound for Trial: The Pretrial Order

   1. Before trial, the parties attend a pre-trial conference presided over by the judge, at which the issueds to be litigated are determined, the witnesses are identified, and the parties' theories are set forth. *Fed.R.Civ.P. 16.*

   2. The pre-trial order that results from the conference supplants the pleadings and becomes a sort of "agenda" for the trial.

   a. The court has wide discretion to allow parties during trial to amend the pre-trial order, and allow the introduction of evidence not contained in the order. *McKey v. Fairburn.*

THE DUE PROCESS CLAUSE IMPOSES LIMITS ON A COURT'S ABILITY TO ENTER
DEFAULT JUDGMENTS AGAINST DEFENDANTS WHO HAVE NOT RECEIVED
ADEQUATE NOTICE

Peralta v. Heights Medical Center

(Guarantor) v. (Hospital)
485 U.S. 80 (1988)

M E M O R Y   G R A P H I C

 ## Instant Facts

The guarantor of hospital debt sought to set aside a default judgment on the grounds that service was a nullity under state law due to delay; but the state court – in spite of the defective service – required the guarantor to show he had a meritorious defense before the it would set aside the judgment.

Black Letter Rule

The fact that a defendant suffers no harm from a default judgment does not alter the rule holding that a default judgment entered without notice or service to the defendant violates the Due Process Clause of the Fourteenth Amendment.

Case Vocabulary

BILL OF REVIEW: A procedure used to start a suit to set aside a previous final judgment.
WRIT OF ATTACHMENT: An order to seize property in satisfaction of a debt or judgment.

Procedural Basis: Appeal to the United States Supreme Court from the decision of the Texas Court of Appeals affirming summary judgment.

Facts: In 1982, Heights Medical Center (Heights) (D) initiated a law suit against Mr. Peralta (P), the guarantor of a hospital debt of $5600. Peralta (P) was personally served 90 days after the summons was issued, a delay which nullified the service of process under state law. Peralta failed to answer and a default judgment was entered against him. The judgment was abstracted and recorded, clouding his title to real property that was eventually sold to satisfy the judgment. In 1984, Peralta (P) began a bill of review proceeding in the Texas courts to set aside the judgment on the grounds that service was defective, and as a result the judgment and subsequent sale were void. Heights (D) filed a motion for summary judgment asserting that Peralta (P) was required to show that he had a meritorious defense to the action in which judgment was entered. The defective service notwithstanding, the Texas courts agreed with Heights (D) and granted summary judgment. The court reasoned that without a meritorious defense, the same judgment would have been entered on retrial, and thus Peralta (P) suffered no harm.

Issue: May a default judgment be sustained against a defendant who has not been properly served or notified on the ground that the defendant was not harmed because he had no defense to the action?

Decision and Rationale: (White, J.) No. Where a person has been deprived of property in a manner inconsistent with due process, it is no answer to say that due process would have led to the same result because he had no defense on the merits. We have held that for a proceeding to be accorded preclusion, due process requires notice reasonably calculated, under the circumstances, to apprise parties of the action and afford them the opportunity to be heard. Yet, the Texas courts held that Peralta (P) was required to show that he had a meritorious defense, apparently, on the ground that the same judgment would be entered against him on retrial, and hence, he suffered no harm. This reasoning is untenable. Had Peralta (P) been notified, he might have impleaded the original debtor, worked out a settlement, or paid the debt. This judgment carried with it serious consequences including a lien encumbering Peralta's (P) property and the property's eventual sale below market value, all without notice. Here, we assume that the judgment entered against Peralta (P) and its ensuing consequences occurred without notice. Therefore, we hold that the holding of the Texas courts violated the Due Process Clause of the Fourteenth Amendment. Reversed.

Analysis:

This case demonstrates that rather than enter a default judgment, courts prefer to see the parties engage on the merits of the dispute. The Court here holds, as it had in previous cases, that due process requires a defendant to be notified of a proceeding against him before he may be deprived of property. The ease with which the case is disposed relies on the assumption that Peralta (P) received no actual notice. This assumption is based on a legal fiction. Although actual notice was given, Texas law nullified any service of process not effectuated within 90 days of its issuance. Had the court assumed that Peralta (P) received actual—although invalid—service, the outcome of the case may have been different. Would it really be unfair to require a person who has been given actual notice of a suit to prove he had a meritorious defense? Maybe not, especially considering that the Due Process Clause does not require a defendant to receive actual notice, it only requires that notice be reasonably calculated to reach him.

FEDERAL COURTS ARE REQUIRED TO GIVE FULL FAITH AND CREDIT TO STATE COURT JUDGMENTS APPROVING SETTLEMENTS, EVEN IF THEY RELEASE A CLAIM WITHIN THE EXCLUSIVE JURISDICTION OF FEDERAL COURTS

Matsushita Elec. Industrial Co. v. Epstein

(Acquiring Corporation) v. (Shareholders of Acquired Corporation)

516 U.S. 367 (1996)

M E M O R Y   G R A P H I C

Instant Facts

Although a state court approved a settlement whereby the class-action plaintiffs agreed to release all present and future state and federal claims, the federal appeals court—before which the class-plaintiff's federal securities claim was pending—held that a state court-approved settlement cannot release those claims within the exclusive jurisdiction of federal courts.

Black Letter Rule

Federal courts must give full faith and credit to state court judgments approving settlements that release claims within the exclusive jurisdiction of federal courts.

Case Vocabulary

CHANCERY COURT: Court of equity. In Delaware the Chancery Court hears all cases arising under corporate law.

Procedural Basis: Appeal to the United States Supreme Court, challenging the decision of the Ninth Circuit Court of Appeals which refused give full faith and credit to a state court-approved settlement.

Facts: The shareholders of MCA (P), an entertainment company acquired by Matsushita (D), brought two sets of class-action suits against Matsushita (D). The first set were federal actions arising under the federal securities laws. The second, filed in Delaware Chancery Court, alleged violations of state fiduciary responsibilities. While the federal cases were on appeal before the Ninth Circuit, the parties to the state action entered into a settlement releasing all claims—state and federal—arising out of the Matsushita-MCA acquisition. The Delaware court approved of the settlement, and entered a judgment incorporating its terms. Matsushita (D) then asserted that the Delaware judgment was a bar to the federal actions before the Ninth Circuit. The Ninth Circuit disagreed, holding that Delaware's approval of the settlement could not preclude litigation of claims within the sole jurisdiction of federal courts.

Issue: May a federal court withhold full faith and credit from a state-court judgment approving a class-action settlement simply because the settlement releases claims within the exclusive jurisdiction of the federal courts?

Decision and Rationale: (Thomas, J.) No. Pursuant to 28 U.S.C. §1738 (the federal statute requiring courts to give state judgments full faith and credit) a federal court must give the judgment the same effect that it would have in the courts of the State in which it was rendered. This act directs federal courts to treat state court judgments with the same respect the judgment would receive in the courts of the rendering state. An examination of Delaware law indicates that these federal claims would be barred in Delaware. In providing for exclusive jurisdiction over federal securities laws, Congress did not impliedly repeal §1738. Thus, pursuant to §1738, the judgment must be given full faith and credit. The shareholders (P) additionally claim that the settlement proceedings should not be accorded full faith and credit because the judgment did not satisfy due process due to inadequate class representation. We first note that the Delaware Chancery Court held that the class was adequately represented. Without determining the accuracy of this finding, we do not address the due process issue because it is outside the scope of the issue presented. Reversed and remanded.

Concurrence and Dissent: (Ginsburg, J.) Under §1738, a state court judgment is not entitled to full faith and credit unless the requirements of the Due Process Clause are satisfied. As the shareholders (P) point out, adequate representation is one of those very requirements. Because the lower court decided the case on other grounds, the due process inquiry remains open for consideration.

Analysis:

The issue in this case arises out of the conflict created by the mandate of the Full Faith and Credit Act, which requires federal courts to give state court judgments the same preclusive effect those judgments would have within the state, and the grant of exclusive subject matter jurisdiction to federal courts over federal securities claims. Matsushita argued before the Court of Appeals that the Full Faith and Credit Act barred the pending claim. The question raised was: how could a state court judgment bar federal claims that the state court had no authority to hear? The Court of Appeals thought the state court could not. The Supreme Court disagreed. It held that Congress did not intend to repeal the Full Faith and Credit Act by granting federal courts exclusive jurisdiction over certain claims. Aside from the preclusion issue, the shareholders alternatively argued that this particular judgment should not be given full faith and credit because the Delaware court failed to abide by due process. Recall *Pennoyer v. Neff* where the court held that judgments not satisfying the Due Process Clause must not be accorded full faith and credit. In any event, the Court suggests—but does not hold—that the Delaware court had decided the issue; and even if it had not, the Court notes the due process issue was not properly before it. Curiously, on remand the Ninth Circuit held that this opinion held that due process was satisfied.

Kalinauskas v. Wong

(Fired Employee) v. (Casino)
151 F.R.D. 363 (D. Nev. 1993)

M E M O R Y   G R A P H I C

Instant Facts

A casino being sued for sexual discrimination by a former employee sought to avoid the deposition of another former employee with whom the casino had previously settled a sexual discrimination suit.

Black Letter Rule

In order to avoid repetitive discovery, courts may modify protective orders or settlement agreements to allow for the discovery of facts otherwise held confidential under the agreement.

Case Vocabulary

PROTECTIVE ORDER: An order issued for the protection of a party, usually as a limit on discovery.

Procedural Basis: Decision by the Federal District Court denying a Motion for a Protective Order.

Facts: Ms. Lin T. Kalinauskas (P), a former employee of Caesar's Palace (D), sued the casino for sexual discrimination. As part of discovery, Kalinauskas (P) sought to depose Donna Thomas, another former employee who had settled a sexual discrimination suit with Caesar's (D). The settlement, which the court had sealed upon stipulation by the parties, provided that Thomas was not to discuss any aspect of her employment at Caesar's (D). Ceaser's (D) sought a Protective Order to prevent Thomas' deposition. The District Court denied the motion.

Issue: Does a settlement agreement, entered into by private litigants, prevent the future discovery of materials or testimony held confidential by the agreement?

Decision and Rationale: (Johnston, M.J.) No. Courts are permitted to modify settlement agreements to place private litigants in a position they would otherwise reach only after a repetition of another's discovery; such modification can be denied only where it prejudices substantial rights of the opposing party, and the prejudice outweighs the benefits of the modification. This case presents a direct conflict between the policies behind the liberal discovery rules and the interest in protecting the secrecy of settlements. To allow full discovery of sealed agreements would discourage such settlements in the future. Because these settlements resolve disputes quickly—serving both public and private interests—they deserve court protection. On the other hand, to prohibit any discovery would condone buying the silence of a witness and would lead to repetitive and wasteful discovery. In the case at hand, Caesar's (D) has not demonstrated any potential injury or prejudice which could arise from allowing the deposition. We also reject Caesar's (D) contention that Kalinauskas (P) must intervene in the Thomas case and seek modification of the order. First, requiring intervention would be wasteful since no live controversy exists in which Kalinauskas (P) can intervene. Moreover, the confidentiality agreement itself provides that a court may order the disclosure of information. The argument that Kalinauskas (P) must show a compelling need to obtain discovery only applies to the specific terms of the settlement, not to the factual circumstances surrounding the case. Accordingly, this court will allow the deposition of Ms. Thomas, but such deposition may not disclose the substantive terms of the agreement. The penalties imposed upon Ms. Thomas by the agreement are inapplicable to the deposition. Motion granted in part and denied in part.

Analysis:

The holding in this case is based primarily on public policy. In this case the District Court holds that the ability of private litigants to enter into confidential settlement agreements must yield to the policies supporting broad discovery whenever the two come into conflict. The opinion recognizes the importance of confidential settlements in an era where courts seek to encourage alternatives to litigation. Nevertheless, the court thought that, in general, the benefits of allowing discovery outweigh the need to encourage settlements. The court, however, does recognize an exception whenever discovery would prejudice the opposing party and that injury would outweigh the benefits of discovery. But because Caesar's (D) failed to demonstrate any prejudice, the court does not state what kind of prejudice is necessary to prevent the discovery. Because many defendants extract these confidentiality agreements for the purpose of avoiding litigation, it is difficult to see how such a showing of prejudice could be made. The holding here prevents future litigants from obtaining one of the major benefits sought from confidential agreements, the ability to avoid future litigation.

PERMITTING PARTIES TO LITIGATION TO STIPULATE A REVERSAL OF A JUDGMENT
TO EFFECTUATE A SETTLEMENT PROMOTES SETTLEMENTS AND PROVIDES FAIRNESS
TO THE PARTIES

Neary v. University of California

(Cattle Rancher) v. (University)
3 Cal. 4th 273 (1992)

M E M O R Y   G R A P H I C

Instant Facts

After the trial court awarded a plaintiff in a libel suit $7 million and while appeals were pending, the parties to the litigation entered into a settlement providing dismissal of the appeals with prejudice, and that the Court of Appeals would vacate the trial court's judgment.

Black Letter Rule

Parties to litigation should presumptively be entitled to a stipulated reversal of a judgment to effectuate settlement.

Facts: George Neary (P) obtained a jury verdict of $7 million in a libel action brought against the University of California (D) and others. The University (D) published a report that asserted that Neary's ranch management practices caused the illness and death of many of Neary's cattle. While an appeal and cross-appeal were pending, the parties entered into a settlement awarding Neary $3 million. The settlement provided that the appeals would be dismissed with prejudice and that the Court of Appeal would vacate the trail court's judgment and remand the case for dismissal with prejudice. Pursuant to this agreement, the parties filed a joint application with the Court of Appeal asking for a reversal. The application was denied.

Issue: May parties to litigation request the reversal of a judgment in order to effectuate their settlement?

Decision and Rationale: (Baxter, J.) Yes. The parties should be entitled to a stipulated reversal to effectuate settlement absent a showing of extraordinary circumstances that warrant an exception to the rule. Although settlement is most efficient at earlier stages of litigation, it benefits do not cease once a judgment is entered. If settlement on appeal is prohibited, the appeal must be heard and decided. If the judgment is reversed and retrial is allowed, considerable expense and resources will be consumed. Fairness also requires that considerable weight be given to the parties' interests. Courts exist for litigants, not vice versa. This case provides a prime example of why the parties should be accommodated. Apart from the substantial costs the parties will incur on appeal and possible retrial, the parties will suffer psychological burdens. These parties spent over twelve years in litigation that was expensive and time consuming, as well as emotionally wrenching and destructively distracting. Refusing to reverse the judgment will frustrate the parties desire to end a 13-year-old dispute. The Court of Appeal's opinion that stipulated reversal undermines the judicial process is based on the faulty premise that litigation is a search for legal truth, and not the disposition of a dispute. Courts resolve real disputes between real people, we do not resolve abstract legal issues. Although public policy may defeat the presumption in favor of stipulated reversal, that policy must be specific, demonstrable, well established, and compelling. No such public interest is present here. Because collateral estoppel is not an issue in this case we do not address the contention that stipulated reversal should be denied whenever a judgment might give rise to collateral estoppel in a future action. Reversed and remanded.

Dissent: (Kennard, J.) Courts are not merely a dispute resolution service. Courts are a part of our government and their function is to administer the laws of this state. Because judgments are an act of government, their annulment must be reconciled with public as well as private interests. Appellate courts should examine the parties' reasons for seeking the stipulated reversal and determine whether the judgment has value for third parties. The ability to dictate an appellate court's actions is subject to abuse; and therefore, courts should ask whether the act is itself proper.

Analysis:

The California Supreme Court's opinion in this case provides one side of a highly debated and controversial subject—the ability of private litigants to vacate judgments by consent. The opinion demonstrates the increasing role courts play in encouraging parties to settle. The California Supreme Court holds that litigants are entitled to a strong presumption in favor of allowing stipulated reversals; and only a compelling public interest will overcome this presumption. The Court reasons that affording litigants this power will encourage settlements at later stages of litigation. The Court dismisses the notion that stipulated reversals discourage early settlement, the stage at which settlement produces most of its benefits. The Court also viewed the issue as one of respect for the litigants' autonomy. In the Court's opinion, fairness demands that the wishes of the litigants be respected, and that courts should not force parties into further litigation. As applied to the facts, the Court thought that 13 years of litigation was sufficient to grant the parties relief. The Court's reasons for permitting stipulated reversals are valid if one assumes, as the Court did here, that the role of the judiciary is simply to provide litigants with a forum for the settlement of disputes. This assumption is questionable. Courts also play a role in shaping the law. Allowing litigants to vacate judgments at will, in one sense, allows litigants to reverse settled law. Simply put, the California Court views the judiciary's role in settling disputes as paramount to its role in administering and interpreting the law. This in turn, could lead to an erosion in the integrity of courts.

U.S. Bancorp Mortgage Co. v. Bonner Mall

(Mortgagee) v. (Mortgagor)
513 U.S. 18 (1994)

M E M O R Y   G R A P H I C

Instant Facts

While their bankruptcy case was pending before the Supreme Court, a mortgagor and mortgagee settled their dispute, thus mooting the case and leading the mortgagor to request a vacatur of the Court of Appeals' judgment.

Black Letter Rule

Mootness by reason of settlement does not justify vacatur of a judgment under review.

Case Vocabulary

REORGANIZATION PLAN: Under Chapter 11 of the Bankruptcy Code, a debtor's plan to pay creditors and reorganize a corporation must be filed with and approved by the Bankruptcy Court.
VACATUR: The act of annulling or setting aside.

Procedural Basis: Appeal to the United States Supreme Court, requesting a vacatur of the Court of Appeals judgment in a bankruptcy case.

Facts: In order to avoid a foreclosure sale, Bonner Mall (Debtor) filed a petition for Bankruptcy; pursuant to Chapter 11 of the Bankruptcy Code, Bonner (Debtor) filed a reorganization plan. Bancorp (Creditor) challenged a portion of the plan. The case worked its way through the federal court system, with Bancorp (Creditor) losing on appeal. While the case was pending before the Supreme Court, the parties consented to a revised reorganization plan, which was approved by the Bankruptcy Court. The settlement mooted the case before the Supreme Court, but Bancorp (Creditor) sought a vacatur of the Court of Appeals judgment. Bonner (Debtor) opposed the motion.

Issue: Should federal appellate courts vacate civil judgments of subordinate courts in cases that are settled after appeal is filed or certiorari sought?

Decision and Rationale: (Scalia, J.) No. Mootness by reason of settlement does not justify vacatur of a judgment under review. Judicial precedents are valuable to the legal community and are not merely the property of private litigants. To allow a party to vacate a judgment would – quite apart from any consideration of fairness to the parties – disturb the orderly function of the federal judicial system. Although permitting vacatur facilitates settlement after the judgment, it deters settlement at an earlier stage. If an unfavorable outcome can be undone, parties are given an incentive to refuse settlement and gamble with the judgment of a court. Moreover, settlement produces most of its efficiencies at earlier stages of litigation. Although mootness by settlement does not justify vacatur, there may exist some exceptional circumstances where vacatur is appropriate. But the fact that the parties settle for vacatur is not one of these exceptional circumstances. The motion to vacate is denied. The case is dismissed as moot.

Analysis:

The Court here takes the position opposite that taken by the California Supreme Court in *Neary v. University of California* [litigants in a libel suit seek to have the judgment reversed as part of their settlement]. The opinion here may be better reasoned than that of the *Neary* court, for Justice Scalia's opinion recognizes the benefits of both sides of the issue. The opinion notes that permitting vacatur on demand is both fair to the parties and encourages settlement in later stages of litigation. Justice Scalia believed, however, that the countervailing arguments – judicial integrity and the need to encourage early settlement – support a presumption against stipulated vacatur, leaving open the possibility obtaining a stipulated vacatur only in "exceptional circumstances." The court simply makes a value judgment in favor of "court autonomy." The Court rejects any notion that litigants "own" a judgment. The opinion notes that courts play a role beyond that of settling disputes, judicial precedents are vital to the public interest. (But, there was no precedent in *Neary*.) According to Justice Scalia, allowing parties to vacate judgments serves no public interest and disturbs the orderly operation of the judicial system.

Lockhart v. Patel

(Injured Patient) v. (Doctor)
115 F.R.D. 44 (E.D. Ky. 1987)

M E M O R Y   G R A P H I C

Instant Facts

An insurance company was declared in default in a medical malpractice suit because, by sending a claims adjuster to a pre-trial settlement conference, the insurer was held to have ignored the judge's order to send a representative with authority to negotiate.

Black Letter Rule

Federal courts have the authority to order attendance of attorneys, parties, and insurers at settlement conferences and to impose sanctions for disregarding the court's orders.

Procedural Basis: After imposing sanctions on a party for its failure to appear at a settlement conference, the Federal District Court discussed its authority to hold such conferences.

Facts: Lockhart (P), a minor plaintiff [he was under age -- he didn't work in a mine], sued his doctor, Patel (D), for malpractice as a result of losing sight in one eye. Following a summary jury trial where Lockhart (P) was awarded $200,000 and after several pretrial and settlement conferences, the court directed the defense attorney to attend a settlement conference and that he bring with him a representative of the Patel's (D) liability insurer, St. Paul's Fire and Marine Insurance Co. (St. Paul's). The court admonished defense counsel to ensure the representative had authority to negotiate. St. Paul's subsequently failed to send the high-level representative the court was seeking. Instead, it sent only a claims adjuster with authority only to settle for a sum no greater than the company's previous offer. The court found that St. Paul's deliberately disregarded its order. It declared the insurance company in default, and ordered a hearing to show cause why criminal contempt charges should not be imposed. The Court eventually accepted St. Paul's apologies and did not impose further sanctions.

Issue: Does a federal court have authority to require the attendance of interested parties at meaningful settlement conferences, and to impose sanctions for failure to attend?

Decision and Rationale: (Bertelsman, J.) Yes. The authority of a federal court to order attendance of attorneys, parties, and insurers at settlement conferences and to impose sanctions for disregard of the court's orders is so well established as to be beyond doubt. Other District Courts have found that Rule 16 of the Federal Rules of Civil Procedure provides courts with the authority to require the presence of parties with full authority to settle a case. The normal caseload of a United States District Judge is about 400 civil cases, in addition to the criminal docket. The drafters of Rule 16 were aware of the heavy caseloads. That is why they encouraged "forceful judicial management" as a means of settling cases. The exigencies of modern dockets require courts to develop novel means of managing litigation, compulsory settlement conferences are merely one. A court cannot require parties to settle, but it may require parties to make a reasonable effort at settlement.

Analysis:

This opinion provides an example of the proactive approach now taken by federal courts in guiding negotiations and settlements. After reviewing another case, the court held that Rule 16 provides courts with the authority to require parties to attend settlement conferences. However, this conclusion is subject to some doubt. After this case was decided, Rule 16 was amended to specifically grant the authority to require attendance at settlement conferences. The amendment casts doubt on the court's conclusion that the pre-amended version granted the same power. The court also justifies its authority to insist on settlement conferences based on the heavy caseload faced by federal courts. But some data suggests that the time saved by court-guided settlement is half that of those cases that are settled without any court action.

Ferguson v. Writers Guild of America, West

(Screenwriter) v. (Writers Guild)
226 Cal. App. 3d 1382 (1991)

M E M O R Y   G R A P H I C

Instant Facts

A screenwriter sought court review of the arbitration proceeding that granted him the screenplay credit and not the story-line credit to a movie he had written.

Black Letter Rule

Courts are limited in their power to review the final decision of arbitration panels.

Case Vocabulary

WRIT OF MANDATE: A court order or command; also *writ of mandamus*.

Procedural Basis: Appeal to the California Court of Appeal from a judgment of the superior court denying a petition for a writ of mandate.

Facts: Larry Ferguson (P), a screenwriter, was hired to write a screenplay for the movie "Beverly Hills Cop II." The Writers Guild (D) awarded Ferguson (P) partial screenplay credit, but gave the story-line credit to two others. The process for determining writing credits was governed by a 369-page agreement entered into by various entities in the entertainment industry, and the Writers Guild West's credits manual. The process is summarized as follows. After each party to the proceeding peremptorily disqualified a reasonable number arbitrators from a list of 400, a Writers Guild secretary selected the arbitrators to hear the case. The arbitrators were then provided with all written material used in the creation of the screenplay. The arbitrators held no hearing, and they deliberated independently of each other. In fact, their identity remained undisclosed to the parties throughout the procedure, and even thereafter. Within 24 hours after the arbitrators reached their decision, Ferguson requested the convening of the policy review board to determine whether the "proceedings" substantially deviated from the policy of the Writers Guild (D). The board was not empowered to review the judgment. The policy review board approved the credit determination, a final decision. In support of his challenge, Ferguson asserted several procedural defects in the process, and as error, the rulings of the superior court denying his requests to (1) depose the writer awarded shared screenplay credit, and (2) compel the Writers Guild (D) to reveal the name of the arbitrators.

Issue: May a court review the appropriateness of procedural rules adopted in an arbitration proceeding?

Decision and Rationale: (Klein, J.A.) No. Judicial review of arbitration proceedings is limited to whether the parties agreed to submit the issue to arbitration and whether the arbitrator exceeded the power granted by the agreement. Under the agreement establishing the arbitration process, disputes over writing credits for movies are nonjusticiable. The writers who constitute the Writers Guild (D) have decided that the credit-determination process can be handled more skillfully and efficiently by arbitration committees than by courts. We note that the procedures adopted in the challenged arbitration have been reviewed for correctness by the policy review board. Because of their expertise, we accord the policy review board considerable deference. Ferguson (P), did not specify to the review board the errors argued before this court. Consequently, Ferguson (P) did not preserve for judicial review the contentions he has made. Even if we were to decide on Ferguson's claims, we find them without merit. Judicial review of the credit determination is restricted to considering whether there was a material and prejudicial departure from the procedures specified in the agreement. No such departure exists in this case. We also reject Ferguson's challenge of the decision of the superior court. Deposition of the writer awarded shared credit would add nothing to Ferguson's claim of sole credit. With respect to the identity of the arbitrators, the Writers Guild has important and legitimate reasons for withholding their identity, including the need to have arbitrators free of pressure, retaliation, and litigation. Although it is unusual for an arbitration to be conducted without an in-person hearing before the arbitrators, discovery of the names in this case would serve no function. Even in arbitration conducted under more familiar rules, the parties have no right to inquire into the arbitrators reasons for reaching a particular decision. Affirmed.

Analysis:

This opinion provides an excellent example of (1) the judicial deference given to arbitration proceedings and their resulting decisions, and (2) the varying procedures adopted by arbitration agreements. The thrust of the California court's holding is that judicial review of arbitration is severely limited. In this case the court bases its decision on two factors, (1) the parties agreed to arbitrate this issue and (2) the arbitration was held in accordance with rules fashioned by the agreement. The court's reliance on the two agreements providing for no judicial determination of credit rights is important because freedom of contract forms the basis for allowing parties to submit their disputes to arbitration. The second factor relied on by the court was that the agreement provided for an internal review of the procedures used in any particular case. The court analogizes the decision of the policy review board with decisions reached by administrative agencies, and hints that they should be accorded similar deference. Extending the analogy, the court "refuses" to entertain Ferguson's procedural contentions because they were not presented to the board. The court finally notes that the particular procedures adopted by the Writers Guild are a deviation from the norm (of courts and other arbitration proceedings), but that there are substantial interests supporting the procedural peculiarities, interests that must be respected.

Engalla v. Permanente Medical Group, Inc.

(Patient) v. (HMO)

15 Cal. 4th 951 (1997)

M E M O R Y   G R A P H I C

Instant Facts

A patient involved in a malpractice dispute with his health maintenance organization broke off arbitration proceedings, filed a suit in state court, and resisted the enforcement of the arbitration agreement on grounds of fraud and unconscionability.

Black Letter Rule

A contracting party's knowledge that an arbitration system is poorly managed may amount to fraud sufficient to resist compelled arbitration.

Case Vocabulary

LOSS OF CONSORTIUM: Cause of action belonging to a spouse who has lost the companionship of the married partner.

Procedural Basis: Not provided.

Facts: Permanente Medical Group (Permanente) (D), a health maintenance organization (HMO), requires that its members submit for arbitration their malpractice disputes. The arbitration program was designed, written, and administered by Permanente (D). The service agreement containing the arbitration provision represented that the program would afford members a hearing in several months time, and that members would find the process fairly protected their rights. Permanente's (D) program provided for a three-arbitrator panel and provided that each party would nominate one arbitrator while the third arbitrator would be named by both parties. The program provided that all selections were to occur within 60 days and that a hearing was to be held within a reasonable time thereafter. Despite these assurances, delays occurred in 90 percent of all arbitrations. In only 1 percent of all cases was a neutral arbitrator appointed within 60 days, in only 3 percent did such appointment occur within 180 days. Furthermore, on average, hearings were conducted almost 2½ years after the appointment of the panel. Prior to his death, Wilfredo Engalla was involved in a malpractice dispute with Permanente (D). Pursuant to the medical services agreement, on May 31 Engalla's sent a demand for arbitration on June 5 or 6. After Permanente (D) received Engalla's demand, there ensued a six-month period during which the parties designated arbitrators that proved to be unavailable. Shortly thereafter, Mr. Engalla died, and Mrs. Engalla (P) filed suit. The delay, and Mr. Engalla's resulting death, caused Mrs. Engalla's (P) claim of loss of consortium to merge with her wrongful death action, reducing the amount of potential damages. Permanente (D) moved to compel arbitration, and Mrs. Engalla (P) resisted on the grounds of fraud and unconscionability.

Issue: Does a contracting party's knowledge of its poorly managed arbitration system amount to fraud sufficient to resist compelled arbitration?

Decision and Rationale: (Mosk, J.) Yes. In order to defeat a petition to compel arbitration on the ground of fraud, the party opposing the petition must show that the asserted fraud goes specifically to the arbitration agreement, rather than the contract in general. Here, Permanente (D) misrepresented the expediency of their proceedings. The facts here support the allegation that Permanente (D) entered into the arbitration agreement with knowledge that it would not comply with its timetable. Permanente was made aware of the delays endemic of the program soon after its institution. We conclude that there is evidence to support the claim that Permanente (D) fraudulently induced the Engallas (P) to enter the arbitration agreement in that it misrepresented the speed of its program, a misrepresentation on which Engalla's employer relied by selecting Permanente's (D) health plan, and that the Engallas (P) suffered delay in the resolution of their dispute as a result of that reliance. We cannot, however, state that the arbitration agreement is unconscionable on its face. The fact that Permanente (D), as a repeat player, has an advantage in appointing arbitrators, and that the company has unlimited power to veto arbitrators proposed by the other party do not make the agreement unconscionable per se. The problem with the arbitration program is not its one-sidedness, but rather the gap between the representations made and the actual workings of the program. Reversed.

Concurrence: (Kennard, J.) This case illustrates the role of courts in ensuring that arbitration be, not only efficient, but also fundamentally fair. Courts must distinguish between arbitration that is efficient and fair and that which is an instrument imposed on a "take it or leave it" basis.

Dissent: (Brown, J.) The majority's decision to validate a party's withdrawal

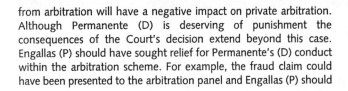

from arbitration will have a negative impact on private arbitration. Although Permanente (D) is deserving of punishment the consequences of the Court's decision extend beyond this case. Engallas (P) should have sought relief for Permanente's (D) conduct within the arbitration scheme. For example, the fraud claim could have been presented to the arbitration panel and Engallas (P) should have requested that they not enforce the provision. They should not be allowed to circumvent the arbitrators altogether. Because the decision will mean that parties to arbitration will have to deal with courts, the exact consequence sought to be avoided by arbitration, I dissent.

Analysis:

The importance of the California Court's opinion does not lie in any generally applicable rule regarding arbitration agreements (if any such rule can be discerned from this case), rather, the opinion provides an example of an exception to the general rule that all contractual disputes arising out of a contract containing an arbitration agreement must be submitted for arbitration. The exception is a product of two concepts. The first is that an arbitration agreement is treated as a separate contract within the general contract. Consequently, the California court required Mrs. Engalla (P) to show fraud specific to the arbitration agreement. Had Mrs. Engalla (P) claimed the entire contract was procured through fraud, that claim would have to be submitted for arbitration. The second concept is an outgrowth of the first and requires that, as a separate contract, the validity of an arbitration agreement is subject to the courts' policing of fraud, unconscionability, duress, and the like. Generally, arbitration agreements, like other contracts, are void if procured through these means. The Court here holds that Permanente's (D) knowledge that its arbitration process suffered from endemic delays, is sufficient to support a claim that its representations regarding the expediency of the process were fraudulent. Therefore, the arbitration agreement itself – not the contract as a whole – is void; and for that reason arbitration cannot be compelled. The dissent is plainly wrong. The issue of fraud in inducing an arbitration agreement cannot be submitted to the arbitration panel because the claim is, essentially, that the arbitration is void. In other words, it never "existed", so a party cannot be held to abide by it.

Celotex Corp. v. Catrett

(Product Manufacturer) v. (Wife of Decedent)
477 U.S. 317 (1986)

M E M O R Y   G R A P H I C

Instant Facts

Charged with several claims for asbestos poisoning that lead to the death of Mr. Catrett, Celotex (D) moved for summary judgment on the grounds that Mrs. Catrett (P) failed to produce evidence to support the claims.

Black Letter Rule

In a summary judgment motion, a moving party may meet its burden of persuasion by demonstrating that the nonmoving party failed to supply sufficient evidence of a genuine dispute of material fact.

Case Vocabulary

BURDEN OF PERSUASION: A party's obligation to establish evidence sufficient to convince the trier of fact that each element of the party's claim or defense is correct.

BURDEN OF PRODUCTION: A party's obligation to produce evidence sufficient to avoid an adverse ruling on an issue, even if this falls short of persuasion.

Procedural Basis: Writ of certiorari reviewing reversal of granting of summary judgment against a party claiming damages for negligence, breach of warranty and strict liability.

Facts: Mrs. Catrett (P) sued Celotex Corp. (D) and others for negligence, breach of warranty, and strict liability, alleging that her husband's death was caused by exposure to products containing asbestos manufactured by Celotex (D) and the other defendants. Celotex (D) moved for summary judgment on the grounds that Catrett (P) failed to produce any evidence that any Celotex (D) product caused the injuries. In response, Catrett (P) produced three documents which she claimed demonstrated that a genuine factual dispute existed. Celotex (D) argued that the three documents, including the husband's deposition and two letters, were inadmissible hearsay. The District Court granted Celotex's (D) motion for summary judgment because there was no showing that Mr. Catrett was exposed to Celotex's (D) product. The Court of Appeals reversed since Celotex (D) made no effort to adduce any evidence, in the form of affidavits or otherwise, in support of its motion for summary judgment. The Supreme Court granted certiorari.

Issue: Must a party moving for summary judgment supply evidence or affidavits showing the absence of a genuine dispute about a material fact?

Decision and Rationale: (Rehnquist, J.) No. A party moving for summary judgment does not necessarily bear the burden of supplying evidence or affidavits showing the absence of a genuine dispute about a material fact. The plain language of Rule 56(c) of the Federal Rules of Civil Procedure mandates the entry of summary judgment, after adequate time for discovery, against a party who fails to establish the existence of an element essential to that party's case, and on which that party will bear the burden of proof at trial. The Court of Appeals misconstrued the holding in *Adickes v. S.H. Kress & Co.* [the party moving for summary judgment must establish the absence of a genuine issue, when viewed in a light most favorable to the opposing party]. This holding should not be construed to mean that the burden is always on the moving party to produce evidence showing the absence of a material fact in dispute. Rather, a summary judgment motion may properly be made in reliance solely on the pleadings, depositions, answers to interrogatories, and admissions on file. Thus, the moving party does not have to submit supporting evidence, as the plain language of Rules 56(a) and (b) indicate. The moving party only bears the initial responsibility of informing the court of the basis for its motion. This responsibility may be met by showing the court that there is an absence of evidence to support the nonmoving party's case. The amendment to Rule 56(e), precluding a party opposing summary judgment from referring only to its pleadings, was intended to broaden the scope of summary judgment motions. However, the Court of Appeal's reasoning tends to make summary judgments more difficult to obtain. In the case at hand, the parties had an adequate opportunity to conduct discovery and establish the evidence needed to prove their cases. The Court of Appeals declined to address whether Catrett (P) had made an adequate showing to carry her burden of proof at trial. For this reason, and based on the foregoing analysis, the judgment of the Court of Appeals is reversed for such a determination. Reversed and remanded.

Concurrence: (White, J.) I agree that a moving party must not always support a summary judgment motion with evidence or affidavits showing the absence of a genuine dispute of a material fact. However, the movant may not simply discharge his burden by asserting that the opposing party has no evidence to prove his or her case. The case should be reversed for the Court of Appeals to consider whether Catrett (P) revealed enough evidence to defeat the motion for summary judgment.

Dissent: (Brennan, J.) The Court has not clearly explained what is required of a moving party seeking summary judgment on the ground that the nonmoving party cannot prove its case. I believe that Celotex (D) has failed to meet its burden of production. The burden on the party seeking summary judgment has two components. First, the party bears the initial burden of production, which shifts to the nonmoving party if satisfied by the moving party. Second, the moving party bears the ultimate burden of persuasion. The decision as to whether the moving party has discharged its initial burden of production depends upon which party will bear the burden of persuasion on the challenged claim at trial. If the moving party will bear the burden of persuasion, it must support its motion with credible evidence that would entitle it to a directed verdict if not controverted at trial. On the other hand, if the burden of persuasion at trial would be on the nonmoving party, then the party moving for summary judgment may satisfy its burden of production in two ways. First, it may submit affirmative evidence that negates an essential element of the nonmoving party's claim. Second, it may demonstrate that the nonmoving party's evidence itself is insufficient to establish an essential element of the nonmoving party's claim. However, the moving party in this scenario may not simply assert a conclusory statement that the nonmoving party's evidence is insufficient. Rather, it must affirmatively show the absence of evidence in the record to support a judgment for the nonmoving party. Based on the facts of this case, Celotex (D) failed to discharge its initial burden of production. Thus, summary judgment is improper.

Analysis:

The majority, led by Justice Rehnquist, clearly desired to expand the scope of summary judgment motions following the restrictive holding in *Adickes v. S.H. Kress & Co.* They accomplished this goal by significantly reducing the burden borne by the party moving for summary judgment. As a result of this holding, a moving party meets its burden by simply alerting the court that the nonmoving party has failed to establish evidence sufficient to prove its claims. Indeed, this holding furthers the general goals of the Federal Rules of Civil Procedure, which were designed to secure speedy and inexpensive determinations of controversies. However, the majority may have been too willing to grant summary judgment. As Justice Brennan's well-reasoned dissent mentions, the Court failed to establish what is required of a moving party. While the Court stated that a moving party cannot simply assert that the nonmoving party has no evidence to prove its case, this seems to be exactly what Celotex (D) did. The dissent presents a more reasoned analysis, predicated on which party will bear the burden of persuasion on the challenged claim at trial. If the moving party will bear the burden of persuasion, then it must produce credible evidence over and above what Celotex (D) produced. However, with respect to the asbestos poisoning, Catrett (D) clearly would bear the burden of persuasion. In this instance, Celotex (D) would only have to demonstrate that Catrett's (D) evidence was insufficient to meet its burden of persuasion. Nevertheless, according to the portions of the opinion reprinted in the book, it seems that Celotex (D) failed to make even this minimal showing. It is interesting to note that, upon remand, the Court of Appeals declined to grant summary judgment, finding that Catrett (P) had produced sufficient evidence of exposure. The majority of the Court of Appeals felt that the potential inadmissibility of Catrett's (P) evidence was no problem, while the dissent felt that the inadmissible evidence should not be considered.

Visser v. Packer Engineering Associates

(Fired Employee) v. (Corporation)
924 F.2d 655 (7th Cir. 1991) (en banc)

M E M O R Y   G R A P H I C

Instant Facts

The defendant in a federal age discrimination suit moved for summary judgment on the ground that there was no showing that the plaintiff was fired on the basis of his age.

Black Letter Rule

Summary judgment must be granted when no rational jury could, on the evidence presented in the summary judgment proceeding, bring a verdict for the party opposing the motion.

Case Vocabulary

IRASCIBLE: Easily angered; quick-tempered.

Procedural Basis: Appeal to the Seventh Circuit Court of Appeals, challenging the District Court's grant of summary judgment.

Facts: Philip Visser (P) sued his former employer, Packer Engineering Associates (Packer) (D), under the Age Discrimination Employment Act (ADEA) [federal legislation which prohibits the dismissal of employees on the basis of age]. After being hired as an officer of Packer, Visser (P) became a member of the firm's board of directors. Years later there arose a dispute between a group of board members, including Visser (P), and the chief executive officer (CEO), Dr. Kenneth Packer. Members of the dissident group, but not Visser (P), eventually quit and started their own firm. The CEO then asked Visser (P) to pledge his loyalty to the CEO personally. Visser (P) refused, and was thus fired at age 64, only nine months before his pension was to vest. In support of his claim, Visser (P) produced evidence that the CEO knew of Visser's (P) age and pension rights. In addition, three members of the dissident group filed affidavits which stated that Visser (P) was fired because of his age. The affidavits, in essence, claimed that the CEO fired Visser and deprived him of his pension in an effort to exact revenge on the dissident group.

Issue: In order to defeat a motion for summary judgment, must a plaintiff show that a reasonable jury could find on his behalf?

Decision and Rationale: (Posner, J.) Yes. If no rational jury could, on the evidence presented in the summary judgment proceeding, bring a verdict for the party opposing the motion – if in other words the moving party would be entitled to a judgment notwithstanding the verdict – then summary judgment must be granted. The evidence presented indicates, as Visser (P) concedes, Visser (P) was fired because he was disloyal to the CEO. We must, however, consider the possibility of mixed motives. To establish liability, the forbidden motive, age in this case, must be the but-for cause of the employee's termination. The only evidence of age discrimination is Packer's knowledge of Visser's (P) age and pension rights. But a trier of fact may not infer action from knowledge alone. In support of his claim, Visser (P) has also submitted the affidavits of three members of the dissident group. These affidavits should be excluded for several reasons, none of which include their self-serving character, the fact that they were drafted by a lawyer, nor that they argue that the CEO is vengeful. These affidavits should be excluded because they are not based on personal knowledge. Rather the affidavits delve into psychoanalysis. They conclude that as a result of the resignation of the dissident group, the CEO felt the need to hurt someone and there being no other targets around, the CEO chose to deprive Visser (P) of his full pension. This comes close to arguing bad conduct from bad character, contrary to the Rules of Evidence. Before Visser (P) could shift the burden of persuasion on causation on to Packer (D) he had to show that a reasonable jury could find that age, or a factor correlated with age, such as concern with the expense of a pension, was a substantial factor in the decision to fire him. This, Visser (P) failed to show. Affirmed.

Dissent: (Flaum, J.) I disagree with the majority's view of the facts before us, and with the substantive law and procedural standards this view leads the majority to apply. The ADEA grants plaintiffs the right to a jury trail on any issue of fact pertinent to the statutory violation they allege. At summary judgment an employer can prevail only if the record shows that its employment decision was not based on discrimination, and the evidence is so strong that a reasonable trier of fact must so conclude. I disagree that this is one of those rare cases. Visser was 64 when he was fired a few months before his pension would vest. The CEO was aware of this and knew the company would be saved some money. Furthermore, Visser was replaced by a 29-year old worker, a factor many courts use in determining the issue before us. I believe that Visser has established a prima facie

Visser v. Packer Engineering Associates (Continued)

case of employment discrimination.

Dissent: (Bauer, C.J.) My dissent is occasioned by my conviction that summery judgment is too rapid a disposition in this case, that sufficient factual questions remain that belong to a jury.

Dissent: (Cudahy, J.) We should be exceedingly cautious in holding that the irascible temperament and apparently unwarranted demands for "loyalty" of a corporate executive may insulate his corporation against age discrimination charges otherwise supported by probative circumstantial evidence.

Analysis:

The Court here decided the other side of the *Celotex Corp v. Catrett* coin [Supreme Court holds that a party moving for summary judgment meets its burden of persuasion by demonstrating that the nonmoving party failed to supply sufficient evidence of a genuine dispute of material fact]. The court decides what kind of evidence is sufficient to create a genuine dispute of a material fact, and thus, successfully oppose a motion for summary judgment. The court concludes that a plaintiff opposing a motion for summary judgment needs to provide evidence that would allow a rational jury to find for the plaintiff. The problem with the court's opinion is the application of this rule to the particular facts of the case. It is apparent that Judge Posner was too willing to discount the plaintiff's evidence. Posner notes that if Visser was fired because of his disloyalty, the natural inference is that he was not fired because of his age. This statement ignores the possibility that the CEO demanded loyalty, knowing that Visser would refuse, and thus giving the company an excuse to deprive him of his pension. Posner states that there is no indication of a pretext to permit a jury to infer that the real reason was age. This reasoning is circuitous for its is based on the assumption that Visser was actually fired because of his disloyalty. Posner fails to answer this question of why disloyalty was not the pretext for the firing. In any event, these are the sort of issues a jury should decide, not the court. Just because facts are not in controversy does not mean that summary judgment should be granted. The jury should decide whether the uncontroverted facts establish the issue, age discrimination in this case.

Sanders v. Union Pacific Railroad Co.

(Injured Employee) v. (Employer)
154 F. 3d 1037 (9th Cir. 1998)

M E M O R Y   G R A P H I C

Instant Facts

The District Court dismissed the plaintiff's action with prejudice after counsel repeatedly missed deadlines and failed to comply with the requirements of the pretrial order.

Black Letter Rule

A court may dismiss an action for prejudice if a party's failure to comply with deadlines and court orders leads to unnecessary delay and expense.

Case Vocabulary

PRETRIAL CONFERENCE: A meeting, usually presided over by the judge, where parties to litigation narrow the issues, secure stipulations, and otherwise streamline the trial.

Procedural Basis: Appeal to the Ninth Circuit Court of Appeals, challenging the District Court's dismissal of the action with prejudice.

Facts: Phillip Sanders (P) sued his employer, Union Pacific Railroad Co. (D), under the Federal Employer's Liability Act, following a work-related injury. The district judge set a trial date for November 19, 1996 and a pretrial conference for November 8. The judge issued an order concerning preparation for the conference. The order set forth a schedule for the filing of motions, oppositions, proposed instructions, and other documents. The order warned that failure to comply would lead to sanctions, even dismissal of the actions. Sanders' (P) counsel failed to comply with any of the requirements of the order. He consistently submitted documents late, and never submitted a trial brief. At the pretrial conference, presided over by the judge's law clerk, Sanders' (P) counsel explained that his inability to meet deadlines was a result of responsibilities in another case. The clerk suggested that the case would be removed from the calendar and the judge would likely take other action. One week later the court dismissed Sanders' (P) action with prejudice.

Issue: Does a court abuse its discretion when it dismisses an action with prejudice for failure to obey an order, without first resorting to lesser sanctions?

Decision and Rationale: (Per Curiam) No. The district court did not abuse its discretion in rejecting lesser sanctions than dismissal. Before dismissing a case for failure to comply with a court order, the factors to be considered are prejudice and availability of lesser sanctions. In this case Sanders' counsel's repeated failures undoubtedly impaired Union Pacific's (D) ability to prepare for trial. By neglecting to inform the court of his inability to meet impending deadlines, Sanders' counsel deprived the court of the opportunity to impose lesser sanctions. Counsel's conduct left the court with last-minute notice of a total failure of preparation, a failure that disrupted the trial calendar. Increased delay and expense threaten to overwhelm our courts. We cannot allow the disregard of judges' orders to increase this threat. We reject Sanders' contention that the dismissal violated the Due Process Clause because he was not notified that dismissal was imminent. The court order expressly advised Sanders that failure to comply could lead to dismissal. The lack of any hearing does not add anything to Sanders' claim.

Dissent: (Canby, S.C.J.) It is true that district courts must be able to manage their dockets, and the conduct of Sanders' counsel cannot be tolerated. Dismissal, however, should only be imposed as a sanction in extreme cases. Although Sanders' counsel was guilty of multiple failures, there consequences were felt at once, the pretrial conference. Dismissal here was sua sponte, which means that counsel should have been advised that dismissal was imminent. A boilerplate warning in a preprinted order should not suffice. Thus, I believe the district court abused its discretion.

Analysis:

This case serves as yet another example of the role courts – particularly federal courts – take in managing litigation. The caseloads faced by courts today demand that courts take a proactive role in assuring the efficiency of the system. The court here thought that counsel's failure, which led to a disruption of the trial calendar, justified the extreme sanctions. Apart from its effect on the efficiency of courts, a failure to meet deadlines can often prejudice one party. There is a difference between simultaneous exchange of information and the preparation of documents after an opportunity to see the other side's. Here, Union Pacific had to prepare for trial and the conference without any opportunity to view Sanders' information. These concerns notwithstanding, this opinion was eventually vacated and reversed after a rehearing en banc. [Thank goodness!] The en banc panel was not so much disturbed with the sanction of dismissal, rather, its concern centered around the manner in which the district court proceeded. A manner which deserved no deference according to the Ninth Circuit. Specifically, the panel noted that the pre-trial conference was presided over by the clerk, and the court dismissed the action *sua sponte* without first holding a hearing.

McKey v. Fairbairn

(Tenant) v. (Landlord's Agent)

345 F. 2d 739 (D.C. Cir. 1965)

M E M O R Y   G R A P H I C

Instant Facts

In a negligence suit against a landlord, the tenant's attorney moved to introduce housing regulations as proof of negligence, but the court denied the motion because the regulations were not contained in the pretrial order.

Black Letter Rule

Trial judges have justifiably large discretion in refusing parties to change their theory during the trial, after a pre-trial order.

Procedural Basis: Appeal to the D.C. Circuit Court of Appeals, challenging the District Court's directed verdict.

Facts: Levi McKey rented a dwelling house from Kenneth Fairbairn (D), agent for the property's owner. Fairbairn was made aware of a leak in one of the house's bedrooms. Shortly thereafter, McKey's mother-in-law (Littlejohn) entered the room, and despite knowing the condition of the floor proceeded to slip and fall, sustaining injuries. After initiating a suit for negligence, Littlejohn died from causes unrelated to the fall, and Helen McKey (P), her administratrix, was substituted as plaintiff. The pretrial order contained McKey's (P) theory of the case. It stated that Littlejohn's injuries were a result of Fairbairn's negligence in failing to repair the roof and eliminate the leak after notice thereof and Fairbairn's promise to repair, all in breach of a duty owed under the lease. During the trial McKey's (P) attorney became aware of housing regulations requiring roofs to be leak-proof. Counsel moved to amend the pretrial order to permit these regulations to be entered into evidence. The court denied the motion and directed verdict for Fairbairn (D).

Issue: Does a court abuse its discretion when it refuses to amend the pretrial order so that pertinent evidence, which came to light during trial, may be admitted; particularly where the other party was aware of the evidence?

Decision and Rationale: (Miller, J.) No. A judge has justifiably large discretion in refusing to permit a party to change its theory during the trial. We need not decide whether the proffered regulations are pertinent to this case. The trail judge acted within his discretion in refusing to admit them. There is also a further reason for upholding the directed verdict. Mainly, Mrs. Littlejohn admitted she knew of the floor's condition and yet failed exercise proper care. Thus, the trial judge would have been justified in instructing the jury that Mrs. Littlejohn was contributorily negligent as a matter of law. Affirmed.

Dissent: (Fahy, J.) There are cases when judges should use their discretion to depart from the pretrial order. The Federal Rules of Procedure provide that the pretrial order controls the course of the action "unless modified at trial to prevent manifest injustice." In deciding the matter of "manifest injustice" the court must weigh the failure of counsel to bring forth this new theory of liability until trial against the possible prejudice to the defendant. The failure in this case was inadvertent. Any prejudice to the defendant could have been obviated by a continuance. Manifest injustice is more likely to occur when the applicable law is precluded from consideration because not referred to in the pretrial order than when the preclusion is of evidentiary matter that takes the adversary by surprise. The court should also not rely on any theory of contributory negligence because the trial court did not rule on the issue.

Analysis:

This case exemplifies the importance of pretrial orders in setting the boundaries for arguments at trial. The pre-trial order issued pursuant to Rule 16 of the Federal Rules of Civil Procedure narrows the issues, guides the trial, and supplants the pleadings. As the court points out, the trial judge has the discretion to hold the litigants to the issues identified in the order. The dissent argues that the trial court should have weighed the benefits of amending the pre-trial order against the detriment to the defendant. This makes sense, but unfortunately for Mrs. McKey, trial courts are given wide latitude in decisions relating to the management of the trial. Appellate review is severely limited.

Chapter 9

This Chapter is important because it concerns *who* will decide the merits of the case. In an earlier chapter you learned how litigation could reach some form of conclusion without trial. But when the case proceeds to the courthouse steps and a trial is about to commence, the case may be won or lost depending upon *who* decides the ultimate outcome of the matter. The *who* could be a choice between one particular judge versus another, or a judge versus a jury, or even one set of jurors versus another set.

When it comes to a judge being the trier of fact, it can make a difference whether you are in federal or state court. Why? In many state courts you can reject a judge for any reason you want, as long as it is done within the proper time frame. This procedure is very helpful, especially where horror stories have been told by lawyers and litigants in other cases about a particular judge.

However, suppose your case is in federal court and you must follow the unfortunate federal procedure of having a reason to get the judge off of your case (pun intended!). What would happen if the judge's son had worked as a law student intern in the prosecutor's office who had tried and convicted your friend and co-conspirator in a related criminal trial before another judge? Would it matter that your judge had watched and admired his son questioning the witnesses in your friend's trial?

Suppose you were one lucky guy and were not convicted of any crime, and were set free. Now you want to file a civil lawsuit against the tenant who rented your house while you were in jail to get her off your property and recover money for the damages done to your house by that no good tenant. Are you entitled to a jury trial? You need to get injunctive relief in order to physically remove the tenant, and you want to collect money from her as well. You must learn about equitable and legal relief to know whether or not you can have a jury or judge decide your case.

Assume that you are allowed to have a jury trial. The tenant you want off your property is an African-American female of the Jewish faith, and you are a white Protestant male. You tell your lawyer that you want a jury that looks just like you, and no blacks, females or non-Protestants. Can you do this? Hopefully, you know the answer without reading any further. If not, read the Chapter very carefully.

Chapter 9

NOTE: THE PURPOSE OF THIS OUTLINE IS TO ORGANIZE THE CASES SO THAT ONE CAN QUICKLY UNDERSTAND THE RELEVANCE OF EACH CASE TO THE COURSE. NO ATTEMPT IS MADE IN THIS OVERVIEW TO ADDRESS EVERY CONCEPT THAT MUST BE STUDIED. BE SURE TO READ THE ENTIRE CASEBOOK AND/OR OTHER MATERIALS TO GAIN A FULL UNDERSTANDING OF ALL CONCEPTS.

I. Judging Judges: Bias and Recusal
  A. The federal system permits disqualification of a judge from hearing a matter only for cause.
  B. The federal statute provides for two categories of recusal, one where certain defined circumstances require mandatory recusal, and another broader category which provides for recusal where the judge's impartiality might reasonably be questioned.
  C. Some state courts permit a peremptory challenge of a judge within a certain time period, without having to give a reason.
  D. Instances where recusal was requested:
    1. The mere appearance of impropriety by the judge will justify recusal. Thus, a judge should have been recused from a criminal trial where his son, a law student and intern for the prosecutor's office, participated in the government's prosecution of a separate, but factually related, criminal trial. *In re Jeffrey C. Hatcher, Sr.*
    2. However, recusal was not required where a judge's law clerk had lived in the same house with one of defendant's counsel for the first eight months of the personal injury case pending before the judge. The reasoning was that it is the judge, and not the law clerk, who decides cases. *O'Bannon v. Union Pacific R.R. Co.*
    3. Recusal should have occurred in cases where the United States was a party and the judge knew he was the subject of a federal grand jury investigation, but the public did not. However, the risk of injustice to the defendants was not so egregious as to require retrial. *United States v. Cerceda.*
    4. Both recusal and setting aside the judgment was required where the judge presided over a criminal trial during a period when he was under investigation by the Circuit Council for judicial misbehavior. The defendant's attorney had testified before the Council concerning the judge's behavior in a series of cases, but before the Council had made a decision. *United States v. Anderson.*
    5. Sometimes, the judge's behavior does not war-

rant recusal, unless it were to continue. Thus, where a judge made statements suggesting racial bias in favor of the African-American plaintiffs, the court of appeals condemned the statements but refused to order recusal. The court of appeal noted that the jury trial had been ongoing for thirty-one days and fifty-eight witnesses, and recusal would require this to be repeated. The court warned the judge to control himself, and reserved the right to reverse on appeal. *In re Chevron U.S.A.*
    6. If the judge has no knowledge of certain facts which would be clear grounds for mandatory recusal, the recusal of the judge is proper under that portion of the statute which provides for recusal where the judge's impartiality might reasonably be questioned. Thus, where the judge was a member of the board of directors for a university but did not know that the university stood to profit or lose from the case before him, recusal was appropriate. *Liljeberg v. Health Services Acquisition Corp.*
    7. The Supreme Court has adopted a policy that does not require recusal of one its members when a relative is a partner in the firm before the court, but not working directly on the case involved. Note that the Supreme Court may not substitute a justice from another court when a member must recuse himself or herself. Instead, the court makes its decision with less than nine justices. *Statement of Recusal Policy.*
    8. Recusal of a black female judge was not required where the case before her alleged sex discrimination and she had previously worked on behalf of blacks who suffered race discrimination as an attorney before becoming a judge. *Blank v. Sullivan & Cromwell.*
    9. In order for recusal to occur based upon information obtained during trial, there must be judicial remarks that reveal such a high degree of favoritism or antagonism as to make a fair judgment impossible. *Liteky v. United States.*
    10. The challenged judge may rule himself on the issue of recusal. *Berger v. United States.*

II. Judge or Jury: The Right to a Civil Jury Trial
  A. Why might it make a difference to have a jury decide the case as opposed to a judge? Consider the following possible differences between the two.
    1. Judges are still predominantly male, white, at

least middle-aged, specialized education, and have years of professional experience in law.

2. Juries, on the other hand, are drawn from the community at large to serve for a short period, they deliberate in secret, announce their verdicts often in general terms, and are unburdened by the requirement of linking facts and law together to reach their conclusions.

B. Historical Reconstruction and the Seventh Amendment

1. The Seventh Amendment provides: "In suits at common law, where the value in controversy shall exceed twenty dollars, the right of trial by jury shall be preserved...."

   a. Thus, suits that could be brought in a court of common law (legal claims) were entitled to a jury trial, but suits that would have been brought before a court of chancery (equitable claims) would not have the right to a jury trial.

2. The courts adopted a "historical test" for deciding the right to jury trial. Under this approach, the court determined whether the claim would have been within the jurisdiction of the common law courts in 1791, when the Seventh Amendment became part of the Bill of Rights. If so, a right to jury trial existed.

C. Applying the Historical Test to New Claims

1. Difficulties developed with the historical test where the claim did not even exist in 1791 when the Bill of Rights was adopted.

2. To determine whether those claims that were not in existence when there were separate courts of law and equity are entitled to a jury trial, a two step inquiry is made. First, a comparison is made between the current action to actions prior to the merger of courts of law and equity to determine if an analogy can be made. Second, a determination is made as to whether the remedy is legal or equitable. Thus, an action against a union for breach of fair representation carries a right to jury trial since the remedy of back pay and benefits is legal in nature. *Chauffeurs, Teamsters and Helpers Local 391 v. Terry.*

3. Most newly created claims that seek money damages as a remedy carry a right to jury trial. Statutory actions under Title VIII of the Civil Rights Act of 1968 and the Age Discrimination in Employment Act carry a right to jury trial.

   a. However, under Title VII, which prohibits discrimination in employment, if the remedy

sought is purely equitable, such as reinstatement or hiring, there is no right to jury trial. The Supreme Court has not ruled on whether a right to jury trial exists if backpay is sought.

4. The Supreme Court has restricted jury trials in patent cases, which were in existence when the Seventh Amendment was ratified. The court held that a particular portion of a patent case—that construing the meaning of a patent "claim"—is not a function of the jury. The basis for the court's ruling was that judges not juries are better suited to find the acquired meaning of patent terms. *Markman v. Westview Instruments.*

5. The Seventh Amendment applies only to federal courts. There is no federal constitutional right that accords the right of jury trial in any civil case. State laws therefore may have differing results regarding jury trials in civil cases. Various state courts have rejected jury trials in contract actions based on promissory estoppel, quiet-title actions, constructive trusts, calculation of damages after breach of contractual covenant not to compete and shareholders' derivative suits.

D. Applying the Historical Test to New Procedures

1. The Seventh Amendment and Changes in Judicial Procedures

   a. After courts of law and equity merged, the issue arose as to whether there was a right to jury trial. The historical test was not useful because it required looking back to a time when equity and law were separate. The Supreme Court determined that the joinder of equitable claims with a legal claim, or an equitable claim with a legal remedy, does not defeat the right to jury trial. *Beacon Theaters, Inc. v. Westovrer* and *Dairy Queen, Inc. v. Wood.*

   b. Federal courts now look at the complaint, and any counterclaims, to determine the type of relief sought. Where both exist, the jury must decide the legal issues. If the claims are not valid, a court may direct the verdict, regardless of the existence of the jury during the trial. The jury will decide factual issues, such as credibility of the witnesses. *Amoco Oil Co. v. Torcomian.*

   c. If a judge decides an issue in an equitable suit, and a second suit for damages is filed involving the same issue, the jury is only entitled to determine damages, and cannot decide issues already decided by the judge in

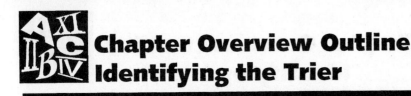

the equitable action. *Parklane Hosiery v. Shore.*

2. The Seventh Amendment and the Structure of Government

   a. The Seventh Amendment does not bar the establishment of administrative agencies that adjudicate issues which, if in court, would be determined by a jury. So long as Congress has entirely removed the claim from the court system, adjudication of issues, even liability for money, by administrative agencies will be upheld.

   b. Federal bankruptcy courts are really somewhere between a federal court and an administrative agency. They operate without juries.

      (1) Litigation of creditor's claims in bankruptcy court without a jury does not violate the Seventh Amendment. *Katchen v. Landy.*

      (2) A fraudulent conveyance suit by a bankruptcy trustee against a preferential creditor requires a jury trial when a demand for one is made. *Granfinanciera, S.A. v. Nordberg.*

E. The Jury's Integrity: Size, Rules of Decision, and the Reexamination Clause

   1. At early common law, the federal jury consisted of twelve persons, the verdict had to be unanimous and the verdict could be attacked by "attaint," a process in which a second, twice as large, jury determines that the first jury has been deliberately untruthful.

   2. In modern times, the federal civil jury is composed of six persons, requiring a unanimous verdict.

   3. The trial and appellate courts however have substantial power to overturn verdicts found to be without evidentiary support. This is so in spite of the Reexamination Clause of the Seventh Amendment which provides "that no fact tried by a jury, shall be otherwise reexamined in any court of the United States than according to the rules of the common law."

F. Choosing Juries

   1. Assembling and Challenging a Pool of Jurors

      a. First, a pool of prospective jurors is *summoned.* Jury summoning generally requires compiling pools of jurors that represent broad cross-sections of the community.

      b. Second, the trial jurors are *selected* from the pool.

      c. Discrimination on the basis of race or gender is an unconstitutional compiling of jury summoning. No one group can be systematically excluded from jury selection summons.

      d. Federal statutes do exempt active members of armed services, police, fire and public officers.

   2. Challenging for Cause

      a. Voir dire is the process of questioning jurors for a particular trial.

         (1) A juror may be disqualified for causes, such as where a juror is a relative or employee of a party.

         (2) Cause exists if it can be shown that the juror is biased and cannot keep an open mind and decide the case only on the basis of the evidence presented.

      b. If a juror lies during voir dire, a verdict will be set aside only if it is shown that the juror failed to answer honestly a material question on voir dire and a correct response would have permitted a challenge for cause.

   3. Peremptory Challenges

      a. Peremptory challenge allows lawyers to strike a juror for any reason, or for no reason at all. In federal court, each side gets three peremptory challenges and additional challenges if alternate jurors are selected.

      b. In 1986, the Supreme Court held that the prosecution's systematic striking of black jurors in a criminal case without a justification based on nonracial factors violated the Equal Protection Clause. *Batson v. Kentucky.*

      c. Exclusion of jurors based on race in a civil action violates the Equal Protection Clause. The trial judge in private civil litigation controls the voir dire process and this is sufficient state action for application of the Equal Protection Clause. *Edmonson v. Leesville Concrete Company, Inc.*

      d. Peremptory challenges based on gender are unconstitutional as well. *J.E.B. v. Alabama.*

In re Jeffrey C. Hatcher, Sr.

(Government) v. (Gang Member)
(1998) 150 F.3d 631

MEMORY GRAPHIC

Instant Facts

Gang member charged with crime sought to have judge recused from case because judge's son had participated as an intern in prosecuting fellow gang member in related case.

Black Letter Rule

A judge should recuse himself from presiding at a trial if, in the eyes of the reasonable, well-informed public, there would be the appearance of impropriety.

Case Vocabulary

INDICTMENT: Document whereby Grand Jury recommends charging one with a crime.

PROFFER: An offer of proof to proceed with action.

RECUSAL MOTION: A method of requesting the disqualification of judge; a motion that the judge be removed as the presiding officer at the trial.

Procedural Basis: Appeal following denial of motion to recuse judge in a criminal proceeding.

Facts: Hatcher (D) filed a motion to recuse the judge from presiding over the criminal trial where he was a defendant. The judge denied the motion and Hatcher (D) appealed. Hatcher (D), a gang member, was named as a defendant in a federal indictment charging him with a variety of federal drug and conspiracy crimes. He was named as a co-conspirator in two other indictments in related cases with almost identical factual and legal allegations. One of the related cases involved criminal charges against Hoover, the head of the gang's drug trafficking business [whose office was located in his own prison cell]. In the criminal proceedings where Hoover was a defendant, Hatcher (D) was named as a co-conspirator. In the criminal proceedings where Hatcher (D) was the defendant, Hoover was named as a co-conspirator. (Get it?) Hatcher (D) contended that the judge was biased and should not be the judge in his criminal trial. (Why you ask?) The basis for the recusal motion was that the judge's son, while a third year law student intern for the U.S. Attorney's office, had assisted the government during the Hoover trial. The son was allowed to present eight witnesses to the jury, and the judge sat in the courtroom's audience section to observe his son. The judge has declared that he has no recollection of the particular evidence presented in the Hoover trial. The judge in the Hatcher (D) case was presented the transcripts of the Hoover case as part of the government's proffer.

Issue: Should a judge be recused from a criminal trial where his son, a law student and intern for the prosecutor's office, participated in the government's prosecution of a separate, but factually related, criminal trial?

Decision and Rationale: (Wood) Yes. We hold that the judge should be recused from the proceedings since there is an appearance of impropriety due to his son having worked on the Hoover case as an intern in the U.S. Attorneys' office. We reach our decision by first considering the various grounds for recusal asserted by Hatcher (D). The fact that the judge's son participated in the Hoover trial is not a basis for mandatory recusal. Mandatory disqualification of the judge is required under the federal statute where the judge or his spouse, or person within the third degree of relationship to the judge or his spouse, is "acting as a lawyer in the proceeding". Although the son qualifies as relative within the third degree, and being a law student intern qualifies as "acting as a lawyer", the Hoover case was not the same "proceeding" as the Hatcher (D) trial. The factual and legal similarities of the two cases do not make them the same proceedings. Therefore, mandatory recusal was not required. The federal statute [luckily for Hatcher (D)] also provides for recusal where the judge's impartiality could be questioned by a reasonable, well-informed observer. Thus, the appearance of impropriety will result in recusal, without need of actual impropriety. The Hoover and Hatcher (D) cases, although separate, are part of one large prosecution of gang members involved in a criminal enterprise. The fact that the son worked on the Hoover case as an intern in the U.S. Attorneys' office is of critical importance to our decision. There is the appearance of impropriety. The judge should be recused so that the criminal trial against Hatcher (D) is seen by the public as a fair proceeding.

Dissent: (Bauer) Since the knowledge the judge obtained by visiting the Hoover trial did not require his recusal, that should end the inquiry. The son did not appear before him in the separate trial, and I disagree that a reasonable person could question the judge's impartiality.

Analysis:

This case is an example of the application of the discretionary recusal provision of the federal statue. It demonstrates that the standard to be applied is whether reasonable members of the public would question the impartiality of the judge. The mere appearance of impropriety is enough to justify recusal. Thus, there need not be proof of actual impropriety. It does not matter that a judge claims that he can be impartial. It does not matter that a party believes the judge will be biased. The standard is an objective one, through the eyes of the reasonable, well-informed public. Note that where the mandatory provision of the federal statute is considered, there is a strict statutory construction involved. This is evident from the court holding that the Hoover case was not the same "proceeding". Hatcher is a federal case, and thus the federal statute concerning disqualification of judges applies. However, many states have their own statutes which permit parties to litigation to exercise one peremptory challenge of a judge. In this situation, no reason whatsoever need be given for challenging the judge. The federal courts have not yet adopted similar legislation.

Chauffeurs, Teamsters and Helpers Local 391 v. Terry

(Labor Union) v. (Employee)
494 U.S. 558 (1990)

M E M O R Y   G R A P H I C

Instant Facts

Several employees sued their union, the Chauffeurs, Teamsters and Helpers Local 391 (D), for alleged violations of the Union's duty of fair representation. Against the Union's protest that the claim was equitable in nature, the District Court and Appellate Court granted a right to jury trial.

Black Letter Rule

An action for breach of fair representation, although analogous to equitable claims at common law, carries a right to jury trial.

Case Vocabulary

COLLECTIVE-BARGAINING AGREEMENT: A labor agreement entered into between employers and a union representing employees.

EQUIPOISE: A point of equal distribution between two opposing claims or sides.

Procedural Basis: Writ of certiorari considering affirmance of denial of motion to strike demand for jury trial in action for back pay for breach of duty of fair representation.

Facts: McLean Trucking Company and the Chauffeurs, Teamsters and Helpers Local 391 (Union) (D) were parties to a collective-bargaining agreement. Terry (P) and 26 other plaintiffs were employed by McLean as truck drivers and were all members of the Union (D). Terry (P) and the others filed a grievance with the Union (D), but the Union (D) declined to refer the charges to a grievance committee. Terry (P) and the other employees then filed an action in District Court, alleging that the Union (D) had violated its duty of fair representation. The complaint sought compensatory damages for lost wages and health benefits. The Union (D) moved to strike Terry's (P) request for a jury trial on the ground that no right to a jury trial exists in a duty of fair representation suit. The District Court denied this motion to strike, and the Fourth Circuit affirmed upon an interlocutory appeal. The Supreme Court granted certiorari to resolve a circuit conflict on the issue.

Issue: Does an employee seeking an award of back pay from a union's alleged breach of fair representation have a right to trial by jury?

Decision and Rationale: (Marshall, J.) Yes. An employee seeking an award of back pay from a union's alleged breach of fair representation does have a right to trial by jury. In order to determine whether a particular action involves legal rights, and hence whether a jury trial is allowed, we conduct a two-step inquiry. First, we compare the statutory action to the 18th-century actions brought in England prior to the merger of law and equity. Second, we examine the remedy sought and determine whether it is legal or equitable in nature. This second inquiry is more important. With respect to the first part of the analysis, there was no such thing as an action for breach of a union's duty of fair representation in 18th-century England; in fact, collective bargaining was unlawful. However, we are persuaded by the Union's (D) analogy between a duty of fair representation action and an action by a trust beneficiary against a trustee for breach of legal duty. Both the union and a trustee have broad discretion in determining how to dispose of claims brought by employees or trustees. We disagree with Terry's (P) analogy to an attorney malpractice action, since a client controls the significant decisions concerning his representation in the attorney-client setting, whereas an individual employee has no such control over a union. Nevertheless, we are not convinced that Terry's (P) claim is wholly equitable. While a duty of fair representation claim is analogous to a common-law equitable action against a trustee, Terry (P) must also prove that the Union (D) breached the collective bargaining agreement. This latter element is comparable to a breach of contract claim, which is a legal issue. Thus, the first part of the analysis does not resolve the issue of whether Terry (P) is entitled to a jury trial. In conducting the second part of the analysis, we note that the only remedy sought by Terry (P) is an award of back pay and benefits. Although this is an award for compensatory damages, we have not held that any award of monetary relief must necessarily be legal in nature. Furthermore, the Union (D) argues that back pay relief must be considered equitable, because the Court has labeled back pay awards under Title VII as equitable. Nevertheless, Congress specifically characterized back pay under Title VII as a form of equitable relief, and Congress made no similar pronouncement regarding the duty of fair representation. We therefore hold that the remedy of back pay is legal in nature, as it is not a form of restitutionary relief but rather an action for the payment of money and benefits. All in all, considering both elements of the Seventh Amendment inquiry, we conclude that Terry (P) is entitled to a jury trial. Affirmed.

Concurrence: (Brennan, J.) I agree that Terry (P) and the other employees seek a remedy that is legal in nature and, hence, that the Seventh Amendment mandates a jury trial. However, I believe that the historical inquiry conducted by the Court can and should be simplified. In expounding the historical test, this Court has repeatedly discounted the significance of the analogous form of action at English common law. I think it is time we dispense with it altogether. Trial judges, who neither have the training nor time necessary to adequately conduct this historical inquiry, should not be required to expend vast judicial resources trying to match a modern claim against an antiquated one. Of course, courts will still be required to examine the nature of the remedies sought and to determine whether they are legal or equitable in nature.

Concurrence: (Stevens, J.) I believe that the Court has made this case unnecessarily difficult by exaggerating the importance of finding a precise common-law analogy. Duty of fair representation suits are ordinary civil actions similar to contract and malpractice disputes. There is no ground for excluding these actions from the right to jury trial.

Dissent: (Kennedy, J.) The Court initially determined that the duty of fair representation action is more similar to cases tried in equity than cases tried in courts of law. Thus, our inquiry should end and there should be no right to jury trial. However, the majority overcomes the equitable nature of the claim by noting that Terry (P) must prove a breach of the collective-bargaining agreement as one element of the claim. I disagree with Justice Marshall's reliance on previous cases to reach this conclusion. Having determined that the duty of fair representation claim is equitable in nature, the cases relied upon by Marshall are inapplicable. Absent certain procedural justifications, we have never parsed legal elements out of equitable claims. The Court also rules that Terry (P) and the other employees have a right to jury trial because they seek money damages. However, we have consistently held that an award of monetary relief must not necessarily be legal in nature. I believe that the injunctive and monetary remedies available make the duty of fair representation suit analogous to an equitable action. I also disagree with the concurrences by Justices Brennan and Stevens, calling for an abandonment of the historical test. Our entire constitutional experience teaches that history must inform the judicial inquiry, and thus we should continue to look to 18th-century England for a resolution of the legal vs. equitable dispute.

Analysis:

This case demonstrates that the majority of the Supreme Court remains committed to an expanded view of the Seventh Amendment right to jury trial. Although the Court recognized the equitable nature of Terry's (P) claim, the majority takes great strides to find that the cause of action was legal in character. Further, the opinion underscores the importance of the two-pronged approach to determining the Seventh Amendment right. Justices Brennan and Stevens, in their concurring opinions, raised valid points about the difficulties courts face in attempting to find analogies between modern causes of action and English common-law claims. While the majority seems unwilling to abandon this historical analysis, it is interesting that the court essentially sidesteps the issue when the result--that the "duty of fair representation" claim parallels a common-law equitable action--argues against the right to jury trial. Thus, perhaps the Court would have been better off abandoning the historical approach altogether. After all, the second prong of the test--whether the remedy is legal or equitable in nature--seems to always decide the issue. On the other hand, the three dissenting justices also raise some valid points in favor of maintaining a strict historical approach to Seventh Amendment issues. In an age of expanding rights to jury trial, however, it may well be that the historical approach should be left behind. Ironically enough, while public and legal criticism of the modern jury system seems stronger than ever, a party's right to jury trial now rests on a solid and expanding foundation.

Amoco Oil Co. v. Torcomian

(Service Station) v. (Operator of Station)

(1983) 722 F.2d 1099

M E M O R Y   G R A P H I C

Instant Facts

Gas station owner and gas station operator filed complaint and counterclaim against each other seeking both equitable and legal relief.

Black Letter Rule

Seeking equitable relief in addition to legal relief does not eliminate the right to a jury trial.

Case Vocabulary

COUNTERCLAIM: Federal court pleading, like a complaint, by defendant against plaintiff or others.

DIRECTED VERDICT: Judge entering judgment for one party before return of jury verdict.

EJECTMENT: Action seeking recovery of land and damages resulting therefrom.

MESNE PROFITS: Profits derived from the land during period of time that it was not in possession of owner.

Procedural Basis: Appeal from a judgment following court trial wherein defendant and counterclaimant was denied a jury trial for legal and equitable claims.

Facts: Torcomian (D) appeals from a judgment denying him the right to a jury trial on the claim by Amoco Oil Co. (Amoco) (P) against him and his counterclaim against Amoco (P). The lower court denied the request for a jury trial because the claims were allegedly equitable in nature. The dispute between the parties involved a service station owned by Amoco (P) and to be run by Torcomian (D) under a franchise agreement. Torcomian (D) operated the station for a short time without executing the franchise agreement. Amoco (P) sued alleging numerous claims, but at the beginning of trial, [thinking it would out smart Torcomian (D)] it amended its complaint to delete many claims that sought money damages, other than for mesne profits. It did so to eliminate any claims that might be construed as legal, so as to foreclose Torcomian's (D) right to jury trial. Torcomian (D) had filed a counterclaim against Amoco (P) seeking an injunction, lost profits for fraud, and attorneys' fees and costs. A bench trial occurred and Torcomian (D) lost. Torcomian (D) appealed contending that there were legal claims and relief sought which should have resulted in a jury trial.

Issue: Does the seeking of equitable relief in addition to legal relief eliminate the right to a jury trial?

Decision and Rationale: (Becker) No. The joinder of an equitable claim with a legal claim does not defeat the right to a jury trial. We must examine the complaint and the counterclaim to determine the type of relief sought. We conclude that Amoco's (P) complaint does seek legal relief. We reject Amoco's (P) [very weak] argument that cases from the state of Pennsylvania control the issue of whether an ejectment action is legal or equitable. It has long been regarded in federal law as legal, and we accept this interpretation. With respect to Torcomian's (D) counterclaim, it sought both equitable relief and damages for the past breach of an agreement which is legal. Accordingly, a jury trial should have been granted unless the error to do so was harmless. The error would be harmless if Amoco (P) would have been entitled to a directed verdict anyway. Since the disposition of the claims rested largely on issues of credibility [in other words, either Amoco (P) or Torcomian (D) was lying], a directed verdict could not have been properly granted on either the claim or counterclaim. Accordingly, because the claim and counterclaim seek legal relief, Torcomian (D) was entitled to a jury trial under the Seventh Amendment. Judgment vacated and case remanded for a new trial.

Analysis:

This case demonstrates the general principle that where a combination of legal and equitable relief is sought, a jury trial is guaranteed under the Seventh Amendment. Remember that at the time the Seventh Amendment was ratified, there were separate courts of equity and law. In order to obtain both equitable and legal relief, two suits were required. The Federal Rules of Civil Procedure resulted in the merger of law and equity, so that one suit could determine both types of actions. However, there was no clear direction as to what to do about the right to jury trial in these combination cases. The court cited to *Beacon Theaters, Inc. v. Westover* and *Dairy Queen, Inc. v. Wood* which held that neither joinder of an equitable claim with a legal claim nor joinder of a prayer for equitable relief with a claim for legal relief as to a legal claim can defeat a right to jury trial. Note that the court here considered whether or not a directed verdict would have been appropriate in order to determine if there was harmless error in denying Torcomian (D) a jury trial. Thus, if there was no basis for either the claim or the counterclaim, and each party would have lost, there would be no need to vacate the judgment and remand. However, the court found that a directed verdict would not have been granted and thus the error in denying a jury trial was not harmless. Also, this case shows Amoco (P) attempting a tactical maneuver prior to trial to prevent a jury trial. Its dismissal of most of its truly legal claims ultimately backfired since the court of appeal found that its claim was legal in nature, and that Torcomian's (D) counterclaims sought legal relief as well.

Edmonson v. Leesville Concrete Company, Inc.

(Construction Worker) v. (Truck Owner)
111 S.Ct. 2077 (1991)

M E M O R Y   G R A P H I C

Instant Facts

Thaddeus Edmonson (P), injured when a truck owned by Leesville Concrete (D) smashed into him, appealed a judgment after Leesville (D) used two peremptory challenges to exclude black jurors.

Black Letter Rule

Peremptory challenges may not be used to exclude jurors on account of their race.

Case Vocabulary

OPPROBRIOUS: Shameful or disgraceful.
PEREMPTORY CHALLENGES: Challenges used to exclude potential jurors without stating the reason for such exclusion.
PETIT JURY: The jury for a civil or criminal trial, as distinguished from a grand jury.

Procedural Basis: Writ of certiorari reviewing affirmance of judgment for damages for negligence.

Facts: Thaddeus Donald Edmonson (P), a construction worker, sued the Leesville Concrete Company (D) in district court for negligence after one of the company's trucks pinned Edmonson (P) against some construction equipment. Edmonson (P) asserted his Seventh Amendment right to jury trial. At voir dire, Leesville (D) invoked two of its three peremptory challenges to remove black persons from the prospective jury. Edmonson (P), a black man, requested that the District Court require Leesville (D) to articulate a race-neutral explanation for the peremptory challenges. [Yes, peremptory challenges used to require no reason whatsoever.] The District Court denied the request on the ground that the cited case, *Batson v. Kentucky* [peremptory challenges cannot be used to excuse black jurors solely on the basis of race], does not apply to civil proceedings. The jury, including eleven whites and one black, found Edmonson (P) 80% contributorily negligent and returned a partial damages verdict for Edmonson (P). Edmonson (P) appealed [apparently feeling that his meager $18,000 award was racially-motivated]. An en banc panel of the Court of Appeals affirmed the judgment, and the Supreme Court granted certiorari.

Issue: May peremptory challenges be used to exclude jurors on account of their race?

Decision and Rationale: (Kennedy, J.) No. Peremptory challenges may not be used to exclude jurors on account of their race. Our *Batson* decision made clear that a prosecutor's race-based peremptory challenge violates the equal protection rights of those people excluded from jury service. Indeed, these constitutional guarantees of equal protection apply in general only to action by the government, and racial discrimination violates the Constitution only when it may be attributed to state action. However, the entire process of jury selection retains an element of state action. A trial judge exercises substantial control over voir dire in the federal system. Further, the objective of jury selection is to determine representation on a governmental body. The fact that the government delegates some portion of the jury-selection process to private litigants does not change the governmental character of the power exercised. When private litigants participate in the selection of jurors, they serve an important governmental function and operate with its substantial assistance. The injury caused by racial discrimination in jury selection is made more severe because the government permits it to occur within the courthouse itself. It only remains to consider whether a prima facie case of racial discrimination has been established in the instant action, requiring Leesville (D) to offer race-neutral explanations for its exclusion of black jurors. We leave it to the trial courts to answer this question. Reversed and remanded.

Dissent: (O'Connor, J.) The decision to strike a juror is entirely up to the litigant and is not encouraged by the judge in any manner. The judge does little more than acquiesce in the decision by excusing the juror. The government only establishes the requirements for jury service, leaving to the private litigant the decision to use peremptory challenges for any reason. Thus, the government is not responsible for everything that occurs in a courtroom, including private challenges by a litigant. No state action is involved in these challenges, and hence the Fifth Amendment's Due Process Clause [and Equal Protection Clause] are not applicable.

Dissent: (Scalia, J.) The majority's decision, as logically applied to criminal cases, will prevent the minority defendant from the certainty of having jurors of his own race, and may result in an all-white jury. In the civil context, the courts now face the added burden of making sure that race is not a factor in the exercising of peremptory challenges. In addition, the decision will permit both sides, in all civil

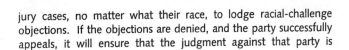
jury cases, no matter what their race, to lodge racial-challenge objections. If the objections are denied, and the party successfully appeals, it will ensure that the judgment against that party is overturned. This only detracts from the merits of the case. I therefore dissent.

Analysis:

This case essentially changes the entire nature of peremptory challenges in civil proceedings. By definition, peremptory challenges to prospective jurors may be made for *any* reason. However, *Batson* had already undermined this basic concept by precluding the use of such challenges to eliminate potential black jurors in criminal proceedings. Nevertheless, in that case, the state-action requirement for equal protection violations was clearly satisfied, since a government prosecutor was engaging in the discriminatory behavior. In the case at hand, conversely, only private litigants are involved in striking certain black jurors. Regardless, the Court desired to eliminate such discriminatory treatment using the only vehicle it saw possible, the equal protection clause. In doing so, the Court quite possibly stretched the concept of state-action beyond its logical extreme. As the strong dissent by three justices accurately noted, peremptory challenges in civil suits involve only the actions of private litigants. The government engages in absolutely no "action" whatsoever. Furthermore, private litigants are not engaging in a governmental function by conducting voir dire; rather, they are simply attempting to win their case for their client. Although racial discrimination at any level is a terrible thing, the Constitution does not necessarily provide recourse for all such discrimination. Nevertheless, the holding stands, essentially redefining the traditional concept of peremptory challenges. Peremptory challenges have now become only a more-flexible form of challenges for cause.

Chapter 10

This chapter looks at the role of the jury, as well as the role of the judge overseeing the jury trial.

The Judge. If the judge concludes that the evidence presented at trial was not legally sufficient to prove the case, he has the power to prevent the jury from rendering a verdict. It is the judge who will then decide the winner and loser. If the case is allowed to go to the jury, the judge still has great power. He can set aside the jury's verdict in favor of one party and declare the other party the winner. Just like that, the case is over! Or, he can set aside the jury's verdict and order a new trial in front of a new and different jury. After the second trial, the judge continues to have the same power as before. The judge even has the power to tell the winner to accept a lesser amount of damages than that awarded by the jury, or else he will grant the loser a new trial.

However, the judge cannot merely disagree with the jury's decision and set aside the verdict and enter a judgment as he sees fit. There are certain legal standards that must be met before the judge can exercise his power of obliterating the jury's verdict. There are things like "inferences" or "weight of the evidence" that the judge must consider when deciding whether to interfere with the jury's decision. The judge has "broad discretion" in making his decision. Do judges decide cases based upon their own opinions of the facts? Yes. Do judges instruct juries on erroneous law? Yes. Do judges reduce the size of jury verdicts that they feel are too great? Yes. Do judges abuse their discretion? Yes. So much for complaining about judges.

The Lawyer. Do lawyers try to get certain people to serve as jurors on their cases? Yes. Do they try to prevent certain people from becoming jurors on their cases? Yes. Do lawyers try to present only favorable evidence? Yes. Do they try to keep the bad evidence from the jury? Yes. Do lawyers make motions trying to prevent the cases from being decided by juries? Yes. Do lawyers beg jurors for excessive damages? Yes. Do lawyers try to have jury verdicts set aside? Yes. Do they seek new trials? Yes. Do they try to get judges to declare winners in spite of juries' verdicts? Yes. And they appeal, appeal and appeal.

The Jurors. Do jurors make irrational decisions? Yes. Do jurors disregard or misunderstand the law? Yes. Do jurors rely on outside influences when making their decisions? Yes. Do jurors make erroneous decisions? Yes. Do jurors award excessive damages? Yes.

Are there clear cut, easily defined rules for judges and jurors to follow? No. But there are rules of procedure which attempt to make the judicial process as fair as possible. This Chapter will address the rules of procedure applicable to trials.

Chapter 10

NOTE: THE PURPOSE OF THIS OUTLINE IS TO ORGANIZE THE CASES SO THAT ONE CAN QUICKLY UNDERSTAND THE RELEVANCE OF EACH CASE TO THE COURSE. NO ATTEMPT IS MADE IN THIS OVERVIEW TO ADDRESS EVERY CONCEPT THAT MUST BE STUDIED. BE SURE TO READ THE ENTIRE CASEBOOK AND/OR OTHER MATERIALS TO GAIN A FULL UNDERSTANDING OF ALL CONCEPTS.

I.   Introduction
   A.   The law seeks to assure that the judge and jury will consider the evidence presented during trial and reach conclusions therefrom that are rationally based. The judge and jury must apply the proper law.
   B.   If the judge in a non-jury trial applies the wrong law, the legal conclusions supporting the judgment will be reversed by the appellate court.
   C.   If the jury is not accurately instructed on the law, the appellate court will reverse the judgment if it concludes that there is a likelihood that the error in law affected the verdict.
   D.   When the judge is the trier of fact, the factual and legal reasoning supporting the judgment must be explained. However, jurors typically are not required to explain how they reached their verdict.
   E.   The law controls what evidence is presented to the jury, and requires that a verdict be set aside if no reasonable person could rationally draw the inferences to support the verdict.
   F.   Generally, the law will not interfere with the jury's reasoning, even if flawed, in order to protect the deliberative process from judicial scrutiny.

II. Rational Inferences
   A.   The law of civil procedure seeks to assure that judgments will be based on inferences that a reasonable person could rationally draw from the evidence. A verdict or judgment should not come from a hunch, partiality, whim or disregard of the law.
   B.   The court has the power to direct a verdict if, by looking at the evidence presented, it determines that the inferences made by the jury from the evidence are not rational.
      1.   For example, where two equal inferences exist to prove a fact, but only one of which can establish liability, there is insufficient evidence to support a verdict. *Reid v. San Pedro, Los Angeles & Salt Lake Railroad.*

   2.   In *Reid*, there was an absence of direct evidence as to how a cow entered onto the railroad tracks before being hit by a train. There were two equal inferences concerning passage onto the tracks, but only one of which would create liability. Thus, there was insufficient evidence to support the verdict in favor of the plaintiff who owned the cow.

III. Procedural Control of Rational Proof
   A.   A jury is many things. It is a fact-finding body, the voice of the community, as well as a temporary, lay and democratic institution. *Juries, Democracy, and Rationality.*
   B.   Rules of trial procedures aim to bring not only truth but fairness to the process. Proof is presented at trial through an adversarial mode where parties take turns in presenting their cases, much like contests. The legal system has devised procedural rules to fit the adversarial presentation of proof. *Adversarial Responsibility for Proof.*
   C.   Two Forms of the Burden of Proof
      1.   The *Burden of Persuasion* may differ depending upon what type of matter or issue is tried. In a criminal matter, the burden of persuasion is "beyond a reasonable doubt". In a civil matter, it is "the preponderance of evidence", also referred to as "more probable than not". Certain issues in civil matters such as fraud, duress or undue influence have an even higher burden of persuasion, that of presenting "clear and convincing" evidence. The burden of persuasion is considered after all the evidence has been presented and is being weighed by the trier of fact.
      2.   The *Burden of Production* requires the party to produce and present evidence in order to remain in court and hopefully prevail at trial.
   D.   Controlling Juries Before the Verdict
      1.   Judgment as a Matter of Law (Directed Verdict)
         a.   A motion for a judgment as a matter of law or "j.m.l." (previously known as a motion for a directed verdict and still referred to as such by state courts) is made by a party at the close of the other party's case. It is an attempt to prevent the jury from considering the evidence and reaching a verdict. The motion is made on the ground that there is no legally sufficient evidentiary basis on which the jury could find

for the party with the burden of proof.

b. Where the facts give equal support to each of two inconsistent inferences, a party has not sustained her burden of proving facts by a preponderance of the evidence. *Pennsylvania Railroad v. Chamberlain*.

  (1) *Pennsylvania Railroad* involved an action for negligence by a train brakeman's heir against a railroad company wherein it was contended that certain rail cars collided killing the brakeman. Proof of the collision was based upon indirect evidence of hearing the collision and inferring that two sets of rail cars were involved.

  (2) There was however equal support for the opposite inference that a collision occurred between other strings of rail cars. Because the evidence gave equal support to each of two inconsistent inferences, it was appropriate to direct a verdict in favor of the railroad company.

c. When ruling on a motion for directed verdict, the court should consider all of the evidence—not just that evidence which supports the non-mover's case—but in the light and with all reasonable inferences most favorable to the party opposed to the motion. *Boeing Co. v. Shipman*.

  (1) The jury is to determine issues of fact, and the judge decides questions of law.

  (2) However, sometimes the facts are not contested but the jury must decide whether or not the uncontested facts constitute negligence. This is the proper role of the jury. *Railroad Co. v. Stout*.

2. Excluding Improper Influences

a. Other procedural methods seek to assure that jurors will not reach verdicts that cannot be sustained by the evidence.

b. Voir dire aims to eliminate jurors who might reach irrational verdicts.

c. The law of evidence, and instructing the jurors on what to do or not to do during the deliberation process, are other methods used to exclude improper influences.

3. Instructions and Comment.

a. Instructions to the jury serve two purposes.

  (1) They instruct the jury on the applicable law, and also

  (2) Provide a vehicle for the appellate court to determine whether there has been a misstatement of the law.

b. Generally, a judge is allowed to comment on the evidence. However, it must be done very carefully so as not to prejudice the jury.

E. Controlling Juries After the Verdict

1. Motion for Judgment as a Matter of Law (Judgment Notwithstanding the Verdict)

a. The grounds for this post verdict motion are identical to those for a motion for directed verdict made pre-verdict, i.e., that there is no legally sufficient evidentiary basis for a reasonable jury to find for the party against whom the motion is made.

b. In federal court, the motion for judgment as a matter of law (or J.N.O.V.) cannot be considered unless the moving party made a motion for directed verdict at the close of all the evidence.

2. Motion for New Trial

a. Flawed Procedures: A new trial may be made where the process leading up to the verdict has been flawed. Examples include:

  (1) An impermissible argument to the jury by the lawyer,

  (2) Error in admission of certain evidence,

  (3) Error in jury instructions, and

  (4) Jury misconduct.

b. Flawed Verdicts

  (1) If the verdict is flawed, a new trial may be granted.

    (a) An example is a quotient verdict where the jury disregards the instructions on how damages should be calculated. The most common ground is that the verdict is against the weight of the evidence.

    (b) However, the judge may not simply decide the case as if a juror and grant a new trial if the jury disagrees.

  (2) The trial judge has wide discretion in determining whether or not a new trial ought to be granted, but he may not set aside the verdict merely because he would have come to a different conclusion than that reached by the jury.

    (a) It is only upon finding that the jury reached a seriously erroneous result that the verdict should be set aside.

    (b) A trial judge therefore abuses his discretion in granting a new trial where he substitutes his judgment concerning the weight of the evidence for that of the jury. *Lind v. Schenley Industries.*

3. Conditional New Trials

   a. A trial judge may grant a partial new trial limited to the issue of damages. *New Trial Limited to Damages.*

   b. A trial judge may order a conditional new trial.

      (1) A *remittitur* is an order for a new trial, unless the plaintiff agrees to accept reduced damages.

      (2) An *additur* is an order for a new trial, unless the defendant consents to an increase in the amount of the verdict. Additur is not allowed in federal courts. The Supreme Court determined it to be in violation of a plaintiff's Seventh Amendment right to jury trial on the issue of damages. *Dimick v. Schiedt.*

      (3) However, many states allow additur. There are three suggested tests for use by the court in determining the appropriate amount of damages when remittitur is ordered. They are:

         (a) Reducing the verdict to the *highest amount* the jury could have awarded;

         (b) Reducing the verdict to a *reasonable amount*; and

         (c) Reducing the verdict to the *lowest amount* the jury could have awarded.

      (4) The Supreme Court has held that a plaintiff must be given a choice between a new trial and accepting reduced compensatory damages. *Hetzel v. Prince William County.*

IV. The Limits of the Law's Control: The Jury as a Black Box

   A. At common law, a juror could not impeach his own verdict. Thus, misconduct had to be established from someone other than the jurors.

1. The Federal Rules of Evidence now govern impeachment of jury verdicts. Rule 606(b) provides that when inquiring into the validity of a verdict, a juror may not testify concerning matters or statements made during the jury's deliberations, such as another juror's mind or emotions influencing a juror to vote in a certain way, or the mental processes involved in the deliberations.

2. An exception exists for extraneous prejudicial information or outside influence which is improperly brought to the jury's attention.

3. Receiving testimony from jurors after they return their verdict for the purpose of ascertaining whether the jury misunderstood the jury instructions is prohibited by Rule 606(b).

4. Therefore, it is error to grant a new trial based upon post verdict statements made to the judge by jurors and relating to the mental processes of the jurors during their deliberations. This is true even if the jurors' comments reveal a lack of understanding of the instructions. *Peterson v. Wilson.*

   B. If there is jury misconduct, such as a juror conducting an experiment at home and reporting his findings to the jury, a new trial is proper. In this situation, juror testimony may be used to show extraneous prejudicial information or outside influence improperly brought to the jury's attention. The jury can render a general verdict or a special verdict.

1. A general verdict can also be accompanied by special interrogatories, which pose questions to the jury.

2. In all but a simple general verdict, there is some clue as to how the jury reached its verdict. However, jurors often are confused by the special verdicts or questions, and sometimes this results in inconsistent answers which then form a basis for challenging the sufficiency of the verdict. *Notes and Problems.*

Reid v. San Pedro, Los Angeles & Salt Lake Railroad

(Cattle Owner) v. (Railroad)
(1911) 39 Utah 617, 118 P. 1009

M E M O R Y   G R A P H I C

Instant Facts

Reid (P) sued Railroad (D) for negligence after her cattle was hit by a train, and the jury found negligence without direct evidence of how the animal entered onto the tracks.

Black Letter Rule

There is insufficient evidence to support a verdict where two equal inferences exist to prove a fact, but only one of which can establish liability.

Case Vocabulary

DIRECT EVIDENCE: Proof of precise fact in question by direct means, such as where a witness sees or hears something.

DIRECTED VERDICT: Judge entering judgment for one party before return of jury verdict.

PREPONDERANCE OF THE EVIDENCE: Proving something by the greater, not just equal, weight of the evidence.

Procedural Basis: Appeal from a judgment following jury verdict in negligence action seeking damages.

Facts: Reid (P) filed suit against San Pedro, Los Angeles & Salt Lake Railroad (Railroad) (D) for damages when her cattle was killed by Railroad's (D) train. Reid (P) contended that Railroad (D) negligently maintained the fence along the railroad so that it was down in certain areas and negligently allowed a gate along the railroad to be opened, so that in either event her heifer strayed onto the railroad tracks and was hit by a train. [Test your farm animal knowledge—Is a heifer a calf, bull, cow, cattle steer, bovine, all of the above or none of the above?] Reid (P) kept the cattle on private land owned by another and located next to the train tracks. Railroad (D) provided the gates for the convenience of the land owner. It was not contended at trial that Railroad (D) left the gate open. The evidence showed that the animal was killed in the immediate vicinity of the open gate and about a mile from the downed portion of the fence. However, there was no direct evidence as to which passage the animal used to reach the tracks. There was no evidence that the train operated negligently. The jury returned a verdict in favor of Reid (P) and Railroad (D) appealed based upon insufficient evidence to support the verdict.

Issue: Is there sufficient evidence to support a verdict where liability is established based upon two equal inferences, one which could establish liability and the other which could not?

Decision and Rationale: (McCarty) No. Reid (P) cannot meet her burden of proof to establish liability by a preponderance of the evidence where there are two equal inferences, only one of which can establish liability. Railroad (D) asserts on appeal that there is insufficient evidence to support the verdict because it cannot be determined where and under what circumstances the cattle got onto the tracks. Statutory law provides that if a railroad company provides gates at private crossings for the convenience of the land owners, the gates must be closed at all times when not in use, and if the owner fails to do so, and his animals stray onto the tracks, the owner cannot recover damages for killed or injured animals. Railroad (D) contends that since the cattle could have passed through the open gate and onto the tracks, resulting in no liability to Reid (P), the verdict must be set aside. The evidence showed that the animal was killed in the immediate vicinity of the gate, and about one mile from the downed fence. However, there was no direct evidence as to how the cattle got onto the tracks. [Maybe it jumped the fence!] The inference is just as strong, if not stronger, that the animal entered through the gate. Reid (P) has the burden of proof to establish liability by a preponderance of the evidence. It is well established that if there are two equal inferences, one which establishes liability and the other which does not, the plaintiff has not met his burden and cannot prevail. In this matter, it was essential for Reid (P) to show by a preponderance of the evidence that the animal entered onto the railroad tracks through the downed fence. Reid (P) did not prove this and thus the verdict is not supported by the evidence. The trial court should have directed a verdict for Railroad (D). [Answer - a heifer is a cow that has not had a calf.]

Analysis:

This case shows that a jury's verdict may be set aside where there is insufficient evidence to support the verdict. There was no direct evidence to prove how the animal got onto the tracks, only indirect evidence based upon inferences. The holding of the case exemplifies that where there are two equal inferences, only one of which can support liability, there is no preponderance of the evidence. Reid (P) did not produce evidence to permit the jury to rationally conclude that it was more probable than not that Railroad's (D) negligence caused the death of the animal. There must be a preponderance of evidence to support the verdict. The judge has the power to set aside the jury's verdict where the evidence presented at trial does not satisfy the burden of proof. Note that the court indicated that the inference was strong, if not stronger, that the animal entered through the open agate. If this were true, there would be no liability because of the statute expressly denying damages to a land owner who leaves a gate open and thereby allows an animal to stray. The case shows that a jury may not engage in irrational speculation concerning non-existent facts. The decision gives no indication as to how or why the jury reached the decision that it did. The court must look at the evidence presented and decide whether or not the inferences made by the jury from the evidence are rational. In this case, since it was just as equally possible for Railroad (D) not to be liable, the jury verdict had to be set aside.

Pennsylvania Railroad v. Chamberlain

(Railroad) v. (Deceased Brakeman's Heir)
(1933) 288 U.S. 333

M E M O R Y G R A P H I C

Instant Facts

Action for negligence by train brakeman's heir against railroad contending that certain rail cars collided killing brakeman based upon indirect evidence of hearing collision.

Black Letter Rule

Where the facts give equal support to each of two inconsistent inferences, a party has not sustained her burden of proving facts by a preponderance of the evidence.

Case Vocabulary

BURDEN OF PROOF: Obligation of proving each necessary element of the cause of action or defense.
CIRCUMSTANTIAL EVIDENCE: Indirect evidence from which inferences from the facts are drawn.

Procedural Basis: Appeal to the United States Supreme Court from a judgment in a negligence action seeking damages for wrongful death.

Facts: The heir of a deceased brakeman, Chamberlain (P), brought a negligence action against Pennsylvania Railroad (Railroad) (D) for the brakeman's wrongful death in the train yard. The decedent was riding on a string of two rail cars while trying to move them onto a certain track. Chamberlain (P) contends that the Railroad's (D) employees were negligent in that they caused another set of rail cars to collide with those ridden by the decedent, causing him to be thrown onto the track, run over by the cars and killed. The evidence at trial established that there were a string of seven cars in front of the decedent's string of two cars, and behind him were a string of nine cars. The basis for the claim of negligence is that the string of nine cars behind the decedent collided with the cars ridden by him. However, the testimony from the Railroad (D) employees riding the nine car string, as well as others close by, was that no such collision occurred. The one witness who testified for Chamberlain (P) was also an employee. He testified that he saw the decedent riding the rail cars, and also saw another string of cars that were placed onto another track, and this was followed by the nine car string. He did not pay further attention but when he looked again, decedent was still on his string of cars directing them to a track, and the string of nine cars was behind him and the speed had increased. While looking away again, he heard a loud crash, but did not immediately look in the direction of the noise since it was not uncommon to hear this kind of noise in train yards. [They must crash a lot of trains in train yards.] When he did turn to look, the decedent was no longer in sight. His distance from where the decedent's body was found was approximately 900 feet. This witness did not testify that a collision occurred, but inferred it because he heard a crash, and thereafter saw the two strings of cars moving together. At the conclusion of the evidence, the trial judge directed the jury to find in favor of Railroad (D). The trial judge believed that all of the testimony, being circumstantial evidence, was so insubstantial and insufficient that it did not justify submission to the jury. The court of appeals reversed the judgment and Railroad (D) appealed to the United States Supreme Court.

Issue: Has a party sustained her burden of proving facts by a preponderance of the evidence where the facts give equal support to each of two inconsistent inferences?

Decision and Rationale: (Sutherland) No. A party has not sustained her burden of proving facts by a preponderance of the evidence where the facts give equal support to each of two inconsistent inferences. In these circumstances, it is proper to not submit the matter to the jury and enter a directed verdict against the party who has the burden of proof. Where there is a direct conflict in the testimony concerning a factual matter, the jury must determine which testimony should be believed. In this case, there is no conflict in testimony concerning the facts. The witnesses for the Railroad (D) testified that there was no collision between the nine car string and the decedent's two car string. The witness for Chamberlain (P) did not testify that there was a collision, rather, he said that he heard a loud crash. It was not unusual for him to hear this type of noise in the train yard, and he did not immediately turn to look when he heard the noise. Thus, there is no direct evidence that the crash by the two strings of cars occurred. At most there was an inference to that effect. However, there is equal support to the opposite inference that a collision occurred between either other strings of cars away from the scene of the accident, or a collision between the cars ridden by the decedent and the seven car string in front of him. Thus, the evidence gives equal support to each of two inconsistent inferences. It does not matter that Chamberlain's (P) sole witness has concluded from what he saw that the string of nine cars was involved in a collision with the decedent. His testimony is considered suspicious and incredible. [Although we are not supposed to weigh the credibility of witnesses, we can't resist.] The distance and angle of vision, near dusk, make it practically impossible of seeing whether the front of the nine car string was in contact with the back of the decedent's two car string. Thus, Chamberlain (P) has not sustained her burden of proof. Accordingly, since neither of the inferences can be established, judgment, as a matter of law, must be against Chamberlain (P), the party who has the burden of proof. Judgment of the court of appeals is reversed and that of the district court affirmed.

Analysis:

This case shows how the court may take the matter from the jury where it determines that the plaintiff has not sustained her burden of proof. In the previous case of *Reid v. San Pedro, Los Angeles & Salt Lake Railroad* [insufficient evidence to support a verdict where two equal inferences exist to prove a fact, but only one of which can establish liability], the jury rendered its verdict and the appellate court set aside the verdict. In this case, the court did not even allow the case to be submitted to a jury for determination. Instead, the court directed a verdict in favor of the Railroad (D). The Supreme Court agreed with the trial judge, and reversed the court of appeals, holding that there were two inconsistent inferences that could be drawn from the testimony. On the one hand, there could be an inference that the collision involved the nine car string, and on the other hand, it could have involved the seven car string or other cars entirely. In fact, it was at best an inference that a collision occurred since the witness for Chamberlain (P) only heard a loud noise sounding like a crash. The court, sounding at times like a trier of fact, comments on the credibility of Chamberlain's (P) sole witness by stating that his testimony is considered suspicious and incredible. The court cannot weigh the evidence. It must instead determine whether there is a factual issue to present to the jury. In this case, there was no direct evidence that a collision occurred. The indirect, or circumstantial evidence from Chamberlain's (P) witness was not sufficient because there were two inconsistent inferences that could be had from his testimony. The testimony gives equal support to each of two inconsistent inferences. Accordingly, the court decided, as a matter of law, that Chamberlain (P) could not sustain her burden of proof by a preponderance of the evidence. The court also noted that even the inference of a collision was contradicted by the direct testimony of other employee witnesses, and as such the inference could not be considered by the jury. Finally, also note that the court would not allow the sole witness for Chamberlain (P) to draw a conclusion about what happened based upon his own inferences.

Lind v. Schenley Industries

(Liquor Sales Manager) v. (Liquor Company Employer)

(1960) 278 F.2d 79

M E M O R Y   G R A P H I C

Instant Facts

Liquor company sales manager obtained jury verdict for breach of contract and liquor company moved for j.n.o.v., and alternatively new trial.

Black Letter Rule

A trial judge abuses his discretion in granting a new trial where he substitutes his judgment for that of the jury concerning the weight of the evidence.

Case Vocabulary

ABUSE OF DISCRETION: A standard of review used by the appellate courts, indicating that a judge has come to a clearly erroneous decision.

J.N.O.V.: Latin initials for judgment non obstante veredicto; otherwise known as judgment notwithstanding the verdict.

MOTION FOR JUDGMENT NOTWITHSTANDING THE VERDICT: Motion made post verdict to have judgment rendered in favor of one party notwithstanding a verdict in favor of the other party.

MOTION FOR NEW TRIAL: Motion made post verdict or post decision by court to have the matter tried again.

Procedural Basis: Appeal from judgment following granting of motion notwithstanding the verdict and alternative motion for new trial after jury verdict in breach of contract action.

Facts: Lind (P), a liquor company sales manager, brought an action against his employer Schenley Industries (Schenley) (D), a liquor company, for breach of oral contract. Lind (P) and his secretary testified as to certain promises made by the company and agents for Schenley (D) [not surprisingly] testified that they did not make such promises. The jury found in favor of Lind (P) and awarded him damages. The trial judge granted Schenley's (D) motion for judgment notwithstanding the verdict and, in the alternative, a new trial. The order granting a new trial was made because the judge concluded that the verdict in favor of Lind (P) was against the weight of the evidence. Lind (P) appealed.

Issue: Does a trial judge abuse his discretion in granting a new trial where he substitutes his judgment for that of the jury concerning the weight of the evidence?

Decision and Rationale: (Biggs) Yes. A trial judge may not substitute his judgment for that of the jury concerning the weight of the evidence. If he does so and grants a new trial, an abuse of discretion occurs. In order to overturn the granting of a new trial on the ground that the verdict was against the weight of the evidence, there must be a clear showing that the trial judge abused his discretion in so doing. There is a closer degree of scrutiny and supervision by the appellate court when the ground for granting a new trial is on the basis of the verdict being against the weight of the evidence, as opposed to other permitted grounds for granting new trials. If the appellate court believes that an injustice may result, it may reverse the trial court. The trial judge has wide discretion in determining whether or not a new trial ought to be granted, but he may not set aside the verdict merely because he would have come to a different conclusion than that reached by the jury. It is only upon finding that the jury reached a seriously erroneous result that the verdict should be set aside. In this case, the subject matter for the jury's consideration was simple and straight forward. Its main function, as trier of fact, was to determine whether or not the witnesses were telling the truth. We conclude [luckily for Lind (P)] that the trial judge substituted his judgment for that of the jury and therefore abused his legal discretion. We reverse and remand the case with direction to reinstate the verdict and judgment in favor or Lind (P).

Dissent: (Hastie) This court has never before reversed an order of a trial judge granting a new trial because of his conclusion that the jury had reached an unjust result. Once a trial judge reaches this conclusion, the appellate court's only function is to see whether there was any basis in reason for the judge's conclusion. In this case, there was sharp conflict in testimony. The trial judge may have reasoned that the amount claimed to have been promised to Lind (P) was so abnormally large, and his concern over nonpayment so unnaturally small, as to make it incredible that the promise ever was made. If so, the conclusion of the judge was neither arbitrary nor an abuse of discretion. I think that the appellate court, rather than the trial judge, has usurped the function of the jury.

Analysis:

Procedurally, this case shows how following a jury's verdict alternative motions are made for judgment notwithstanding the verdict ("j.n.o.v.") or, in the alternative, for a new trial. The grounds for the motion for j.n.o.v. are the same as for a motion for directed verdict, i.e., insufficient evidence to support the verdict. The only differences are when the motions are made -- one before the verdict and one following. One ground for making a motion for new trial is that the verdict is against the weight of the evidence. There is a fine line between the permissible granting of the motion on this ground and the erroneous substituting of the trial judge's opinion in place of the jury's opinion. This case examines that fine line. Note that the appellate court felt that the matter for the jury's determination was a simple function of deciding whether or not the witnesses were telling the truth. The dissenting Justice Hastie examined the sharp conflict in testimony and supported the trial judge's conclusion, calling it neither arbitrary nor an abuse of discretion. The majority opinion reviews the standard to be applied by trial judges in ruling on a motion for new trial on the ground of the verdict being against the weight of evidence. It also discusses the standard that the appellate court should apply in reviewing the order granting the new trial. Finally, note that the case analyzes the abuse of discretion standard as applied to new trial motions on only the ground that the verdict is against the weight of the evidence.

Peterson v. Wilson

(Fired Employee) v. (Person Who Fired)
(1998) 141 F.3d 573

M E M O R Y   G R A P H I C

Instant Facts

Employee of University successfully obtained a jury verdict, but new trial was ordered based upon statements made by jurors to judge and employee thereafter lost on re-trial.

Black Letter Rule

It is error to grant a new trial based upon post verdict statements from jurors relating to the mental processes of the jurors during their deliberations.

Case Vocabulary

EX PARTE: Application made by one party [in this case it was the judge] without notice to the other.
INTERROGATORY: A written question.
MOTION FOR J.M.L.: Name used in federal court for motion for judgment as a matter of law. Formerly called motion for judgment notwithstanding the verdict.
QUA: Indicating in the capacity "as" or by virtue of being "as".
SUA SPONTE: Acting in a voluntary manner.

Facts: Peterson (P) brought suit for federal statutory and constitutional claims after being fired, allegedly arbitrarily and capriciously, from Texas Southern University where he worked as a grant director. The jury returned a verdict in Peterson's (P) favor and awarded him damages. Following the verdict, Wilson (D), the person who made the decision to terminate Peterson (P), renewed his motion for judgment as a matter of law, and supplemented it with an alternative motion for new trial. Four months later, the judge granted the new trial for the following specified reason: "The court concludes, based on the jury's verdict and *comments the jurors made to the court after returning the verdict* [and outside the presence of the parties and their respective counsel], that the jury completely disregarded the Court's instructions. Instead, it appears that the jury considered improper factors in reaching its verdict. Accordingly, the Court deems it in the interest of justice to grant a new trial (emphasis added)." Peterson (P) unsuccessfully moved for reconsideration. The case was re-tried and a jury verdict was rendered in favor of Wilson (D). [This is why jury trials are similar to flipping a coin, you never can predict the verdict.] Peterson (P) appealed.

Issue: Is it error to grant a new trial based upon post verdict statements from jurors relating to the mental processes of the jurors during their deliberations?

Decision and Rationale: (Wiener) Yes. It is improper to impeach a verdict based upon the jurors' mental processes during deliberations. It is clearly apparent that the trial judge relied upon information he obtained from the jurors post verdict, and outside the presence of the parties and counsel. Meeting with the jurors alone was impermissible. [But it did not end there. The judge did more.] The judge relied upon the jurors' comments to grant a new trial. The Federal Rules of Evidence govern impeachment of jury verdicts. Rule 606(b) provides that when inquiring into the validity of a verdict, a juror may not testify concerning matters or statements made during the jury's deliberations, such as another juror's mind or emotions influencing a juror to vote a certain way, or the mental processes involved in the deliberations. An exception exists for extraneous prejudicial information or outside influence which is improperly brought to the jury's attention. It is also well settled in case law that juror testimony may not be used to impeach a jury verdict. [Obviously the trial judge didn't know the law on how not to impeach a verdict.] In *Robles v. Exxon Corp.* we held that receiving testimony from jurors after they had returned their verdict, for the purpose of ascertaining whether the jury misunderstood the jury instructions is prohibited by Rule 606(b). It is clear in the case before us that the jurors' statements to the judge related directly to matters that transpired in the jury room, and that these matters comprehended the mental processes of the jurors in their deliberations. These statements formed the foundation of the court's impeachment of the verdict. Such conduct clearly violates *Robles.* We therefore must reverse the trial court's grant of a new trial, vacate the court's judgment rendered on the basis of the jury verdict in the second trial, and reinstate the results of the first trial. We remand the case to the district court for entry of judgment in favor of Peterson (P) and against Wilson (D).

Analysis:

This case demonstrates that a jury verdict cannot be impeached even where the trial judge believes that they did not understand the instructions given. There are express rules, both federal and state, which set forth the specific grounds for impeaching a verdict. Since this was a federal case, Rule 606(b) of Federal Rules of Evidence applied. It was error to impeach the verdict because it was based upon the *deliberation process* of the jurors. If, however, a juror had brought something into the jury room from the outside, such as a dictionary, and it was used as part of the deliberation process, the verdict could be impeached. Note that the judge obtained the information from the jurors outside the presence of the parties and their counsel. The court of appeals referred to this as "impermissible". This case also examines appellate procedure. When a motion for new trial is granted, the order granting the new trial is not immediately appealable because it is not a final judgment. Peterson (P) tried, unsuccessfully, to have the judge reconsider his granting of Wilson's (D) motion for new trial. When that failed, Peterson (P) had to wait for the outcome of the second trial. Since he lost and judgment was entered on the verdict in favor of Wilson (D), Peterson (P) appealed from the judgment in the second trial. However, note that Peterson (P) can, and did, claim error in the granting of the new trial following for the first trial. After Peterson (P) won on appeal, the court of appeal reinstated the verdict in Peterson's (P) favor from the first trial.

Chapter 11

In many ways, appealing resembles the start of a new lawsuit, rather than continuing the same one. Appellate courts and trial courts do not supervise each other's decisions. Furthermore, there are numerous doctrinal walls that place restrictions on the availability of appellate review. These walls limit the persons that may seek review of a trial court decision, limit when trial court decision may be appealed, and limit the depth and scrutiny of appellate review.

There are numerous restrictions that limit which parties may seek review of a trial court decision. Appeals are only allowed by parties who have not settled, and have received a judgment "adverse" to the one that party desired. Thus, in a case where a party wins on one legal theory, but loses on another, that party may not have standing to appeal if the relief sought on the winning theory is the same as the losing theory. Furthermore, according to the doctrine of mootness, a party will not be allowed to appeal if changes in certain circumstances make relief no longer possible. For instance if the claim being litigated is settled during the trial, an adverse decision will not give the losing party standing to contest.

The doctrine of waiver may also prevent the ability to appeal if a party did not present the contention on which it wants a ruling to the trial court. Generally, arguments not used during trial are deemed "waived," and may therefore not be use on appeal by appellants, or on cross-appeal by appellees. Moreover, new issues may not generally be raised during appeal, even due to a change in law. However some courts may entertain a new issue on appeal if a change in law is deemed sufficiently fundamental, or where a "plain error" has seriously affected the fairness, integrity, or public reputation of judicial proceedings.

There are also numerous restrictions which limit when a trial court decision may be appealed. Generally, a party may only appeal after a "final judgement." More specifically, a party may only appeal after a final decision that ends litigation on the merits, leaving only for the court to execute the judgment.

Many exceptions to the final judgement rule exist. The most common of these exceptions is the collateral order doctrine. This doctrine allows a party to appeal prejudgment orders by the trial court, that are final determinations of rights collateral and separable to rights asserted in the action. However, these rights must also be too important to be denied immediate review. For instance, the United States Supreme Court has determined that the right to sued, but not the right to be sued in a different forum, is a right too important to be denied immediate review.

Other exceptions to the "final judgment" rule include, first, 28 U.S.C. section 1292(a), which allows a party to appeal interlocutory or prejudgment orders of a district court, which grant, continue, modify, refuse, or dissolve injunctions, or refuse to dissolve or modify injunctions. The reason for this is the special nature of injunctions and their potential for harm. Second, 28 U.S.C. Section 1292(b), allows a district court judge who wishes to create the possibility for an interlocutory appeal, to certify that the order involves a controlling question of law, has a substantial ground for difference of opinion, and that immediate review may advance the termination of litigation. However, this exception is not heavily used, nor often successful. Finally, a writ of mandamus, obtained in an original proceeding in the court that issues the writ, can order a judge of a lower court to certify an interlocutory appeal.

Lastly, there are restrictions that limit the scope of appellate review. First, although a decision is final, the court of appeals must certify that the question is worth review, and is not obligated to review the lower court decision. Second, when a decision is reviewed by an appellate court, a "clearly erroneous" standard, rather than an "de novo" review, is used. Put simply, if based upon the evidence presented to the trial court, the decision may have reasonably gone either way, the judgment will not be set aside. Finally, even if an appellate court, applying a "clearly erroneous" standard, finds that the trial court committed an error, it will not necessarily reverse. 28 U.S.C. section 2111 forbids federal courts to reverse judgments, based on errors or defects that did not affect the substantial rights of the parties. Thus, an appellate court may not reverse a decision, if it believes that the trial court's mistake amounted to nothing more than "harmless error."

Chapter 11

NOTE: THE PURPOSE OF THIS OUTLINE IS TO ORGANIZE THE CASES SO THAT ONE CAN QUICKLY UNDERSTAND THE RELEVANCE OF EACH CASE TO THE COURSE. NO ATTEMPT IS MADE IN THIS OVERVIEW TO ADDRESS EVERY CONCEPT THAT MUST BE STUDIED. BE SURE TO READ THE ENTIRE CASEBOOK AND/OR OTHER MATERIALS TO GAIN A FULL UNDERSTANDING OF ALL CONCEPTS.

I. Parties Allowed to Appeal
  A. Appeals may only be made by a party to the lawsuit who has not settled.
    1. The principle of "adverse" judgments requires that the relief granted to the party who wishes to appeal, be different from the relief requested.
    2. The doctrine of mootness holds that a party may not appeal if changes in circumstances make relief no longer possible.
      a. Mootness may also result from settlement. *U.S. Bancorp Mortgage Co. v. Bonner Mall.*
      b. One exception to this doctrine, is found in cases where plaintiff's claim has been satisfied, but the question raised is likely to recur. *Sosna v. Iowa.*
  B. The doctrine of waiver may prevent the ability to appeal, if a party did not present the contention on which it wants a ruling to the trial court.
    1. An appellant may not use an argument on appeal, that the appellant did make in the trial court.
    2. If a party who prevails at trial cross-appeals, the party may only raise those arguments made at trial.
      a. However, an appellee may urge in support of a decree, any matter that appears in the record, although his argument may involve an attack upon the reasoning of the lower court or upon a matter overlooked by the lower court. *United States v. American Ry. Exp. Co.*
  C. An issue may not be raised on appeal, due to a change in law between the time of the trial and the appeal.

    1. However, some courts may entertain the new issue brought about by a change in the law, if the change is sufficiently fundamental. *Carson Products Co. v. Califano.*
    2. The "plain error" rule may allow a new issue to be raised at the appellate level, where an error has seriously affected the fairness, integrity, or public reputation of judicial proceedings.
    3. An appealing party, in addition to raising the matter in the trial court, must also raise an issue in the appellate court.

II. When Decision May Be Reviewed
  A. Under section 1291, the "final judgement" rule, a party may only appeal from a final decision of the district courts.
    1. A final decision is a decision that ends litigation on the merits, leaving the court only to execute the judgment. *Catlin v. United States.*
    2. Interlocutory orders, such as a partial summary judgment, are not "final judgments" and are therefore not appealable. *Liberty Mutual Insurance Co. v. Wetzel.*
    3. However, rule 54(b) gives a judge discretion with regard to the question of appealability, when matters that could have been raised separately have been joined in one case under liberal joinder rules.
  B. Rule 58 provides that final judgments shall be set forth on a separate document.
    1. The F.R.A.P. 4(a)(2) may allow appeals from decisions reasonably believed to be final, despite the lack of a separate document embodying the judgment, treating a notice of appeal as filed on the date of the entry of judgement.
  C. Exceptions to the Final Judgment Rule
    1. The collateral order doctrine allows a party to appeal prejudgment orders that finally determine claims of right collateral and separable from rights asserted in the action, which are too important to be denied immediate re-

view. *Cohen v. Beneficial Industries Loan Corporation*.

    a. The right to be sued in a different forum, unlike the right to stand trial, is not a claim of right that is too important to fall within the collateral order doctrine. *Lauro Lines s.r.l. v. Chasser*.

  2. 28 U.S.C Section 1292

    a. 28 U.S.C Section 1292(a), allows appeals from interlocutory orders of the district courts, which grant, continue, modify, refuse, or dissolve injunctions, or refuse to dissolve or modify injunctions.

    b. 28 U.S.C. Section 1292(b), though not often successful, allows a district court judge, who wishes to create the possibility for an interlocutory appeal, to certify that the order involves a controlling question of law with a substantial ground for difference of opinion, and that immediate appeal may advance the termination of litigation.

  3. A writ of mandamus, obtained in an original proceeding in the court that issues the writ, can order a judge of a lower court to certify an interlocutory appeal.

III. Scope of Review

  A. Even if a decision is final, the appellate court is not obligated to review the lower court decision.

    1. An appellate court must utilize a "clearly erroneous" standard rather than an "de novo" review when reviewing findings of fact, and therefore may not disturb the judgments of a lower court if there are two permissible views of the evidence. *Anderson v. City of Bessemer City*.

    2. Rule 52(a) states that, "Findings of fact whether based on oral or documentary evidence, shall not be set aside unless clearly erroneous."

  B. 28 U.S.C. Section 2111, will not allow a federal court to reverse a lower court decision, if the defects and errors of the lower court decision amounted to *"harmless error,"* and did not effect the substantial rights of the parties.

Liberty Mutual Insurance Co. v. Wetzel

(Employer) v. (Employee)
424 U.S. 737 (1976)

M E M O R Y   G R A P H I C

Instant Facts
Liberty Mutual Insurance Co. (D) appealed the grant of partial summary judgment against it, and the Supreme Court now considers the jurisdiction of the appellate court.

Black Letter Rule
A grant of partial summary judgment on the issue of liability is an interlocutory order and is not appealable.

Case Vocabulary

INTERLOCUTORY: An order occurring during a proceeding which is not final and does not ultimately resolve the issues in dispute.

Procedural Basis: Writ of certiorari reviewing jurisdiction of Court of Appeals following affirmance of partial summary judgment finding liability for violations of the Civil Rights Act.

Facts: Wetzel (P) sued Liberty Mutual Insurance Co. (D) in federal district court, alleging that Liberty Mutual's employee insurance benefits and maternity leave provisions violated Title VII of the Civil Rights Act of 1964. Wetzel (P) sought a declaratory judgment, an injunction, and damages. The District Court granted Wetzel (P) partial summary judgment on the issue of liability, holding that the policies did indeed violate Title VII. However, the judgment did not provide any of the relief sought by Wetzel (P). Liberty Mutual (D) appealed this grant of partial summary judgment. The Third Circuit Court of Appeals held that it had jurisdiction and affirmed the judgment. The Supreme Court granted certiorari, and the Supreme Court now analyzes the jurisdiction of the Court of Appeals.

Issue: Does a Court of Appeals have jurisdiction to review the granting of partial summary judgment.

Decision and Rationale: (Rehnquist, J.) No. A Court of Appeals does not have jurisdiction to review the granting of partial summary judgment. Such orders are interlocutory in nature, and thus are not final judgments within the meaning of 28 U.S.C. § 1291. Moreover, § 1292 is not applicable as a basis for jurisdiction in the instant action. If the District Court had granted injunctive relief, this interlocutory order would have been appealable under § 1292(a)(1). However, the District Court granted no relief whatsoever when it decided on the issue of Liberty Mutual's (D) liability. In addition, Rule 54(b) does not apply to cases like this, which are actions on a single claim, and the requirements of § 1292(b) are not satisfied. Were we to allow the Court of Appeals to exercise jurisdiction over cases like this, we would condone the procedure whereby any district court could render an interlocutory decision on liability which would be immediately appealable. Although Congress has provided for exceptions to the "final judgment" rule, none are applicable in the case at hand. Vacated and remanded, with instructions to dismiss Liberty Mutual's (D) appeal.

Analysis:

As a general rule, only final decisions are appealable to higher federal courts. While there are numerous exceptions, which are addressed throughout this chapter, this case involves a straightforward application of the final judgment rule. The only difficult task is defining what exactly constitutes a final judgment. According to many commentators, a final judgment is one rendered after all possible issues have been determined by a trial court. Stated differently, a final judgment ends the litigation on the merits and leaves nothing for the court to do but execute the judgment. Thus, a decision addressing only liability but not considering possible remedies, as in this case, is not a final judgment. Consider briefly the rationale for the final judgment rule. Trial courts make several decisions, ranging from minor orders to grants of summary judgment, throughout the course of the trial. It would obviously cause a substantial disruption in the trial process if each decision were appealable. On the other hand, if one of these decisions is erroneous, it appears to be a tremendous waste of judicial resources to litigate the case to conclusion only to have the entire case reversed on appeal and retried. As the Supreme Court mentions in this opinion, Congress has attempted to reconcile these two arguments by providing limited exceptions to the final judgment rule.

EXCEPT IN RARE CIRCUMSTANCES, AN APPEAL CAN ONLY BE MADE AFTER A JUDGMENT IS FINAL; CLAIMS THAT THE SUIT WAS REQUIRED TO BE FILED IN A DIFFERENT COURT ARE NO EXCEPTION

Lauro Lines s.r.l. v. Chasser

(Yacht Owner) v. (Passengers)
490 U.S. 495 (1989)

M E M O R Y   G R A P H I C

Instant Facts

An interlocutory order denying an Italian company's motion to dismiss, based on a contractual forum-selection clause, is held not to come within the collateral order doctrine exception to the final judgment rule, and therefore cannot be immediately appealed.

Black Letter Rule

Passengers on a cruise ship bring suit against the owner of the ship for deaths caused by terrorists. The cruise ship (D) claims suit must be filed in Italy according to the ticket.

Case Vocabulary

COLLATERAL ORDER DOCTRINE: An exception to the final judgment rule, which allows the appeal of prejudgment orders that finally determine claims of right collateral to rights asserted in the action, and which are too important to be denied immediate review.

Procedural Basis: Certification to the United States Supreme Court of an interlocutory order by the United States District Court denying a motion to dismiss.

Facts: On October 1985, the cruise ship Achille Lauro, owned by Lauro Lines s.r.l (Lauro) (D), an Italian company, was hijacked by terrorists in the Mediterranean. Plaintiffs, who were the passengers, or represent the estate of passengers who were aboard the Achille Lauro at the time, filed suit against Lauro (D) in the District Court for the Southern District of New York, for injuries sustained and for the wrongful death of Leon Klinghoffer. Lauro (D) moved before trial to dismiss the actions, pursuant to the forum clause printed on the back of each passenger ticket. This clause stated that all passengers were obligated to institute any suit arising in connection with the contract in Naples, Italy, and renounce the right to sue elsewhere. The District court denied Lauro's (D) motion to dismiss, holding that the ticket did not give reasonable notice to passengers that they were waiving the opportunity to sue in a domestic forum. Lauro (D) then sought to appeal the District Court's order. The Court of Appeals for the Second Circuit denied Lauro's (D) appeal on the ground that the District Court's orders denying petitioner's motions to dismiss were interlocutory and could be appealed according to section 1291 [which provides that appeals to the court of appeals may only be from final decisions handed down by the district courts]. Furthermore, the Court held that the orders did not fall within an exception to the final judgment rule. The Supreme Court granted certiorari.

Issue: Is an interlocutory order denying a motion to dismiss based on a contractual forum-selection clause, appealable under the collateral order doctrine exception to the final judgment rule?

Decision and Rationale: (Brennan, J.) No. An interlocutory order denying a motion to dismiss based on the right to be sued elsewhere, cannot be appealed under the collateral order doctrine exception to the final judgment rule. A "final judgment" in general, is a decision that ends litigation on the merits and leaves nothing for the court to do but execute judgment. An order denying a motion to dismiss based on a contractual forum-selection clause is not a decision on the merits that ends litigation. It in fact ensures that litigation will continue in the District Court. Therefore, section 1291 will only permit an appeal if the order falls within the narrow exception to the final judgment rule, the collateral order doctrine, as held in Cohen v. Beneficial Industries Loan Corporation [which stated that an exception applies to orders that finally determine claims separable and collateral to rights asserted in the action, too important and too independent of the cause itself to be deferred until the whole case is settled]. The three requirements of this exception are: 1) The order must conclusively determine the disputed question, 2) resolve an important issue completely separate from the merits of the action, and 3) be effectively unreviewable on appeal from a final judgment. The order in this case fails to satisfy the third requirement. An order is unreviewable only when the order involves an asserted right which would be destroyed if it were not vindicated before trial. For instance we have held that the denial of a motion to dismiss, based upon a claim of absolute immunity from suit, is immediately appealable prior to final judgment because of the right of not having to answer for conduct in a civil action. On the other hand, we have held that the collateral order doctrine is not applicable where a district court has denied a claim that the defendant is not properly before the particular court for lack of jurisdiction. In the instant case, Lauro (D) argues their right not to be tried by tribunals outside the agreed forum, cannot be vindicated by appeal after trial in an improper forum. However, an entitlement to avoid suit is different from an entitlement to be sued only in a particular forum. Lauro's (D) claim that it may be sued only in Naples, is as adequately vindicable by appeal after the trial, as the claim that the court lacked personal jurisdiction over the defendant. Therefore the third requirement of the collateral order doctrine has not been fulfilled. Affirmed.

Concurrence: (Scalia, J.) The law does view the right to be sued elsewhere, important enough to be vindicated by an injunction against its violation obtained through interlocutory appeal. The collateral order doctrine permits appeal of final interlocutory determinations of claims that are not only collateral to the rights asserted in the action, but that are also too important to be denied review. The right to be sued elsewhere is not important enough to overcome the policies militating against interlocutory appeals.

Analysis:

This case presents the collateral order doctrine, a well-recognized exception to the final judgment rule. As illustrated by this opinion, the collateral order doctrine is a very narrow exception. As stated in the concurring opinion, final interlocutory determinations of claims must not only be collateral and separable from the rights asserted in the action, the claims must also be too important to be denied review in order to fall within the exception. If the appellate court's review of a claim, after a trial on the merits, would not infringe upon an essential right, then the claim is not appealable until the final judgment of the case has been handed down. In other words, the most important limitation on the availability of the collateral order doctrine, is that the court would necessarily have to find that a denial of immediate review, would most likely preclude any review whatsoever.

Anderson v. City of Bessemer City

(Applicant) v. (Government)
470 U.S. 564 (1985)

M E M O R Y   G R A P H I C

Instant Facts

The appellate court conducted a new review of the district court's findings of fact in a discrimination case, reversing the district court's ruling.

Black Letter Rule

An appellate court must utilize a "clearly erroneous" standard rather than an "de novo" review when reviewing findings of fact.

Case Vocabulary

DE NOVO: A standard of review where the appellate court conducts a new review of the facts and law of the case.

Procedural Basis: Writ of certiorari reviewing reversal of finding of discrimination.

Facts: Anderson (P) sued Bessemer City (D) for discrimination, alleging that she was overlooked for a position because she was a woman. The District Court found that Anderson (P) was the most qualified candidate, and entered other findings of fact and conclusions of law. The Court of Appeals for the Fourth Circuit reversed, holding that the District Court's findings were clearly erroneous. The Supreme Court granted certiorari.

Issue: When reviewing factual findings, is the function of an appellate court to conduct a de novo review?

Decision and Rationale: (Justice Not Stated) No. When reviewing factual findings, the function of an appellate court is not to conduct a de novo review. Rather, the appellate court is bound by the "clearly erroneous" standard. Where there are two permissible views of the evidence, the factfinder's choice between them cannot be clearly erroneous. In the instant action, it was plausible, in light of the entire record, that Anderson (P) was the most qualified candidate for the job. In light of a trial court's capacity to rule on issues of fact, we must give deference to the District Court's finding that Anderson (P) was indeed the most qualified. The Court of Appeals improperly conducted a de novo review of the record. If it had conducted a "clearly erroneous" review, it would have determined that nothing in the record mandates reversal of the District Court's findings. Reversed.

Analysis:

This case presents perhaps the best explanation and rationale for the "clearly erroneous" standard. The Supreme Court has revealed that District Court findings of fact should be given great deference. Where there are two equally plausible views of the evidence, and the lower court has adopted one of them, the appellate court should not conduct an independent review and choose the other. Furthermore, the Court notes that this standard applies even when district court's findings are based on physical or documentary evidence. When the district court's findings rest on credibility determinations, even more deference must be given to the trial judge's findings, since the trial judge was present at the examination of the witnesses.

Chapter 12

Imagine that, in an unfortunate accident, an airplane falls from the sky and crashes in the middle of a cornfield. Fortunately no one is killed, but two passengers, John and Jessica, are injured—John with a broken arm and Jessica with a broken leg. To recover the costs of their medical bills, John and Jessica, in separate cases, sue the company that owns the airplane, Junk-It Airlines.

Imagine further that Jessica goes to trial first and wins her suit, recovering $2,000.00 for her broken leg. She isn't happy with the result, however, so two days later Jessica decides to sue Junk-It Airlines for damage caused to her laptop computer (on which she had the only copy of her recently-written novel that would have been a best-seller). Is it fair to Junk-It Airlines if Jessica is allowed to bring this second suit? How about a third suit for the destruction of a valuable antique vase that she had stored in her suitcase? How about a fourth for the big scar that now covers her stomach? Should Junk-It have to defend against a different suit every week, each one stemming from a single airplane crash? Or should Jessica have to bring all her claims against Junk-It at one time?

Or imagine that Jessica's attorney, in a hard-fought battle, wins $200,000.00 for his injured client based on what the judge trying the case calls "horribly gross negligence" on the part of Junk-It Airlines. A week later, in the same courtroom, John's trial for medical damages stemming from his broken arm begins. In Jessica's suit it was established that Junk-It Airlines was negligent. Should John have to establish negligence in his suit, which arose from the same plane crash and the same negligent actions as Jessica's suit? Or can he simply rely on the judgment of negligence made in Jessica's suit and focus his suit only on damages? Would it be fair to allow Junk-It, in John's suit, to argue that they were not in fact negligent, when it had earlier been determined that they were? Would it be fair to allow them to do so even when it might result in inconsistent verdicts on the issue of negligence?

Situations such as John's and Jessica's are not uncommon, and to deal with these situations the law has developed two doctrines: the doctrine of claim preclusion and the doctrine of issue preclusion. These doctrines serve a number of purposes. First, they promote finality—an eventual end to litigation when the time is right for it to end. Second, they promote a complete adjudication of disputes, so that an accurate and just outcome occurs. Finally, they set forth guidelines for dealing with the way in which prior judgments effect later judgments. In sum, the doctrines of issue and claim preclusion deal with the respect that the law has for finalized judgments, the subject of this chapter.

Chapter 12

NOTE: THE PURPOSE OF THIS OUTLINE IS TO ORGANIZE THE CASES SO THAT ONE CAN QUICKLY UNDERSTAND THE RELEVANCE OF EACH CASE TO THE COURSE. NO ATTEMPT IS MADE IN THIS OVERVIEW TO ADDRESS EVERY CONCEPT THAT MUST BE STUDIED. BE SURE TO READ THE ENTIRE CASEBOOK AND/OR OTHER MATERIALS TO GAIN A FULL UNDERSTANDING OF ALL CONCEPTS.

I. Respect for Judgments - An Introduction
  A. The law requires that states, people, and other courts respect judicial determinations made in the courts of our states and nation.
  B. To ensure that this respect is given, the law recognizes the doctrines of claim preclusion and issue preclusion.
    1. While these doctrines are strong bars to collateral attack of prior judgments, a look at the case law shows that they are not always absolute.

II. Claim Preclusion
  A. Introduction
    1. Claim preclusion, also termed *res judicata*, is an affirmative defense that bars parties from litigating a second time, claims that have already been litigated in an earlier proceeding.
    2. There are three essential elements of claim preclusion:
      a. A prior decision on identical issues;
      b. A final judgment on the merits in a prior suit; and
      c. The involvement of the same parties that were involved in the original suit, or the involvement of parties in privity with the original parties.
    3. The goals of claim preclusion are efficiency, finality, and an avoidance of inconsistency.
  B. Suits Presenting the Same Claim
    1. Efficiency
      a. Claim preclusion promotes efficiency by encouraging parties to bring all claims resulting from a single transaction at one time.
      b. Where the parties and the causes of action in two different suits are identical, the first suit precludes the second under the doctrine of claim preclusion. *Frier v. City of Vandalia.*
    2. Consistency
      a. Claim preclusion promotes consistency by disallowing one claim to be resolved by two courts in two different ways.

  b. Claim preclusion treats a judgment on the merits as an absolute bar to relitigation between parties and those in privity with them of every matter offered and received to sustain or defeat the claim or demand and to every matter which might have been received for that purpose. *Martino v. McDonald's System, Inc.*
  C. Suits Between the Same Parties
    1. A person is in privity with another when he is so identified in interest with another that he represents the same legal right as that other person; privity means one whose interest has been legally represented at the time.
    2. Claim preclusion can only be asserted against a person or entity who was a party or in privity with a party in a prior suit. *Searle Brothers v. Searle.*
  D. Following a Judgment on the Merits
    1. A court must have jurisdiction over a matter to render a final judgment on the merits for the purpose of claim preclusion.
    2. A final judgment by a state court upon a cause of action over which the adjudicating court had no subject matter jurisdiction does not have claim preclusive effect in any subsequent proceedings. *Gargallo v. Merrill, Lynch, Pierce, Fenner & Smith.*

III. Issue Preclusion
  A. An Issue Actually Litigated and Determined
    1. Slightly different from claim preclusion, issue preclusion prohibits a party from putting in issue in a subsequent suit facts or questions determined and adjudicated in an earlier case.
    2. When a prior judgment may have been based on one of two issues, a party wishing to invoke issue preclusion in a subsequent suit on one of the same two issues must show that the prior decision was based upon one particular issue and not the other; otherwise, the question will be open to a new contention. *Illinois Central Gulf Railroad v. Parks.*
  B. Parties Affected by Issue Preclusion
    1. Parties to issue preclusion—the precludee and the precluder—do not need to be the same parties that participated in the prior suit; non-parties can

take advantage of the doctrine of issue preclusion.
  a. When a party has had a full and fair opportunity to litigate a particular matter, a person not a party to the original litigation can invoke issue preclusion against the party who had the full opportunity.
2. Issue preclusion does not need to be applied in every potential situation in which it might be applied.
  a. Courts have broad discretion in determining when and where offensive collateral estoppel should be applied. *Parklane Hosiery Co. v. Shore*.
  b. If the circumstances are such that a court's confidence in the integrity of a prior judicial determination is severely undermined, or that the result would likely be different in a second trial, it would work an injustice to deny the litigant another opportunity to present his case. *State Farm Fire & Casualty Co. v. Century Home Components*.

IV. The Outer Boundaries of Preclusion
  A. Introduction: As has been mentioned, claim and issue preclusion are not constitutional principles and are not set in stone. There are times when these doctrines must give way.
  B. Claim Preclusion: Claim preclusion will not be applied in a few situations, including those in which parties have stipulated to claim splitting, a court has reserved a party's right to bring a second suit, or jurisdictional rules disallowed a party from seeking certain forms of relief.
  C. Issue Preclusion: The following, among others, provide exceptions to the application of issue preclusion:
    1. There was no opportunity for appellate review of the prior judgment,
    2. The issue is one of law and a new trial is necessary in order to account for a change in the law, or
    3. The burden of proof on the party against whom preclusion is sought was greater in the prior trial.

D. Judicial Estoppel
  1. Judicial estoppel is a doctrine that precludes a party from adopting a position inconsistent with a stance taken in prior litigation.
  2. At least one federal circuit requires that three elements be met:
    a. The party sought to be estopped must assert a position of fact inconsistent with that taken in prior litigation;
    b. The prior inconsistent position must have been accepted by the court; and
    c. The party sought to be estopped must intentionally have misled the court to gain an unfair advantage.

V. Collateral Attack and the Reopening of Judgments
  A. In addition to issue and claim preclusion, the Full Faith and Credit clause prohibits collateral attack on prior judgments. However, a court, in some instances, does have the option of reopening a prior final judgment.
  B. Full Faith and Credit—A Bar to Collateral Attack
    1. Full faith and credit generally requires every state to give to a judgment at least the res judicata effect which the judgment would be accorded in the state which rendered it. *Durfee v. Duke*.
  C. Reopened Judgments—An Alternative to Collateral Attack
    1. In some cases, a prior judgment can be reopened by means of an independent action.
    2. An independent action should be available, however, only to prevent a grave miscarriage of justice. Independent actions must be reserved for those cases of injustices which, in certain circumstances, are deemed sufficiently gross to demand a departure from the rigid adherence to the doctrine of res judicata. *United States v. Beggerly*.

Frier v. City of Vandalia

(Car Owner) v. (City Government)

770 F.2d 699 (1985)

M E M O R Y   G R A P H I C

Instant Facts

A car owner brought suit against the city in which he lived for multiple towings of a number of cars that he tended to park illegally.

Black Letter Rule

Where the parties and the causes of action in two different suits are identical, the first suit precludes the second under the doctrine of claim preclusion.

Case Vocabulary

CLAIM PRECLUSION: A doctrine of civil procedure that bars two or more parties from litigating a claim that has already been litigated in a prior suit.

"CORE OF OPERATIVE FACTS": The factual basis for a lawsuit, or the facts that make up the basis of a cause of action under the law.

DUE PROCESS CLAUSE: A portion of the 14th Amendment which states that "No state shall . . . deprive any person of life, liberty, or property, without due process of law."

ESTOPPEL BY JUDGMENT: As used in this case, estoppel by judgment is a third name or term for the doctrine of claim preclusion. Other courts, however, have used this same term to refer to issue preclusion.

REPLEVIN: An action brought by one wrongfully deprived of personal property to regain possession of that property.

RES JUDICATA: Another name or term for the doctrine of claim preclusion.

"SAME TRANSACTION": Broadly defined by some to include matters related in time, space, origin, and motivation, a transaction is an occurrence that is the basis for a cause of action under the law. For example, a car accident is a "transaction" for the purposes of claim preclusion.

Procedural Basis: Certification to the Seventh Circuit Court of Appeals of a district court decision dismissing a citizen's claim against the City of Vandalia (D) for failure to state a claim on which relief can be granted.

Facts: Charles Frier (P), a citizen of the small city of Vandalia (D), had a "problem" with parking his cars illegally on a narrow street, which forced others to drive on another citizen's lawn in order to get past Frier's (P) car. During 1983, the police had four of Frier's (P) cars towed to various garages in the city. Frier (P) balked at paying the $10 garage fee, and instead filed suits in Illinois state court seeking replevin. In each suit Frier (P) named as defendants the City of Vandalia (D) and the garage that had towed the car. One of the suits was voluntarily dismissed when Frier (P) got his cars back, but the two other cases were consolidated and litigated. Frier's (P) writ of replevin was denied in each case. After losing in state court, Frier (P) turned to federal court, arguing that the city (D) had not offered him a hearing either before or after it took the cars and that it is the "official policy" of the City (D) not to do so. The complaint invoked the Due Process Clause and 42 U.S.C. § 1983, and it sought equitable relief in addition to $100,000.00 in compensatory and $100,000.00 in punitive damages. The district court dismissed Frier's (P) complaint for failure to state a claim on which relief may be granted. Frier (P) appealed.

Issue: Can a plaintiff bring the same suit against the same defendant more than once?

Decision and Rationale: (Easterbrook, J.) No. A court ought not resolve a constitutional dispute unless that is absolutely necessary. Here it is not. Frier (P) had his day in court in the replevin action. The City (D) has argued that this precludes further suits. The district court bypassed this argument because, it believed, Frier (P) could not have asserted his constitutional arguments in a replevin action. This is only partially correct. Frier (P) could not have obtained punitive damages or declaratory relief in a suit limited to replevin. But he was free to join one count seeking such relief with another seeking replevin. As such, the law of Illinois, which governs the preclusive effect to be given to the judgment in the replevin actions, would bar this suit. The City (D) is therefore entitled to prevail on the ground of claim preclusion, although the district court did not decide the case on that ground. Illinois recognizes the principles of claim preclusion, also called res judicata or estoppel by judgment. Under that doctrine, one suit precludes a second where the parties and the cause of action are identical. Causes of action are identical where the evidence necessary to sustain a second verdict wold sustain the first, i.e., where the causes of action are based on a common core of operative facts. Two suits may entail the same cause of action even though they present different legal theories, and the first suit operates as an absolute bar to a subsequent action, not only as to every matter which was offered and received to sustain or defeat the claim or demand, but as to any other admissible matter which might have been offered for that purpose. In this case the City (D) was a defendant in each replevin action. Frier (P) could have urged constitutional grounds as reasons for replevin. He also could have joined a constitutional claim seeking punitive damages and declaratory relief to his demand for replevin, and therefore he had a full and fair opportunity to litigate. The actions also involve both the same common core of operative facts and the same transactions; the operative facts in the replevin and § 1983 actions are therefore the same. The replevin actions diverged from the path of this § 1983 suit only because the state judge adjudicated on the merits the propriety of the seizures. Having found the seizures proper, the judge had no occasion to determine whether the City (D) should have offered Frier (P) an earlier hearing. But this divergence does not mean that the two causes of action require a different core of operative facts. The courts of Illinois sometimes put the inquiry as whether the two theories of relief allege the same conduct by the defendant, and Frier (P) has attacked the same conduct in all of his suits. Here the replevin theory contained the elements that make up a due process theory, and we are therefore confident that the courts of Illinois would treat both theories as one case of action. The final question is whether it makes a difference that only two of the replevin actions went to judgment, while here Frier (P) challenges the towing of four cars. Under Illinois law the answer is no. The defendant may invoke claim preclusion when the plaintiff litigated in the first suit a subset of all available disputes between the parties. If Frier (P) had filed the current suit in state court, he would have lost under the doctrine of claim preclusion. Under 28 U.S.C. § 1738 [requiring federal courts to follow state claim preclusion rules] he therefore loses in federal court as well. Affirmed.

Concurrence: (Swygert, J.) In my view, the majority has

simply applied the wrong analysis to the problem at hand. Rather than trying to squeeze a res judicata solution into a mold that does not fit, I would review the facts to determine whether Frier's (P) procedural due process claims could withstand a summary judgment motion. Because I believe the City (D) was entitled to summary judgment, I concur in the result. Illinois adheres to a narrow, traditional view of claim preclusion, as opposed to the broader approach codified in the Restatement (Second) of Judgments. Under the modern view, all claims arising from a single transaction—broadly defined to include matters related in time, space, origin, and motivation—must be litigated in a single, initial lawsuit, or be barred from being raised in subsequent litigation. Under that approach, I would agree that Frier's (P) claims are barred, but under the traditional approach that Illinois takes, they are not.

Analysis:

Near the end of the court's opinion, Justice Easterbrook sets forth the purpose of the doctrine of claim preclusion—the benefits that the law of civil procedure recognize as stemming from the doctrine. The court states that claim preclusion is designed to impel parties to consolidate all closely related matters into one suit. Doing so, the court points out, "prevents the oppression of defendants by multiple cases, which may be easy to file and costly to defend." Thus the doctrine of claim preclusion protects potential defendants from both possible harassment and a potentially steep financial burden that litigation tends to incur. In this same vein, the court also states that "[t]here is no assurance that a second or third case will be decided more accurately than the first and so there is no good reason to incur the costs of litigation more than once. When the facts and issues of all theories of liability are closely related, one case is enough." This last statement provides the key to proper claim preclusion: claim preclusion is necessary and proper when the facts, issues, and theories of liability are close enough related that there is no need for a second or third lawsuit. The following key principles apply to claim preclusion: "Under that doctrine, one suit precludes a second where the parties and the cause of action are identical. Causes of action are identical where the evidence necessary to sustain a second verdict would sustain the first, i.e., where the causes of action are based on a common core of operative facts. Two suits may entail the same cause of action even though they present different legal theories, and the first suit operates as an absolute bar to a subsequent action, not only as to every matter which was offered and received to sustain or defeat the claim or demand, but as to any other admissible matter which might have been offered for that purpose." These concepts form the basis for proper claim preclusion.

Martino v. McDonald's System, Inc.

(Former Restaurant Owner) v. (Fast Food Chain)

598 F.2d 1079 (1979)

M E M O R Y   G R A P H I C

Instant Facts

A former restaurant owner brought suit against the McDonald's (D) franchise for violation of the Sherman Act.

Black Letter Rule

Res judicata treats a judgment on the merits as an absolute bar to relitigation between parties and those in privity with them of every matter offered and received to sustain or defeat the claim or demand and to every matter which might have been received for that purpose.

Case Vocabulary

COMPULSORY COUNTERCLAIM: A compulsory counterclaim is a counterclaim that is logically related to the initial claim set forth by the other party, and which also arises out of the same facts or subject matter that is the basis for the original claim. In some cases, if a compulsory counterclaim is not asserted, it is lost and cannot be brought up in a subsequent action.

CONSENT JUDGMENT: Also called an agreed judgment, a consent judgment is a settlement between the parties to a lawsuit that becomes an official court judgment upon a judge's sanctioning approval.

GRAVAMEN: The significant or material part of a complaint or claim.

JUDGMENT ON THE MERITS: A final judgment based not on technical or procedural grounds, but on actual evidence going to the substance of the issue before the court.

SHERMAN ACT: A federal antitrust act, passed in 1890 and amended in 1914, that prohibits any interference, whether direct or indirect, with the free movement of goods interstate.

Procedural Basis: Certification to the United States Court of Appeals for the Seventh Circuit of a federal district court decision granting summary judgment against Martino (P) under the doctrine of res judicata.

Facts: In 1962 Martino (P) and his brothers entered into a franchise and lease agreement with McDonald's (D) for the operation of a McDonald's restaurant in Ottumwa. The contract which the parties signed provided that neither Martino (P) nor a member of his immediate family would acquire a financial interest in a competing business without written consent from McDonald's (D). In 1968, Martino's (P) son purchased a Burger Chef franchise in Pittsburg, Kansas [traitor!]. Martino (P) [hereafter referred to as "Big Mac"] financed the transaction. On the basis of this transaction, McDonald's (D) brought suit for breach of contract. The lawsuit, which began in 1972, ended in 1973 with a consent judgment to which the district court appended findings of fact and conclusions of law. The court order also provided that the parties had entered into an agreement for the sale of the Ottumwa franchise back to McDonald's (D) for $140,000.00. The sale was completed. Martino (P) brought suit in 1975, alleging that enforcement of the restrictions on acquisition in the original agreement violated Section 1 of the Sherman Act. The district court entered summary judgment against Martino (P) on Count I of his complaint, and Martino (P) appealed.

Issue: Can a consent judgment form the basis for an application of claim preclusion?

Decision and Rationale: (Pell, J.) Yes. McDonald's (D) argues that the district court correctly held that Count I of Martino's (P) complaint is precluded by FRCP 13(a) ["a pleading shall state as a counterclaim any claim which at the time of serving the pleading the pleader has against any opposing party, if it arises out of the same transaction or occurrence that is the subject matter of the opposing party's claim and does not require for its adjudication the presence of third parties of whom the court cannot acquire jurisdiction"], as claims not coming within the definition of "compulsory counterclaim" are lost if not raised at the proper time. Rule 13(a), however, by its own terms, does not apply unless there has been some form of pleading. Martino (P), in the prior action, filed no pleading as defined by the FRCP. As such, Rule 13(a) does not apply to bar Martino's (P) claim. Although Rule 13(a) does not dispose of Martino's (P) antitrust claim, longstanding principles of res judicata establish a narrowly defined class of common law compulsory counterclaims. We hold that the antitrust claims set forth in Count I of Martino's (P) complaint falls within this narrow class of claims and that the res judicata effect of the earlier consent judgment is a bar to raising it again now. Res judicata treats a judgment on the merits as an absolute bar to relitigation between parties and those in privity with them of every matter offered and received to sustain or defeat the claim or demand and to every matter which might have been received for that purpose. The conclusion of the earlier contract lawsuit with a consent judgment does not prevent the earlier judgment from having a res judicata effect. Having determined that the prior consent judgment is an adjudication on the merits, we conclude that this judgment precludes Count I of the antitrust action. The gravamen of Count I of Martino's (P) antitrust complaint is the 1973 lawsuit. In fact, it is impossible to interpret this count as anything but a direct challenge to the outcome of that suit. The 1973 lawsuit concluded that termination was justified, and Martino (P) now contends that termination was not justified, because the federal antitrust laws forbade it. The well-settled rule for the purpose of determining the res judicata effect of a judgment is that a cause of action comprises defenses, such as the alleged antitrust violation here, that were or might have been raised. As the Supreme Court said in *Cromwell v. County of Sac.*, "[A judgment on the merits] is a finality as to the claim or demand in controversy, concluding parties, and those in privity with them, not only as to every matter which was offered and received to sustain or defeat the claim or demand, but as to any other admissible matter which might have been offered for that purpose." Because the alleged antitrust violation constitutes a separate ground for recovery as well as a defense to the suit to terminate the franchise, however, Martino (P) argues that Count I of this action constitutes a different cause of action for the purpose of res judicata and that the prior judgment does not preclude relitigation of the defendant's termination rights under the antitrust laws. When facts form the basis of both a defense and a counterclaim, the defendants failure to allege these facts as a defense or a counterclaim does not preclude him from relying on those facts in an action subsequently brought by him against the plaintiff. The logic of this rule in circumstances not subject to Rule 13(a) is manifest. Should the earlier litigation end in its very first stage, no great burden on the courts results from permitting a counterclaim to be raised at a more convenient time and place.

Notions of judicial economy give way to fairness. The defendant in the earlier action has his day in court when and where he sees fit. The rule is not absolute, however. Both precedent and policy require that res judicata bar a counterclaim when its prosecution would nullify rights established by the prior action. McDonald's (D) has terminated and repurchased Martino's (P) franchise in reliance on the trial court's 1973 judgment telling them they were justified in doing so. Now Martino (P) seeks to impose significant financial liability on McDonald's (D) for this action. We cannot hold that the counterclaim exception to the res judicata rule, based merely on notions of convenience, permits Martino (P) here to wage this direct attack on the rights established by the prior judgment. Concluding that Martino's (P) claim set forth in Count I of his complaint is a direct attack on the termination rights established in the earlier judgment, we hold that Martino (P) is barred from raising that claim. Affirmed.

Analysis:

While it clearly sets forth the basics of the law of claim preclusion or res judicata, this decision provides important detail as well—detail necessary for something more than a surface understanding of claim preclusion. First, one important element of the doctrine of claim preclusion is the existence of a final judgment on the merits of a particular case. Of course a decision rendered by a judge or jury is usually going to be seen as a final judgment on the merits, but this case makes it clear that a consent judgment can also form the basis for res judicata—the fact that a judgment is a consent judgment does not in any way preclude the application of the doctrine (meaning litigants must be careful as to what they consent to, because there may just be no going back). *Martino* also sets forth the outer limits of the doctrine of claim preclusion when it states that a cause of action comprises defenses that were or *might have been* raised in a prior action. Thus, claim preclusion not only precludes a party from relitigating a defense raised in a prior case, but it cuts off all defenses that were not but could have been raised in that same prior case. This means, at the very least, that a particular plaintiff and his or her attorney needs to very carefully assess all aspects of a particular case before filing suit or responding to a complaint. Thus, this case demonstrates that, in a sense, the doctrine of claim preclusion requires a person to lay all their cards on the table at one time. In so doing it promotes both consistency (as all claims will be decided with the same outcome) and efficiency (the court will not be burdened with multiple suits over the same issue). Finally, this case also makes clear the point that the law will give the utmost respect, for the most part, to the judgments of other courts. The *Martino* court explicitly states that a second suit cannot be brought to challenge the outcome of a prior suit, which, in this case, the court felt that Martino (P) was trying to do. The reasoning behind this rule is clear: if a person were able to challenge the outcome of a suit already decided on the merits and the facts, litigation would be endless. Both sides of a particular case would very possibly continue to pursue litigation until they were either victorious (in which case the other side would sue to attack the judgment), or until they ran out of money. Neither result is desirable, and as such the law recognizes the importance of final judgments and the further importance of respecting those judgments. If nothing else, res judicata, then, keeps the courts from becoming more clogged with litigation than they already are.

Searle Brothers v. Searle

(Partnership) v. (Divorcee)
588 P.2d 689 (1978)

M E M O R Y   G R A P H I C

Instant Facts

A partnership brought suit against a recently divorced woman who was, in a divorce decree, awarded ownership of property belonging partly to the partnership.

Black Letter Rule

A person is in privity with another when he is so identified in interest with another that he represents the same legal right as that other person; privity means one whose interest has been legally represented at the time.

Case Vocabulary

COLLATERAL ESTOPPEL: An affirmative defense that precludes a party in a prior suit from relitigating an issue that was decided in the prior suit (such as a finding of negligence in the first suit stemming from a multi-car accident). The doctrine applies even when the second action differs significantly from the first.

FULLY LITIGATED: A case is fully litigated when there no longer exist any issues that need to be decided at the trial level, but all have been resolved.

ISSUE PRECLUSION: Another name or term for collateral estoppel (not to be confused with res judicata or estoppel by judgment, both of which are names of the separate doctrine of claim preclusion).

PRIVIES: Persons in privity with another.

PRIVITY: People are in privity with another when they are so identified in interest with each other that they represent the same legal right.

Procedural Basis: Certification to the Utah Supreme Court of a lower state court judgment barring Searle Brothers' (P) claim against Edlean Searle (Edlean) (D) on grounds of claim and issue preclusion.

Facts: In a divorce settlement between Edlean (D) and Woodey Searle, the court gave Edlean (D) a piece of property known as the Slaugh House, which had been recorded in Woodey's name but was considered part of the marital property. Despite Woodey's contention that he only owned half of the property, the entire property was given to Edlean (D). The other half, he claimed, belonged to a partnership known as the Searle Brothers (P), of which he and his sons were members. Following the divorce decree, the Searle Brothers (P) brought suit seeking a return of its portion of the property.

Issue: Are agents and principles in privity with one another for the purposes of claim and issue preclusion?

Decision and Rationale: (Ellett, C.J.) No. In general, a divorce decree, like other final judgments, is conclusive as to parties and their privies, and operates as a bar to any subsequent action. In order for res judicata to apply, both suits must involve the same parties or their privies and also the same cause of action. If the subsequent suit involves different parties, those parties cannot be bound by the prior judgment. Collateral estoppel, on the other hand, arises from a different cause of action and prevents parties or their privies from relitigating acts and issues in a second suit that were fully litigated in the first suit. This means that the plea of collateral estoppel can be asserted only against a party in the subsequent suit who was also a party or in privity with a party in a prior suit. The following factors apply in determining whether collateral estoppel applies: [1] Was the issue decided in a prior adjudication identical with the one presented in the action in question? [2] Was there a final judgment on the merits? [3] Was the party against whom the plea is asserted a party or in privity with a party to the prior adjudication? [4] Was the issue in the first case competently, fully, and fairly litigated? With respect to the third factor, it is clear that the Searle Brothers partnership (P) was not a party to the first action; hence, the only way it can be barred from pursuing this second suit is if it were in privity with the parties to the divorce action. The legal definition of a person in privity with another, is a person so identified in interest with another that he represents the same legal right. This includes a mutual or successive relationship to rights in property. Privity means one whose interest has been legally represented at the time. In this case, the Searle Brothers' (P) interest was neither mutual or successive. It claims no part of the interest owned by Woodey Searle, but asserts its own independent partnership interest. The rights are similar, but not identical. The first and fourth tests previously outlined also do not permit the application of collateral estoppel in this case. The partnership interest was not legally represented in the divorce suit, as Woodey Searle was acting in his own individual capacity as the husband of Edlean (D) and not as a representative of the partnership. Edlean (D) argues that Woodey was acting as an agent for the partnership, and therefore the Searle Brothers (P) is bound by the results of the prior action. However, the general rule is that agents and principals do not have any mutual or successive relationship to rights of property and are not, as a consequence, in privity with each other; therefore, a principal is not bound by any judgment obtained against an agent unless the principal became a party or privy thereto by actually and openly defending the action. Further, the right to intervene as a party in a prior suit does not bind the party in the subsequent suit where he failed to so intervene. Based on the foregoing, collateral estoppel is not available to defeat the Searle Brothers' (P) claim. The Searle Brothers (P) cannot be bound by the decree entered in the previous suit, nor is it estopped from litigating its own claim against the property in a subsequent suit. Reversed.

Dissent: (Crockett, J.) I am unable to agree with the majority. Upon a survey of the circumstances, I think that the trial court was justified in its ruling. The property at issue was owned solely in the name of Woodey Searle. The Searle Brothers partnership (P) even admit that he was the managing partner of the claimed partnership and had control of the property in dispute and the income therefrom; he should thus be regarded as representing and protecting whatever interests they and the claimed partnership had therein. Further, the Searle Brothers (P) itself was fully aware of the disputation concerning the ownership of the property. The Searle Brothers (P) actively participated in the lawsuit, but asserted no claim for itself. Instead, it stood by until the determination was made adverse to its interests. Such claim as it has in contesting the record title to the property is based solely on supposed oral declarations made within the family, and self-serving declarations at that. The purpose of collateral estoppel is to protect a party from being subjected to harassment by being compelled to litigate the same controversy more than once. This case is a good example of a situation where the trial court was justified in applying that doctrine and concluding that the plaintiffs should now be estopped from seeking the relief they ask against their mother (the brothers constituting the Searle Brothers (P) were Edlean's (D) sons).

Analysis:

In *Searle*, the court states that collateral estoppel, or issue preclusion, arises from a different cause of action and prevents parties or their privies from relitigating acts and issues in a second suit that were fully litigated in a prior suit. The most important aspect of *Searle* is its discussion on the meaning of the word "privity" (which applies to both claim and issue preclusion). This decision teaches the following principles about privity: First, a person is in privity with another when he is so identified in interest with that other person that he represents the same legal right. This includes a mutual or successive relationship to rights in property. Second, the general rule is that agents and principles do not have any mutual or successive relationship to rights of property and are not, as a consequence, in privity with each other. This means that a principal is, in the usual case, not bound by any judgment obtained against an agent, though this is not the case when the principal becomes a party or privy thereto by actually and openly defending the action. Finally, *Searle* also makes it clear that the right to intervene as a party in a prior suit does not bind the party in the subsequent suit where he failed to so intervene. Understanding these limitations on the privity doctrine will help an attorney to determine the applicability of issue and claim preclusion to persons closely connected with a party in a prior lawsuit.

UNDER OHIO LAW A COURT MUST HAVE JURISDICTION OVER A MATTER TO RENDER A FINAL JUDGMENT ON THE MERITS FOR THE PURPOSE OF CLAIM PRECLUSION

Gargallo v. Merrill, Lynch, Pierce, Fenner, & Smith

(Investor) v. (Broker)
918 F.2d 658 (1990)

M E M O R Y   G R A P H I C

Instant Facts

A disgruntled investor brought suit against his broker on grounds of violations of federal securities law.

Black Letter Rule

A final judgment by a state court upon a cause of action over which the adjudicating court had no subject matter jurisdiction does not have claim preclusive effect in any subsequent proceedings.

Case Vocabulary

COLLUSION: A secret agreement made to further a deceitful or illegal purpose.

CONCURRENT JURISDICTION: Concurrent jurisdiction exists when more than one tribunal has both personal and subject matter jurisdiction over an issue. For instance, when a claim can be brought in both federal and state court (at the party's choice), there exists concurrent jurisdiction.

COURT OF COMPETENT JURISDICTION: A court of competent jurisdiction is one in which jurisdiction, both personal and subject matter, is proper.

DISMISSAL WITH PREJUDICE: A dismissal with prejudice is a dismissal which bars a party from bringing suit again on the same issue or claim. In contrast, a dismissal is "without prejudice" if the party whose suit is being dismissed has leave of the court to re-file a similar action.

EXCLUSIVE JURISDICTION: A court has exclusive jurisdiction when no other court has jurisdiction over a particular case. In *Gargallo*, the court mentions that the federal courts have exclusive jurisdiction over violations of federal securities laws, meaning a state court is not competent to adjudicate such claims.

FULL FAITH AND CREDIT: A principle of law, embodied both in the federal constitution and federal statutory law, that requires one state to enforce the judicial decisions of another state.

Procedural Basis: Certification to the Sixth Circuit Court of Appeals of a federal district court decision barring a securities law claim based on grounds of res judicata.

Facts: Miguel Gargallo (P) opened an account with Merrill Lynch (D) in 1976. He maintained that account until 1980, when his investments went awry and losses occurred, resulting in a debt of $17,000.00 owed to Merrill Lynch (D). When Gargallo (P) refused to pay, Merrill Lynch (D) brought suit for collection in Ohio state court. In response, Gargallo (P) filed a counterclaim alleging, among other things, violations of federal securities laws. The state court eventually dismissed the claim with prejudice for Gargallo's (P) refusal to comply with discovery requests and orders. Gargallo (P) then filed suit in federal district court, charging Merrill Lynch (D) with violations of various securities laws. The district court dismissed the suit on res judicata grounds, finding that the issues, facts, and evidence to sustain Gargallo's (P) action were identical to the claims asserted in his counterclaim, which was dismissed with prejudice. Gargallo (P) appealed.

Issue: Does a federal court have to apply state claim preclusion law in deciding whether a prior state court judgment on subject matter over which only a federal court has exclusive jurisdiction is a bar to a subsequent federal court claim upon the identical cause of action?

Decision and Rationale: (Ryan, J.) Yes. The securities law claims asserted against Merrill Lynch (D) in this case are the same as those Gargallo (P) previously asserted in the counterclaim he filed in state court. As will be explained later, Ohio law governs this situation. Consequently, we must decide whether the state judgment dismissing Gargallo's (P) first lawsuit would operate as a bar, under Ohio law, to the action now brought in this federal court. In Ohio, the requirements for claim preclusion are as follows: "The doctrine of res judicata is that an existing final judgment rendered upon the merits, without fraud or collusion, by a court of competent jurisdiction, is conclusive of rights, questions and facts in issue, as to the parties and their privies, in all other actions in the same or any other judicial tribunal of concurrent jurisdiction." Under Ohio law, the dismissal with prejudice of Gargallo's (P) state court counterclaim was a final judgment on the merits. Whether a final judgment on one claim precludes the filing of another depends on whether the second embodies the same cause of action as the first. Here, Gargallo's (P) suit against Merrill Lynch (D) complains of the same transactions and alleged violations. We agree that the issues, facts, and evidence to sustain this action are identical to the claims asserted in the counterclaim, and we are satisfied that the federal claim giving rise to this appeal is the same claim or cause of action asserted in prior litigation. It is clear to us that Ohio claim preclusion law would bar Gargallo's (P) federal claim. However, the district court is not an Ohio court, but a federal tribunal. Consequently, we must decide whether a federal district court may give claim preclusive effect to an Ohio judgment regarding federal securities laws that are within the exclusive jurisdiction of the federal courts. In *Marrese v. Academy of Orthopaedic Surgeons*, the Supreme Court held that under the full faith and credit statute, federal courts are required to determine the preclusive effect of prior state court judgments, pursuant to the law of the state in which the judgment was entered, even as to claims within the exclusive jurisdiction of the federal courts. That is what we must do here. Ohio takes the position that a judgment rendered by a court lacking subject matter jurisdiction ought not to be given preclusive effect. It seems clear, then, that in Ohio, a final judgment by a court of that state, upon a cause of action over which the adjudicating court had no subject matter jurisdiction, does not have claim preclusive effect in any subsequent proceedings. In sum, we hold that the Ohio court judgment dismissing Gargallo's (P) securities law claims against Merrill Lynch

(D) may not be given claim preclusive effect in a subsequent federal court action asserting those same claims because Ohio courts would not give claim preclusive effect to a prior final judgment upon a cause of action over which the Ohio court had no subject matter jurisdiction. Reversed.

Analysis:

Gargallo stands for the proposition that a judgment must be "on the merits" in order for claim preclusion to apply. In this case, which applies Ohio law, Gargallo's (P) second claim, filed in federal district court, alleged violations of federal securities laws by Merrill Lynch (D). His first suit, adjudicated in state court, made the same allegation. Normally, an adjudication in state court would bar a litigant from bringing a similar suit in federal court (under the issue of claim preclusion), but in Gargallo's (P) case, there was no preclusion. This is because, under the law, federal securities law violations can only be adjudicated in federal court (i.e., state courts are not of competent jurisdiction to address federal securities law issues as they have no subject matter jurisdiction over such issues). As such, the state court's decision was deemed to not be a "decision on the merits." Thus, this case demonstrates the principle that, at least in Ohio, only when subject matter jurisdiction is proper (along with personal jurisdiction and venue) can issue or claim preclusion apply. This rule, however, is not absolute. Citing prior Supreme Court authority, the Sixth Circuit lays down the principle that when addressing issues of preclusion, federal tribunals are to follow the claim and issue preclusion law of the state in which the first judgment was entered. Because Ohio law held that courts without subject matter jurisdiction could not make a judgment that is final and "on the merits" for claim preclusion purposes, that is the rule that the Sixth Circuit followed in reaching the result in this case. If Ohio law had been to the contrary—i.e., recognizing the judgments of courts without subject matter jurisdiction as final and "on the merits"—the result would have been different.

Illinois Central Gulf Railroad v. Parks

(Railroad Company) v. (Accident Victim)

181 Ind. App. 141, 390 N.E.2d 1078 (1979)

M E M O R Y   G R A P H I C

Instant Facts

An accident victim brought a second suit against the railroad company that crashed into his car, after having not been successful in a first suit.

Black Letter Rule

Where a judgment may have been based upon either or any of two or more distinct facts, a party desiring to plead the judgment as an estoppel by verdict or finding upon the particular fact involved in a subsequent suit must show that it was previously decided upon that fact, or else the question will be open to a new contention.

Case Vocabulary

ESTOPPEL BY VERDICT: Another name or term, used by the *Park* court, to refer to issue preclusion.

Procedural Basis: Certification to the Indiana Court of Appeals of a trial court decision rejecting a railroad company's defense of claim preclusion in a suit for accident injuries.

Facts: Jessie Parks (P) and his wife Bertha were injured when their car, driven by Jessie (P), collided with an Illinois Central Gulf Railroad (D) train. Both sued Illinois Central Gulf (D), and Bertha received $30,000.00 for injuries. Jessie (P) sued for loss of services and consortium, and received nothing. He then, in a separate suit, sued Illinois Central Gulf (D) for his own injuries. On a motion for summary judgment by the railroad (D), the trial court held that Park's (P) claim was not barred by the doctrine of claim preclusion. The trial court also held that the prior suit did not establish that Park (P) was contributorily negligent. The trial court held as it did on the theory that it was not possible to determine if Jessie (P) lost because he was contributorily negligent or because he could not prove damages. Illinois Central Gulf (D) appealed.

Issue: When a prior case was determined on one of two separate issues, and it is not clear which issue it was decided on, can issue preclusion be used to prohibit a suit that will raise one of the two issues?

Decision and Rationale: (Lybrook, J.) No. Claim preclusion does not apply in this case, but issue preclusion does. The causes of action in this suit and Park's (P) prior suit are not the same, but if the case at bar were to go to trial on all the issues raised in the pleadings and answer, some facts or questions determined and adjudicated in the earlier case would again be put in issue in this subsequent suit between the same parties. To protect the integrity of the prior judgment by precluding the possibility of opposite results by two different juries on the same set of facts, the doctrine of issue preclusion allows the judgement in the prior action to operate as an estoppel as to those facts or questions actually litigated and determined by the prior action. The problem at hand, then, is to determine what facts or questions were actually litigated in the prior case. In this respect, we agree with Illinois Central Gulf (D) that because the prior case established that the railroad (D) was negligent, in order for the jury to have returned a verdict against Park (P) it had to have decided that he either sustained no damages or that his own negligence was a proximate cause of his damages. This places upon Illinois Central Gulf (D) the heavy burden outlined by Judge Shake in *Flora v. Indiana Service Co.*: "[W]here a judgment may have been based upon either or any of two or more distinct facts, a party desiring to plead the judgment as an estoppel by verdict or finding upon the particular fact involved in a subsequent suit must show that it went upon that fact, or else the question will be open to a new contention. The estoppel of a judgement is only presumptively conclusive, when it appears that the judgment could not have been rendered without deciding the particular matter brought in question. It is necessary to look to the complete record to ascertain what was the question in issue." The railroad (D) argues that, because Park's (P) evidence as to his loss was uncontroverted, the jury's verdict had to be based upon a finding of contributory negligence. Park (P) counters with a contention that, although the evidence was uncontroverted, it was minimal and, thus, could have caused the jury to find no compensable damages. We reviewed the complete record in the companion case and hold that the jury verdict against Park (P) in that case could mean that he had failed in his burden of proving compensable damages. We hold that Illinois Central Gulf (D) has failed its burden of showing that the judgment against Park (P) in the prior action could not have been rendered without deciding that he was contributorily negligent in the accident which precipitated the two lawsuits. Consequently, the trial court was correct in granting partial summary judgment estopping the railroad from denying its negligence and in limiting the issues at trial to whether Park (P) was contributorily negligent, whether any such contributory negligence was a proximate cause of the accident, and whether Park (P) sustained personal injuries and compensable damages. Affirmed.

Analysis:

At first blush, the opinion in *Park* can be somewhat confusing, but once the facts and law are clear, this decision presents an important concept in the area of issue preclusion. Park (P) brought two suits against the railroad (D). The first, in state court, resulted in his receiving nothing in the way of compensation. However, the basis or reasoning behind that decision was not made clear. Thus, as far as the second court knew, the decision could have been based on one of two issues or reasons: [1] The jury found that Park (P) had sustained no compensable injuries; or [2] Park (P) was contributorily negligent to the degree that he deserved no compensation. After Park (P) brought suit a second time, the railroad tried to raise the defense of issue preclusion. The court held, however, that because there was no clear evidence as to the basis of the first court's decision, it would be improper to allow the railroad to raise the defense. This was because, if the court allowed the railroad to raise the issue, it might be precluding Park (P) from litigating an issue that was not decided earlier. At this point, the court brought in the requisite burden of proof, stating that in order for the railroad to preclude the litigation of one of the two issues, it had to prove that the prior court made its decision based on that particular issue, and therefore it had already been litigated. This Illinois Central Gulf (D) was unable to do. This case brings forth an important doctrine of issue preclusion: in order for issue preclusion to apply, there has to be solid proof that a particular issue has already been litigated. If it cannot be demonstrated that a particular issue has been litigated, but simply a possibility that it has been, issue preclusion cannot apply. While issue preclusion seeks to prevent a person from litigating the same issue twice, this case stands for the proposition that a person deserves to have his or her day in court, and only when it is clear that the day has been had will a court disallow bringing suit.

Parklane Hosiery Co. v. Shore

(Corporation) v. (Shareholder)

Supreme Court of the United States, 1979, 349 U.S. 322, 99 S.Ct. 645, 58 L.Ed.2d 552

M E M O R Y   G R A P H I C

Instant Facts

Shore (P), a stockholder in Parklane Hosiery Co. (D) ("Parklane") brought a class action against the latter alleging that Parklane (D) had issued a materially false and misleading proxy statement in connection with a merger.

Black Letter Rule

Trial courts have broad discretion to apply the doctrine of offensive collateral estoppel, even in cases where the defendant will be deprived of a jury trial.

Case Vocabulary

IN PERSONAM: "Into or against the person"; in pleading, the term refers to an action against a person or persons founded on personal liability, and requiring jurisdiction over the person sought to be held liable.

NON-MUTUAL COLLATERAL ESTOPPEL: Where a party who is not bound by an earlier judgment may use the judgment against a party who is bound by the judgment.

OFFENSIVE COLLATERAL ESTOPPEL: Offensive collateral estoppel refers to a situation where a plaintiff is seeking to estop a defendant from re-litigating the issues which the defendant previously litigated and lost in an earlier action.

Procedural Basis: Certiorari to the United States Court of Appeals for the Second Circuit in stockholder class action suit.

Facts: Shore (P), a stockholder, brought a class action suit against Parklane (D) alleging that the latter had issued a materially false and misleading proxy statement in connection with a merger. Before, the instant case reached trial, the SEC filed suit against Parklane (D) based on the same allegations as Shore (P). In that action, the District Court ruled in favor of the SEC, and entered a declaratory judgment to that effect. The Court of Appeals for the Second Circuit affirmed. Subsequently, Shore (P) moved for summary judgment, asserting that Parklane (D) was collaterally estopped from litigating the same issues which had been resolved against it in the suit by the SEC. The District Court denied the motion on the ground that the estoppel would deny Parklane (D) its Seventh Amendment Right to a jury trial. The Court of Appeals for the Second Circuit reversed. The Supreme Court of the United States granted certiorari.

Issue: 1) Can a party be precluded from re-litigating facts resolved adversely to the party in prior equitable proceedings where the court determines that the party has had full and fair opportunity to litigate the facts? 2) Would the use of offensive collateral estoppel violate such party's Seventh Amendment right to a jury trial?

Decision and Rationale: (Stewart, J.) (1) Yes. A party can be precluded from re-litigating facts resolved adversely to the party in prior equitable proceedings where a court has determined that the party has had a fair and full opportunity to litigate the facts. This case involves offensive collateral estoppel, where a plaintiff is seeking to estop a defendant from re-litigating the issues which the defendant previously litigated and lost in an earlier action. This court resolved that the *Blonder-Tongue* case involved defensive collateral estoppel. Contrary to defensive collateral estoppel, offensive collateral estoppel does not promote judicial economy. Since the plaintiff will be able to rely on a previous judgment against a defendant but will not be bound by that judgment if the defendant wins, the plaintiff has every incentive to wait before bringing an action against the defendant, in the hope that the first action by another plaintiff will result in a favorable judgment. Also, offensive collateral estoppel may be unfair to the defendant if the defendant had little incentive to defend vigorously in the first action. However, the preferable approach is not to rule out offensive collateral estoppel altogether, but to allow judges broad discretion to determine when it should be applied. Thus, where a plaintiff could have easily joined the earlier action, where for other reasons the application of offensive collateral estoppel would be unfair to the defendant, a trial judge should not allow its use to the plaintiff. In this case, the use of offensive collateral estoppel should be allowed because the plaintiff most probably could not have joined in the injunctive action brought by the SEC. Also, there is no unfairness to Parklane (D) because the latter had every incentive to litigate the SEC lawsuit fully and vigorously in light of the gravity of the charges and the foreseeability of private lawsuits which could follow. Additionally, there are no procedural opportunities in this action that were not available in the SEC action. (2) No. The use of offensive collateral estoppel would not violate the party's Seventh Amendment right to a jury trial. Parklane (D) argues that the Seventh Amendment should be interpreted based on its scope in 1791, and that since the common law at that time permitted collateral estoppel only where there was mutuality, collateral estoppel can not be applied where there is no mutuality. There is no persuasive reason however, why the meaning of the Seventh Amendment should depend on the existence of mutuality. A litigant who has lost in an equity action is equally deprived of a jury trial whether he is estopped from re-litigating the same facts and issues against the same or a different party.

In either case, there are no more factual issues to be decided by the jury because the facts were already resolved in the previous action. The development of collateral estoppel is not repugnant to the Seventh Amendment simply because they did not exist in 1791. (Affirmed.)

Dissent: (Rehnquist, J.) The contents of the Seventh Amendment right to jury trial should be judged based on historical standards. If a jury would have been impaneled in a particular case in 1791, the Seventh Amendment requires a jury trial today. No one can doubt that at common law, as it existed in 1791, Parklane would have been entitled to a jury trial to determine whether the proxy statement was false and misleading as alleged. The development of non-mutual collateral estoppel is a substantial departure from the common law and its use in this case completely deprives Parklane of its right to have a jury determine contested issues of fact.

Analysis:

Remember that traditionally, collateral estoppel could be used by a party only if that party was bound by the earlier judgment. That is I could use collateral estoppel against you if and only if you could use collateral estoppel against me. However, in this case, the party seeking to assert collateral estoppel against the other party was not even involved in the earlier action. We did encounter the same scenario in the *Blonder* case. However, the collateral estoppel in that case was called defensive collateral estoppel. This means that the defendant in that case, was asserting collateral estoppel against a party who was a plaintiff in the earlier action. In this case however, we are encountered with offensive collateral estoppel, where the plaintiff in the instant action is asserting the judgment of the court against the defendant in the earlier action. Note that in both cases the party asserting the estoppel was not involved in the earlier action. That is why we call the doctrine "non-mutual" collateral estoppel.

State Farm Fire & Casualty Co. v. Century Home Components

(Neighboring Warehouse Owner) v. (Warehouse Owner)

275 Or. 97, 550 P.2d 1185 (1976)

M E M O R Y   G R A P H I C

Instant Facts

Suit regarding the propriety of employing issue preclusion where three cases regarding the negligence of a house builder in starting a fire reached inconsistent results.

Black Letter Rule

Where, in a prior case, there are extant determinations that are inconsistent on the matter in issue with those made in a subsequent case, it is a strong indication that the application of collateral estoppel would work an injustice.

Case Vocabulary

COMPROMISE VERDICT: A verdict that is reached when some jurors concede on certain issues so other issues can be settled in the way they would like them to be.

GENERAL VERDICT: A verdict in which a jury simply finds in favor of one side or the other, as opposed to resolving particular specified questions of fact.

Procedural Basis: Certification to the Oregon Supreme Court of a state trial court decision finding that collateral estoppel barred Century Home (D) from contesting liability in suits following one in which it was held liable for negligence.

Facts: Century Home (D) was in the business of constructing prefabricated housing, which it did primarily in a large shed. State Farm (P) stored some of its property in a warehouse about sixty feet from Century Home's (D) shed. On a Sunday morning in the summer of 1968, a fire started in Century Home's shed, which spread to engulf and destroy State Farm's (P) warehouse. The cause of the fire was disputed, but potentially the result of the actions of Century Home's janitor. Eventually, more than 50 lawsuits were filed against Century Home (D). In the first three, two resulted in judgment for the plaintiffs (i.e., Century Home (D) was found negligent) (*Pacific N. W. Bell* and *Hesse*), and one resulted in a judgment for Century Home (D) (i.e., they were not negligent) (*Sylwester*). Following the entry of judgment in *Pacific N. W. Bell* and *Hesse*, State Farm (P) and a number of other plaintiffs filed amended complaints to match those cases, and asserted that the judgments therein should preclude Century Home (D) from again litigating the question of liability. Century Home (D) relied on the verdict in *Sylwester* to argue that it was not negligent and should not have to re-litigate negligence.

Issue: When prior cases are inconsistent in their verdicts, can a court refuse to apply collateral estoppel in a third suit?

Decision and Rationale: (Holman, J.) Yes. There is no foundation in either experience or policy for accepting the suggestion that a decision rendered after a full and fair presentation of the evidence and issues should be considered either substantially suspect or infected with variables indicating the question might be decided differently in another go-around. However, we are not free to disregard incongruous results when they are looking us in the eye. If the circumstances are such that our confidence in the integrity of the determination is severely undermined, or that the result would likely be different in a second trial, it would work an injustice to deny the litigant another chance. Thus, where it is apparent that the verdict was the result of a jury compromise, the losing party should not be precluded by the judgment. It has also been held that if the prior determination was manifestly erroneous the judgment should not be given preclusive effect. And the existence of newly discovered or crucial evidence that was not available to the litigant at the first trial would provide a basis for denying preclusion where it appears the evidence would have a significant effect on the outcome. Further, where outstanding determinations are actually inconsistent on the matter sought to be precluded, it would be patently unfair to estop a party by the judgment it lost. We agree that, where there are extant determinations that are inconsistent on the matter in issue, it is a strong indication that the application of collateral estoppel would work an injustice. There seems to be something fundamentally offensive about depriving a party of the opportunity to litigate the issue again when he has shown beyond a doubt that on another day he prevailed. State Farm (P) contends that the determinations are not inconsistent because the issues in *Hesse* and *Pacific N.W. Bell* were not identical with the issues in *Sylwester*. It is true that the phrasing of the allegations of negligence differed and that certain specifications of negligence were not submitted to the jury in *Sylwester*. We do not give much weight to variations in the working of the pleadings, however, where essentially the same acts and omissions are alleged. The thrust of State Farm's (P) argument must be that the jury in *Hesse* and the court in *Pacific N.W. Bell* adjudicated Century Home (D) negligent in respects which were not considered by the jury in *Sylwester*. The records of these cases, however, do not permit such a conclusion. Since the jury in *Hesse* returned a general verdict, we do not know in which respects it found Century Home (D) negligent and, given the similarity of some of the allegations and the basic thrust of negligence alleged, we are unable to conclude that it found

Century Home (D) negligent on the basis of conduct not submitted to the jury in *Sylwester*. We conclude that the prior determinations are basically inconsistent and that the circumstances are such that it would be unfair to preclude Century Home (D) from relitigating the issue of liability. Reversed.

Analysis:

While *State Farm* demonstrates the proper application of issue preclusion under the law, it also shows the importance of fairness in the use of issue preclusion. One of the most significant reasons supporting the doctrine of issue preclusion is the fact that to allow a party to re-litigate issues that have already been decided against them would work unfairness in that it would produce potentially conflicting results and decisions. However, this case demonstrates that fairness goes the other way as well. The Supreme Court of Oregon makes it clear that when it would be unfair to apply issue preclusion, such as when a prior decision was reached through jury compromise, issue preclusive effect should be denied to prior judgments. Additionally, when an issue has been tried more than once and the cases have rendered inconsistent verdicts, it would similarly be unfair to apply issue preclusion. In sum, fairness is the key to issue preclusion. When it is fair to apply it, issue preclusion will be applied. When it is unfair, it will not be applied. It is up to the judge to decide when it would and wouldn't be fair to apply issue preclusion.

Durfee v. Duke

(Not Stated) v. (Not Stated)
375 U.S. 106 (1963)

M E M O R Y   G R A P H I C

Instant Facts

Suit regarding the preclusive effect of a prior decision as to the ownership of certain bottom land on the Missouri River.

Black Letter Rule

A judgment is entitled to full faith and credit, even as to the question of jurisdiction, when the second court's inquiry disclosed that those questions have been fully and fairly litigated and finally decided in the court which rendered the original judgment.

Case Vocabulary

ACCRETION: The increase, growth, or enlargement of land caused by the action of natural forces.

AVERMENTS: A declaration or affirmation that a particular fact is true, such as an allegation in a legal pleading.

AVULSION: A separation or cutting-off of land by the change in course of a river or other body of water.

BOTTOM LAND: A piece of low-lying land near a river or other watercourse.

COLLATERAL ATTACK: An attack on a judgment outside of the proceeding in which it was entered. The usual intent of a collateral attack is to have the prior judgment overturned or impeached.

FEDERAL PREEMPTION: A principle of constitutional law holding that, under the Supremacy Clause, federal law supercedes state law that is inconsistent with federal law.

SOVEREIGN IMMUNITY: The principle that a sovereign cannot be sued in its own courts without its prior consent.

TRIAL DE NOVO: A new trial of a particular case, addressing both questions of fact and issues of law, that is conducted as if the original trial had never taken place.

Procedural Basis: Certification to the United States Supreme Court of a federal appellate court decision not to give res judicata effect to a Nebraska Supreme Court judgment regarding the title to a certain piece of land.

Facts: In 1956, the petitioners brought a quiet title action against the respondent in Nebraska state court seeking title to certain bottom land situated on the Missouri River. The main channel of that river forms the boundary between Missouri and Nebraska. The Nebraska court had jurisdiction over the subject matter of the controversy only if the land in question was in Nebraska. Whether the land was in Nebraska depended on whether a shift in the river's course had been caused by avulsion or accretion. The respondent appeared in Nebraska court and fully litigated the issues of the case, all the while contesting subject matter jurisdiction. The court found in favor of the petitioners and quieted title to them. The respondent appealed, and the Supreme Court of Nebraska affirmed. Two months later, the respondent filed suit against the petitioners in a Missouri court to quiet title to the same land, alleging that the land in question was in Missouri. The suit was removed to federal district court, which held that the land was in fact in Missouri, but that all the issues had been litigated and determined in the Nebraska litigation, and that the judgment of the Nebraska Supreme Court was res judicata and "binding on this court." The Court of Appeals reversed, holding that the district court was not required to give full faith and credit to the Nebraska judgment, and that normal res judicata principles did not apply because the controversy involved land and a court in Missouri was therefore free to retry the question of Nebraska's subject matter jurisdiction. This appeal followed.

Issue: When an issue has been fully and fairly litigated and finally decided in a particular court, must other courts give full faith and credit to that judgment?

Decision and Rationale: (Stewart, J.) Yes. The constitutional command of full faith and credit requires that "judicial proceedings . . . shall have the same full faith and credit in every court within the United States . . . as they have by law or usage in the courts of such State . . . from which they are taken." Full faith and credit thus generally requires every State to give to a judgment at least the res judicata effect which the judgment would be accorded in the State which rendered it. By the Constitutional provision for full faith and credit, the local doctrines of res judicata become part of the national jurisprudence, and therefore the federal questions cognizable here. It is not questioned that the Nebraska courts would give full res judicata effect to the Nebraska judgment quieting title in the petitioners. It is the respondents' position, however, that whatever effect the Nebraska courts might give to the Nebraska judgment, the federal court in Missouri was free independently to determine whether the Nebraska court in fact had jurisdiction over the subject matter, i.e., whether the land in question was actually in Nebraska. In support of this position, the respondent relies on the many decisions of this Court which have held that a judgment of a court in one State is conclusive upon the merits in a court in another State only if the court in the first State had jurisdiction to render the judgment. However, while it is established that a court in one State, when asked to give effect to the judgment of a court in another State, may constitutionally inquire into the foreign court's jurisdiction to render that judgment, the modern decisions of this Court have carefully delineated the permissible scope of such an inquiry. From these decisions there emerges the general rule that a judgment is entitled to full faith and credit, even as to the question of subject matter jurisdiction, when the second court's inquiry disclosed that those questions have been fully and fairly litigated and finally decided in the court which rendered the original judgment. One trial of an issue is enough. It is just as important that there should be a place to end as that there should be a place to begin litigation. After a party has his day in court, with opportunity to present his evidence and his view of the law, a collateral attack upon the decision as to jurisdiction there rendered merely retries the issue previously determined. To be sure, the general rule of finality or jurisdictional determinations is not without exceptions. Doctrines of federal preemption or sovereign immunity may in some contexts be controlling, but no such overriding considerations are present here. In sum, for the reasons stated, we hold that the federal court in Missouri had the power and, upon proper averments, the duty to inquire into the jurisdiction of the Nebraska courts to render the decree quieting title to the land in the petitioners. We further hold that when that inquiry disclosed, as it did, that the jurisdictional issues had been fully and fairly litigated by the parties and finally determined in the Nebraska courts, the federal court in Missouri was correct in ruling that further inquiry was precluded. The Court of Appeals is reversed.

Concurrence: (Black, J.) I concur in today's reversal of the Court of Appeal's judgment, but with the understanding that we are not deciding the question whether the respondent would continue to be bound by the Nebraska judgment should it later be authoritatively decided, either in an original proceeding between the States in this Court or by a compact between the two States that the disputed tract is in Missouri.

Analysis:

The common law doctrines of claim and issue preclusion require that courts in the same state must give preclusive effect to the decisions of other courts in the same state. Under the Full Faith and Credit Clause (Article IV) and the Full Faith and Credit Statute (28 U.S.C. § 1738), this requirement of giving preclusive effect to prior decisions is extended to the United States as a whole; under the clause courts in one state must apply preclusive effect to the decisions of courts in other states or the federal government. This makes the United States as a whole a single unit for the purpose of issue and claim preclusion. For a time, however, there was one problem that affected the viability of issue preclusion applying throughout the nation: courts would invalidate the judgments of other courts based on an alleged lack of jurisdiction in the prior court. *Durfee* is one of the first cases to deal with this issue, holding that when jurisdiction, along with the other issues in the case, has been fully and fairly litigated, subsequent courts will be required to accept decisions as to jurisdiction made by the prior court. In this case, that meant that even though the federal district court in Missouri found that the Nebraska trial court had no jurisdiction over the case, it acted as if that court did because the issue of jurisdiction had been fully and fairly litigated. Thus, *Durfee* at least partially plugs the hole and disallows the use of jurisdictional objections to ignore issue and claim preclusion. For this reason, it is a significant decision. In a different vein, it is important to note that, after the Nebraska Supreme Court found jurisdiction to be proper, the case, and the issue of subject matter jurisdiction, was not appealed to the United States Supreme Court. Had the petitioner done so, and won, the second suit would have been completely unnecessary and the doctrine of issue preclusion would not have stopped him from getting the land that he thought was rightfully his.

United States v. Beggerly

(Federal Government) v. (Land Owner)

524 U.S. 38 (1998)

M E M O R Y   G R A P H I C

⚡ Instant Facts

A purported land owner sought to reopen a suit over the ownership of a particular piece of land.

⚖ Black Letter Rule

Independent actions must be reserved for those cases of injustices which, in certain circumstances, are deemed sufficiently gross to demand a departure from the rigid adherence to the doctrine of res judicata.

📖 Case Vocabulary

AUDITA QUERELA: A common law writ in which a party brought an action seeking relief against a judgment already entered on the ground that some defense has arisen since the entry of judgment that could not be taken advantage of unless the judgment is re-opened.

BILL IN THE NATURE OF REVIEW: A common law bill brought in equity to cancel judicial proceedings before the entry of judgment.

BILL OF REVIEW: A common law bill brought to have a decree of a court reviewed, altered, set aside, or reversed.

CORAM NOBIS: A writ of error used to correct errors of fact, and to bring before a court which has entered judgment matters of fact which, if known at the time the judgment was entered, would have prevented its entry.

CORAM VOBIS: A writ of error entered by an appellate court instructing a trial court to correct an error of fact.

"GRAVE MISCARRIAGE OF JUSTICE": An action creates a "grave miscarriage of justice" when it results in a decision that is inconsistent with or prejudicial to the substantial rights of one of the parties.

INDEPENDENT ACTION: As used in this case, an independent action is an action independent and separate from a prior action (i.e., not an appeal) that is brought to set aside the prior action.

ORIGINAL ACTION: Used in this case as another name for "independent action."

Procedural Basis: Certification to the United States Supreme Court of a federal appellate court decision to allow the reopening of a prior judgment.

Facts: In 1979, as a part of creating a National Seashore, the federal government (D) brought a quiet title action (the *Adams* litigation) against Beggerly (P) in the Southern District of Mississippi. The issue in that case was the ownership of certain beach-front property. More specifically, the case turned on whether, before the Louisiana Purchase in 1803, the land in question had been deeded to a private individual. If so, Beggerly (P) owned the land. If not, the U.S. government (D) already owned it, and would not have to purchase it from Beggerly (P). On the eve of trial, the case settled, and a small sum was provided to Beggerly (P) by the government (D); Beggerly (P) agreed to settle because there was not strong proof of his claim. Judgment was entered based on the settlement agreement. Twelve years later in 1994, however, Beggerly (P) brought suit in the same court, seeking to have the settlement agreement set aside. Beggerly (P) also sought a damage award. The new suit was based on a document found by a genealogical record specialist in the National Archives in Washington, D.C. The specialist found materials that, according to her, showed that on August 1, 1781, Bernardo de Galvez, then the Governor General of Spanish Louisiana, granted Horn Island to a private party, meaning that Beggerly (P) had been the owner of the land. The District Court found that it was without jurisdiction to hear Beggerly's (P) new suit and dismissed the complaint. The Court of Appeals, however, reversed, concluding that the suit satisfied the elements of an "independent action," and was therefore proper under Federal Rule of Civil Procedure 60(b). The United States (D) appealed.

Issue: Can completed litigation be reopened when new evidence is found?

Decision and Rationale: (Rehnquist, J.) Yes, but only in special circumstances. The Government's (D) primary contention is that the Court of Appeals erred in concluding that it had jurisdiction over Beggerly's (P) 1994 suit. The Government (D) argues that there was no statutory basis for the Beggerlys' (P) 1994 action, and the District Court was therefore correct to have dismissed it. We think the Government's (D) position is inconsistent with the history and language of Rule 60(b) [allowing a new trial to be granted in certain circumstances]. The 1946 Amendment to the rule made clear that nearly all of the old forms of obtaining relief from a judgment, i.e., coram nobis, coram vobis, audita querela, bills of review, and bills in the nature of review, had been abolished. The revision make equally clear, however, that one of the old forms, i.e., the "independent action," or the "original action," still survived. The Advisory Committee notes confirm this view. The Government (D) is therefore wrong to suggest that an independent action brought in the same court as the original lawsuit requires an independent basis for jurisdiction. This is not to say, however, that the requirements for a meritorious independent action have been met here. If relief may be obtained through an independent action in a case such as this, where the most that may be charged against the Government is a failure to furnish relevant information that would at best form the basis for a Rule 60(b)(3) motion, the strict one-year limit on such motions would be set at naught. Independent actions must, if Rule 60(b) is to be interpreted as a coherent whole, be reserved for those cases of injustices which, in certain circumstances, are deemed sufficiently gross to demand a departure from the rigid adherence to the doctrine of res judicata. Under the Rule, an independent action should be available only to prevent a grave miscarriage of justice. In this case, it should be obvious that the Beggerlys' (P) allegations do not nearly approach this demanding standard. It surely would work no "grave miscarriage of justice," and perhaps no miscarriage of justice at all, to allow the judgment to stand. We therefore hold that the Court of Appeals erred in concluding that this was a sufficient basis to justify the reopening of the judgment in the *Adams* litigation. Reversed.

Analysis:

In the usual case, a losing party attacks a judgment entered against them through the standard appellate process. The final judgment in a case, perhaps made by the Supreme Court, is then generally protected from reversal by the doctrines of issue and claim preclusion, as well as the requirements of the full faith and credit clause and statute. Sometimes, however, restricting an attack on a judgment to the appeals process may work an injustice. For instance, in a case in which one side hides evidence from the other, in contravention of a proper discovery request, and that hiding of evidence is not discovered until after the appeals process is complete, there is no chance for further appeal. In cases such as this, litigants are given the opportunity to reopen a judgment, the subject of *Beggerly*. Today, at least in the federal system, the opportunity to reopen a judgment is given by FRCP 60 - Relief from Judgment or Order. The rule states that when justice requires it, a court may "relieve a party . . . from a final judgment, order, or proceeding" because of mistake, inadvertence, surprise, newly discovered evidence that could not have been brought to light in time for trial, fraud, and a number of other reasons. Time limits are placed upon these options. *Beggerly* is an important case because it demonstrates the use of this option in a real-life fact situation. *Beggerly* is also important in that it makes clear that FRCP 60, while "not limit[ing] the power of a court to entertain an independent action to relieve a party from a judgment," does abolish a number of common law writs used to attack judgments.

Chapter 13

There are numerous situations where a group of plaintiffs, each of whom would be free to sue separately, may consider it desirable to pool their resources and join in a single action. They are permitted to do so, subject only to the requirements that their rights grow out of the same transaction, occurrence, or series of transactions or occurrences and that some question of law and fact common to all of them will arise in the action. Such joinder may not only be advantageous to the parties, but also serve the public interest by preventing relitigation of the same facts in a succession of actions – and with a possibility of inconsistent results. The party-structure of a lawsuit is determined in the first instance by the plaintiff instituting the action. But he is not entirely free to do as he pleases. There are outer limits on who *may* be joined as "proper" parties, and inner limits to tell the plaintiff who *must* be joined. These limits are enforced by the defendant or the court.

There are rules making provision for a plaintiff who is doubtful which of two or more defendants is liable to him. But what of the prospective defendant who is in doubt as to which of two or more claimants is entitled to payment of a debt admittedly owed to one of them? There is an escape from this dilemma, called interpleader. B may commence a suit against C and D and require them to make their respective claims in the same action, thus avoiding the hazard of double liability. Additionally, a defendant may wish to extend the lawsuit in another way. He may want to reach a third person, not joined in the action, who he believes is or may be liable to him for all or part of the claim that the plaintiff is making against him. Impleader permits such a defendant to bring the third person into the case as a party if he can be reached by effective service of process.

Once it is recognized that there may be several plaintiffs, several defendants, and several third-party defendants in an action, the possibility of conflict among the co-parties becomes apparent. Thus, co-parties are permitted, but not compelled, to assert against one another claims that bear certain prescribed relations to the rest of the controversy. Such claims are called cross-claims.

Finally, the class action is a way by which persons may sue or defend not merely on their own behalf, but on the behalf of others not before the court as parties. If each person had to commence his own individual action (or defend an action brought against him alone), there would be repetitious proceedings with a large expenditure of time and money. There would also be the possibility of inconsistent results. Accordingly, under stated conditions and subject to certain safeguards, one or a few members may sue (or defend) on behalf of the class.

Chapter 13

NOTE: THE PURPOSE OF THIS OUTLINE IS TO ORGANIZE THE CASES SO THAT ONE CAN QUICKLY UNDERSTAND THE RELEVANCE OF EACH CASE TO THE COURSE. NO ATTEMPT IS MADE IN THIS OVERVIEW TO ADDRESS EVERY CONCEPT THAT MUST BE STUDIED. BE SURE TO READ THE ENTIRE CASEBOOK AND/OR OTHER MATERIALS TO GAIN A FULL UNDERSTANDING OF ALL CONCEPTS.

I. Introduction: There are two distinguishing features of modern civil procedure in the United States.
   A. Discovery increases the depth of any given lawsuit.
   B. Joinder of claims and parties increases the breadth of a lawsuit.

II. Joinder of Claims
   A. A plaintiff may have more than one claim against a defendant, and a defendant may have claims against the plaintiff.
   B. Joinder of Claims by Plaintiff
      1. Historical Background
         a. At common law, the plaintiff could join only claims using the same writ, but could do so regardless of whether the claims were factually related.
         b. Misjoinder was a mistake which could lead to a successful demurrer or even upsetting of a verdict.
      2. Federal Rules
         a. The Rules eliminated all barriers to joinder of claims by a plaintiff.
         b. The Rules also solve trial management problems by permitting the judge to sever claims for trial convenience.
         c. While joinder is permitted, it is not compulsory. However, there are powerful incentives for plaintiffs to join claims anyway.
      3. Joinder and Jurisdiction
         a. Federal courts are tribunals of limited jurisdiction: They do not have jurisdiction unless a provision of the Constitution and a statute grant it to them.
         b. Supplemental jurisdiction depends on three variables:
            (1) The basis of the original jurisdiction over the case;
            (2) The identity of the party (plaintiff or defendant) seeking to invoke supplemental jurisdiction; and
            (3) The rule authorizing the joinder of the party or claim over whom supplemental jurisdiction is sought.
   B. Claims by the Defendant: Counterclaims
      1. At common law, a defendant who had a claim against a plaintiff could not himself recover in the original action; he had to either bring a separate suit, or "set off" his claim against the plaintiffs.
      2. Rule 13 permits defendants to bring claims against plaintiffs in the same action. Counterclaims are either compulsory or permissive.
      3. An action on an underlying debt in default is a compulsory counterclaim that must be asserted in a suit by the debtor on a truth-in-lending cause of action. *Plant v. Blazer Financial Services.*
      4. A lender's claim for debt against a borrower who sues for violation of the Truth-in-Lending Act has none of the characteristics associated with a compulsory counterclaim. *Whigham v. Beneficial Finance Co.*
      5. Two consequences flow from deciding a counterclaim is compulsory: first, it must be brought at the risk of losing it; and second, if it is brought, supplemental jurisdiction extends to cover it.
      6. There is a penalty for omitting a counterclaim that is later held to be compulsory, but there is no penalty for including a counterclaim that is found not to be compulsory.
      7. A counterclaim is compulsory if it bears a "logical relationship" to an opposing party's claim. *Great Lakes Rubber Corp. v. Herbert Cooper Co.*

III. Joinder of Parties
   A. By Plaintiffs
      1. The difficulties in ultimately adjudicating damages to the various plaintiffs are not so overwhelming as to require severance of the plaintiffs' causes of action. *Mosely v. General Motors Corp.*
      2. Under Rule 21, a defendant can challenge joinder of parties, with the result that the parties found to be improperly joined will have their cases severed.
      3. Rule 42 gives the judge independent power and discretion to consolidate and sever claims.
   B. By Defendants: Third-Party Claims
      1. A third party complaint is appropriate only where the third party defendant is held liable to the plaintiff. *Watergate Landmark Condominium Unit Owners' Association v. Wiss, Janey, Elstner Associates.*

2. Because Rule 14 permits impleader only where the substantive law permits the defendant to pass on liability to another party, most of the difficult problems in impleader cases are substantive.

3. The original version of Rule 14(a), which has been retained by some states that base their procedures on the Federal Rules, permitted a defendant to force another defendant into the suit, even if the plaintiff initially chose not to sue that defendant.

C. More Complex Litigation

1. Locating the line between permissible and impermissible extensions of supplemental jurisdiction requires both a close reading of the statute and a consideration of the underlying concept of the statute. It also involves thinking strategically along with the parties as they invoke the Rules and the principles of jurisdiction.

2. OPPD (D) used impleader as a form of "litigation insurance" and denied liability as its central defense. The Court held that OPPD (D) owed no duty to James Kroger, and, as such, is not liable for his death. *Kroger v. Omaha Public Power District.*

3. A federal court does not retain jurisdiction over an action, based on diversity of citizenship, when the plaintiff adds a pendent party defendant who destroys complete diversity. *Owen Equipment & Erection Co. v. Kroger.*

4. In determining whether jurisdiction over a non-federal claim exists, the context in which the nonfederal claim is asserted is crucial. Supplemental jurisdiction typically involves claims by a defending party brought into court against his will.

D. Compulsory Joinder

1. Rule 19 embodies the propositions that litigation often affected people who weren't formal parties, and if the effects were serious enough and the affected persons could be joined, they should be.

   a. The Rule does not require the joinder of anyone who might be affected by precedent, nor does it require that lawsuits be brought in efficient packages.

   b. In the typical Rule 19 case, the indispensable party issue is raised in the trial court, and it is a given that the assertedly desirable party is not subject to jurisdiction.

2. It is generally recognized that a person does not

become indispensable to an action to determine rights under a contract simply because that person's rights or obligations under an entirely separate contract will be affected by the result of the action. *Helzberg's Diamond Shops v. Valley West Des Moines Shopping Center.*

3. Supplemental jurisdiction is generally denied where there is no independent basis for diversity jurisdiction. It is said that if the courts permitted ancillary jurisdiction in this situation, it would open the door to collusive manipulation of jurisdiction.

IV. Intervention

A. Rule 24 allows some (but not all) who might wish to be involved in a lawsuit to join.

1. Rule 24 is divided into two major categories: intervention of right (Rule 24(a)) and permissive intervention (Rule 24(b)).

2. Intervention of right contains four requirements. The intervention must be timely; the intervenor may not lie in wait until the litigation is on the brink of resolution. The intervenor must have an "interest" in the property or transaction that is the subject of the suit, and that interest must be in some strong way at risk. Finally, even an applicant meeting all these criteria will be denied intervention if those already in the lawsuit are adequately representing the interest.

B. Applicants satisfying their burden of the three requirements of Rule 24(a)(2) should be allowed to intervene in an action. *Natural Resources Defense Council v. United States Nuclear Regulatory Commission.*

C. Occasionally, courts have hinted that knowledge of a pending action in which one could intervene suffices to make the judgment binding on such a person, even though he had not in fact intervened.

D. A party seeking a judgment binding on another cannot obligate the latter to intervene in the action without mandatorily joining that person in the action. *Martin v. Wilks.*

1. Those in the suit share with the court the responsibility for joining the absentees. The penalty for failing to locate and join all absentees is that one must face the prospect of subsequent litigation when the absentees do assert their interests.

2. If one believes that parties should be encouraged or required to intervene in a pending action in which their interests may be affected, one will be

tempted to enforce that belief by refusing to hear a later action. If, on the other hand, one believes strongly in party autonomy, one may be reluctant to require intervention in the original suit and accordingly to permit the later action.

V. Interpleader

A. Congress enacted the Federal Interpleader Act which broadens the circumstances in which interpleader is available, eliminating some restrictions that older equity doctrines had imposed. It also removes limitations on federal subject matter jurisdiction, permits nationwide service of process, and expands venue provisions to permit venue where any claimant resides. *28 U.S.C. Secs. 1335, 1397, 2361.*

B. Rule 24 of the Federal Rules of Civil Procedure allows anyone, upon timely application, to intervene in an action if the applicant claims an interest relating to the property or transaction which is the subject of the action, and that interest is subject to possible prejudice and lack of adequate representation. *Cohen v. The Republic of the Philippines.*

VI. Class Actions

A. Introduction

1. Rule 23 permits one or more parties to sue or be sued as representative parties on behalf of all those similarly situated. The underlying concept is that if many persons find themselves in the same situation, advantages may flow from aggregating many lawsuits into one.

2. When the availability of class actions increases the number of claims that are brought rather than simply facilitating the bringing of large numbers of claims that would have been brought separately, the impact of the underlying substantive law may be greatly heightened.

   a. Some argue that this effect is a regrettable aspect of the rule, while others say that the increased potential for deterring wrongdoers and forcing wider compliance with the law is a powerful argument in favor of the device.

B. Statutory Requirements

1. To become certified, a class action must meet both the requirements of Rule 23(a) and also fit into one of the three categories of Rule 23(b).

   a. The four requirements of Rule 23(a) are referred to as numerosity, commonality, typicality, and adequacy of representation.

(1) Numerosity is established if the class representative can show that enough persons are in the class to make joining them as individuals impractical.

(2) Commonality means that the class should consist of persons who share characteristics that matter in terms of the substantive law involved.

(3) Typicality is the requirement that class representatives stand, in significant respects, in the same shoes as the average class member.

(4) Adequacy of representation focuses on factors such as: the class member must have some stake in the litigation himself, the lawyer should have no conflicts that would cloud the representation, the lawyer has to be sufficiently skillful and equipped with sufficient support and resources to handle the case, and the lawyer's or firm's financial ability to finance protracted litigation.

   b. Having surmounted the hurdles of Rule 23(a), the litigation must also fit into one of the three categories in Rule 23(b).

(1) The 23(b)(1) class is essentially a mass-production version of Rule 19.

(2) Rule 23(b)(2) provides for class actions where the party opposing the class has acted or refused to act "on grounds generally applicable to the class."

(3) Rule 23(b)(3) comprises all class actions not captured in 23(b)(1) and 23(b)(2). In particular, it includes all claims in which the plaintiffs are seeking primarily money damages.

2. A class is not maintainable merely because the complaint parrots the legal requirements of Rule 23; a hearing may be necessary for the court to probe behind the pleadings before coming to rest on the certification question. *Communities for Equity v. Michigan High School Athletic Assn.*

3. The decision to certify (or to refuse to certify) a proposed class action is often critical for the outcome of the litigation. Certification gives the class representative immense bargaining power, refusal to certify means that the defendant is facing only a single plaintiff or a handful of plaintiffs, with much less at stake.

4. Where the district court has given due consideration to all the relevant factors within the context of a rigorous analysis and has not relied upon impermissible factors, it is unable to find an abuse

of discretion. *Heaven v. Trust Company Bank.*

5. Certification of a class has another important consequence in that an adequately represented class is bound by a judgment or settlement.

    a. Because of the important consequences, Rule 23(c)(1) requires that the court shall determine whether to certify a case as a class action "as soon as practicable after the commencement of the action."

    b. Because certification is difficult, and because it so sharply changes the dynamics of the litigation, sometimes parties and judges drag their feet, leaving the class uncertified even after a decision on the merits.

C. The Class Action and the Constitution

1. Representative Adequacy

    a. Fundamental to the class action is the idea that a suit, conducted by a representative on behalf of a number of persons who are not formal parties, may nevertheless bind the entire represented class.

    b. Granting res judicata effect to a class action judgment, in which the prerequisites and procedures for class action were not satisfied, violates due process. *Hansberry v. Lee.*

    c. A judgment in a class action binds absentee members of a class only if they have been adequately represented.

    d. The problem of the binding power of a class action usually boils down to a question of fairness to parties who may not have been adequately represented.

2. Jurisdiction

    a. In class actions, personal jurisdiction does not require that each class member have minimum contacts with the forum state, but the forum state must have sufficient interests in the claims to assert its state law to all claims. *Phillips Petroleum v. Shutts.*

    b. The *Uniform Securities Litigation Standards Act of 1988* restricts state law securities class actions by, first, stating that federal law preempts state securities laws, but only in class actions alleging fraud in the purchase and sale of securities. Second, it provides that all class actions filed in state courts and alleging securities fraud shall be removable to federal district courts without regard to diversity or amount in controversy. *15 U.S.C. Sec. 77p(c).*

D. Settlement of Class Actions and the "Settlement Class"

1. Settlement presents several difficult problems unique to the class action. Most of these problems flow from the circumstance that the litigative group is organized only for purposes of the lawsuit.

2. Fees

    a. Courts regularly award the class lawyer a fee taken directly from the fund created by the litigation.

    b. Setting fees presents problems because most class actions settle, and the fee award is made in the context of a settlement approval hearing required by Rule 23(e).

2. Damages and Injunctive Relief

    a. Damages pose an issue in class actions which rarely arises in ordinary cases: making sure that the class recovery finds its way into the hands of the class members. Class members are often unaware of the class action and subsequent recovery, and consequently don't claim damages.

    b. Fluid class recovery provides that in the case of a class consisting of past consumers that dealt with a company, damages would be distributed to future consumers through rate reductions lasting long enough to exhaust the recovery.

3. Settlement and Dismissal

    a. Class actions are supposed to bind members of the class, so it is particularly important that class members be informed, if possible, of settlement proposals.

    b. In determining the propriety of a settlement–only class certification, the requirements of Rule 23(a) and (b)(3) Fed. R. Civ. P. must be satisfied, and the settlement must be taken into account as well. *Amchem Products, Inc. v. Windsor.*

Plant v. Blazer Financial Services

(Debtor) v. (Lender)
598 F.2d 1357 (1979)

M E M O R Y   G R A P H I C

Instant Facts
Plant (P) borrowed $2,520 from Blazer Financial (D), made no payments for eight months, then sued Blazer Financial (D) under the Truth-in-Lending Act.

Black Letter Rule
An action on an underlying debt in default is a compulsory counterclaim that must be asserted in a suit by the debtor on a truth-in-lending cause of action.

Case Vocabulary

ANCILLARY JURISDICTION: the federal court acquires jurisdiction over the entire case, even though some of the matters would not independently be subject to federal jurisdiction.

COMPULSORY COUNTERCLAIM: Arises out of the same transaction or occurrence as the present claim.

DIVERSITY JURISDICTION: The federal courts have jurisdiction over cases involving citizens of different states.

FEDERAL QUESTION JURISDICTION: The federal courts have jurisdiction over all cases arising under the U.S. Constitution and certain federal statutes.

PERMISSIVE COUNTERCLAIM: Does not arise out of the present claim.

TRUTH-IN-LENDING ACT: A federal law requiring that persons applying for commercial credit be provided with accurate and understandable information relating to the cost of credit.

Procedural Basis: Plaintiff's appeal from the trial court's ruling that the defendant's counterclaim on the underlying debt was compulsory.

Facts: Theresa Plant (P) executed a note in favor of Blazer Financial Services, Inc. (D) for $2,520 to be paid in monthly installments of $105. No payments were made on the note. Eight months later, Plant (P) commenced a civil action under the Truth-in-Lending Act for failure to make disclosures required by the Act. Blazer Financial (D), counterclaimed on the note for the unpaid balance. Based on Blazer Financial's (D) failure to disclose a limitation on an after-acquired security interest, the trial court held the disclosures inadequate and awarded Plant (P) the statutory penalty of $944.76 and $700 in attorney's fees.

Issue: Is an action on an underlying debt in default a compulsory counterclaim?

Decision and Rationale: (Roney, J.) Yes. Plant (P) challenges the trial court's ruling that Blazer Financial's (D) counterclaim on the underlying debt was compulsory. The issue of whether a state debt counterclaim in a truth-in-lending action is compulsory or permissive is one of first impression in this Circuit, has never, to our knowledge, been decided by a court of appeals, and has received diverse treatment from a great number of district courts. Rule 13(a), Federal Rules of Civil Procedure, provides that a counterclaim is compulsory if it "arises out of the transaction or occurrence" that is the subject matter of the plaintiff's claim. The test which has commended itself to most courts, including our own, is the logical relation test. This test is a loose standard which permits "a broad realistic interpretation in the interest of avoiding a multiplicity of suits." The hallmark of this approach is its flexibility. Applying the logical relationship test literally to the counterclaim in this case suggests its compulsory character because a single aggregate of operative facts, the loan transaction, gave rise to both Plant's (P) and Blazer Financial's (D) claims. Because a tallying of the results from the district courts which have decided this question, however, shows that a greater number have found such a counterclaim merely permissive, we subject the relationship between the claims to further analysis. The purpose of the Truth-in-Lending Act is to assure a meaningful disclosure of credit terms so that the consumer will be able to compare more readily the various credit terms available to him and avoid the uninformed use of credit. It has been argued that this purpose would be frustrated if federal courts were entangled in the myriad factual and legal questions essential to a decision on the debt claims but unrelated to the truth-in-lending violation. Additionally, courts have predicted a flood of debt counterclaims, greatly increasing the federal court workload. Other courts have suggested that regarding such debt counterclaims as compulsory would infringe on the power of states to adjudicate disputes grounded in state law. After careful consideration of these factors relied upon to find counterclaims permissive, we opt for the analysis applied by courts in several states in determining debt counterclaims to be compulsory. Emphasizing the goal of judicial economy furthered by a single presentation of facts, one court observed that suits on notes will inevitably deal with the circumstance of the execution of the notes and any representation made to induce the borrowing. We add to these arguments the observation that one of the purposes of the compulsory counterclaim rule is to provide complete relief to the defendant who has been brought involuntarily into the federal court. Absent the opportunity to bring a counterclaim, this party could be forced to satisfy the debtor's truth-in-lending claim without any assurance that his claims against the defaulting debtor arising from the same transaction will be taken into account or even that the funds he has been required to pay will still be available should he obtain a state court judgment in excess of the judgment on the truth-in-lending claim. In addition, a determination that the underlying debt was invalid may have a material effect on the amount of damages a debtor could recover on a truth-in-lending claim. To permit the debtor to recover from the creditor without taking the original loan into account would be a serious departure

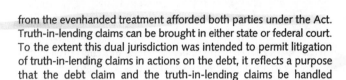

from the evenhanded treatment afforded both parties under the Act. Truth-in-lending claims can be brought in either state or federal court. To the extent this dual jurisdiction was intended to permit litigation of truth-in-lending claims in actions on the debt, it reflects a purpose that the debt claim and the truth-in-lending claims be handled together. We conclude that the obvious interrelationship of the claims and rights of the parties, coupled with the common factual basis of the claims, demonstrates a logical relationship between the claim and counterclaim under the logical relation test. We affirm the trial court's determination that the debt counterclaim is compulsory.

Analysis:

The issue in this case is jurisdictional. A permissive counterclaim must have an independent jurisdictional basis, while it is generally accepted that a compulsory counterclaim falls within the ancillary jurisdiction of the federal courts even if it would ordinarily be a matter for state court consideration. In this case, there is no independent basis since neither federal question nor diversity jurisdiction is available for the counterclaim. Consequently, if the counterclaim were to be treated as permissive, Blazer Financial's (D) action on the underlying debt would have to be pursued in the state court. The split of opinion on the nature of debt counterclaims in truth-in-lending actions appears to be, in large part, the product of competing policy considerations between the objectives of Rule 13(a) and the policies of the Truth-in-Lending Act, and disagreement over the extent to which federal courts should be involved in state causes of action for debt. While Rule 13(a) is intended to avoid multiple litigation by consolidating all controversies between the parties, several courts and commentators have observed that accepting creditors' debt counterclaims may obstruct achievement of the goals of the Truth-in-Lending Act. Courts which have concluded that debt counterclaims are to be permissive have found the nexus between the truth-in-lending violation and debt obligation too abstract or tenuous to regard the claims as logically related. One claim, they reason, involves the violation of federal law designed to deter lender nondisclosure and facilitate credit shopping and the other concerns merely a default on a private duty. The Court in this case spent a great deal of time exploring and explaining the arguments *against* making the debt counterclaim compulsory, then out of the blue throws out a terrific argument and conclusion that indeed the debt counterclaim *is* compulsory. The opinion is confusing and the direction the Court is taking is unclear right up to the end. Far too much time is spent on the arguments which do not sway the Court, rather than the arguments the Court eventually adopts. The correct result was achieved in the end, however the path to it is unnecessarily occluded.

Mosley v. General Motors Corp.

(Black Employee) v. (Discriminating Employer)
497 F.2d 1330 (1974)

M E M O R Y   G R A P H I C

Instant Facts

Mosely (P) and nine others joined together to bring suit against General Motors (D) for discrimination against blacks and women.

Black Letter Rule

The difficulties in ultimately adjudicating damages to various plaintiffs in a class are not so overwhelming as to require severance of the plaintiffs' causes of action.

Case Vocabulary

DECLARATORY RELIEF: A judgment of the court to express an opinion of the court on a question of law without ordering anything to be done.
ET SEQ.: "Et sequentia"; and the following; used in denominating page reference and statutory section numbers.
INJUNCTIVE RELIEF: Requires a party to refrain from doing or continuing to do a particular action.
INTERLOCUTORY APPEAL: Provisional, temporary.
JOINDER: Uniting of several causes of action or parties in a single unit.

Procedural Basis: Application to permit an interlocutory appeal after district court ordered each plaintiff to bring separate causes of actions.

Facts: Nathaniel Mosely (P) and nine others joined in bringing this action individually and as class representatives alleging that their rights guaranteed under 42 U.S.C. Sec. 2000 et seq. and 42 U.S.C. Sec. 1981 were denied by General Motors (D) and the local Union by reason of their color and race. Each of the ten had, prior to the filing of the complaint, filed a charge with the Equal Employment Opportunity Commission (EEOC) asserting the facts underlying these claims. Pursuant thereto, the EEOC made a reasonable cause finding that General Motors (D) and the Union had engaged in unlawful employment practices in violation of Title VII of the Civil Rights Act of 1964. Accordingly, the charging parties were notified by EEOC of their right to institute a civil action in the appropriate federal district court. All of the individual plaintiffs requested injunctive relief, back pay, attorneys' fees and costs [dig deep]. The class counts of the complaint also sought declaratory and injunctive relief, back pay, attorneys' fees and costs. The district court ordered that "insofar as the first ten counts are concerned, those ten counts shall be severed into ten separate causes of action," and each plaintiff was directed to bring a separate action based upon his complaint, duly and separately filed. Upon entering the order, and upon application of the plaintiffs, the district court found that its decision involved a controlling question of law as to which there is a substantial ground for difference of opinion and that any of the parties might make application for appeal under 28 U.S.C. Section 1292(b). This court granted the application to permit this interlocutory appeal.

Issue: Are the issues of ten plaintiffs claiming unlawful employment sufficient to sustain joinder under Federal Rules of Civil Procedure 20(a)?

Decision and Rationale: (Ross, J.) Yes. To determine whether the district court's order was proper herein, we must look to the policy and law that have developed around the operation of Rule 20. The Supreme Court has said that under the Rules, the impulse is toward entertaining the broadest possible scope of action consistent with fairness to the parties. Joinder of claims, parties and remedies is strongly encouraged. Permissive joinder is not, however, applicable in all cases. The rule imposes two specific requisites to the joinder of parties: (1) a right to relief must be asserted by, or against, each plaintiff or defendant relating to or arising out of the same transaction or occurrence, or series of transactions or occurrences; and (2) some question of law or fact common to all the parties must arise in the action. Here, Mosely (P) and the other plaintiffs have asserted a right to relief arising out of the same transactions or occurrences. Each of the ten plaintiffs alleged that he had been injured by the same general policy of discrimination on the part of General Motors (D) and the Union. We conclude that a company-wide policy purportedly designed to discriminate against blacks in employment similarly arises out of the same series of transactions or occurrences. Thus Mosely (P) and the others meet the first requisite for joinder under Rule 20(a). The second requisite necessary to sustain a permissive joinder under the rule is that a question of law or fact common to all the parties will arise in the action. The rule does not require that *all* questions of law and fact raised by the dispute be common. Yet, neither does it establish any qualitative or quantitative test of commonality. With respect to employment discrimination cases under Title VII, courts have found that the discriminatory character of a defendant's conduct is basic to the class, and the fact that the individual class members may have suffered different effects from the alleged discrimination is immaterial for the purposes of the prerequisite. The right to relief here depends on the ability to demonstrate that each of the plaintiffs was wronged by racially discriminatory policies on the part of General Motors (D) and the Union. The discriminatory character of General Motors' (D) and the Union's conduct is thus basic to each plaintiff's recovery. The fact that each plaintiff may have different effects from the alleged discrimination is immaterial for the purposes of determining the common question of law or fact. Thus we conclude that the second requisite for joinder under Rule 20(a) is also met by the complaint. For the reasons set forth above, we conclude that the district court abused its discretion in severing the joined actions. The difficulties in ultimately adjudicating damages to the various plaintiffs are not so overwhelming as to require such severance. If appropriate, separate trials may be granted as to any particular issue after the determination of common questions. The judgment of the district court disallowing joinder of the plaintiffs' individual actions is reversed and remanded with directions to permit Mosely (P) and the other plaintiffs to proceed jointly.

Analysis:

Rule 20(a) of the Federal Rules of Civil Procedure provides that "all persons may join in one action as plaintiffs if they assert any right to relief jointly, severally, or in the alternative in respect of or arising out of the same transaction, occurrence, or series of transactions or occurrences and if any question of law or fact common to all these persons will arise in the action." Rule 20(b) and Rule 42(b) vest in the district court the discretion to order separate trials or make such other orders as will prevent delay or prejudice. In this manner, the scope of the civil action is made a matter for the discretion of the district court, and a determination on the question of joinder of parties will be reversed on appeal only upon a showing of abuse of that discretion. The purpose of Rule 20 is to promote trial convenience and expedite the final determination of disputes, thereby preventing multiple lawsuits [we don't want to overwork these poor judges]. Single trials generally tend to lessen the delay, expense and inconvenience to all concerned. In ascertaining whether a particular factual situation constitutes a single transaction or occurrence for purposes of Rule 20, a case by case approach is generally pursued. No hard and fast rules have been established under the rule, however construction of the terms "transaction or occurrence" as used in the context of Rule 13(a) counterclaims offers some guide to the application of this test. "Transaction" has been held to be a word of flexible meaning. It may comprehend a series of many occurrences, depending not so much upon the immediateness of their connection as upon their logical relationship. Accordingly, all logically related events entitling a person to institute a legal action against another generally are regarded as comprising a transaction or occurrence. The analogous interpretation of the terms as used in Rule 20 would permit all reasonably related claims for relief by or against different parties to be tried in a single proceeding. Absolute identity of all events is unnecessary. The Court applied the reasoning used in other cases to arrive at the most logical result in this case [will wonders never cease?]. The district court made a much too narrow reading of the facts, finding that the joint actions had only one common problem, that is the defendant, General Motors and the Union. This Court astutely stepped back a bit to see that the issues of each plaintiff truly do have one common thread: discrimination. The fact that each plaintiff may have suffered differing damages really is irrelevant to the determination of General Motors' liability for its unlawful employment practices. [Kudos to the Court!]

Watergate Landmark Condominium Unit Owners' Association v. Wiss, Janey, Elstner Associates

(Condo Association) v. (Engineers)
117 F.R.D. 576 (1987)

M E M O R Y   G R A P H I C

 ## Instant Facts

A condominium association, relying on engineering specifications drawn, hired a waterproofing firm, which unsuccessfully attempted to repair condo balconies.

 ## Black Letter Rule

A third party complaint is appropriate only where the third party defendant is held liable to the plaintiff.

Case Vocabulary

DERIVATIVE (SECONDARY) LIABILITY: Arises only when the party directly liable fails to perform.

IMPLEADER: Procedure used to bring a third party into a suit between a plaintiff and defendant, where that third party may be liable, so as to settle all claims in a single action.

JOINT TORTFEASORS: Two or more persons who are jointly and individually liable for an injury.

PUTATIVE: Alleged, supposed.

THIRD PARTY COMPLAINT: Claim against someone other than the original plaintiff and defendant.

Procedural Basis: Motion to dismiss the amended third party complaint pursuant to Rule 12(b)(6) of the Federal Rules of Civil Procedure.

Facts: Watergate Landmark Condominium Unit Owners' Association (P), a condominium association, hired a real estate management firm, Legum & Norman (D), to oversee maintenance of the units. When owners reported that their balconies were crumbling, Legum & Norman (D) hired an engineering firm, Wiss, Janey, Elstner Associates (D), to draw specifications for repairing the balconies. On the basis of those specifications, Watergate (P) hired Brisk Waterproofing to do the repairs. When the repairs failed to satisfy the owners, they invoked diversity jurisdiction and sued Wiss, Janey (D), and Legum & Norman (D), but not the waterproofers, Brisk. [Aw c'mon, go for the deep pockets!] In response to the complaint, Legum & Norman (D) filed an answer, a cross-claim against Wiss, Janey (D) and a third party complaint against Brisk Waterproofing, the company that performed the repairs. The amended third party complaint alleges that Brisk negligently performed the repairs and is solely liable to Watergate (P). Brisk moved pursuant to Rule 12(b)(6), Federal Rules of Civil Procedure, to dismiss the amended third party complaint.

Issue: Are third party claims permissible in the absence of derivative or secondary liability?

Decision and Rationale: (Ellis, J.) No. The question presented is whether Legum & Norman's (D) third party claim is maintainable under Rule 14(a) Fed. R. Civ. P. Central to this question is whether the third party claim asserts that Brisk's liability is derivative of, or secondary to, Legum & Norman's (D) liability to Watergate (P). Legum & Norman (D) does not claim that Brisk is derivatively or secondarily liable. Nor indeed could such a claim be made, for Watergate's (P) complaint concedes that the repair work was performed non-negligently in accordance with the specifications. Whether Brisk's work was negligent is not part of the main claim of Watergate (P) against Legum & Norman (D). Thus, Legum & Norman's (D) claim against Brisk is independent of the outcome of the main claim. Given this, the third party claim against Brisk is manifestly inappropriate in this case. Derivative liability is central to the operation of Rule 14. It cannot be used as a device to bring into a controversy matters which merely happen to have some relationship to the original action. Other courts' use of the Rule 14 derivative liability principle confirms the inappropriateness of the claim against Brisk in this case. In Struss v. Renault, U.S.A., Inc. [plaintiff, whose two minor children were injured in an auto accident, sued the auto manufacturer on a crashworthiness theory], the manufacturer's effort to implead the driver failed where it was based on the theory that the driver's negligence was the sole cause. Similarly, in another case, impleader was held improper where plaintiff claimed defendant was the seller of the doormat that caused her injuries and defendant denied this and claimed that the proposed third party defendant was the actual seller of the accused doormat (Barab v. Menford). Legum & Norman (D) cannot avoid this result by claiming that it is seeking contribution from Brisk. Although a right of contribution is generally a proper basis on which to file a third party complaint, Virginia's contribution statute does not apply to this action. Section 8.01-34 provides that, "Contribution among wrongdoers may be enforced when the wrong results from negligence and involves no moral turpitude." Legum & Norman (D) and Brisk are not joint wrongdoers within the meaning of the statute. Additionally, the statute has been held to give a right of contribution only where the person injured has a right of action against two persons for the same indivisible injury. Here, the acts which are involved in the main claim are separate and distinct from the acts alleged to give rise to the third party claim. The main claim against Legum & Norman (D) involves the hiring of Wiss, Janey (D) and the delivery of the specifications. The third party complaint deals with Brisk's alleged negligent performance of the repairs, a separate event which occurred later in time and, significantly, an event that is specifically disclaimed by the complaint as a basis for the action. Accordingly, Legum & Norman's (D) third party complaint against Brisk is dismissed. This Court, of course, intimates no view as to whether Legum & Norman's (D) theory that Brisk's negligence caused Watergate's (P) damages may provide a defense to the main claim. Similarly, no view is expressed here on the merits of any separate claim Watergate (P) or Legum & Norman (D) may have against Brisk for negligent workmanship. And finally, it may be worth noting that a different result would obtain here had Watergate's (P) claim been broad enough to include a claim for recovery based on inadequate workmanship. An appropriate order has been entered.

Analysis:

It is settled beyond dispute [if that can ever really happen] that a third party claim can be maintained only if the liability it asserts is in some way derivative of the main claim. Typically, proper third party claims involve one joint tortfeasor impleading another, an indemnitee impleading an indemnitor, or a secondarily liable party impleading one who is primarily liable. Absent such derivative liability, a third party claim must fail. In other words, a third party claim is not appropriate where the defendant and putative third party plaintiff says, in effect, "It was him, not me." Such a claim is viable only where a proposed third party plaintiff says, in effect, "If I am liable to plaintiff, then my liability is only technical or secondary and partial, and the third party defendant is derivatively liable and must reimburse me for all or part (one-half, if a joint tortfeasor) of anything I must pay plaintiff." This is why Legum & Norman's (D) claim against Brisk is a "him, not me" situation and therefore must fail. The Court was correct in its assessment that the two claims involved are separate and distinct. Legum & Norman (D) is alleged to have breached its contract with Watergate (P) and its duties as an agent of Watergate (P). The third party complaint deals with Brisk's alleged negligent performance of the repairs. Brisk is not alleged to have participated in the selection of Wiss, Janey (D) or in the failure to deliver information to Watergate (P). Thus, because Legum & Norman (D) and Brisk did not share a common duty to Watergate (P) and the acts giving rise to the main claim and third party claim were separate in time, place and consequences, the alleged injuries to Watergate (P) were not indivisible.

Kroger v. Omaha Public Power District

(Administratrix) v. (Original Owner of Transmission Lines)
523 F.2d 161 (1975)

M E M O R Y   G R A P H I C

Instant Facts
Steel worker was killed when the crane he was working with came too close to power lines and he was electrocuted.

Black Letter Rule
Sumary judgment may be granted on the issue of duty if the court concludes that, as a matter of law, the defendant owed no duty.

Case Vocabulary

SUMMARY JUDGMENT: Preverdict judgment rendered by the court because there is no real factual dispute as a matter of law.
WRONGFUL DEATH ACTION: Cause of action for any wrongful act, neglect, or default which causes death.

Procedural Basis: Appeal from the district court's granting of the defendant's motion for summary judgment.

Facts: James Kroger was employed by Paxton & Vierling Steel Company at one of its factories. James was involved in the movement of a large steel tank by means of a crane with a 60-foot boom. While one man drove the crane and another operated the boom, James walked alongside the tank to steady it. During this maneuver, the boom came close enough to high-tension lines that electricity from those lines arced over to the boom. Another arc of electricity arced from the tank over to James and killed him [shocking!]. Omaha Public Power District (OPPD) (D), a public corporation of the state of Nebraska, had at one time owned the transmission lines involved. Six years prior to the accident which killed James, OPPD (D) sold the lines and equipment to Paxton & Vierling. OPPD (D) thereafter sold electricity to Paxton & Vierling, and when so requested, made repairs upon the lines and equipment. Geraldine Kroger (P), as administratrix of the estate of James Kroger, brought suit based on diversity jurisdiction for damages resulting from the decedent's wrongful death by electrocution. The district court found that OPPD (D) owed no duty to James, and granted OPPD's (D) motion for summary judgment.

Issue: Does OPPD (D) owe a duty to James Kroger, the breach of which would give rise to liability?

Decision and Rationale: (Nangle, J.) No. The District Court based its order of summary judgment on the fact that ownership of the transmission lines lay indisputably with Paxton & Vierling, that OPPD (D) had no duty to maintain the lines, that OPPD (D) had not been requested to discontinue the flow of electricity on the date of the accident and that OPPD (D) had not been put on notice that a crane was being operated in the vicinity of the lines. As a result, there was no duty owed by OPPD (D) to James Kroger, the breach of which would give rise to liability. We agree with the findings of the District Court and thus affirm the order of summary judgment.

Analysis:

The Court found that OPPD (D) could not have been held liable in a wrongful death action in this case because it owed no duty to James Kroger. OPPD (D) was far enough removed from the circumstances surrounding the accident that liability could not attach. OPPD (D) had not owned the transmission lines for six years and, although it did occasionally perform maintenance on the lines and equipment, it was under no obligation to do so. Finally, since OPPD (D) had not been requested to cut off the electricity, nor was it given notice of crane work in the area, there was no opportunity for OPPD (D) to have taken steps to try to prevent the accident. There is simply no cause for holding OPPD (D) responsible for the accident which claimed James Kroger's life. The Court correctly granted OPPD's (D) motion for summary judgment. From the facts, one might think that Paxton & Vierling might be a better choice for defendant. In most states, workers' compensation laws give employees the right to receive compensation for on-the-job injuries and death without the necessity of proving fault. In return for this right, however, workers' compensation laws bar torts suits against employers. Thus, Paxton & Vierling are immune from prosecution in this case. Owen Equipment might also pose a logical choice as defendant. In fact, OPPD (D) impleaded Owen Equipment and the case went to trial against Owen as sole defendant two years after OPPD (D) won its summary judgment motion [don't these things just drag on and on?].

Owen Equipment & Erection Co. v. Kroger

(Crane Company) v. (Wife)
437 U.S. 365 (1978)

MEMORY GRAPHIC

Instant Facts

In a wrongful death suit for the electrocution of her husband, Mrs. Kroger (P) attempted to obtain federal diversity jurisdiction over Owen Equipment and Erection Company (D), a nondiverse party, by alleging pendent party jurisdiction.

Black Letter Rule

A federal court does not retain jurisdiction over an action, based on diversity of citizenship, when the plaintiff adds a pendent party defendant who destroys complete diversity.

Case Vocabulary

ANCILLARY JURISDICTION: Jurisdiction obtained when a party injects a claim lacking an independent basis for jurisdiction by way of a counterclaim, cross-claim, or third party complaint.

IMPLEAD: The act of bringing a new party, who is part of the subject matter of a claim, into an action.

THIRD-PARTY COMPLAINT: Complaint brought against a person or entity who was not formerly a party to the lawsuit.

Procedural Basis: Writ of certiorari from affirmation of denial of motion to dismiss, for lack of subject matter jurisdiction, an action for damages for wrongful death.

Facts: Mrs. Kroger's (P) husband was electrocuted while walking next to a steel crane which came too close to a high tension electric line. Mrs. Kroger (P), a citizen of Iowa, sued the Omaha Public Power District (OPPD) (D), a Nebraska corporation which allegedly negligently operated the power line [how do you negligently operate a power line?], for wrongful death. Kroger (P) brought the suit in federal court based on diversity of citizenship. OPPD (D) filed a third-party complaint against Owen Equipment and Erection Company (Owen) (D), alleging that Owen's (D) negligence proximately caused the death [this certainly seems more reasonable]. Mrs. Kroger (P) then amended her complaint to name Owen (D) as a defendant, alleging that Owen (D) was a Nebraska corporation with its principal place of business in Nebraska. However, as revealed at trial, Owen's (D) principal place of business was actually Iowa [surprise, surprise!]. Thus, complete diversity of citizenship was lacking. After OPPD (D) was granted summary judgment, Owen (D) moved to dismiss based on a lack of subject-matter jurisdiction. The District Court denied the motion, the Court of Appeals affirmed, and the Supreme Court granted certiorari.

Issue: Does a federal court retain jurisdiction over an action, based on diversity of citizenship, when the plaintiff adds a pendent party defendant who destroys complete diversity?

Decision and Rationale: (Stewart, J.) No. If a plaintiff obtains jurisdiction based on diversity of citizenship, the plaintiff cannot later add a defendant, who would destroy the complete diversity, as a pendent party. The jurisdiction of federal courts is limited both by the Constitution and by Acts of Congress. Pursuant to the *Gibbs* test, the constitution allows for pendent jurisdiction provided that the federal and nonfederal claims arise from a common nucleus of operative fact. However, as noted in *Aldinger*, congressional intent underlying the jurisdictional statute must be examined when pendent party jurisdiction is attempted. With regards to the relevant statute in this case, 28 U.S.C. §1332(a)(1), Congress has consistently required complete diversity of citizenship. Thus, no plaintiff can be a citizen of the same state as any defendant. Mrs. Kroger (P) could not have originally brought suit against both Owen (D) and OPPD (D) based on diversity jurisdiction, since Owen's (D) principal place of business is the same state in which Mrs. Kroger (P) lives [don't you think she probably knew this?]. Likewise, Mrs. Kroger (P) should not be allowed to obtain federal jurisdiction by naming only the diverse party, OPPD (D), in her original suit, and by waiting for OPPD (D) to implead the nondiverse party, Owen (D). This procedure, if allowed, would permit plaintiffs to circumvent the complete diversity requirement of §1332(a)(1). Furthermore, considerations of convenience and judicial economy do not suffice to extend pendent or ancillary jurisdiction over Owen (D) in this case.

Analysis:

As the Supreme Court correctly decided, Mrs. Kroger's (D) attempt at circumventing the complete diversity requirement for federal jurisdiction--whether disingenuous or forthright--should not succeed. An alternative holding would all but destroy the complete diversity requirement of §1332(a)(1). Certainly Mrs. Kroger (D) knew, or should have known, that Owen (D) was at least partially responsible for negligently operating the crane and proximately causing Mr. Kroger's electrocution. Even if OPPD (D) negligently operated the power line--the court obviously disagreed by granting summary judgment in OPPD's (D) favor--Mrs. Kroger should have known that OPPD (D) would want Owen (D) in the suit in order to reduce OPPD's (D) negligence. It is interesting to note that the district court allowed OPPD (D) to bring Owen (D) into the suit, apparently without questioning the fact that Owen (D) destroyed complete diversity [maybe they were just asleep]. Perhaps courts are more willing to allow a defendant to obtain ancillary jurisdiction than to allow a plaintiff to obtain pendent jurisdiction over the same party. This approach may be reasonable, since the plaintiff, but not the defendant, could have chosen a more suitable forum originally.

Helzberg's Diamond Shops v. Valley West Des Moines Shopping Center

(Jewelry Store) v. (Shopping Mall)
564 F.2d 816 (1977)

M E M O R Y   G R A P H I C

Instant Facts

A jewelry store sued the shopping mall for violating its lease agreement and allowing four full line jewelry stores lease spaces in the mall.

Black Letter Rule

It is generally recognized that a person does not become indispensable to an action to determine rights under a contract simply because that person's rights or obligations under an entirely separate contract will be affected by the result of the action.

Case Vocabulary

ADJUDICATED: Final judgment of the court.
ENJOINED: Legally prevented from doing a certain act.
"LONG ARM" STATUTE: Allows local courts to obtain jurisdiction over nonresident defendants.
PERSONAL JURISDICTION: Refers to the court's power over the parties involved in a particular lawsuit.
SUBJECT MATTER JURISDICTION: Refers to the competency of the court to hear and determine a particular category of cases.

Procedural Basis: Appeal from the district court's order denying the defendant's motion to dismiss pursuant to Rule 19, Federal Rules of Civil Prodecure.

Facts: On February 3, 1975, Helzberg's Diamond Shops, Inc. (P) and Valley West Des Moines Shopping Center (D) entered into a written lease agreement. The lease agreement granted Helzberg (P) the right to operate a full line jewelry store at space 254 in the Valley West Mall. Section 6 of Article V of the lease agreement provided that Valley West (D) "agrees it will not lease premises in the shopping center for use as a catalog jewelry store nor lease premises for more than two full line jewelry stores in the shopping center in addition to the leased premises." Subsequently, Helzberg (P) commenced operation of a full-time jewelry store in the Valley West Mall. During the next twenty one months, Valley West (D) and two other corporations entered into leases for spaces in the Valley West Mall for use as full line jewelry stores. Pursuant to those leases, the two corporations also initiated actual operation of full line jewelry stores. On November 2, 1976, Valley West (D) and Kirk's Incorporated, doing business as Lord's Jewelers, entered into a written lease agreement granting Lord's the right to occupy space in Valley West Mall "only as a retail specialty jewelry store (and not as a catalogue or full line jewelry store)." However, Lord's intended to open and operate what constituted a full line jewelry store at space 261 [surely just a small misunderstanding]. In an attempt to avoid the opening of a fourth full line jewelry store in the Valley West Mall and the resulting breach of the Helzberg (P)-Valley West (D) lease agreement, Helzberg (P) instituted suit seeking preliminary and permanent injunctive relief restraining Valley West's (D) breach of the lease agreement. The suit was filed in the United States District Court for the Western District of Missouri. Subject matter jurisdiction was invoked pursuant to 28 U.S.C. Sec. 1332 based upon diversity of citizenship between the parties and an amount in controversy which exceeds $10,000. Personal jurisdiction was established by service of process on Valley West (D) pursuant to the Missouri "long arm" statute. Valley West (D) moved to dismiss pursuant to Rule 19 because Helzberg (P) had failed to join Lord's as a party defendant [always looking for the easy way out]. The motion was denied. The district court went on to order (in part) that pending the determination of the action on the merits, Valley West (D) is enjoined and restrained from allowing, and shall take all necessary steps to prevent, any other tenant in its Valley West Mall (including but not limited to Lord's Jewelers) to open and operate a fourth full line jewelry store. From this order Valley West (D) appeals.

Issue: Did the district court properly deny the motion to dismiss for failure to join an indispensable party?

Decision and Rationale: (Alsop, J.) Yes. Because Helzberg (P) was seeking and the District Court ordered injunctive relief which may prevent Lord's from operating its jewelry store in the Valley West Mall in the manner in which Lord's originally intended, the District Court correctly concluded that Lord's was a party to be joined if feasible. Therefore, because Lord's was not and is not subject to personal jurisdiction in the Western District of Missouri, the District Court was required to determine whether or not Lord's should be regarded as indispensable. After considering the factors which Rule 19(b) mandates be considered, the District Court concluded that Lord's was not to be regarded as indispensable. We agree. We think that Lord's absence will not prejudice Valley West (D) in a way contemplated by Rule 19(b). Valley West (D) contends that it may be subjected to inconsistent obligations as a result of a determination in this action and a determination in another forum that Valley West (D) should proceed in a fashion contrary to what has been ordered in these proceedings. It is true that the obligations of Valley West (D) to Helzberg (P), as determined in these proceedings, may be inconsistent with Valley West's (D) obligations to Lord's. However, we are of the opinion that any inconsistency in those obligations will result from Valley West's (D) voluntary execution of two lease agreements which impose inconsistent obligations rather than from Lord's absence from the present proceedings. Valley West's (D) contention that it may be subjected to inconsistent judgments if Lord's should choose to file suit elsewhere and be awarded judgment is speculative at best. In the first place, Lord's has not filed such a suit. Secondly, there is no showing that another court is likely to interpret the language of the two lease agreements differently from the way in which the District Court would. Therefore, we also conclude that Valley West (D) will suffer no prejudice as a result of the District Court's proceeding in Lord's absence. Rule 19(b) also requires the court to consider ways in which prejudice to the absent party can be lessened or avoided. The District Court afforded Lord's the opportunity to intervene in order to protect any interest it might have in the outcome of this litigation. Lord's chose not to do so. In light of Lord's decision not to intervene we conclude that the District Court acted in such a way as to sufficiently protect Lord's interests. Similarly, we also conclude that the District Court's determinations that a judgment rendered in Lord's absence would be adequate and that there is no controlling significance to the fact that Helzberg (P) would have an adequate remedy in the Iowa courts were not erroneous. It follows that the District Court's conclusion that in equity and good conscience the action should be allowed to proceed was a correct one. In sum, it is generally recognized that a person does not become indispensable to an action to determine rights under a contract simply because that person's rights or obligations under an entirely separate contract will be affected by the result of the action. We conclude that the district court properly denied the motion to dismiss for failure to join an indispensable party. The judgment of the District Court is affirmed.

Analysis:

Rule 19(b) requires the court to look to the extent to which a judgment rendered in Lord's absence might be prejudicial to Lord's or to Valley West (D). It seems axiomatic that none of Lord's rights or obligations will be ultimately determined in a suit to which it is not a party [duh]. Even if, as a result of the District Court's granting of the preliminary injunction, Valley West (D) should attempt to terminate Lord's leasehold interest in its space in the Valley West Mall, Lord's will retain all of its rights under its lease agreement with Valley West (D). None of its rights or obligations will have been adjudicated as a result of the present proceedings, proceedings to which it is not a party. Therefore, Lord's would not be prejudiced under Rule 19(b) as a result of this action. Additionally, Helzberg seeks only to restrain Valley West's (D) breach of the lease agreement to which Helzberg (P) and Valley West (D) were the sole parties. Certainly, all of the rights and obligations arising under a lease can be adjudicated where all of the parties to the lease are before the court. Thus, in the context of these proceedings, the District Court can determine all of the rights and obligations of both Helzberg (P) and Valley West (D) based upon the lease agreement between them, even though Lord's is not a party to the proceedings. The Court's principle that a person does not become indispensable to an action to determine rights under a contract simply because that person's rights or obligations under an entirely separate contract will be affected by the result of the action, applies equally to an action against a lessor who has entered into other leases which also may be affected by the result in the action in which the other lessees are argued to be indispensable parties. Thus, the Court correctly [on a roll!] assessed the evidence and necessarily affirmed the District Court's ruling.

Natural Resources Defense Council v. United States Nuclear Regulatory Commission

(Environmentalists) v. (Licensing Agency)

578 F.2d 1341 (1978)

M E M O R Y   G R A P H I C

Instant Facts

A complaint was filed to prevent NRC (D) from issuing licenses for the operation of uranium mills without first preparing environmental impact statements.

Black Letter Rule

Applicants satisfying their burden of the three requirements of Rule 24(a)(2) should be allowed to intervene in an action.

 ## Case Vocabulary

AMICUS CURIAE BRIEF: Submitted by one not a party to the lawsuit on behalf of third parties who will be affected by the resolution of the dispute.

FRCP 24(a): " . . . [A]nyone shall be permitted to intervene in an action: . . . . (2) when the applicant claims an interest relating to the property or transaction which is the subject of the action and the applicant is so situated that the disposition of the action may as a practical matter impair or impede the applicant's ability to protect that interest, unless the applicant's interest is adequately represented by existing parties."

INTERVENTION: A proceeding allowing a person to enter into a lawsuit already in progress.

LACHES: Doctrine providing a party an equitable defense where long-neglected rights are sought to be enforced against the party.

RES JUDICATA: Final judgment has been made in a court.

STARE DECISIS: Principles announced in former decisions will be upheld.

Procedural Basis: Appeal from the district court's denial of the applicants' motion to intervene.

Facts: The American Mining Congress and Kerr-McGee Nuclear Corporation seek review of the district court's order denying their motions to intervene as a matter of right or on a permissive basis, pursuant to Rule 24(a)(2) [applicant claims interest relating to the property or transaction, and disposition of the action may impair or impede ability to protect that interest, unless interests are adequately protected] and (b), Fed. Rules Civil Proc. The underlying action in which the movants requested intervention was instituted by the Natural Resources Defense Council (P) and others. In the action, declaratory and injunctive relief is directed to the United States Nuclear Regulatory Commission (NRC) (D) and the New Mexico Environmental Improvement Agency (NMEIA), prohibiting those agencies from issuing licenses for the operation of uranium mills in New Mexico without first preparing environmental impact statements. Kerr-McGee and United Nuclear are potential recipients of the licenses. Congress, in the Atomic Energy Act of 1954, has authorized the NRC (D) to issue such licenses. NMEIA is involved because under Sec. 274(b) of the Act, the NRC (D) is authorized to enter into such agreements with the states allowing the states to issue licenses. Thus the action in effect seeks to prevent the use of Sec. 274(b) of the Act so as to avoid the requirement of an impact statement for which provision is made in the National Environmental Policy Act. The complaint alleges that such statements are now prepared by the NRC (D) in states that have not entered into agreements with the NRC (D), but that the NRC (D) does not prepare such statements where there is an agreement with a state such as New Mexico. The relief sought by the National Resources Defense Council's (P) complaint is, first, that NRC's (D) involvement in the licensing procedure in New Mexico is, notwithstanding the delegation to the state, sufficient to constitute major federal action, whereby the impact statement requirement is not eliminated. Second, that if an impact statement is not required in connection with the granting of licenses, the New Mexico program is in conflict with Sec. 274(d)(2) of the Atomic Energy Act. The motion of United Nuclear Corporation to intervene was not opposed by the parties and it was granted. On the date the complaint was filed, NMEIA granted a license to United Nuclear to operate a uranium mill. The complaint seeks to enjoin the issuance of the license thus granted. It was after that, that Kerr-McGee, American Mining Congress, and others filed motions to intervene. These motions, insofar as they sought intervention as of right, were denied on the ground that the interests of the parties or movants would be adequately represented by United Nuclear [too many cooks]. Permissive intervention was also denied. Kerr-McGee and American Mining Congress both appeal denial of both intervention as of right and permissive intervention.

Issue: Was the Court's denial of intervention correct under Rule 24(a) of the Federal Rules of Civil Procedure?

Decision and Rationale: (Doyle, J.) No. Our issue is a limited one. We merely construe and weigh Rule 24(a) of the Fed. R. Civ. P. (intervention as of right) and decide in light of the facts and considerations presented whether the denial of intervention was correct. The position adopted by the trial court that Kerr-McGee was adequately represented dispensed with the need for the court to consider the question whether Kerr-McGee had an interest in the litigation before the court. The question then is whether the contention made is a correct concept of interest. Strictly to require that the movant in intervention have a *direct* interest in the outcome of the lawsuit strikes us as being too narrow a construction of Rule 24(a)(2). Thus we are asked to interpret interest in relationship to the second criterion in Rule 24(a)(2), impairment or impeding ability to protect the interest.

The Supreme Court has said that the interest must be a significantly protectable interest. The matter of immediate interest is the issuance and delivery of the license sought by United Nuclear. However, the consequence of the litigation could well be the imposition of the requirement that an environmental impact statement be prepared before granting any uranium mill license in New Mexico, or, secondly, it could result in an injunction terminating or suspending the agreement between NRC (D) and NMEIA. Either consequence would be felt by United Nuclear and to some degree, of course, by Kerr-McGee, which is said to be one of the largest holders of uranium properties in New Mexico. A decision in favor of the Natural Resources Defense Council (P), which is not unlikely, could have a profound effect upon Kerr-McGee. Hence, it does have an interest within the meaning of Rule 24(a)(2). The next question is whether, assuming the existence of an interest, the chance of impairment is sufficient to fulfill the requirement of Rule 24(a)(2). The question of impairment is not separate from the question of existence of an interest. The Natural Resources Defense Council (P) contend that Kerr-McGee and the American Mining Congress would not be bound by the results of the case if they are not participants, therefore their interests are not impaired. Kerr-McGee points out that even though it may not be res judicata, still it would have a stare decisis effect. Moreover, with NRC (D) and NMEIA as parties, the result might be more profound than stare decisis. The Rule refers to impairment "as a practical matter," thus the court may consider any significant legal effect in Kerr-McGee's and the American Mining Congress' interest and is not restricted to a rigid res judicata test. Hence, the stare decisis effect might be sufficient to satisfy the requirement. We are of the opinion, therefore, that Kerr-McGee and the American Mining Congress have satisfied the impairment criterion. The final question is whether the trial court was correct in its conclusion that United Nuclear would adequately represent Kerr-McGee and the American Mining Congress. United Nuclear has already been granted its license, thus Kerr-McGee urges that United Nuclear may be ready to compromise the case by obtaining a mere declaration that while environmental impact statements should be issued, this requirement need be prospective only, whereby it would not affect them. While we see this as a remote possibility, we gravely doubt that United Nuclear would opt for such a result. It is true, however, that United Nuclear has a defense of laches that is not available to Kerr-McGee or the others. There are other reasons for allowing intervention. There is some value in having the parties before the court so that they will be bound by the result. American Mining Congress represents a number of companies having a wide variety of interests. This can, therefore, provide a useful supplement to the defense of the case. The same can be said of Kerr-McGee. Thus Kerr-McGee and the American Mining Congress have satisfied their burden of the three requirements of Rule 24(A)(2). Consequently, they should be and they are hereby allowed to intervene. The order of the district court is reversed and the cause is remanded with instructions to the trial court to grant Kerr-McGee's and the American Mining Congress' motions to intervene.

Analysis:

The district court's order denying intervention by the several corporations focused on whether the interest of the party seeking to intervene was adequately represented by a fellow member of the industry. The court decided that the interests of Kerr-McGee and the American Mining Congress were adequately protected by United Nuclear, which possessed the necessary experience and knowledge in a complex area of business, whereby the representative's capability was competent to meet the demands. The court thought that to allow the intervention would engender delay and produce unwieldy procedure, and that the Kerr-McGee and the American Mining Congress requirements were met by allowing the filing of amicus curiae briefs. To say, as the Natural Resources Defense Council (P) attempted to argue, that the issue could be repeatedly litigated is not an answer, for the chance of getting a contrary result in a case which is substantially similar on its facts to one previously adjudicated seems remote. This Court made a better decision that the interests of Kerr-McGee and the American Mining Congress in the subject matter were sufficient to satisfy the requirements of Rule 24 and that the threat of loss of their interest and inability to participate is of such magnitude as to impair their ability to advance their interest.

Martin v. Wilks

(City) v. (Firefighters)

Supreme Court of the United States, 1989, 490 U.S. 755, 109 S.Ct. 2180, 104 L.Ed.2d 835

M E M O R Y   G R A P H I C

Instant Facts

Pursuant to consent judgments between the City of Birmingham ("City") and the Jefferson County Personnel Board ("Board") with black firefighters, the white firefighters filed a suit against the City and the Board alleging reverse discrimination.

Black Letter Rule

A party seeking a judgment binding on another cannot obligate the latter to intervene in the action without mandatorily joining that person in the action.

Case Vocabulary

INTERVENTION: A proceeding permitting a person to enter into a lawsuit already in progress. This term refers to admission of a person not an original party to the suit, so that the person can protect some right or interest which is allegedly affected by the proceeding.

JOINDER: Uniting of several causes of action or parties in a single suit. Mandatory joinder refers to the mandatory joining of certain parties which are required for the just adjudication of a controversy.

Procedural Basis: Certiorari to the United States Court of Appeals for the Eleventh District in discrimination suit.

Facts: The City of Birmingham ("City") and the Jefferson County Personnel Board ("Board") entered into a consent judgment with black firefighters for discrimination in hiring and promotion of the latter. Subsequently, white firefighters ("Martin") (P) brought an action against the City and the Board (D), alleging that the promotions were in violation of federal law because they were based on race. The City and the Board (D) defended on the ground that the consent judgment precluded the current suit. The District Court, holding in favor of the City and the Board (D), declared that the consent judgment was a defense to the reverse discrimination alleged by the white firefighters (P). The Court of Appeals reversed on the ground that the consent judgment did not preclude the current suit because the white firefighters (P) were not parties to the previous judgment. In the Supreme Court, the City and the Board (D) argued that the white firefighters could have intervened in the first suit.

Issue: May a party seeking a judgment binding another obligate the latter to intervene in the action without mandatorily joining that party in the action?

Decision and Rationale: (Rehnquist, C.J.) No. A party seeking a judgment binding on another cannot obligate the latter to intervene in the action without mandatorily joining that person in the action. Generally, one is not bound by a judgment in which he was not a party, or was not made a party by service of process. The City and the Board (D) argue that because the white firefighters (P) failed to voluntarily intervene in the earlier action, their suit is impermissible, especially in light of their knowledge that the consent judgment would affect them. This court, however, is in agreement with Justice Brandeis' view in *Chase National Bank v. Norwalk*, that a person entitled to a hearing does not have the burden of voluntary intervention in a suit in which he is not a party. The drafters of the Federal Rules of Civil Procedure have determined that the concern for finality and completion of a judgment is better served by mandatory joinder procedure and not by permissive intervention. FRCP 19(a) provides for mandatory joinder in circumstances where a judgment rendered in the absence of a person may impose a risk of incurring inconsistent obligations in a party. Joinder as a party, rather than knowledge of a lawsuit and an opportunity to intervene, is the method by which potential parties are subjected to the jurisdiction of the court and bound by a judgment or decree. The parties in a suit know better the nature and scope of the relief sought in the action, and at whose expense the relief might be granted. Thus, the burden should be on these parties to bring additional parties where such a step is indicated, rather than potential additional parties to intervene upon gaining knowledge of the suit. The City and the Board (D) argue that mandatory joinder will be burdensome because the potential claimants may be numerous and difficult to identify, and that if they are not joined, there is potential for inconsistent judgments. Such difficulties, although possible, are not alleviated by allowing voluntary intervention. Again, plaintiffs who seek the aid of the courts to alter existing employment opportunities, or the employer who might be subject to conflicting decrees, are best able to bear the burden of designating those who would be adversely affected if the plaintiffs prevail. (Affirmed.)

Dissent: (Stevens, J., Brennan, J., Marshall, J., Blackmun, J.) While the consent decree in this case could not deprive the white firefighters of their contractual rights, such as seniority or other legal rights, there is no reason why the consent judgment might not produce changes in conditions at the white firefighters' place of employment that may have a serious effect on their opportunities for employment or promotion. The fact that one of the effects of the decree is to curtail the opportunities of nonparties does not mean that the nonparties have been deprived of legal rights or that they have standing to appeal

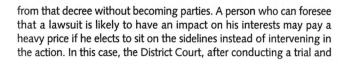

from that decree without becoming parties. A person who can foresee that a lawsuit is likely to have an impact on his interests may pay a heavy price if he elects to sit on the sidelines instead of intervening in the action. In this case, the District Court, after conducting a trial and carefully considering the firefighters' arguments, concluded that the effort of the City and the Board to eradicate discrimination through a consent decree was lawful. Thus, the firefighters have already had their day in court and have failed to carry their burden.

Analysis:

Compare this case to the previous case, *In Re Multi-district Civil Actions* [issue preclusion can be applied to a person who was not a party to the earlier action]. Do the results seem inconsistent? In the latter case all the actions were the same and each party brought an action against the defendant. In this case, however, the white firefighters had not intervened and had not been joined in the previous consent judgment. Thus, they really did not have a day in court. Note, however, this case was subsequently overruled by an act of Congress which prohibits challenges to employment consent decrees by individuals who had actual notice and reasonable opportunity to intervene, or those whose interest were adequately represented. In this case, we see that the court distinguishes between a voluntary intervention and mandatory joinder. As the word itself suggests, voluntary intervention is "voluntary"; a party whose interests are at stake may choose to join in the action. Mandatory joinder, on the other hand, is when a party to the case seeks to join other parties as plaintiffs or defendants. The decision of the court in this case indicates that even if a party's rights may be affected, the party is not obligated to intervene. However, when a party in a case wants to make the judgment binding on a nonparty, that party must join the nonparty in the action under the mandatory joinder rules of the Federal Rules of Civil Procedure.

Cohen v. The Republic of the Philippines

(Art Dealer) v. (Country)
146 F.R.D. 90 (1993)

M E M O R Y   G R A P H I C

Instant Facts

A fight between an art dealer, Imelda Marcos and her agent, and the Philippine Government over true ownership of paintings which hung in Marcos' home.

Black Letter Rule

Rule 24 of the Federal Rules of Civil Procedure allows anyone, upon timely application, to intervene in an action if the applicant claims an interest relating to the property or transaction which is the subject of the action, and that interest is subject to possible prejudice and lack of adequate representation.

Case Vocabulary

COLLATERALIZED: Property is subject to a security interest.

INTERPLEADER: A party places property in the hands of the court to decide who should reightfully receive the property; used to avoid double or multiple liability on the part of the debtor.

SECURITY INTEREST: Interest in personal property which secures the payment of an obligation.

Procedural Basis: Motion to intervene in the interpleader action.

Facts: This is an interpleader action initiated by Marc Cohen and Marc Cohen & Co. (collectively "Cohen") (P) against Klaus Braemer and The Republic of the Philippines (D). The action is presently before the Court on the motion of Imelda R. Marcos for leave to intervene. At issue in this interpleader action is the ownership of four paintings whose total value is nearly $5 million. In late 1991 or 1992, Cohen (P) received the paintings on consignment from Braemer (D), who was Marcos' agent entrusted to run her New York home in which the paintings had previously hung. Braemer (D) demanded return of the paintings in March of 1992, but Cohen (P) refused because he was uncertain who actually owned the paintings. Consequently, Cohen (P) brought this interpleader action. Braemer (D) claims that Marcos authorized him to sell the paintings, and he asserts a direct interest in the paintings originating from a loan he made to Marcos, and a loan he guaranteed for Marcos, both of which were collateralized by the paintings. The Philippines (D) claims that the paintings were acquired with Philippine Government funds for the benefit of the Philippines (D), or that the paintings were acquired with funds which Marcos or her husband illegally obtained during Ferdinand Marcos' tenure as President of the Philippines [nah, all that went to shoes!]. In either case, the Philippines (D) claims to be the rightful owner of the paintings. Marcos now seeks to intervene in this action, claiming that the paintings were acquired with her personal funds and remain her property. She denies that a lien or security interest in the paintings was given to Braemer (D) and, in the alternative, claims a right to the paintings after payment of the amount due Braemer (D).

Issue: May a person intervene in an action if he or she has an interest relating to property which is the subject of the action?

Decision and Rationale: (Conner, J.) Yes. Rule 24 of the Federal Rules of Civil Procedure allows anyone, upon timely application, to intervene in an action if the applicant claims an interest relating to the property or transaction which is the subject of the action, and that interest is subject to possible prejudice and lack of adequate representation. Marcos' decision to apply for intervention was made approximately five months after the initial complaint was filed. We believe Marcos' delay was not unreasonable given the complex and politically sensitive international implications of this action. The existing parties have not been unduly prejudiced by the delay because the addition of Marcos does not require altering a scheduled trial date on which they may have relied. However, Marcos' interest is very likely to be prejudiced if her intervention is denied. Marcos has alleged and affirmed an interest in the paintings sufficient to support her motion to intervene, and this interest may be impaired by the action if she is not allowed to intervene. Additionally, Marcos' interest is not adequately protected by the existing parties. Marcos' alleged interest is contrary to the interest of both existing parties. Marcos claims an interest in the paintings superior to that of the Philippines (D), and she disputes Braemer's (D) security interest in the paintings. Thus, Braemer (D) can not adequately protect Marcos' interest. We will not deprive Marcos of her day in court simply to allow the speedy but possibly unjust disposition of the action before us. Marcos fulfills all the requirements of Rule 24(a)(2), and her motion to intervene is, therefore, granted.

Analysis:

The Court ruled that Marcos complied with the requirements of Rule 24(a)(2) of the Fed. R. Civ. P., and thus her motion to intervene should be granted. To succinctly summarize, Marcos' intervention motion is timely, she has an interest in the paintings which are the subject of this interpleader action, her interest is likely to be prejudiced by the action, and the existing parties are unlikely to adequately protect Marcos' interest. Timeliness is a flexible determination made in the discretion of the Court. Among the factors to be considered in determining whether a motion to intervene is timely are (1) how long the applicant knew of his interest before making the motion; (2) prejudice to the existing parties from any such delay; (3) prejudice to applicant if the motion is denied; (4) other unusual circumstances. While Marcos' decision to apply for intervention came five months after the filing of the complaint, all the parties knew of her potential intervention from the inception of the action, and the delay was caused by settlement discussions between Marcos and the Philippines in another action. The Court recognized that there would not be undue prejudice in allowing Marcos to intervene, however if her motion is denied, Marcos' interest would very likely be prejudiced. Marcos filed an affidavit with her motion claiming the paintings were acquired with her personal funds, and she disputes the alleged lien Braemer (D) claims on the paintings. Additionally, the Philippines (D) holds Marcos' residence in a constructive trust for the Philippines (D), however this judgment does not include the contents of the premises, i.e. the paintings. Marcos also has a significantly different interest which is contrary to the interest of both Braemer (D) and the Philippines (D). Thus the Court was correct in asserting that there is a lack of adequate representation on Marcos' behalf if her motion is denied. The court placed conditions upon the granting of Marcos' motion, including the requirement that she make all necessary applications to the Government to allow her to travel to New York for a deposition, or, if the Government does not allow her to travel to New York, that she make herself available for a deposition in the Philippines. These conditions are reasonable, and the Court wisely protected the interests of all parties by instituting these conditions.

Communities for Equity v. Michigan High School Athletic Assn.

(Female High School Athletes) v. (High School Athletic Department)

1999 U.S. Dist. LEXIS 5780 (1999)

M E M O R Y   G R A P H I C

Instant Facts

High school girls sued their high school athletic association for gender discrimination with regard to the athletic programs, which favor boy's athletics.

Black Letter Rule

A class is not maintainable merely because the complaint parrots the legal requirements of Rule 23; a hearing may be necessary for the court to probe behind the pleadings before coming to rest on the certification question.

Case Vocabulary

CLASS ACTION: Lawsuit brought by a representative member of a large group of persons on behalf of all the members of the group.

COMMONALITY: Common questions of law and fact.

MOOTNESS: Judgment which cannot have any practical effect upon the existing controversy.

TYPICALITY: The case is typical of other claims against a petitioner because of common questions of law and fact.

Procedural Basis: Application to the Court on the plaintiff's motion for class certification.

Facts: Communities for Equity (P) bring this suit against the Michigan High School Athletic Association (D) and its Representative Council, alleging that they have been excluded from opportunities to participate in interscholastic athletic programs and have received unequal treatment and benefits in these programs. They contend that this putative exclusion and unequal treatment constitute gender discrimination, in violation of (1) Title IX of the Education Amendments of 1972; (2) the Equal Protection Clause of the Fourteenth Amendment; and (3) Michigan State laws. The alleged discrimination is made manifest, according to Communities for Equity (P), in Michigan High School Athletic Association's (D): (1) refusing to sanction girls' ice hockey and water polo; (2) requiring that the Communities for Equity (P) Class play its sports in non-traditional seasons; (3) operating shorter athletic seasons for some girls' sports than for boys' sports; (4) scheduling the competitions of the Communities for Equity (P) Class on inferior dates; (5) providing, assigning, and operating inferior athletic facilities to the Communities for Equity (P) Class in which to play Michigan High School Athletic Association (D)-sanctioned games; (6) requiring that the Communities for Equity (P) Class play some sports under rules and/or conditions different from those in the NCAA or other governing organizations, unlike boys; and (7) allocating more resources for the support and promotion of male interscholastic athletic programs than for female programs. Communities for Equity's (P) motion for Class Certification asks the Court to define the proposed class as follows: all present and future female students enrolled in Michigan High School Athletic Association (D) member schools who participate in interscholastic athletics or who are deterred from participating in interscholastic athletics because of Michigan High School Athletic Association's (D) discriminatory conduct and who are adversely affected by that conduct.

Issue: Does a group of high school female athletes meet the requirements of Rule 23, Fed. R. Civ. P. to certify a class action?

Decision and Rationale: (Enslen, C.J.) Yes. According to the United States Supreme Court, this Court must conduct a "rigorous analysis" into whether the prerequisites of Federal Rule of Civil Procedure 23 are met before certifying a class action. The "rigorous analysis" requirement means that a class is not maintainable merely because the complaint parrots the legal requirements of Rule 23. Although a hearing prior to the class determination is not always required, it may be necessary for the Court to probe behind the pleadings before coming to rest on the certification question. In this case, the extensive briefing filed by the parties, the Court's past review of motions, and the documentary evidence and affidavits filed make the hearing of evidence unnecessary because the Court is able to probe behind the pleadings without additional evidence or argument. In this case, the numbers themselves justify a conclusion of numerosity and impracticability of joinder. Under Communities for Equity's (P) theory of liability, thousands of female high school athletes and would-be athletes are subjected to Michigan High School Athletic Association's (D) alleged discriminatory practices. The Court concludes that the numerosity requirement is satisfied by the proposed class. Next, the Rule requires commonality. Here, the common questions of fact and law are obvious enough. The overarching question is, did Michigan High School Athletic Association (D) and its Representative Council act in a manner inconsistent with Title IX, the Equal Protection Clause of the Fourteenth Amendment, and/or the Michigan State laws? The answer turns on the resolution of factual questions regarding Michigan High School Athletic Association's (D) decisionmaking process and outcomes, and determination of the legal consequences of those facts. The "typicality" requirement is the one demanding the closest attention in this matter. The Court must determine whether, on the facts of this case, the Supreme Court's decision in *Gen. Tel. Co. v. Falcon* precludes a finding of typicality, given the breadth of Communities for Equity's (P) claims. In *Falcon*, a Mexican-American employee who alleged that he had been denied a promotion because of race discrimination brought a class action against his employer. The class included all Mexican-American employees and Mexican-American applicants for employment who had not been hired. The Supreme Court held that there were no questions of law or fact common to all members of the class he sought to represent, thus it was not typical of other claims against the petitioner by Mexican-American employees and applicants. That decision, at first glance, appears applicable in this case, as a number of different harms are alleged here which have not been suffered uniformly among the proposed class representatives. There are two reasons, however, why that decision does not bar the certification of this class. First, the various discrete harms alleged by the plaintiffs are all allegedly suffered by members of Communities for Equity (P), a proposed class representative. More importantly, however, the mere fact of some distinction between the particular claims of named plaintiffs and the diverse manifestations of discrimination alleged here is insufficient to extinguish typicality. Rule 23(a) requires that the class members and their counsel be prepared to provide fair and adequate representation to the class. Two issues in this matter raise the potentiality for conflict. First, it is quite possible that members of the class have no desire to pursue this action, and are not unhappy with the status quo. However, this sort of putative conflict generally fails to bar class certification. A second type of potential conflict may be that achieving certain types of relief in this case could come at the expense of other types. To the extent that the underlying issue in this case is one of unequal treatment and discrimination, the matter of whether to sanction a particular sport appears to be one relating to relief, rather than liability. The Court determines that the requirements are met. Michigan High School Athletic Association (D) argues that a class is unnecessary, because relief granted to the named plaintiffs would inure to the benefit of the class. The Sixth Circuit has disclaimed any necessity requirement for Rule 23(b)(2) certification. Even if such a requirement existed, mootness concerns would suggest the necessity of certification. Therefore, it is the conclusion of this Court that the motion for Class Certification shall be granted. The class action is certified as to the following class: all present and future female students enrolled in Michigan High School Athletic Association (D) member schools who participate in interscholastic athletics or who are deterred from participating in interscholastic athletics because of Michigan High School Athletic Association's (D) discriminatory conduct and who are adversely affected by that conduct.

Analysis:

In addition to the requirement that joinder be an impracticality, commonality, typicality, and adequacy of representation are factors to be considered by the Court when making a determination of class certification. As to commonality, not every common question suffices. What is necessary for certification are common issues the resolution of which will advance the litigation. In cases involving the question of whether a defendant has acted through an illegal policy or procedure, commonality is readily shown because the common question becomes whether the defendant in fact acted through the illegal policy or procedure. Where the nature of the legal claims are such that individuals would have to submit separate proofs in order to establish liability, class actions are disapproved due to lack of commonality. When discussing the typicality requirement, it should be noted that the *Falcon* Court did provide for the possibility of broad-based attacks on discrimination if there were proof of an underlying policy of discrimination. Here, the variety of alleged manifestations of discrimination, such as inequitable facilities, scheduling, sanctioning, and rules, present a sufficient case of an underlying policy or practice of discrimination. The Court determines that differences between sanctioning water polo and scheduling basketball are less significant in this matter than the typicality of claims that female high school athletes are discriminated against in violation of the various laws invoked by Communities for Equity (P). The Court also correctly decided that the class members are adequately represented in this case. Even if there are some female athletes who are not unhappy with the way things are, those people can be adequately represented by Michigan High School Athletic Association (D). To the extent that Michigan High School Athletic Association (D) discriminates against female athletes through unequal treatment, it acts or refuses to act on grounds generally applicable to the class. Injunctive relief is, of course, an appropriate remedy for discriminatory treatment. The Court presented a well thought out and thorough analysis of the facts in this case ["rigorous" even!], and arrived at the correct conclusion that the Communities for Equity's (P) motion for class certification should be granted.

Heaven v. Trust Company Bank

(Car Leaser) v. (Leasing Company)
18 F.3d 735 (1997)

M E M O R Y   G R A P H I C

Instant Facts

Heaven (P) leased a car from Sun Trust (D) and then sued them for failure to comply with disclosure requirements of the Consumer Leasing Act.

Black Letter Rule

Where the district court has given due consideration to all the relevant factors of FRCP Rule 23 within the context of a rigorous analysis and has not relied upon impermissible factors, there is no abuse of discretion in denying a class action.

Case Vocabulary

ABUSE OF DISCRETION: The standard of review the appellate court uses to determine whether the decisions made by the trial court are consistent with the facts and circumstances before the court, and that the deductions made are reasonable.
STANDARD OF REVIEW: The measure used to reexamine the proceedings of a court.

Procedural Basis: Appeal from the district court's denial of Heaven's (P) motion for class certification.

Facts: Ranae Heaven (P) leased a Ford Taurus from Sun Trust (D), signing a preprinted lease agreement provided by Sun Trust (D). Later, Heaven (P) brought this action alleging that Sun Trust failed to comply with the strict disclosure requirements of the Consumer Leasing Act (CLA) and Regulation M (implementing the Act) [she probably just didn't like her car anymore]. Heaven (P) sued for the statutory penalty and attorney fees but alleged no actual damages. She sought to certify a class pursuant to Rule 23(a) [class so numerous that joinder of all is impractical, common question of law or fact, claims and defenses of representatives are typical, representatives will fairly and adequately represent interests of class] and (b)(3) of the Fed. R. Civ. P. [common questions or law or fact predominate, class action is superior to other approaches; pertinent findings include the interest of members of class in individually controlling prosecution of separate actions, extent litigation already commenced, desirability of concentrating litigation, difficulties in managing the class]. Sun Trust (D) counterclaimed on the alternative grounds that individual class members had (a) defaulted on the terms of their lease agreements, and/or (b) made false statements in their lease applications. The district court denied certification of the class.

Issue: Was the district court's denial of the motion to certify a class consistent with the facts and circumstances before the court?

Decision and Rationale: (Burns, J.) Yes. The district court ruled that Heaven had established the four prerequisites of Rule 23(a). We see no need to revisit that aspect of the court's ruling. The district court concluded Heaven (P) had not established that her action met the requirements of subdivision (b)(3). The district court recognized that the question of appropriateness of class certification in this case was very close. We agree with that assessment. First, the court determined that Sun Trust's (D) counterclaims were compulsory under Fed. R. Civ. P. 13(a). We agree that this conclusion is compelled by the case law of this circuit. Heaven (P) does not dispute that debt counterclaims are compulsory in CLA cases as a general matter. However, she contends that the presence of counterclaims cannot be a basis for denying class certification. The court below considered the nature of Sun Trust's (D) counterclaims and determined that individual lessee counterclaim defendants would be compelled to come forward with individual defenses. This would require the court to engage in multiple separate factual determinations. The court also determined that the interests of some individual class members in controlling their own case would be compromised. Their exposure as counterclaim defendants could well exceed the amount they might recover for statutory penalties as class members. The statutory claims asserted by the class would be against the interests of these individual class members. Where the district court has given due consideration to all relevant factors within the context of a rigorous analysis and has not relied on impermissible factors, we are unable to find an abuse of discretion. If, after such an evaluation, the district court is convinced that a class action is not superior to other available methods for the fair and efficient adjudication of the controversy, we cannot second guess that conclusion under the applicable standard of review. Affirmed.

Analysis:

The Court had an easy time with this one. Basically, it just reiterated everything the district court concluded and tacked on a "we agree" to the end of each sentence. It was a bit redundant, and the Court seemed to have nothing new to add. The Court does try to differentiate its decision from the district court's by adding that it did not intend to suggest that compulsory counterclaims should preclude the maintenance of class actions in cases under the CLA as a general rule. It ruled only that it is a proper exercise of discretion for the district court to evaluate the nature of the counterclaims and the difficulties they present and to consider the usefulness of breaking the proposed class into subclasses to avoid those difficulties. The decision to certify or not to certify a proposed class action is a major determination which has broad repercussions for all parties concerned [think hard]. In "small claims" classes, the decision to certify may face the defendant with a potentially huge liability claim, which it may feel compelled to settle almost without regard to the merits. In that same case, a refusal to certify will end not just the class, but any individual actions. Another important consequence of certifying a class is that an adequately represented class is bound by a judgment or settlement.

IN A CLASS ACTION SUIT, WHERE A CLASS MEMBER WAS NOT ADEQUATELY REPRESENTED, GIVING RES JUDICATA EFFECT TO THE JUDGMENT VIOLATES DUE PROCESS

Hansberry v. Lee

(Buyer) v. (Covenantor)
311 U.S. 32 (1940)

M E M O R Y   G R A P H I C

 Instant Facts

Hansberry (D), the black purchaser of land that was subject to a racially restrictive sales covenant, sought to avoid a prior class action holding that the covenant was valid.

Black Letter Rule

Granting res judicata effect to a class action judgment, in which the prerequisites and procedures for class action were not satisfied, violates due process.

Case Vocabulary

CLASS SUIT: An action brought, on behalf of a large number of people, by a representative who is similarly situated and who purports to represent the interests of the absent parties.

Procedural Basis: Writ of certiorari from order affirming res judicata effect of prior decree.

Facts: This class action suit was brought in an Illinois state court to enforce a racially restrictive covenant involving some land in Chicago. The covenant provided that it was not effective unless signed by 95% of the landowners. In the complaint, Lee (P), a white person, sought to enjoin the purchase of some restricted land by Hansberry (D), a black. Lee (P) alleged that the seller had signed the covenant, and that an earlier state court decision had held that the covenant was effective, since 95% of the landowners had signed the agreement. Hansberry (D) and other defendants argued that they were not bound by the res judicata effect of the earlier judgment, since they had not been parties to the suit. Thus, Hansberry (D) and the others argued that their due process rights were being violated. The Illinois Circuit Court and Supreme Court held that the original action was a class suit, and therefore that the holding was binding on all class members, including Hansberry (D) and the sellers. The United States Supreme Court granted certiorari.

Issue: Where the procedural requirements for class action have not been satisfied, is the judgment res judicata and therefore binding on absent parties?

Decision and Rationale: (Stone, J.) No. Where the procedure and course of litigation in a class action do not insure the protection of absent parties, a judgment entered in the action is not binding on those absent parties. An alternative holding would violate the due process rights of the absent members. In a typical litigation, notice and an opportunity to be heard are requisite to due process, and a judgment in which a person is not designated as a party does not have a res judicata effect on that person. An exception exists, however, in the class action context [Just when you thought you understood due process, class actions confuse the issue!]. Judgments entered in class or representative suits may bind members of the class or those represented who were not made parties to it. However, there is a failure of due process where the procedure adopted does not fairly insure the protection of the interest of absent parties who are to be bound by it. In the original case at hand, which found the covenant effective, the procedure did not adequately protect the interests of Hansberry (D) and the sellers. First, the restrictive agreement did not purport to create a joint obligation or liability. Rather, the racially restrictive covenant was a series of several obligations of the signers. Second, the signers seeking to enforce the agreement cannot be considered members of the same class as those signers seeking to challenge the validity of the agreement or to resist its performance. The signers such as Lee (P) attempting to enforce the agreement have conflicting interests with the parties such as Hansberry (D) and the sellers attempting to challenge the agreement. Thus, the mere fact that all of the parties had signed the agreement does not make them the same class, and the absent parties in the original litigation were not provided due process protections in asserting their interests. Reversed.

Analysis:

This case presents a different type of due process analysis from the jurisdictional cases encountered early in this book. While due process in the jurisdictional context typically focused on the adequacy of notice and opportunity to be heard, the Supreme Court now focuses on the adequacy of class representation. This makes sense in the class action context, given the potentially sever res judicata effects of a judgment on an absent class member. In effect, the Court is saying that people such as Hansberry (D) and the sellers were not adequately represented in the original litigation. Thus, they are not to be considered members of the original class. Conversely, if they were class members, the Court asserts, then the original judgment would be binding. Note that the "adequacy of representation" argument presents a timing problem, namely, at what point in time should the adequacy of representation be judged? The U.S. Supreme Court apparently assumed that the adequacy of representation in an original action could be analyzed in a later action. The logic of this approach is sound, since a final determination of the adequacy of representation could only be made through subsequent challenges to the res judicata effect of the suit. As Rule 23(c)(3) states, a class action decree should define the members of the class, presumably to aid in future determinations of the judgment's binding effect. The original court hearing the class action cannot predetermine the binding effect of its judgment, since this construction of Rule 23 would arguably be substantive in nature and thus violate the Rules Enabling Act, 28 U.S.C. § 2072.

Phillips Petroleum Co. v. Shutts

(Lessee) v. (Lessor)
472 U.S. 797 (1985)

M E M O R Y   G R A P H I C

Instant Facts

Shutts (P) and several other holders of royalty interests brought a class action against Phillips Petroleum (D) to recover royalty payments. The Kansas court obtained personal jurisdiction over all parties and applied Kansas law to all claims.

Black Letter Rule

In class actions, personal jurisdiction does not require that each class member have minimum contacts with the forum state, but the forum state must have sufficient interests in the claims to assert its state law to all claims.

Case Vocabulary

PRO FORMA: A required format with which procedures must comply.
RARA AVIS: Literally "a rare bird"; a unique person or thing.

Procedural Basis: Writ of certiorari reviewing affirmance of class action judgment in favor of class for damages for contractual violations.

Facts: Phillips Petroleum (D) obtained natural gas from leased land in eleven different states. Shutts (P) and several other lessors brought an action against Phillips Petroleum (D) in a Kansas state court, seeking to recover interest on royalty payments due under the leases. The Kansas trial court certified a class consisting of 33,000 royalty owners, and the class representatives provided each class member with notice by mail and with an opportunity to opt out of the class action. [Don't worry, the $100,000 in postage could later be recovered by the representatives!] The final class consisted of 28,100 class members residing in all fifty states and in foreign countries. Nevertheless, the trial court asserted personal jurisdiction and applied only Kansas contract law, finding Phillips Petroleum (D) liable for interest on suspended royalties to all class members. Phillips Petroleum (D) argued that the Due Process Clause prevented the Kansas court from adjudicating the claims of the non-resident class members, and that the Full Faith and Credit Clause prohibited the application of Kansas law to all of the claims. The Kansas Supreme Court affirmed the trial court's ruling, and the U.S. Supreme Court granted certiorari.

Issue: (1) May a court exercise personal jurisdiction over absent class members even if the members do not possess the minimum contacts with the forum which would support personal jurisdiction over a defendant? (2) Does a mailed notice and opt out provision satisfy the notice requirements for due process purposes? (3) May a forum state apply that state's law to every claim in a class action where the state does not have a significant contact and interest in every claim asserted by each member of the class?

Decision and Rationale: (Rehnquist, J.) (1) Yes. A court may exercise personal jurisdiction over absent class members even if the members do not possess the minimum contacts with the forum which would support personal jurisdiction over a defendant. As this Court has held in several cases, due process requires that a defendant have sufficient minimum contacts with the forum state in order for a court to obtain personal jurisdiction over a defendant. Phillips Petroleum (D) argues that, likewise, the Kansas courts may not assert personal jurisdiction over class members who neither affirmatively consent to jurisdiction nor have sufficient minimum contacts with Kansas. However, there are significant differences between jurisdiction over a defendant and jurisdiction over a class of plaintiffs. While defendants deserve due process protections from being haled into a distant state with which the defendants have no contacts, plaintiffs in class actions are not haled anywhere to defend themselves upon threat of default judgments. In class actions, both the court and the class representatives protect the interests of absent class members. Moreover, absent class members do not have to hire counsel or appear, are not subject to coercive or punitive remedies, and are not bound by adverse judgments for damages. Thus, the due process rights afforded to defendants, who should not be forced to travel to and appear in distant states with which they have no minimum contacts, do not apply equally to plaintiff class members. (2) Yes. A mailed notice including an opt out provision satisfies the due process requirements to provide notice to all interested litigants. This notice must be reasonably calculated to apprise the interested parties of the pendency of the actions and present them an opportunity to be heard. In the case at hand, the class representatives reasonably used first class mail to notify all 33,000 royalty owners of the pending action. Moreover, this notice provided the parties an opportunity to opt out of the litigation so as to avoid the binding effect of any judgment, allowing such members to bring separate claims. Phillips Petroleum (D) maintains that notice in class actions must provide an "opt in" provision, and that jurisdiction is improper over all distant plaintiffs who do not voluntarily opt in to the litigation. We do not think that the Constitution requires the State to sacrifice the obvious advantages in judicial efficiency resulting from the opt out approach for the protection of the onerous opt in approach. (3) No. Where a forum state does not have a significant contact and interest in every claim asserted by each member of the class, the state may not apply that state's law to every claim in a class action. In the case at hand, the Kansas state court applied Kansas contract law to every claim, notwithstanding that over 99% of the leases and 97% of the plaintiffs had no apparent connection to Kansas. Phillips Petroleum (D) contends that the application of Kansas substantive law in this situation violates the Due Process Clause and the Full Faith and Credit Clause, and we agree. Kansas must have a significant contact to the

claims asserted by each member of the plaintiff class, creating sufficient state interests, in order to ensure that the application of Kansas law is not arbitrary or unfair. However, Kansas did not have a sufficient interests in claims unrelated to the state. Moreover, the Kansas laws conflict with laws of jurisdictions such as Texas, in which many class members reside. In addition, there is no indication that the leases contemplated an application of Kansas law to all claims arising out of the leases. Therefore, the application of Kansas law to every claim in this case is sufficiently arbitrary and unfair as to exceed constitutional limits. In conclusion, we affirm the judgment of the Supreme Court of Kansas insofar as it upheld Kansas jurisdiction over all claims, but we reverse its judgment insofar as it held that Kansas law was applicable to all of the transactions. Remanded for further proceedings not inconsistent with this opinion.

Analysis:

Justice Rehnquist presents a thorough and logical analysis of difficult issues in class actions, including requirements for personal jurisdiction and the application of appropriate law. The holdings regarding notice and personal jurisdiction are sensible. The due process protections afforded to defendants in ordinary civil actions simply do not parallel the protections necessary for plaintiffs in class actions, since class action plaintiffs do not suffer similar hardships and are adequately protected by the court and by the class representatives. Phillips Petroleum's (D) arguments, that every class member must "opt in" to class actions and must have minimum contacts with the forum state, would obliterate class actions involving numerous plaintiffs residing in several different states and countries. Clearly, the efficiencies provided by class actions outweigh the minimal needs to obtain consent or for the forum to have minimum contacts with each class member. In the case at hand, the 33,000 potential class members were treated fairly, as 3,400 opted out of the litigation and an additional 1,500 were excluded because the notice was undeliverable. However, previous Supreme Court decisions regarding personal jurisdiction explicitly stated that *all* assertions of state-court personal jurisdiction must be evaluated on a minimum contacts standard. The instant case alters this requirement, justifying jurisdiction despite a lack of minimum contacts on one of two grounds: either consent to jurisdiction is inferred by the members' failure to opt out, or class action plaintiffs are not entitled to (and do not need) the same due process protections. In all likelihood, the latter interpretation is the most probable. With regard to the choice-of-law issue, the Court retreats from a flexible approach to class actions. Consider the practical difficulties inherent in the holding that Kansas law should not apply to every claim. This means that the Kansas court would have to ascertain which plaintiffs were covered by other laws, and would have to apply these disparate laws to various subclasses. Since the class members resided in all fifty states and even in some foreign countries, application of so many various laws would probably effectively undermine the efficiencies inherent in the class action [although it certainly would keep law clerks very busy!]. Possibly recognizing this litigation nightmare, the Kansas Supreme Court, upon remand of this case, found that *none* of the other state laws was in conflict with the law of Kansas. Thus, the court entered a new judgment reflecting no change in the original outcome!

Amchem Products, Inc. v. Windsor

(Asbestos Producer) v. (Exposed Class)
521 U.S. 591 (1997)

M E M O R Y   G R A P H I C

Instant Facts
People exposed to asbestos products created a settlement-only class to settle current and future asbestos-related claims.

Black Letter Rule
In determining the propriety of a settlement–only class certification, the requirements of Rule 23(a) and (b)(3) Fed. R. Civ. P. must be satisfied, and the settlement must be taken into account as well.

Case Vocabulary

JUSTICIABLE: Capable of being tried in a court of law or equity.
OPT-OUT CLASS: Those potential plaintiffs who choose to not be part of the class action.
RIPE CLAIM: A case which is ready to be adjudicated.
SETTLEMENT-CLASS CERTIFICATION: A class action not intended to be litigated, but merely for settlement purposes.
STIPULATION: An agreement made by the parties relating to the matter before the court.

Procedural Basis: Appeal from the Court of Appeals' reversal of the trial court, thus denying the class certification.

Facts: This case concerns the legitimacy under Rule 23 of the Federal Rules of Civil Procedure of a class-action certification sought to achieve global settlement of current and future asbestos-related claims. The class proposed for certification potentially encompasses hundreds of thousands, perhaps millions, of individuals [is that all?] tied together by this commonality: each was, or some day will be, adversely affected by past exposure to asbestos products manufactured by one or more of 20 companies (D). The class action thus instituted was not intended to be litigated [no courtroom big enough?]. Rather, within the space of a single day, the settling parties presented to the District Court a complaint, and answer, a proposed settlement agreement, and a joint motion for conditional class certification. As requested by the settling parties, the District Court conditionally certified, under Fed. R. Civ. P. Rule 23(b)(3), an encompassing opt-out class. Various class members raised objections to the settlement stipulation, and the Judge granted the objectors full rights to participate in the subsequent proceedings. Objectors urged that the settlement unfairly disadvantaged those without currently compensable conditions in that it failed to adjust for inflation or to account for changes, over time, in medical understanding. Strenuous objections had also been asserted regarding the adequacy of representation, a Rule 23(a)(4) requirement. Objectors maintained that class counsel and class representatives had disqualifying conflicts of interest. In particular, objectors urged, claimants whose injuries had become manifest and claimants without manifest injuries should not have common counsel and should not be aggregated in a single class. Declaring the class certification appropriate and the settlement fair, the District Court preliminarily enjoined all class members from commencing any asbestos-related suit against Amchem (D) in any state or federal court. The Court of Appeals reversed, finding that "serious intra-class conflicts precluded the class from meeting the adequacy of representation requirement" of Rule 23(a)(4). The objectors maintain in this Court an array of jurisdictional barriers. Most fundamentally, they maintain that the settlement proceeding is not a justiciable case or controversy within the confines of Article III of the Federal Constitution. In the main, they say the proceeding is a nonadversarial endeavor to impose on countless individuals without currently ripe claims and administrative compensation regime binding on those individuals if and when they manifest injuries. Like the Third Circuit, the Supreme Court declined to reach these issues because they "would not exist but for the class action certification."

Issue: Does settlement play a role when determining the propriety of a settlement–only class certification?

Decision and Rationale: (Ginsburg, J.) Yes. Among current applications of Rule 23(b)(3), the "settlement only" class has become a stock device. Although all Federal Circuits recognize the utility of Rule 23(b)(3) settlement classes, courts have divided on the extent to which a proffered settlement affects court surveillance under Rule 23's certification criteria. We granted review to decide the role settlement may play, under existing Rule 23, in determining the propriety of class certification. Contrary to the Third Circuit's opinion, we hold that settlement is relevant to a class certification. Confronted with a request for settlement-only class certification, a district court need not inquire whether the case, if tried, would present intractable management problems, for the proposal is that there be no trial. But other specifications of the rule – those designed to protect absentees by blocking unwarranted or overbroad class definitions – demand undiluted, even heightened, attention in the settlement context. Such attention is of vital importance, for a court asked to certify a settlement class will lack the opportunity, present when a case is litigated, to adjust the class, informed by the proceedings as they unfold. The safeguards provided by the Rule 23(a) and (b) class-qualifying criteria, we emphasize, are not impractical impediments – checks shorn of utility – in the settlement class context. Federal courts, in any case, lack authority to substitute for Rule 23's certification criteria a standard never adopted – that if a settlement is "fair," then certification is proper. Applying to this case criteria the rulemakers set, we conclude that the Third Circuit's appraisal is essentially correct. Although the court should have acknowledged that settlement is a factor in the calculus, a remand is not warranted on that account. The Court of Appeals' opinion amply demonstrates why – with or without a settlement on the table – that sprawling class the District Court certified does not satisfy Rule 23's requirements. We address first the requirement of Rule 23(b)(3) that "common questions of law or fact predominate over any questions affecting only individual members." We hold that the predominance requirement is not met by the factors on which the District Court relied. The benefits asbestos-exposed persons might gain from the establishment of a grand-scale compensation scheme is a matter fit for legislative consideration, but it is not pertinent to the predominance inquiry. Nor can the class approved by the District Court satisfy Rule 23(a)(4)'s requirement that the named parties "will fairly and adequately protect the interests of the class." As the Third Circuit pointed out, named parties with diverse medical conditions sought to act on behalf of a single giant class rather than on behalf of discrete subclasses. Because we have concluded that the class in this case cannot satisfy the requirements of common issue predominance and adequacy of representation, we need not rule, definitively, on the notice given here. The argument is sensibly made that a nationwide administrative claims processing regime would provide the most secure, fair, and efficient means of compensating victims of asbestos exposure. Congress, however, has not adopted such a solution. And Rule 23, which must be interpreted with fidelity to the Rules Enabling Act and applied with the interests of absent class members in close view, cannot carry the large load Amchem (D), class counsel, and the District Court heaped upon it.

Concurrence and Dissent: (Breyer, J.) The issues in this case are complicated and difficult. The District Court might have been correct. Or not. Subclasses might be appropriate. Or not. I cannot tell. And I do not believe that this Court should be in the business of trying to make these fact-based determinations. That is a job suited to the district courts in the first instance, and the courts of appeal on review.

Analysis:

The settlement-class certification evolved in response to an asbestos-litigation crisis. The most objectionable aspects of asbestos litigation have been listed as: dockets in both federal and state courts continue to grow; long delays are routine; trials are too long; the same issues are litigated over and over; transaction costs exceed the victims' recovery by nearly two to one; exhaustion of assets threatens and distorts the process; and future claimants may lose altogether. The settling parties, in sum, achieved a global compromise with no structural assurance of fair and adequate representation for the diverse groups and individuals affected. Although the named parties alleged a range of complaints, each served generally as representative for the whole, not for a separate constituency. The Court found no assurance here, however, either in the terms of the settlement or in the structure of the negotiations, that the named plaintiffs operated under a proper understanding of their representational responsibilities. As a result, the class could not satisfy the requirements under Rule 23 and, as such, the Court was required to deny the motion. Overall, this was just another long-winded opinion by the Court, which really did not add anything illuminating or insightful to the District Court's decision, except for a stamp of approval [all that matters in the end].